Mahogany

Mahogany

THE COSTS OF LUXURY
IN EARLY AMERICA

Jennifer L. Anderson

HARVARD UNIVERSITY PRESS
CAMBRIDGE, MASSACHUSETTS
LONDON, ENGLAND
2012

Library of Congress Cataloging-in-Publication Data

Anderson, Jennifer L., 1966–
Mahogany : the costs of luxury in early America / Jennifer L. Anderson.
p. cm.
Includes bibliographical references and index.
ISBN 978-0-674-04871-3 (alk. paper)
1. Mahogany industry–United States–History–18th century.   2. Mahogany–United
States–History–18th century.   3. United States–Social life and customs–To 1775.
4. United States–History–Colonial period, ca. 1600–1775.   I. Title.

HD9769.M33U625 2012
338.4'7674142–dc23   2012010780

FOR MARTIN

Contents

Illustrations

Odious upon a Walnut-Plank to Dine!
No, the red-veined Mohoggony be Mine!
Each Chest and Chair around my Room that Stands,
Was shipped thro' Dangerous Seas from Distant Lands.

—THOMAS WHARTON (1748)

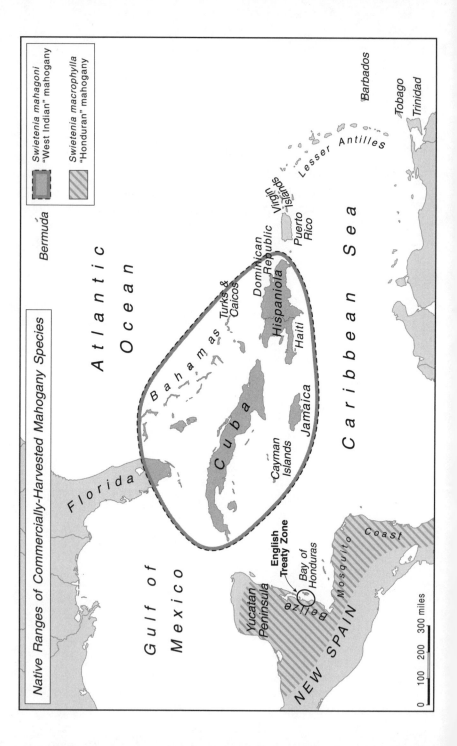

Native Ranges of Commercially-Harvested Mahogany Species

Swietenia mahagoni "West Indian" mahogany

Swietenia macrophylla "Honduran" mahogany

Bermuda

Atlantic Ocean

Gulf of Mexico

Florida

Bahamas

Turks & Caicos

Cuba

Cayman Islands

Jamaica

Hispaniola

Dominican Republic

Haiti

Virgin Islands

Puerto Rico

Lesser Antilles

Barbados

Tobago

Trinidad

Caribbean Sea

Yucatan Peninsula

English Treaty Zone

Bay of Honduras

Belize

Mosquito Coast

NEW SPAIN

0 100 200 300 miles

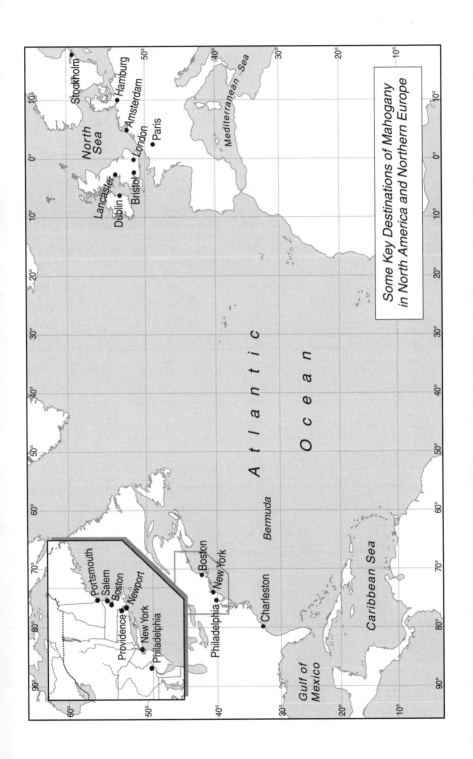

Some Key Destinations of Mahogany
in North America and Northern Europe

Introduction

*I*N 1748, Pehr Kalm, a protégé of the famous Swedish botanist Carl
Linnaeus, embarked on a three-year tour of North America to identify valuable trees that might thrive in chilly Scandinavia. Travelling
from the Eastern Seaboard to the Appalachian frontier, he was deeply
impressed with the land's vast forests as well as the prodigious quantities of high-quality timber its inhabitants consumed and exported. Yet
after visiting the well-furnished homes of many people along the way,
including such luminaries as Benjamin Franklin in Philadelphia and
Cadwallader Colden in New York, he reported that colonial Americans
exchanged their native timber for "true mahogany, which grows in Jamaica [where it] is at present almost all cut down."[1]

Most people in British North America in the mid-eighteenth century would have found the first half of his statement, at least, unsur-
prising. If he had extended his journey farther, Kalm would have found
that the use of this imported tropical hardwood was widespread
throughout the colonies. Hard-driving merchants and ship captains
in New England, prosperous farmers and minor gentry in the Mid-
Atlantic, debt-ridden Virginia planters, and aristocratic Carolina rice-
growers all owned, and often prominently displayed, mahogany furnishings. Although these objects might differ in appearance (reflecting

stylistic and regional preferences, distinctive vernacular traditions and local craft practices, changing fashions, and quirks of personal taste), the use of mahogany as a primary wood was an important commonality. Rare and exotic only a few decades earlier, mahogany—while still a luxury commodity—was no longer novel or exclusive to the wealthy few. More middling Americans now also sought out this favored wood to add a touch of refinement to their modest homes, if only a few chairs, a small table, or a tea caddy. Even Americans who did not own any mahogany were likely familiar with it from neighbors' houses, cabinetmaking workshops, stores, churches, the courthouse, or even the local tavern.

If you had accompanied Kalm on one of his evening social calls — perhaps to a leading Philadelphia family—you would have observed an impressive array of mahogany furniture. Imagine entering a brightly painted parlor where a tall chest-on-chest towers against the far wall on elegant curved legs; the swirling grain of its facade and shiny brass handles and escutcheons gleam in the candlelight. Along the opposite wall stands a sofa, its red silk upholstery set off by its dark brown mahogany frame. Before the marble fireplace a pair of mahogany armchairs, clambering with carved vines and flowers, flank a round tea table with a piecrust edge. In adjacent rooms, you glimpse still more mahogany—a looking glass topped with a gilded phoenix, a pair of card tables, a delicate sewing table, perhaps a grand desk and bookcase or a stately grandfather clock. The unseen private chambers likely contain mahogany as well—four-poster beds, washstands, dressing tables, maybe an armoire—arranged alongside plainer maple and pine objects. In the formal dining room, you find a veritable showroom of mahogany furniture. The sideboard looms like a battleship, laden with sparkling glasses, silver candlesticks, and Chinese porcelain tureens and platters. Matching knife boxes display ivory-handled cutlery and a lead-lined cellarette contains bottles of fine French wine. In the middle of the room, centered under a crystal chandelier and surrounded by a dozen matching chairs, stands the *pièce de résistance*—a twelve-foot dining table. When you are seated at the table, however, its gorgeous expanse of wood remains concealed until just before the dessert course. When at last the servants ceremoniously remove the white damask cloth, its smooth, polished surface is revealed, allowing everyone at the table to admire their shimmering reflections within its lustrous depths.

Amidst such abundance, most colonial Americans would have scoffed at the second half of Kalm's remark—about mahogany's imminent depletion in Jamaica—since the wharves of American seaports heaved with imported mahogany logs, and cabinetmaking shops regularly turned out all manner of mahogany creations for sale to anyone who could afford them. His claim, however, was largely accurate. The accessible trees were indeed rapidly disappearing on Jamaica, the main mahogany supplier to England and colonial America since its introduction in the 1720s. This unfortunate reality gave rise to an ongoing search for the two commercially harvested species of New World mahogany, a search that eventually extended throughout their native ranges from the Northern Caribbean to Central and South America, and beyond. In the face of rising consumer demand, the drive to find, access, and control mahogany sources intensified over the course of the eighteenth century, giving rise to fierce competition and violent conflicts over remaining supplies. It also contributed to increased exploitation of slave labor and widespread deforestation. In the West Indies, where mahogany often was felled in the process of clearing land for plantation agriculture, its extraction coincided with the very vanguard of European colonial expansion. Moreover, as the search for mahogany heated up, it exacerbated interpersonal and broader interimperial tensions over access to land, labor, and natural resources. Although the Anglo-American and British contexts in which mahogany was used are the main focus of this work, mahogany was also exported to France, Spain, Denmark, and the Netherlands from their respective West Indian colonies (as well as to other destinations in Europe).[2]

The historical significance of mahogany, and the very substance of the material itself, cannot be fully understood apart from the living trees from whence it came and the contentious human circumstances surrounding its production. The health, maturity, growth patterns, and particular species of the mahogany trees felled at any given point in time dictated the character of wood available to consumers. As the largest, healthiest trees with the best reproductive capacity were systematically cut down, those harvested subsequently became increasingly unpredictable and inconsistent in size and quality, which directly impacted the international mahogany market. Most significantly, what trees were felled (as well as how, where, and by whom) was inextricably linked with changing social, political, economic, and environmental conditions within their native ranges. Although not always aware of these underlying causes, consumers experienced their effects, directly and indirectly, as they were forced to redefine their conceptions of mahogany and recalibrate their expectations in the face of market fluctuations and deteriorating wood stocks. In 1780, even the intrepid Benjamin Franklin expressed confusion about mahogany, noting, "there is a great deal of difference in woods that go under that name." Over time, mahogany depletion and the ensuing search to find new sources fundamentally reshaped how it was valued, used, and perceived. This direct correlation, however, has not always been evident, then or now, to those who appreciate this sublime but disembodied material.[3]

Known colloquially in English by a name likely derived from the Yoruban *M'Oganwo*, since slaves purportedly found it reminiscent of an African tree, the vast majority of New World mahogany consumed in the eighteenth and early nineteenth centuries was one of two species of the genus *Swietenia* of the *Meliaceae* family: short-leaf West Indian mahogany (*Swietenia mahagoni* Jacquin) and big-leaf Honduran mahogany (*Swietenia macrophylla* King). The native range of the former was limited to the North Central Caribbean, including the tip of Florida, Jamaica, Cuba, the Bahamas, Hispaniola (now Haiti and the Dominican Republic), and the smaller surrounding islands of the northern Antilles. Given the relatively small sizes of these landmasses, its geographical scope was quite circumscribed. The native range of the Honduran species, by contrast, was vast, encompassing parts of Central and South America from southern Mexico to the Amazon. Since this was Spanish territory for most of the eighteenth century, however, British woodcutters were officially restricted to limited areas, defined by international treaties, in the Bay of Honduras (now Belize). They also cut mahogany along the Mosquito Shore (now Nicaragua and Honduras) with cooperation from the indigenous Miskito Indians, who resisted Spanish claims of sovereignty. A third species of New World mahogany (*Swietenia humilis*), indigenous to the Pacific coast and smaller in size, was not exported to any significant extent.[4]

Logging mahogany trees was especially challenging and labor intensive because of their highly dispersed growth habit. In a healthy tropical forest environment, *Swietenia* species typically avoid crowding each other by growing singly or in small clusters scattered across vast acres (with an average density of one tree per two and a half acres and clusters of up to twenty trees per acre), intermingling with an average of forty to sixty other tree species. In addition, the trees, which average eighty to one hundred feet tall, with diameters of four to twelve feet, are slow growing and do not easily regenerate once virgin forest is felled. In an undisturbed forest setting, parent trees disperse their seeds seasonally, resulting in large numbers of seedlings, most of which eventually die as they are shaded out by competing flora. But if a seedling receives adequate water and a strong infusion of light at the right moment to trigger continued growth (such as caused by the fall of a neighboring tree), it will grow rapidly into a tall, skinny juvenile, shooting upward until it reaches the height of the surrounding canopy. After that initial spurt, however, its growth slows considerably as its energy is redirected into developing outstretched crowning branches and expanding the girth of its trunk. It takes many years for a tree to reach maturity, much less achieve its full potential size. The age of a mahogany tree, not evident in annual growth rings, is usually estimated based on the diameter of its trunk; a tree with a diameter of six feet, for example, is probably several hundred years old. Mahogany reproduction is also believed to be facilitated by cataclysmic events, such as hurricanes and fires, that periodically create large rifts in the forest canopy. In a typical scenario, high winds or raging flames decimate competing tree species, leaving standing only the largest mahogany trees, which are protected by their sturdy buttressed trunks and thick fire-resistant bark. Taking advantage of the disruption, these trees maximize their reproductive capacity by scattering their seeds in the natural clearing; bathed in nurturing sunlight, the seeds take root and begin to sprout. This survival strategy allows their progeny to gain a foothold before faster-growing trees have a chance to catch up and engulf them. The mahogany trees that grow back in a given area after such an event are all of about the same age and size.[5]

In the eighteenth and early nineteenth centuries, mahogany logging was largely an extractive industry that relied on two main modes of production—clear-cutting and selective cutting. Analogous to strip mining, clear-cutting entailed removing *all* the trees across a wide area to eradicate whole forests, usually as the precursor to plantation agriculture. On many West Indian islands, mahogany-rich forests competed unfavorably for space on what proved to be prime sugar-growing lands. Whereas natural cataclysms similarly felled many trees at once, usually enough mature individuals were left standing that the forest could eventually recover, with its original diversity and vigor intact. On man-made clear cuts, however, the land, denuded of trees and bereft of protection from heavy rains and the scorching sun, eroded and lost fertility, while tender mahogany saplings died of exposure. Secondary forests might eventually spring up in the wake of clear-cutting, but mahogany usually did not revive, especially not if all the mature, seed-bearing trees had been removed. Selective cutting singled out *only* the mahogany trees from a given area, leaving behind less desirable species. While less destructive to the forest as a whole, this method still required that miles of logging roads be cut through the forest to reach each mahogany tree. Since the largest, healthiest mahogany trees were removed first, their reproductive cycles were similarly disrupted, and remaining seedlings were crowded out by faster-growing species. In the wake of either logging method, the relatively slow-growing, ecologically complex *Swietenia* seldom recovered after such man-made disruptions. Consequently, as once-abundant mahogany became rare in many places by the mid- to late-eighteenth century, the realization that mahogany supplies were finite encouraged a "wild west" mentality throughout the circum-Caribbean as people hastened to seize a one-time bounty.

While many historians have investigated the commodification of tropical flora (from sugar, tobacco, and chocolate to coffee, rubber, and bananas), mahogany offers a very different case study. For although its initial introduction and popularization were similar to that of other tropical commodities, its long-term history followed a very different trajectory because of three key factors: its limited availability, its durability, and its increasing scarcity; these same characteristics were shared with other now-endangered species that were similarly commodified (such as elephants for their ivory tusks and sea turtles for their mottled shells) but in relatively smaller quantities. Slow-growing mahogany proved difficult to raise "in captivity," so to speak. Its lifecycle, so intimately intertwined within the larger rain forest ecology, was not easily replicated under artificial conditions, and efforts to cultivate mahogany trees on plantations within their native Atlantic ranges were of limited success during the colonial period. *Swietenia* therefore provides an important counterexample to the more general plantation model of the commodification of nature in which rare species of trees and plants were transformed into highly regimented, quality-controlled, mass-produced agricultural products. Mahogany continued to be taken almost exclusively from the wild and initially only from within the proscribed limits of its natural propagation. Until significant breakthroughs in understanding its ecology and its relationship to its tropical environment were made in the twentieth century, mahogany was, for all intents and purposes, a nonrenewable resource.[6]

Mahogany's durability also set it apart from other more ephemeral, if addictive, plantation-grown commodities such as sugar, tea, coffee, and tobacco. Whereas these tropical staples became increasingly accessible to more people and in ever greater quantities, those who partook of them had little to show for it beyond their immediate gratification. Once these products were imbibed or used, nothing was left—except, perhaps briefly, some unburned calories, an acrid aftertaste, or a cloud of smoke. Mahogany, on the other hand, was converted into substantial, long-lasting, material artifacts—physical *things*—that people gradually imbued with a range of cultural connotations that held shared meaning. Eventually as abolition sentiments advanced in England and North America, some consumers drew a moral distinction between mahogany's solid substance and the ephemeral character of most tropical produce, even though all were slave-produced commodities. In 1807, in a critique of West Indian sugar planters who were demanding protectionist policies because their produce so enriched the British Empire, William Spence argued that, to the contrary, sugar was "so *transient* or *fugitive*," that it offered little benefit to anyone. If only, he noted, consumers would invest in goods "as durable as the mahogany which is imported from Jamaica," they would enjoy long-term value "for years, perhaps for half a century, and . . . obtain by selling them at least a portion of their original cost. But what have the consumers of Rum and Sugar . . . to show for the ten millions of these luxuries which they consumed last year? Nothing." Mahogany objects, on the other hand, tended to retain, or even gain, economic, sentimental, and historical value over time.[7]

While the particular historical context of mahogany's introduction in colonial America during the early eighteenth century had much to do with its positive reception, people's appreciation for this material and its enduring cultural significance were (and are) predicated foremost on its physical and aesthetic properties that made it an extraordinarily durable, versatile, and attractive wood, well suited for a wide range of applications. Although the separate species of *Swietenia* trees are readily differentiated based on their external appearances—*Swietenia macrophylla* grows taller and wider and has longer, rounder leaves than *Swietenia mahogoni*—their close heredity is evident in cellular structures so similar that even twenty-first century wood identification experts, armed with high-powered microscopes, cannot definitively distinguish them based just on wood samples. Moreover, both species share important characteristics and, as tropical hardwoods, are categorically different in a number of significant ways from hardwood trees of more temperate regions. Most North American and European hardwoods, for example, have clearly visible seasonal bands of growth (wider or narrower depending on annual rainfalls and growing conditions) such that a tree's age can easily be estimated by counting the resulting rings on a cross-section of its trunk. Since the tropics have a continuous growing season, however, mahogany trees have especially dense, tightly-packed growth rings that are not readily discernible to the naked eye in the fibers of their trunks or branches. (Indeed, Europeans were often confounded by their inability to assess the age of the seemingly ancient mahogany trees they encountered.) Like other tropical hardwoods, *Swietenia* tends to have especially solid, fine-grained wood that is extremely hard, heavy, strong, and durable. Whereas all woods swell or shrink with changes in humidity due to their permeable cell structures, its density makes it more stable

than most other woods as well as warp-resistant and relatively impervious to insect damage. Fully mature mahogany trees, although seldom found today, can also attain gargantuan sizes, exceeding all European and North American species (with the exception of tulip trees
and sequoias); those initially harvested during the colonial period
yielded boards of extraordinary widths.[8]

The strength, insect resistance, and large sizes of mahogany (especially the larger Honduran species) made it a preferred material for
shipbuilding, construction, and architectural woodwork. Shipwrights
found that its density largely prevented problems with worms and dry
rot that could shorten the longevity of ocean-going vessels. Its stability made it well suited for making musical instruments, such as vio-
lins and guitars, and the housings of delicate scientific instruments.
Some Old Masters even painted on panels of mahogany when they
could get their hands on it, as Rembrandt did for his 1634 self-portrait.
Cabinetmakers and carvers deemed it excellent as well for furniture
making, lending itself especially well to the "art and mystery" of their
crafts. As long as large trees were available, some tabletops were fabricated out of a single mahogany slab, making for a uniform, stable surface that minimized the problems of warping, shrinking, and cracking
that could occur when smaller boards were pieced together. Mahogany
was so strong that cabinetmakers in some regions dispensed with traditional structural reinforcements, such as chair stretchers. Solid mahogany, however, was quite heavy, a disadvantage for card tables, chairs,
and the like that were routinely moved around; the late eighteenth-
century shift to veneers solved that problem by sheathing lighter woods
in a thin mahogany layer.[9]

At the same time, mahogany also offered enormous aesthetic potential that opened up new artistic possibilities for eighteenth-century artisans because both species came in a wide range of colors, textures, and
densities—variables determined by the unique situation and growing

conditions of particular mahogany stands or even of individual trees. Myriad factors (such as patterns of rainfall, soil conditions, light levels, exposure, proximity to other trees, or environmental stresses) affected a tree's physiology, which translated directly into the quality, size, character, and, ultimately, the value of its resulting timber. In other words, each tree's autobiography was written in the grain of its body, with seemingly infinite variations. Depending on the particular chemical composition of the soil, for example, its wood might develop a surprising array of colors—from dark to light brown, deep maroon to reddish orange, greenish yellow to golden blonde. If a *Swietenia* tree of either species took root in a sunny, well-watered, fertile spot and grew up unimpeded, it would generally develop even-grained, slightly porous, bland wood composed of an open, net-like cellular structure; if that same tree started life instead on rocky, dry soil, crowded by other trees or clinging to a steep mountainside, it would grow more slowly and gnarly, resulting in harder, denser wood, possibly with more vivid color and a tighter, more closed cellular structure. In addition, wherever the tree twisted, bent, or branched (such as around its buttressed roots or at the crotch of its trunk), the stresses on the wood fibers caused irregularities and malformations in the grain, resulting in patterns of mottles, swirls, whorls, feathering, and other distinctive figures. Since most *Swietenia macrophylla* grew in the former conditions, it gained a reputation for lighter, spongier, plainer wood that was long regarded as inferior for cabinetmaking to *Swietenia mahagoni,* a negative perception that became less pronounced as availability of the preferred West Indian species declined.[10]

Nevertheless, in the hands of a skilled woodworker, the diverse physical characteristics of both species could be manipulated to achieve a remarkable array of visual and tactile effects. The elaborate grain patterns were only fully revealed, for example, when the wood was cut in particular ways that required judgment and skill acquired through long experience. Dense mahogany, *without* a figured grain, proved to be a superior carving wood from which carvers coaxed delicate ornaments (impossible to accomplish in less sturdy woods), achieving a level of crispness, clarity, swooping articulation, and deep surface contrasts that, in the best work, imparted to the inert wood a stimulating sense of movement and vigor. Carvers' intricate designs, often embellished with twining tendrils, shells, and blossoms characteristic of the sophisticated rococo and chinoiserie styles that became fashionable during the mid-eighteenth century, introduced a new dimension of stylized nature to the parlors and dining rooms of colonial Americans.

Adding to mahogany's appeal was that, when the rough wood was finished and polished, it resulted in a satiny smooth texture with a shiny, reflective surface. Grain patterns in some figured mahogany were reminiscent of the then-fashionable moiré silks that were specially woven or passed between iron rollers to create iridescent effects. Mahogany's reflective, chameleon-like aspect continued to fascinate people long thereafter. In 1853, *The Cabinet-maker's Assistant* noted that its beauty varied "as the observer alters his position, the lights and shades dissolving into, and alternating with each other. This illusion of change defies the imitation of the painter, and is unconsciously one of the chief attractions which mahogany furniture presents." Thanks to the seemingly infinite diversity of mahogany, each object made from it was to some degree unique, the enduring legacy of once-living trees.[11]

Satisfying the British Empire's appetite for mahogany required a veritable army of people, spread out across the Atlantic hemisphere— enslaved Africans, itinerant woodcutters, colonists, and planters in the West Indies and Central America, ship captains, sailors, and stevedores, as well as merchants, cabinetmakers, and laborers in England and its northern colonies. In the rain forest, workers sought out and felled each huge tree, extricated the massive trunks, laboriously hauled them to the closest waterway to be floated to the coast and loaded on waiting ships. Across the ocean, other workers unloaded, sorted, graded, measured, and sawed up the raw wood while others transformed it into all kinds of objects (tables, chairs, desks, etc.) that furniture buyers conveyed to their homes. All of these people experienced mahogany as a part of their material surroundings but in very different contexts.

Enslaved Africans in the West Indies and Central America, as well as Miskito Indians and other indigenous peoples, were also drawn into the search for mahogany, playing integral roles in finding and harvesting forest resources and, in some cases, serving as important brokers of environmental information. They thus contributed to investing part of the natural world with exchange value, transforming it into a commodity, and activating its economic potential in the Atlantic marketplace. By parlaying geographical and ethnobotanical knowledge to serve their own strategic purposes, they also gained some negotiating power within an otherwise exploitative labor system. Beginning as early as the mid-eighteenth century in some areas, however, their lives were also significantly impacted by the negative effects of unbridled woodcutting and ensuing geopolitical and economic crises.

On the consumption side, Americans' growing familiarity with mahogany resulted from a tangled learning process of encountering, experiencing, and assimilating the new. Cabinetmakers, merchants, and furniture buyers acted together, sometimes in overlapping roles—as makers, sellers, and consumers—to create a meaningful, value-laden cultural context for this novelty. Critical to this process was that its aesthetic qualities coincided with eighteenth-century Anglo concepts of beauty, gentility, refinement, and modernity that most culturally literate people of the day appreciated; mahogany objects thus became desirable status symbols among the social elite. Whether they surrounded themselves with lavish furnishings or saved up for a hard-earned few, colonial Americans sought out mahogany—from cradles to coffins.[12]

Beginning in the 1760s, as mahogany began to be imported from more locales, craftsmen and their customers developed preferences for the produce of specific places, indicated by the proliferation of geographical monikers, although all still referred to one or the other of the same two species. West Indian mahogany *(Swietenia mahagoni)* was also called True Mahogany, Island Wood, Jamaica Wood, Providence Wood (after New Providence in the Bahamas), or, later, Cuban, Santo Domingan, or Spanish mahogany (after various French and Spanish islands). Honduran mahogany *(Swietenia macrophylla)* was called Bay Wood (after the Bay of Honduras), Mosquito wood (after the Mosquito Shore), or Ruatan mahogany (after an island off the coast of Belize). This popular nomenclature, variations of which are still used as trade terms by antique dealers, bespeaks the shifting geographical sources (actual or perceived) of the mahogany trade over the course of its convoluted history. As mahogany sources became more variable and unpredictable, however, such place-name labels had more to do with marketing that catered to consumers' preconceptions than with any objective reality regarding where wood was actually sourced. As preferred types ceased to be available, furniture makers and buyers alike had to modify their preferences and adapt to the shifting range of geographical options. Whereas Jamaican mahogany defined consumers' standard of excellence in the 1720s, for example, its declining quality and rapid depletion increasingly forced them to seek out mahogany from other places, such as the Bay of Honduras, that they had previously spurned. By 1803, Thomas Sheraton, the famous English cabinetmaker whose furniture design books circulated widely in the new United States, described Honduran wood as "the principal kind of mahogany in use amongst cabinetmakers." Although surges in mahogany production periodically glutted the Atlantic marketplace as new sources were found and made available, the overall long-term trend was toward greater scarcity as they too were eventually tapped out, especially the West Indian species that was less abundant from the outset.[13]

While mahogany gained a reputation for its versatility for many utilitarian purposes, colonial Americans appreciated its aesthetic properties as much or more; they seemed to respond to mahogany's look and feel on a visceral level—they were fascinated by its silky, polished surfaces, deep saturated colors, and intriguingly figured grains. By reifying mahogany as superior to other materials, colonial Americans breathed new life into dead wood. Mahogany thus has a dual history, that of wild living organisms and of cultural artifacts. Once the mahogany trees were felled, people reinterpreted their carcasses first as a raw material (lumber), then as a commodity with exchange value, and ultimately, as finished products to be owned, utilized, and displayed. The trees were no longer a flourishing part of nature, no longer mere wood. Like Marx's dancing table, mahogany was transubstantiated through human effort into objects—useful, beautiful, and often status-laden—but completely disassociated from its organic origins. This sylvan alchemy appealed deeply to many Anglo-Americans precisely because it placed the wild, unfettered natural world at a safe remove.[14]

Many people assume that mahogany has always been regarded as a luxury material, but its conception as such was very much a cultural construct, one among many mutable meanings that have been applied to this material at various points in time. Depending on the historical context, mahogany has been regarded as utilitarian (cheap and abundant), precious (expensive and rare), desirable (sensual and exotic), respectable (refined and genteel), deceptive (duplicitous and false), and nostalgic (elegiac and reminiscent). So although colonial Americans initially considered mahogany remarkable, exciting, and refreshingly modern, by the mid-nineteenth century, fashion-conscious people had come to regard it as tiresomely familiar, stodgy, and *retardataire* compared to rosewood and other newly available specialty woods, while at the same time traditionalists began to revere its antiquity and historical associations. Significantly, these conflicting re-envisionings of mahogany both began at the point of consumption—either in booming factories and showy furniture emporiums or in the imagined hands of idealized, independent artisans and virtuous American homes—overlooking the contestation and vast slave-driven imperial network that brought tropical hardwoods to northern shores.

Today, both *Swietenia* species verge on extinction and are protected under the CITES treaty throughout their native ranges within the American neotropics. While *Swietenia mahogoni* is commercially extinct within the Caribbean, *Swietenia macrophylla* is still logged under heavy regulation in parts of Central and South America, although illegal cutting persists. Throughout the Americas, commercial logging of both species is defunct, declining, or strictly limited. Consequently, since the twentieth century, mahogany has become a fetishized commodity once again, connoting sumptuousness and luxury for many people in ways that other once-precious commodities simply do not. We are quick to toss used teabags, coffee grounds, and banana peels on the compost heap, but old mahogany furniture more often ends up in auction houses, antique shops, and museums.[15]

While some people today still regularly use and enjoy mahogany objects, both antique and contemporary, for most of us, their high cost and limited availability have placed them largely outside of our everyday realms into a bygone world of desire. On those rare occasions when we have the opportunity to examine and contemplate actual mahogany objects from the colonial period—perhaps spot-lit in a museum gallery, behind a velvet rope at a historic site, or on a Sotheby's auction block—we may marvel at their beauty and craftsmanship but perhaps not pause to ponder their rain forest origins, the consequences of their production, or what they meant to those who once yearned to possess them. Where colonial Americans once admired their shimmering reflections deep in the heart of the mahogany, we can still catch glimpses of ourselves mirrored in well-polished facades. But just as those perfect, glancing surfaces conceal the raw, unfinished wood of objects' underbellies, hidden guts, and wall-facing posteriors, so too the mahogany trade had a decidedly less glamorous aspect. Nevertheless, its compelling history is one of transformation—creative and destructive—from its introduction in the early eighteenth century, to its prominence from the mid- to late-eighteenth century, to its relative decline by the mid-nineteenth century. While the benefits of the mahogany trade were great for some, if one considers the effects that its production had on many of the people and places where it originated, fulfilling consumers' desires for mahogany came at a high price. These connections bring together the polish and the rough that made the Age of Mahogany.[16]

CHAPTER ONE

A New Species of Elegance

I N 1698, Philadelphia merchant Jonathan Dickinson ordered a "Few fine woods for ye Joyners & Some Mahogany . . . in board or Plank for Chest of Drawers & Tables" from Jamaica. Having lived for many years on that island where he was born in 1663 and still owned two plantations, Dickinson was well-informed about its various tropical hardwoods and their uses. In Philadelphia, however, he initially found little interest in his imported timber. North American forests abounded with excellent furniture woods that were readily available, inexpensive, and already extensively utilized by local craftsmen. Why import wood from hundreds of miles away? He eventually found buyers among his acquaintances, including joiner Abraham Hooper who acquired some planks from him in 1701. In the meanwhile, Dickinson furnished his own home with mahogany tables, chests of drawers, and a clothes press. When he died in 1722, his probate inventory listed eighteen pieces of mahogany furniture, as well as "11 Mohogany planks Each 11 foot long 5 Inches Thick and 2 foot wide." By the time of his death, demand for mahogany was just beginning to take off in England and, more slowly, in colonial America; by mid-century, it had become *the* preferred wood for fine furniture. Although he introduced at least some of his fellow Philadelphians to this exotic wood, Dickinson was a man ahead of his time.[1]

Colonial Americans' adoption of mahogany and their elevation of it to luxury status were by no means preordained. Rather, knowledge of and appreciation for this novel material developed over time through a dynamic, reciprocal exchange of information predicated on four main factors: first, the convergence of economic and social preconditions that made tropical commodities more available and gave rise to new consumption patterns; second, a change in governmental policy in England that reduced the price of mahogany, indirectly impacting the colonial market; third, the active engagement of colonial merchants, cabinetmakers, and furniture buyers in promoting mahogany as a worthwhile addition to Americans' repertoire of raw materials; and fourth, by the serendipitous alignment of mahogany's characteristic physical properties with eighteenth-century English aesthetics and values that made it appear beautiful, desirable, and meaningful to many eyes. In particular, mahogany's smooth, polished surfaces seemed to epitomize the ideal of refinement, then considered an essential aspect of civility.

Where mahogany was concerned, which developed first—demand or supply—was somewhat of a chicken-and-egg question in colonial America as they were mutually reinforcing; American merchants, cabinetmakers, and furniture buyers (in roles that sometimes overlapped) generated, responded to, and expanded both. Mahogany's rising social status in England, however, certainly primed colonial Americans' receptivity to it. As they incorporated this new material into their physical surroundings and social rituals, they were participating in a broader, transatlantic cultural phenomenon. In 1787, the London *Times* reported: "Modern refinement has substituted mahogany instead of walnut timber, for the purposes of furniture in the houses of the rich, and even of the middling orders of the people. . . . The superior elegance of the mahogany to any species of our native timber must be admitted." Colonial Americans, especially Anglo Americans, likewise aspired to possess this new species of elegance.[2]

Mahogany's Early Uses

Europeans first encountered West Indian mahogany during their initial forays into the Caribbean where they extolled the lush verdure of this strange New World. When Columbus spied the tall, green trees of Hispaniola, he immediately speculated about their physical properties and economic value. He was especially impressed by the natives' large canoes, hollowed out of single tree trunks, and their curiously carved wooden stools, called *duhos,* that were reserved for priests and chieftains. These objects may very well have been made out of mahogany, which Tainos and other Arawak peoples in the Greater Antilles traditionally employed for both utilitarian and spiritual purposes during the pre-Columbian period.[3]

Mahogany began to be logged by early Spanish settlers on Hispaniola and Cuba for use in proto-industrial, military, and naval contexts, for such purposes as building fortifications, barracks, warehouses, sugar mills, and basic furnishings. Once the essential colonial infrastructure was established, they commenced to export some mahogany, or *caoba* as they called it (a name possibly derived from Taino), to Spain where it was used for architectural woodwork, church decor, and fine furniture. In 1578, Felipe II proposed mahogany to adorn the monastery of San Lorenzo el Real. By 1590, José de Acosta's *Natural and Moral History of the Indies* noted his countrymen's growing appreciation for "Precious woods such as ebony, mahogany, *granadillo,* cedar, and other woods about which I know nothing [that] are brought to Spain from . . . the island of Cuba, where there are an immense number of these trees." Having ascertained that West Indian mahogany was an excellent shipbuilding material—strong, rot resistant, and shatterproof even when pummeled by cannonballs—the Spanish Royal Navy commandeered as much as possible to construct galleons. In short order, Cuba became one of the most important shipbuilding centers in the Spanish empire.[4]

English ships also returned home from the East and West Indies carrying so-called "fancy woods" (including mahogany, ebony, rosewood, and cedar, as well as other unnamed species) but in such small quantities at first that artisans used them only for ornamentation, such as in marquetry, a technique of gluing tiny jewel-like pieces of contrasting woods in elaborate designs on cabinet doors, tabletops, or small boxes. Ownership of such rarified objects, however, remained exclusive to the aristocracy.[5]

In addition, some mahogany bark was also imported for its purported curative powers. Used as a medicinal by Indians in the Caribbean and Central America, it joined the growing pharmacopeia yielded by European exploration and appropriation of indigenous knowledge in the Americas. Steeped as a tea or ground into powder, mahogany bark was administered for a variety of ailments. Although taken as a purge or an anti-fever drug, its precise health benefits remained a subject of great interest and debate among European medical practitioners and naturalists.[6]

Quite apart from such limited encounters with exotic woods, the English were interested in securing American trees of all kinds to meet even their basic timber needs. Throughout their home isle, widespread deforestation had long made chronic timber shortages an unwelcome fact of life. What forests remained, outside of restricted Royal preserves, were heavily regulated or off-limits to the general populace. Yet during this period, wood served myriad purposes, such as for houses, ships, furniture, and fuel. Given the dearth of timber, however, people were forced to rely on wood supplies imported from Scandinavia, Germany, and elsewhere in Northern Europe. Even the most venerated English oak and walnut trees, long favored as furniture woods, were no longer domestically available. Securing an abundant, reliable wood supply was absolutely vital to the nation's future and one of the prime attractions of colonization.[7]

By the early seventeenth century, as more English ships traversed the Caribbean, they began to buy wood from local Indians or settlers or to simply take trees from unoccupied islands to fill out their return cargos. Having audaciously claimed the entire Caribbean region, the Spanish Crown sought to halt such activities which it saw as undermining its sovereignty. Accordingly, whereas Cuba's forests had previously been treated as an open commons, in 1552, the Havana city council banned nonresidents and ships of foreign flags from felling and exporting trees. Much to the annoyance of Cuban residents, however, in 1622, the Spanish Crown placed large forest tracts off-limits to the local populace as well in order to ensure the navy's long-term timber supply. Thereafter, Cuban mahogany became virtually unavailable in Spain. Long after surrounding islands were deforested, this restrictive policy effectively preserved the island's mahogany trees until the late eighteenth century.[8]

As Spain struggled to protect the fruits of its conquest, England, France, the Netherlands, Denmark, and other European powers all vied to secure land and natural resources in the West Indies. Not surprisingly, some of the earliest documented mahogany arrived in England by way of captured Spanish ships. When English privateers seized a sturdy mahogany vessel, it was usually recommissioned for naval service or, if battle-damaged, the wood was salvaged to repair other vessels. In 1654, Oliver Cromwell launched his Western Design, an ambitious military campaign intended to rout Spain from the Caribbean. During the invasion, an English commander gleefully announced the capture of a Dutch vessel en route from Surinam to Amsterdam, laden with cedar and "speckled wood," a tropical timber (also called snakewood) with distinctive dark markings. To his superiors' disappointment, however, this prize wood was spirited away on two Flemish ships just before the English fleet arrived. Nonetheless, their excitement at this report intimates some of what the English hoped to gain from this aggressive gambit.[9]

Despite lofty aims, the poorly planned assault on Hispaniola proved a dismal failure, as the English miscalculated the forces needed to rout the Spanish. As a fall-back plan, their retreating fleet invaded Spanish-held Jamaica which, after several years of protracted struggle, finally came under English control. Although not successful in ousting the Spanish entirely from the region, this conquest enabled the English to extend their strategic presence in the Caribbean beyond their former foothold in the Lesser Antilles. Initially regarded as a sorry consolation prize, Jamaica eventually proved a great addition to the nation's growing portfolio of colonial possessions. Before becoming a successful sugar producer, it served as a convenient entrepôt for woodcutters, privateers, and contraband traders plumbing the greater Caribbean. Much of the island was also densely forested. In 1678, colonial promoter Richard Blome enumerated Jamaica's "great variety of Woods . . . Cedar, Mothogency [mahogany], Brasiletto, Lignum Vitae, Ebony, . . . and many other sweet smelling and curious woods fit for choice works, whose names are as yet not known, nor indeed their excellencies."[10]

Although the Jamaican landscape was still scarred years after the earlier Spanish settlers departed, leaving behind shadowy ruins, overgrazed ranges, and eroded wastelands, few English colonizers paid attention to the lessons of past land uses, including their own. By all measures, the island, with its large, diverse land mass and abundant natural resources, seemed a more promising venue for long-term economic development than smaller islands, like Barbados, with their sugar monocultures. In particular, Jamaica's forests seemed to contemporary observers to be of such abundance that, in the words of Blome, they promised an "infinite store." With "the Commodities that this Island produceth," Blome asserted, "if well *improved* [it] would soon become the best, the richest Plantation that ever the English were, (or are like to be) Masters of." With the acquisition of Jamaica, West Indian mahogany was also available for the first time on English territory.[11]

During the colony's early years, few settlers exported much timber although they felled thousands of trees to make room for sugar cultivation. Impressed and awed by the magnificent trees of the West Indies that were larger and more diverse than any they had previously encountered, they were also somewhat intimidated by and fearful of tropical forests. In particular, many shared the common belief of the time that an overabundance of trees caused miasmas, noxious fumes that were thought to cause life-threatening fevers. Settlers were determined to commence planting and to reduce any health dangers by reshaping the land as quickly as possible according to their own pastoral ideals. In their rush to push back the dense phalanxes of forest, prodigious quantities of West Indian mahogany went to waste. Clearing the land, however, was a key part of English colonizing rhetoric that emphasized "improvements," namely investments of labor and capital to develop ostensibly unoccupied or underused land, as the basis for both individual land claims and broader assertions of national sovereignty. A precedent for this concept may be found in the English enclosure movement, which privatized traditionally common lands and emphasized "improvements," such as fencing fields and draining fens. Robert Marzec argues convincingly that "before England began to colonize open, wild, and uncultivated land and subjects abroad, it created an apparatus for colonizing its open land and subjects at home—an apparatus that could readily be transplanted to distant territories." Replacing a wilderness of forests with tended fields and recognizable built environments, British subjects gained a sense of personal sovereignty, which extended to the national project as England enlarged and strengthened its colonial grasp.[12]

Richard Ligon's 1657 treatise about Barbados exemplifies both English colonizers' embrace of the concept of improvement in the West Indies and their anxieties about tropical forests. On the one hand, he evoked a benevolent image of the island's "lofty trees . . . [that] seem'd to be beholding to the earth and roots that gave them such plenty of sap for their nourishment, as to grow to that perfection of beauty and largeness, whilst they in gratitude return[ed] their cool shade." He marveled at unusual trees and plants that equaled "the strangest works and beautifullest forms that I have seen fit to be kept as a rarity, in the Cabinets of the greatest Princes." On the other hand, he was overwhelmed by their seemingly infinite diversity and abundance; noting that "to mention all were to loose [i.e. lose] my selfe in a wood," he reassured himself that "as the Woods are cut down, the Landscapes will appear." Already, the settlers "bent all their endeavors to advance their knowledge in the planting and making of Sugar." Given the combination of this single-minded goal and their discomfort with the forests, English colonizers cleared much of Barbados within the span of a few decades, profoundly altering the island's ecology. By the end of the seventeenth century, it was said that in some parts of Barbados it had become "as rare to meet a Wood . . . as it was to meet with a House" in Ligon's day. Hence when England took over Jamaica, it was greeted as a haven for planters fleeing deforestation and environmental problems elsewhere. Blome, for one, described Jamaica as "so large and so fertile, it is capable of receiving those great numbers of people, that are forced to desert the Caribbe Iles: Their plantations being worn out, and their woods wasted."[13]

On most West Indian islands during this period, tropical hardwoods were used locally for construction, housing, furniture, flooring, and even shingles, but enormous quantities of excess wood were burned or left to rot in the fields, where workers had to maneuver awkwardly around them. The monster trees were simply too many, too large, and too unwieldy to be worth the tremendous effort needed to extricate them. When European indentured servants proved inadequate to the land-clearing task, planters imported growing numbers of enslaved Africans, who later became the backbone of mahogany production even as many islands were transformed into plantation-based slave societies. As long as removing the plethora of trees cost more than the land itself, however, planters opened only enough acreage to commence cultivation and had no incentive to launch more organized commercial logging enterprises.

At some point during the late seventeenth century, the first Honduran mahogany also arrived in England from the Central American coast, most likely as ballast for shipments of logwood *(Haematoxylon campechianum),* which was much more prized at the time than mahogany because of its importance as an essential dye ingredient used by Europe's textile industry. Because shrubby logwood branches had to be packed with a heavier material to prevent dangerous shifting of the cargo in heavy seas, Honduran mahogany was convenient for this purpose since it grew in close proximity to the coastal lagoons where logwood thrived. When off-loaded in England, this mahogany ballast, although considered of lesser account than the precious logwood, did not go to waste but was used by the navy for shipbuilding or occasionally was disposed of at public auction. Since both woods grew mainly on Spanish-claimed territories, however, other nations that desired them either had to negotiate with Spain or acquire them by other means, such as through privateering or the contraband trade. As access first to logwood, and then to mahogany, became a potent bargaining chip among competing imperial powers, these specialty woods became the source of chronic international conflict that periodically flared up, and the focus of extensive diplomatic negotiations, with serious consequences for their native regions.[14]

The greatest obstacle to mahogany's initial conversion into an export commodity was the lack of an established consumer market for it. During the first quarter of the eighteenth century, the British navy already used mahogany for building warships, but it was slower to make inroads in the English domestic market. While this seems surprising in light of the general population's hunger for timber, potential buyers were deterred by high shipping costs and a heavy customs duty that inflated the price of mahogany (which in 1720 averaged £8 per ton in London) by almost 70 percent. Although shipping costs were largely fixed, in 1721 the Naval Stores Act eliminated customs duties on key military stores exported from British colonies, which included tar, turpentine, hemp, and certain tall North American pines (reserved as masts for His Majesty's Navy). Jamaican planters successfully lobbied for the inclusion of mahogany and other tropical hardwoods as well in order to boost sales of the timber that was an unavoidable by-product of their drive to clear land.[15]

While naval officials favored this law as a cost-cutting measure, it inadvertently transformed mahogany from a war material into a luxury material. Faced with shortages of domestic woods as well as of continental walnut (then the preferred furniture wood) that was suffering from a blight and still carried a heavy import duty, cabinetmakers turned to mahogany out of necessity. In the wake of the Naval Stores Act, demand for mahogany increased as it became a more affordable alternative, at least for the upper echelons of English society. Although lesser grades continued to be used in shipbuilding, construction, and other industries, the best mahogany was increasingly reserved for making fine furniture. Contemporary commentators specifically commended the change in tax policy for aiding the nation's cabinetmakers. As English craftsmen and consumers inquired after this "fancy wood" and merchants sought out more, Jamaica quickly became the world's leading exporter of West Indian mahogany.[16]

Whereas changes in tax policy served as an important catalyst, the subsequent upsurge of interest in mahogany in England, and later in the North American colonies, must also be understood as part of a longer trajectory of economic and social trends that resulted in new

consumption patterns. Beginning in the late sixteenth and early seventeenth centuries, expanding English industry and international trade
brought new prosperity to much of its populace. Domestic manufactured wares proliferated and foreign goods and commodities flowed in
from the East and West Indies, including tea, silks, tobacco, spices,
dyestuffs, ivory, ceramics, and "fancy woods." Endowed with more dis-
cretionary income than previous generations, many people, particularly among the landed gentry and rising mercantile classes, partook
of these new luxury goods. Artisans, manufacturers, and importers,
in turn, increased and diversified their products to offer a greater
range of types, prices, and quantities of merchandise. The gyroscopic
market forces thus set in motion have been aptly characterized as a
"consumer revolution" that accelerated during the eighteenth century.
What made this phenomenon truly revolutionary was how far down
the social hierarchy it eventually permeated. From urban centers to
provincial and even rural areas, British men and women at all rungs
of society participated to varying degrees.[17]

Most significantly, this phenomenon encouraged people to recast
themselves as "consumers" who could proactively reshape themselves
and their surroundings through the goods and commodities that they
selected, bought, ingested, wore, used, and displayed. Conspicuous consumption, especially of luxurious materials, became a potent, highly
visible form of self-expression and a means of enhancing one's social
standing in the eyes of others. Although likely apocryphal, an oft repeated story in furniture lore emphasizes this theme even as it pur-
ports to pinpoint mahogany's introduction in England to a specific
serendipitous event. Supposedly around 1724, Dr. Gibbons, a prominent physician, received some wooden planks from his sea captain
brother who brought them from the West Indies as ballast. Later finding himself in need of a candle box, Gibbons sent the unfamiliar wood
to his cabinetmaker, who rejected it as too hard for his tools. After insisting the man find stronger tools, Gibbons finally received his fin-

ished box as well as a bureau. Immensely pleased with their rich color and fine polish, he "invited all his friends to come see," including a duchess who ordered similar items for herself, setting off a fashion craze among the aristocracy for this extraordinary new wood. Given the haphazard way in which mahogany initially arrived in England, of course, it is impossible to attribute its introduction definitively to any one person or event. What is revealing about this "origins" myth is that from an early date, mahogany was associated with emulative consumption, aristocratic patronage, and notions of discovery, mystery, exoticism, modernity, and delight.[18]

The impact of new consumption patterns was most evident in people's homes where the quantity and diversity of domestic furnishings expanded dramatically beyond previous norms. Before then, most householders, even among the nobility, had houses with multipurpose rooms and relatively little furniture. In a typical dwelling, people might sit on stools or shared benches, store their clothes in unpartitioned wooden trunks, and take their meals at a communal table. Much of this material culture was little changed in form or function since the Middle Ages. As new consumption patterns solidified during the late seventeenth century, however, many of these tradition-bound modes of living slowly changed, beginning with the more affluent members of society. Houses became more architecturally complex, separating private rooms from public spaces intended for entertaining. Furniture underwent dramatic transformation as well thanks to new materials, furniture forms, and woodworking techniques. The fabrication of innovative objects, such as chests-of-drawers and high chests, was made possible with the introduction of cabinetmaking, a technique in which boards were conjoined with dovetail joints, allowing for lighter, less visible construction than traditional joinery (which overlapped and nailed or pinned boards together). By the early eighteenth century, these new objects could be had in mahogany as well as in walnut.

The consumer revolution altered people's daily routines as well—from how they ate, dressed, behaved, and amused themselves to how they perceived and interacted with others. New consumables, such as tea, coffee, chocolate, and tobacco, gave rise to accompanying rituals that required fluency in changing social conventions and specialized equipment, fixtures, and architectural settings. Activities, such as tea drinking, card playing, and formal dining, gave rise to new classes of objects that had not existed a generation or two earlier. Tea drinking, for example, involved elaborate preparations and a veritable shopping list of supporting objects: a brass or copper tea kettle, a kettle stand, a tea pot, handless ceramic teacups, a tea tray (usually mahogany), silver tea spoons and a strainer, and a lockable tea box to secure the costly leaves. With all the requisite accoutrements in place, people would prepare and partake of this libation together around a "tea table" (usually a small, round or rectangular, folding or tilting table that was stored carefully away when not in use), where, in a newly gendered role, the lady of the house would usually preside. The syncretic elements of this modified tea ceremony—Chinese porcelain, Indian tea, Barbadian sugar, South American silver, Jamaican mahogany—bespoke British subjects' assimilation of the products of global trade and colonialism into their own shared social rituals and material culture.[19]

French-style formal dining, introduced in England during this period, also gave rise to new categories of consumer goods. A special table, even a whole room, dedicated to dining elevated the mundane bodily function of taking sustenance into a highly choreographed social performance. As mahogany came into fashion, the large, flat surfaces of dining tables became showy displays of this new material; in elegant homes, it became a common practice for the servants to dramatically remove the protective cloth before the last course to show off the beautifully polished surface, bestowing a sense of privilege upon those gathered around it. A guest to Thomas Jefferson's Monticello, for example, noted that "no wine was set on the table till the

FIG. 1.1 Tilt-top Tea Table, unattributed, Philadelphia, PA, circa 1765–1775. Mahogany with iron. 29×37 in. Collection of Winterthur Museum; Gift of Henry Francis du Pont. (1959.3404).

When not in use, this Philadelphia tea table was designed to tilt, so as to conserve space and to display the remarkable figured mahogany used in its top, which comprises a single board with a carved edge. The v-shaped configurations of the table top's grain, that appear as waves, reveal that this piece of wood was likely cut from the main crotch of a mature tree where its trunk diverged into large branches.

cloth was removed" at the end of the meal, presumably by his house slaves. In the eighteenth century, a host or hostess with the wherewithal to invite others to join them around "the Mahogany" demonstrated their civility and skill in maneuvering within a realm of coded meanings. To realize the desired effect, of course, others had to be equally well versed in interpreting such unspoken messages. Mahogany objects served a critical function in this new material world by reinforcing new ways of living, behaving, and relating.[20]

Introducing Mahogany to Colonial North America

For colonial Americans, the choice of mahogany was less a matter of necessity, economy, or convenience than of sheer desire. In much of eastern North America, forests remained abundant so there was no real *need* for imported woods. But as colonists looked to the metropole for their fashions, they were heavily influenced by its denizens' new consumption patterns, including the emerging taste for imported tropical hardwoods. Indeed, some of the earliest mahogany objects with North American histories of ownership are believed to be English made, ordered from London or brought over by arriving immigrants.

On those West Indian islands where native mahogany was initially abundant, settlers redefined it as a preferred fine furniture wood only after it was labeled thus in Europe. In St. Domingue, for example, since mahogany was exported to France as a raw material and then returned to the island in the form of expensive furniture, it was the metropole that "gave form and meaning to the finished product." Ironically, as Chaela Pastore has argued, because mahogany came to connote luxury in France, its relative accessibility to the French Creole population of St. Domingue was disparaged by Parisians as a sign of colonial decadence. On Jamaica, seventeenth century probate inventories indicate that while early settlers' furnishings included basic, traditional forms (such as turned-leg tables, stands, and chests), they were fabricated from many different island woods, including machineel, cedar, so-called plumwood, and mahogany. But as English demand for mahogany increased in the early eighteenth century, it gained prestige in Jamaica as well, although cedar was still favored because of its insect resistance. In the urban centers of the Northern Antilles, settlers increasingly acquired at least some island-made furniture produced by European or enslaved African craftsmen who made ample use of the native mahogany.[21]

As the British colonies in North America thrived during the mid-eighteenth century, many Anglo-Americans, eager to reinforce their status as full-fledged subjects, partook of new English consumer goods and fashions as a means of drawing into closer connection with the mother country and the imperial marketplace. Colonial members of the landed gentry, royal appointees, and the rising merchant class looked to England to educate themselves about what was current, cosmopolitan, and appropriate for persons of their status. Fashionable mahogany furnishings became vehicles of conspicuous consumption in the colonies, connoting affluence, taste, and social caché in ways that readily available local woods simply did not. Quite apart from their mundane functions—a place to sit, to sleep, to take a meal—mahogany objects also served a less prosaic purpose as highly visible status symbols for others to see, admire, and covet.[22]

For many years after Jonathan Dickinson proactively tested the waters with his Jamaican woods, mahogany arrived in the northern colonies only in small, random lots, carried aboard American ships returning from the Caribbean or left over from larger shipments trans-shipped to Europe. When these early parcels came into the hands of colonial cabinetmakers, they were passed on to consumers in the form of objects. But for the most part, American merchants initially sent what little mahogany came their way directly to London and were understandably reluctant to import larger quantities to North America as

long as buyers remained uncertain. Following passage of the Naval
Stores Act in 1721 and with growing demand for mahogany first in the
metropole and then in the colonies, the tropical timber trade became
more palatable for American merchants, particularly since many of
their ships already routinely traveled regions where West Indian and
Honduran mahogany could be found. They increasingly sought it out
and gave consideration to emerging colonial markets as well as those
elsewhere in England and Europe, including Sweden, Ireland, Germany, the Netherlands, and Russia.

Typically, colonial merchants added this new product into the mix
of their already diversified coastal and circum-Caribbean trade. Private
and jointly owned vessels sailed regularly from North America to the
Caribbean laden with agricultural produce, oak barrel staves, lumber,
livestock, dried fish, food stuffs, and English-made textiles and hardware. They returned with cargos of plantation produce (sugar, rum,
cotton, pimento, ginger, and coffee) and wild-harvested commodities
(logwood, balsam, sarsaparilla, lignum vitae, and other tropical woods).
To acquire a few mahogany logs, whether for re-sale or for their own
use, American merchants turned to existing exchange networks with
West Indian planters or Anglo woodcutters in Central America who
already supplied them with logwood. American merchants, from New
England to Charleston, soon faced increasing competition from more
well-financed English merchants, whose mahogany imports dwarfed
those of American carriers, and from their colonial counterparts who
engaged in similar trading patterns. In New York, Philip Livingston,
John Watts, Gabriel Ludlow, Jonathan Beekman, John Cruger, and
Samuel Townsend all became involved in importing tropical woods.
Within a few years, Townsend's ship, the *Solomon,* made at least four-
teen documented voyages from Long Island to the Bay of Honduras
for logwood and mahogany. The total volume of the colonial mahogany trade is difficult to quantify, however, because, depending on the
wood's intended use and the available labor, it was often shipped in

non-equivalent forms, such as by the ton or itemized as whole logs, sawn planks, or oddly-shaped pieces cut from the swirling grain of a tree's crotch or roots. Export records did not always indicate where exactly mahogany shipments originated, especially if they were trans-shipped from intermediate locales, or where they were ultimately bound as they were sent throughout the British empire and, sometimes in violation of navigation laws, to multiple other destinations, including Amsterdam, Hamburg, Dublin, and Stockholm.[23]

When a load of mahogany arrived at a North American seaport, the ship captain or receiving merchant typically sold it wharf-side or at public vendues, reaching potential buyers via local newspaper advertisements. In 1737, *The Boston Gazette* advised its readers of "Mahogany and Other Woods. To be Sold . . . on the Long Wharffe" (along with lignum vitae, boxwood, ebony, and cinnamon bark) and "50 Pieces of fine Mahogany in 10 Lots" slated for auction at the Exchange Tavern. Interested parties were advised to inspect the wood prior to the sale. In June 1742, the *Boston News-Letter* announced an auction of mahogany from "the cargo of a Spanish prize ship brought into Newport, R.I."[24]

Colonial merchants and ship captains quickly learned that the mahogany trade, by its very nature, was quite a risky business. Compared with sugar, coffee, or tobacco that could be easily measured, packed, and stowed in uniform barrels, mahogany was a bulky, unwieldy commodity, difficult and costly to transport. Expenses included insurance, lading, wharfage, and warehouse space. So although the largest logs usually commanded the highest prices, they were also the most expensive to move, stow, and store. In many port cities, merchants shelled out more money to pay the fees of official wood surveyors who were responsible for evaluating, measuring, and grading in-coming timber before it could be sold. This governmental post was usually entrusted to a master cabinetmaker. In Newport, various members of the esteemed Townsend-Goddard family of cabinetmakers firm held the post for many years. While some merchants plied the wood surveyor with drinks to ensure that their timber was generously measured, Portsmouth merchant George Boyd was less subtle, advising an associate that "a little Money with your Surveyors will do the thing . . . Capt. Hart got a Large measure Once by giving a Guinea or two which saved Twenty." Other unexpected costs and variables, often beyond a merchant's control, made it difficult to anticipate projected mahogany sales. Abrupt price fluctuations, periodic gluts and shortages, labor problems, war and political upheavals, minor shipping disruptions, and even natural disasters—hurricanes, floods, and drought—could wreck havoc on a merchant's best-laid plans. At those times, profit margins could be quite narrow and sometimes nil.[25]

Moreover, as merchants discovered through painful experience, mahogany was an unpredictable, seemingly deceptive commodity, especially if one was not vigilant. Only good quality wood was worth the freight. A merchant could lose his entire investment if a large log, that appeared fine on its exterior, proved defective when it was sawn open. Moreover, since flaws were not always immediately apparent, mahogany purchasers were typically allowed a grace period of up to a year to pay. Some merchants thus preferred to ship mahogany as pre-cut boards but that might reduce its potential value for fabricating large-scale objects. Adding to the inherent challenges of the mahogany trade was the still nebulous, imperfect state of knowledge about tropical hardwoods and the difficulties of asserting quality control over long distances. Sometimes altogether different species arrived misidentified as mahogany. Other times, inferior mahogany was sent surreptitiously or deliberately misrepresented by mahogany purveyors. Accordingly, most colonial merchants limited mahogany to only one facet of their diversified trade. By juggling many commodities simultaneously, they hedged their risks and could more easily absorb occasional losses, adapt to fluctuating prices and demand levels, and ride out volatile market conditions. By the mid-eighteenth century, the success of this strategy was evident. Many merchants became wealthy and their burgeoning trade helped North America's busy seaports grow significantly in population and prosperity.[26]

The emergence of a strong merchant class was a critical factor in the development of furniture industries along the Eastern Seaboard. In addition to supplying cabinetmakers with mahogany, merchants provided them with patronage and access to other markets. While imported English objects still appealed to some buyers, most colonial Americans, especially in urban areas, increasingly expected comparable productions from the workshops of local craftsmen. In many of the leading port cities, merchants commissioned furniture as venture cargo, sometimes supplying mahogany, cedar, and other raw materials to fill their orders. Consigned on vessels bound for the West Indies or for the coastal trade, these objects were shipped off on speculative voyages in hopes of finding buyers in distant venues. As early as 1734, the British Council of Trade and Plantations reported that many New Englanders, discouraged by the poor soil and harsh climate, had turned to furniture-making and other forms of manufacturing, so successfully "that not only escritoires [desks], chairs, and other wooden manufactures, but hoes, axes, and other iron utensils, are now exported from thence to the other plantations."[27]

While not all affluent American merchants traded or speculated in mahogany during this period, most certainly did become ardent consumers of mahogany objects. However they made their money, lavish mahogany furnishings seemed a great way to spend it. Many indulged in colossal desks and over-sized dining tables that were rather ostentatious displays of affluence. The Brown family of Providence, for example, derived immense wealth from sugar, the China trade, and the African slave trade. A substantial chunk of their profits went to acquiring elegant mahogany furnishings made by the Townsend family of Newport. With illustrious patrons willing to pay handsomely for such bespoke work, the Townsends used the finest mahogany, in the words of one furniture historian and curator, "joyously, extravagantly, and apparently without regard to economy." Several magnificent mahogany objects with Brown family provenances are still extant in Rhode Island museums. Boston merchant Nicholas Boylston likewise enjoyed an unprecedented degree of domestic comfort made possible by his successful trade that extended from the West Indies to Europe, Africa, and Russia. After dining at Boylston's mansion in 1766, John Adams described its sumptuous interiors as fit "for a nobleman, a prince" and was astounded to learn that the furniture alone cost £1,000. While Adams looked askance at such extravagance, it clearly made a big impression on him. As colonial merchants filled their houses with monumental mahogany objects, others were encouraged to follow suit, although their acquisitions were usually of more modest proportions.[28]

From the point of wood purchase to the point of furniture sale, American cabinetmakers too played a central role in the introduction and diffusion of mahogany. In the late seventeenth century, most furniture makers in colonial North America had emigrated from provincial regions of England and cleaved to familiar furniture designs (such as dower chests, high-crested Great Chairs, and trestle tables) and woodworking techniques, such as joinery and turning, that were centuries old. Whenever possible, they sought out the same woods traditionally used for English furniture, especially oak and walnut, which were well suited to their skills and tools. During the first half of the eighteenth century, however, an influx of more urbane cabinetmakers, trained in London, Paris, or Edinburgh, began arriving in North America's growing seaports. While they eagerly took advantage of many excellent American woods, they also brought with them prior experience working with mahogany and a repertoire of innovative furniture design ideas. Through the combined influx of English-made objects (that served as prototypes for American copies), skilled craftsmen, and some of the first publications of furniture designs, more colonial Americans became acquainted with mahogany and with new furniture forms.[29]

Accordingly, American cabinetmakers increasingly offered imported mahogany as an option for their high-end products, typically in combination with cheaper, native secondary woods (for structural and hidden furniture parts). How exactly they transformed mahogany into objects, however, varied widely by region, depending on to what degree they abandoned, adapted, or retained their traditional vernacular styles, construction techniques, and artisanal practices. They also catered to their clientele's tastes and pocketbooks; those with more sophisticated or fashion-conscious customers typically adhered more closely to metropolitan English furniture designs, while those in more conservative or rural regions typically produced more idiosyncratic or creolized designs. Over time, many regions in colonial America thus developed distinctive furniture styles, especially in those places dominated by non-English ethnic groups. Given its large German immigrant population, Pennsylvania furniture tended to have heavier construction and a more baroque flavor. In parts of New York, Dutch and Huguenot influences were evident in some furnishings. Boston cabinetmakers developed the so-called bombé style (with distinctive swell-bases). Rhode Island cabinetmakers concurrently innovated their blockfront style, emphasizing the use of choice woods but minimal carving. In South Carolina, people favored very English-looking furniture but scaled with larger proportions to suit their high-ceilinged plantation houses adapted to the warm climate. In the Anglophone West Indies as well, while wealthy planters still imported fine furniture from England or North America (even supplying wood for this purpose), many also patronized the small cohort of émigré furniture makers in Kingston and other cities who, although mostly London trained, also developed their own regional variations.[30]

In all of these contexts, a cabinetmaker's success depended on many variables such as his available capital, labor force, suppliers, and access to markets. More fundamentally, he needed training, skill, and creative intuition to be able to conceive, replicate, or adapt designs to his particular intentions and to translate them into finished objects using his available materials and technology. In particular, he needed intimate knowledge of the physical characteristics and woodworking properties of the entire repertoire of woods available to him—whether strong, flexible hickory for chair spindles; cheap, easy-to-work pine for a hidden drawer back; or showy mahogany for a desk front. In selecting wood for a particular purpose, he had to confirm its soundness (avoiding rotten areas, knots, or other imperfections), determine the direction of its grain, and evaluate the potential structural effects of its natural movement. Any miscalculations could undermine the integrity and attractiveness of his finished product.

Where mahogany was concerned, long experience was required in order to fully exploit its particular qualities, especially given that each piece varied depending on the age, health, and life history of the tree from whence it came. Yet cabinetmakers' wood selections were also highly subjective. Depending on what they were making, their client's wishes, as well as their own aesthetic sensibilities, individual cabinetmakers developed preferences for certain geographical sources or grades of mahogany. Even after selecting a mahogany log, cutting it open so as to maximize its useable timber with minimal waste required considerable skill. In urban areas that allowed for greater specialization, many cabinetmakers hired professional sawyers or sent their logs to sawmills accustomed to handling mahogany. In addition, cabinetmakers had to anticipate their future timber requirements constantly because wood needed to dry for a long period before use (for a minimum of two to three years, preferably for many years). Laying in a large store of wood to season called for a significant investment, although any extra wood might be later sold off wholesale. When Philadelphia cabinetmaker Joseph Claypoole retired in 1738, for example, he advertised for sale "the largest and oldest Stock of Timber, of the Produce of this country and the West-Indies of any in this Province, some of which having been in Piles near 25 Years."[31]

During the 1720s to 1730s, Philadelphia joiner John Head used predominately locally-sourced black walnut for furniture making, as well as cherry, maple, and pine. His clientele seems to have been quite diverse, including both merchants and tradesmen. His best selling items were chests of drawers, which would have been a relatively new and extremely useful form, but, as befitted his clientele, he made a wide range of utilitarian objects such as dough kneading trays, brick molds, candle-making equipment, coffins, and even a quilting form—all of which were apparently made of common domestic woods. He did make some early use of imported mahogany for his more expensive fabrications, although the choice of wood did not always correlate with a higher price and there is no indication of where precisely his supply originated. In a typical order in 1720, he made a mahogany cradle and oval table for Thomas Masters, who also ordered a bedstead later that same year made of an unspecified wood. Head's other mahogany productions included chests of drawers, tall clock cases, and high chests.[32]

In Boston, the gradual adoption of mahogany can be similarly tracked in the records of Samuel Grant, an upholsterer and cabinetmaker, whose surviving account book spans from 1737 to 1760. During the early years of his career, Grant's account book indicates that he used locally sourced black walnut and maple almost exclusively. Around 1739, he initiated some "Petty Adventures to Jamaica," sending some walnut chairs and other furnishings there in exchange for logwood from the Bay of Honduras that he later sold in London. His first recorded entry of mahogany was in April 1743, when he sold Samuel Wentworth a dozen mahogany chairs with leather seats for £5 each (similar chairs in walnut were £3 each and in maple, only £2.5 each). Thereafter, although walnut continued to be Grant's primary wood, mahogany slowly assumed a larger share of his production. Seven

years after delivering Wentworth's chairs, Grant's commissions included numerous sets of mahogany chairs ordered by the dozen, an
"Easie Chaire [with] Carvd Mohogy feet," and a mahogany bedstead
with "squared carved gothic fretwork." His accounts included the
names of many wealthy Bostonians, which suggests the fashionable
clientele who were buying his new mahogany objects.[33]

During this same period, Newport cabinetmakers developed a
strong trans-regional market for their furniture that rested heavily on
its earned reputation for excellence. To meet growing demand, several
hundred cabinetmakers, journeymen, and apprentices were kept busy,
contributing significantly to the city's wealth. In Newport, two contrasting organizational models of furniture production briefly coex-
isted: the traditional, patriarchal master-apprentice model and a newer,
less hierarchical model based on wage labor. The Townsend-Goddard
dynasty exemplified the former; their family-based workshop (which
included as many as twenty interrelated cabinetmakers) was headed
by master craftsmen who trained numerous apprentices and journeymen drawn from an extended kinship sphere, as well as a small number of enslaved Africans. This organizational structure persisted in
Newport much longer than in other urban areas, such as New York
and Philadelphia, because intermarriages among closely-knit cabinetmaking families kept artisanal knowledge, valuable tools, timber
stocks, and capital within their circle. Like most New England cabinetmaking firms, the Townsends and Goddards made furniture for export
as well as for a loyal local and regional clientele, including many influential merchants. As Quakers, they also benefitted from strong patronage within their spiritual community. Located in Newport, their proximity to incoming mahogany shipments kept their workshops well
supplied.[34]

By contrast, John Cahoone, although himself a joiner's son, followed the newer model of production by relying on wage labor. In
addition to hiring full-time journeymen in his shop, he jobbed out

FIG. 1.2 Blockfront Bureau table, attributed to John Townsend, Newport, RI, 1785–95. Mahogany, chestnut, tulip poplar, white pine, maple. 34½ × 5 × 37½ × 21 in. Collection of Winterthur Museum; Gift of Henry Francis du Pont. (1959.2645).

This object, made with a single-board top, combines a central concave shell cut from the solid, with convex shells applied at either side, creating its so-called block front form, a distinctive New England design.

work to part-time cabinetmakers to fabricate ready-made retail stock and wholesale goods for export. Using timber supplied by Cahoone, they made either complete objects or standardized parts (such as chair legs) to be assembled later. Paid by the piece, they received more for work done using mahogany, which required extra time and care to avoid costly mistakes and wasted materials. In 1752, for example, Cahoone paid a workman £12 for his labor on a maple desk but £22 for one made of mahogany. Cahoone passed this cost differential on to his customers, charging on average a third each for materials, labor, and profit.[35]

According to his account book, the woods that Cahoone used or sold wholesale were predominately Native American species, including maple (most frequently), elm, oak, chestnut, and black walnut. The only imported woods he used were mahogany and cedar, which he usually acquired through trade with incoming ship captains. In 1757, for example, Cahoone received 243 feet of mahogany and 13 feet of black walnut from Captain Joseph Arnold in return for which he fabricated a desk, a tea table, and three tables. Early in his career, Cahoone likely received mahogany from his uncles, William and Elijah Cahoone, former mariners who had become woodcutters in the Bay of Honduras and who maintained close New England ties. Cedar desks, one of Cahoone's best-selling items, were especially popular in the South and West Indies likely because their aromatic wood was so insect resistant. Between 1749 and 1760, the most expensive items that Cahoone produced were almost all made of mahogany, including tables (from three to five feet long), tea tables, desks, and bookcases. While he did not record exact specifications, here again one can get a sense of how materials factored into an object's overall cost. As a point of comparison, the least expensive mahogany desk made by Cahoone was £66 (ranging up to £160) whereas a maple desk cost on average only £30. In 1760, Cahoone charged Major Godfrey Malbone £50 for a maple desk, £100 for a cedar desk, and £110 for a mahogany desk. His close competitor, Job Townsend, Jr., whose primary woods during the 1760s were also mahogany and maple, had similar prices and usually charged a third to half again as much for the former. A standout entry in Cahoone's account book was £250 billed to Samuel Goldthwait in 1759 for a custom-made "mahogany OG Case of Drawers;" the fashionable use of ogee curves (double curves) to create a serpentine front took great skill and certainly explains why this case piece commanded such a high price. For such an important commission, Cahoone would have undoubtedly selected the very finest mahogany to showcase his workmanship.[36]

Other special commissions Cahoone fulfilled suggest the important and, at times, highly personal role that cabinetmakers played in their communities and in their customers' lives. On 9 November 1759, for example, Cahoone billed Jonathan Easton the sum of £55 to make a "Mahogany Coffin for your Wife." While coffin making was a sorrowful but reliable part of Cahoone's business, he usually made them out of less expensive materials; this was the first mention of a coffin made of mahogany. Was this extravagant choice motivated by an anguished man's love for his deceased wife—to honor her in death as in life? Or was it intended more as a gratuitous display for those who stood graveside? There is no knowing. By the mid-eighteenth century, mahogany coffins (often with silver handles and engraved silver name plates to boot) began to appear in colonial America, both for adults and children, although deceased slaves usually went into the earth in plain pine boxes. Evidence suggests that mahogany was not generally used for coffins until the latter half of the eighteenth century. In Philadelphia, for example, John Head's account book, included numerous orders for coffins during the 1720s to 1730s, but they were usually made of walnut or blackened pine, with no recorded instances of mahogany. By the 1770s, however, David Evans offered Philadelphians mahogany coffins in a range of prices, suggesting that he used varying grades of wood. In Rhode Island, likewise, from 1762 to 1776, Job Townsend, Jr. regularly made mahogany coffins. Rather astoundingly, whole groves of mahogany ended up planted in the burying grounds of early America. This phenomenon suggests quite literally how deeply mahogany was becoming integrated into the important social rituals of many people's lives.[37]

Overall, as American cabinetmakers experimented with mahogany's various physical characteristics—through their hands, tools, and senses—they acquired a deep familiarity with and understanding of its particular physical properties and aesthetic possibilities that they passed on to their journeymen and apprentices. Drawing on this type of acquired experiential knowledge, cabinetmakers' perspectives were vital in expanding consumers' range of choices, shaping their expectations and standards, and fueling their desire for mahogany. Their customers, in turn, sought to educate themselves as they tried to get their footing in this new realm of consumption.

Mahogany as the Pinnacle of Style and Refinement

In the wake of the Seven Years War, which ended in 1763 with the defeat of Spain and France, the British Empire emerged more powerful than ever. After weathering serious wartime trade disruptions and soaring mahogany prices, American merchants resumed their mercantile activities with renewed fervor to meet pent-up demand. Those merchants who, during Britain's occupation of Havana had profited from a brief influx of Cuban mahogany had to regroup once the island was restored to Spain and that supply was cut off. But otherwise, from New England to Charleston, the leading mercantile families solidified their wealth and elevated their social status through propitious marriages, strong kinship ties, widespread land acquisitions, and strategic business partnerships. They also asserted their place in the world with greater confidence, assured of the American colonies' centrality to the future economic and political power of the British Empire. One reflection of this attitude was evident in people's robust consumption of imported luxury goods and commodities, including mahogany. If Pehr Kalm had returned to America during the late 1760s or early 1770s, he would have seen even more lavish use of this material than at mid-century.[38]

During this period, Philadelphia emerged as the foremost stylistic center in North America, where London-trained artisans flocked to take advantage of ample patronage. Carpenters, cabinetmakers, carvers, gilders, upholsterers, and other skilled craftsmen found employment building and furnishing sumptuous townhouses and country estates. Drawing on their intimate knowledge of materials, tools, and design, these craftsmen transformed raw wood into objects of exquisite beauty. The proliferation of published design books made the latest metropolitan fashions readily available in the colonies. The influence of Thomas Chippendale's *Gentleman and Cabinetmaker's Directory*, first published in London in 1754, with its fanciful amalgam of Gothic, Chinese, and rococo elements, is evident, for example, on Benjamin Randolph's elaborately bordered trade card (circa 1769) that advertised cabinetmaking services "performed in the Chinese and Modern Tastes."[39]

Among the most extravagant commissions of the day were the furnishings made for General John and Elizabeth Cadwalader's home in 1769. Since their recent marriage combined two substantial fortunes, and there was no need to scrimp, they commissioned furniture from Philadelphia's leading cabinetmakers, including Benjamin Randolph, William Savery, and Thomas Affleck. Although General Cadwalader ordered all their fine furniture in solid mahogany (with American secondary woods), there is no indication that he specified where his mahogany should be sourced. Rather, by selecting the best available craftsmen, he was counting on (and paying for) their wood expertise, as did most people during this period. The Cadwaladers' elaborate parlor suite is attributed to the workshop of the Scotsman Thomas Affleck, a highly-skilled, London-trained cabinetmaker and experienced timber dealer. Thanks to Affleck's discriminating knowledge of materials and his judicious decision to subcontract the carving to the shops of Nicholas Bernard and Martin Jugiez and of James Reynolds, the final result was a set of sensuous, visually striking objects with forceful design, robust carving, and rich materials. The matching card tables were comprised of powerful scrolls, with carved volutes, a frieze-like edge, and polished tops. On successfully executed objects, such as these,

FIG 1.3 Trade Card, Benjamin Randolph, Philadelphia, PA, circa 1769. Engraved and etche by James Smither. Collection of The Library Company of Philadelphia.

Cabinetmaker Benjamin Randolph's trade card advertises his services "Performed in th Chinese and Modern Tastes." Its elaborate rococo border and inset images of chairs, table and cabinets illustrate the type of carving for which mahogany was especially well suited.

cabinetmakers and carvers used strong visual and spatial contrasts (height and depth, voids and spaces, smooth and rough surfaces, symmetry and asymmetry, light and dark) to create a sense of movement, plasticity, and multidimensionality. The Cadwaladers' satisfaction with the craftsmen's artistic achievement is confirmed by the fact that when Charles Willson Peale painted their family portrait in 1772, they posed with their little daughter Anne next to one of these very card tables.[40]

Just as the Cadwaladers spared no expense on their furniture, the rooms that contained it were equally elaborate with ornate plasterwork ceilings, gilded friezes, and carved architectural details. The rooms were further enriched with an abundance of costly textiles ordered from some of Philadelphia's leading upholsterers. Making the silk damask upholstery and tasseled draperies provided weeks of employment for many skilled workers (including the accomplished young seamstress who gained later fame for making the nation's first flag). Altogether, the Cadwaladers' completed parlors must have been an impressive sight; they were widely regarded at the time as among colonial America's most elegant interiors.[41]

Following General Cadwalader's death in 1786, however, their household was dispersed. Over the course of several generations, their fabulous furniture was variously bequeathed, sold, stored away, or lost. Happily, in the twentieth century, some of these objects were rediscovered and brought back from obscurity. Most notably, in 1986, the Cadwaladers' long-lost easy chair was found in the hallway of a private school where the students had subjected it to no end of abuse, until a sharp-eyed visitor recognized its distinctive lion-carved feet. The following year, it sold at Sotheby's for $2.5 million, setting a record for the then highest hammer price for a piece of American furniture. Regarded as masterpieces of American craftsmanship, several other objects with Cadwalader family histories of ownership are preserved and exhibited at the Metropolitan Museum of Art, Winterthur Museum, and the Philadelphia Museum of Art. In this context, the objects are not only valued today, as they were in the eighteenth century, for their superlative materials, design, and craftsmanship but also for their historical provenance of having belonged to one of America's influential colonial families—the trend-setters and taste-makers of their day.[42]

The Allure of Mahogany

Mahogany appealed to Anglo-Americans in the mid-eighteenth century foremost because its silky smooth, polished surfaces aligned with the contemporary fascination with refinement as an important aspect of beauty. In the words of one essayist, "beauty arises from that species of elegance, which we call smoothness.... The higher the marble is polished, the brighter the silver is rubbed, and the more the mahogany shines, the more each is considered as an object of beauty: as if the eye delighted in gliding smoothly over a surface." Edmund Burke's *Philosophical Inquiry into the Origin of Our Ideas of the Sublime and Beautiful* likewise noted that smoothness was such a "considerable" component of beauty that if one gave an object "a broken and rugged surface ... however well formed it may be in other respects, it pleases no longer." Silky mahogany, however, was a sensory delight.[43]

From an artisanal perspective, refinement literally meant the distancing of a raw material from its natural state (such as rough ore refined into pure gold). Master craftsmanship required that design, tools, materials, and skill came seamlessly together resulting in perfectly integrated objects that gave no hint of the labor invested in them, the raw materials used in their fabrication, or the structural elements that actually held them together. Silversmiths thus buffed away all evidence of their hammering techniques (the physical manifestation of their labor) creating perfectly unblemished teapots and bowls. The goal for cabinetmakers was the same but, in their case, this transformation entailed using razor-sharp planes to systematically remove layers of wood, reducing its rough exterior down to a less coarse undersurface that was then sanded with a series of abrasives from coarse to fine. This process removed any bumps or burrs until the wood's texture was as silky smooth as a baby's skin. The finished wood was then polished (often with linseed oil and brick dust) until it shone. Some cabinetmakers particularly favored wood cut from the base of a mahogany tree that took "the highest polish, with a singular lustre, so firm as even to reflect objects like a mirror." In some larger cabinetmaking firms, the labor-intensive task of polishing completed objects was done by full-time finishing specialists while in smaller shops it might be delegated to apprentices; either way, it required careful attention to detail and the subtle nuances of surfaces. While hidden parts of a completed object (such as the back or underside) might be left in the rough, no one was ever meant to see the wood in its natural state or to be able to discern any tool marks, nails, or pins marring the visible perfection of its facade.[44]

Polishing did not end, however, when mahogany objects left a cabinetmaker's shop. To the contrary, keeping their surfaces in good condition required on-going maintenance. In finer homes, cleaning, dusting, and polishing the furniture were regular, recurring assignments for household servants and slaves that consumed untold hours of domestic labor. In his autobiography, Juan Manzano, a Cuban slave, recalled as a child cleaning the furniture every half hour, "whether it was dusty or not . . . I was sent to polish the mahogany so that I would not spend my time weeping." In a well-ordered household, however, workers were expected to remain in the background and not call attention to themselves; only their faults would be noticed when a handprint or smudge left by a housemaid or slave shattered the illusion of perfect refinement. Robert Roberts's *House Servant's Directory* (1827) gave detailed instructions on how properly to clean mahogany furniture,

FIG. 1.4(A–C) Desk and Bookcase (with interior details), attributed to John Welch, Boston, MA, circa 1750. Mahogany. Courtesy of the Chipstone Collection; photograph by Gavin Ashworth. (1991.10).

(*continued*)

As revealed in these details of the inside of the desk drawers and the desk's removable central compartment, which is a hidden drawer (top image), the interiors and reverse sides of mahogany objects were often left in the rough while the visible portions were finished with a high polish.

insisting that servants had to "pay a great deal of attention to cleaning furniture to make it look well." To achieve the requisite "beautiful and brilliant polish," he advised multiple rounds of rubbing with oil or beeswax, ending with a final polish using a silk handkerchief to "give it a good gloss."[45]

During this period, socially ambitious people strived to improve themselves by cultivating an aura of refinement—from their furnishings and domestic interiors to their personal appearance, dress, manners, and speech. In the homes of affluent Americans, mahogany furnishings, often with shiny brass hardware or gilded decorative details, were typically combined with other equally polished or reflective objects, such as silver tea services, brass candlesticks and andirons, large looking glasses, cut-crystal chandeliers, and mirrored wall sconces. In the evenings, these shimmering elements caught, refracted, and magnified the candlelight dancing off people's lustrous silk clothing, gold or silver buttons, and shiny metallic lace or embroidery, giving the interiors as well as their occupants an enchanting glow. In this world, as Richard Bushman stated in *The Refinement of America*, a "polished environment was as much the essence of gentility as polished manners."[46]

In eighteenth-century portraiture as well, artists often sought to create an aura of refinement around their subjects by depicting them alongside appropriately evocative objects. Accordingly, as mahogany became a mark of status, it began to appear in portraits. The ability to conjure the illusion of mahogany in paint—with all its superlative smoothness, reflectivity, and polish—was considered a great test of an artist's skill and talent. Appreciation for those who could convincingly render images of precious materials (such as gold, silver, pearls, gemstones, silks, velvets, ivory, ebony, tortoiseshell, and furs) began in the Renaissance when wealthy European patrons commissioned artists to record their luxurious goods for display. This new "aesthetic of expenditure," as Lisa Jardine termed it, was meant to evoke in onlookers a "fantasy of possession, which was independent of any real possibility of owning such wonders themselves." In colonial America, portraits were themselves a rarified art form, accessible mainly to the wealthy and even then usually commissioned only to mark an important event (such as a marriage) or achievement in a person's life. For those who had their likenesses painted, the experience may have been a self-conscious moment as they had to decide literally how to put their best face forward.[47]

In New England, John Singleton Copley catered to his elite patrons' preferences by depicting them in elegant settings which quite often included what appear to be mahogany tables or chairs, often of recognizable designs. Since he sometimes choreographed his subjects' dress, accoutrements, and surroundings using both actual and fictive elements, the mahogany objects thus depicted may have represented his patrons' actual furniture, studio props, or purely imaginary conceits. As he helped his sitters stage their poses, he indirectly offered them guidance in comportment and in how to present themselves. Among his subjects were members of many of the leading families in colonial New England, including Nicholas Boylston, Hannah Fayerweather Winthrop, Dorothy Skinner, Elizabeth Goldthwait, Mary Devereux, Miles Sherbrook, William Vassall, Sylvester Gardiner, and Isaac and Jemima Winslow.[48]

In his 1773 portrait of the Winslows, Copley depicted the couple seated with their hands resting upon a simple gate-leg table which appears in several of his paintings. Since the Winslows were very wealthy and lived in a large, well-furnished mansion in Roxbury, Massachusetts, that Copley resorted to a convenient prop suggests that the portrait was done in his Boston studio. Nevertheless, Copley gave the requisite attention to depicting the gleaming surface of the table, adding an aura of gentility to the careful composition of their juxtaposed hands. In Copley's famous portrait of Paul Revere, he similarly evoked reflective surfaces to enhance his subject's surroundings. Although this portrait has often been interpreted as an homage to the working

FIG. 1.5 *Paul Revere,* John Singleton Copley, Boston, MA, 1768. Oil on Canvas. 35¹⁄₈ × 28¹⁄₂ in. Collection of the Museum of Fine Arts, Boston; Gift of Joseph W. Revere, William B. Revere, and Edward H. R. Revere. (30.781). Photograph © Museum of Fine Arts, Boston.

man, the famous silversmith is not, in fact, actually shown at work—rather we see Revere deep in contemplation, cradling a silver teapot in his hand with his tools at rest before him, leaning on what appears to be a mahogany table or countertop. With no evident manufacturing residue or any sign of exertion, the glowing orb in his hand seems to have sprung forth fully formed from his unruffled mind; Revere is the very picture of refinement.[49]

In Charles Willson Peale's charming group portrait of the Cadwalader family, he carefully recorded their appearance along with that of one of their mahogany card tables. If one compares the actual three-dimensional table with its two-dimensional simulacrum, one can appreciate the difficulty of translating the nuances of this polished wood into paint. Nonetheless, Peale successfully captured its essence as well as his subjects' silk garments, shiny buttons, and glistening jewelry. While the painting's primary emphasis is on the relationship among the three sitters, the table creates an elegant backdrop that seems their natural habitat. Similarly, when New York merchant Jeremiah Platt commissioned his portrait from John Mare in 1767, mahogany was central to his self-presentation. With erect posture, forthright gaze, and distinguished costume, Platt stands with his hand possessively on the crest rail of a Chippendale chair. Foregrounded in this manner, the chair—of the latest style and status-laden exotic wood—seems to announce its owner's claims on a lofty place in the world. Did contemporary viewers interpret this image as an expression of justifiable pride or perhaps of arrogance? Despite his bold display of self-confidence (or perhaps, in part, because of it), Platt's career later ended in insolvency, although his inventory recorded a house filled with fine furnishings. Desirous of the costly trappings of gentility, he apparently lived beyond his means. The only legacy of his better days is this painted image, now in the portrait collection of the Metropolitan Museum of Art, which immortalized his idealized self alongside the iconic chair.[50]

During the 1760s and 1770s, colonial artists and cabinetmakers both became agents of self-fashioning for their customers, helping them to shape their personal identities and public personas. Their efforts to capture mahogany's elusive beauty and sensuality—whether in three dimensions or two—and their patrons' willingness to pay for the results became another means through which this material transcended the pedestrian existence of mere wood. Mahogany's physical properties and its metaphorical meanings were mutually reinforcing in colonial America. While some inquisitive individuals no doubt sought out deeper understandings of the raw materials, technical processes, and labor embodied in mahogany objects and their painted images, most were content to merely use them to project an aura of prosperity, poise, and polish as they staked out their positions in a shifting social hierarchy of taste and power.

While the Cadwalader furniture represented a high point in the annals of American furniture, by the mid-eighteenth century, mahogany's assimilation in colonial North America began to extend beyond the elegant parlors of the affluent few. Imported mahogany, although still more expensive than native woods, was no longer so prohibitive as to remain exclusive. Although the pace varied by region and economic level, the ongoing consumer revolution permeated further down the social strata and across a wider geographical range, eventually reaching even into quite rural areas. Many formerly rare, exotic goods and commodities, once the prerogative of the wealthy, became more accessible to the general populace. Studies of probate inventories in both the New England and Chesapeake colonies document that consumers at almost all economic levels increased the quantity and quality of their household artifacts over the course of the eighteenth century.

As mahogany furnishings became the standard of domestic comfort among the social elite, less affluent people also acquired them, although usually in smaller numbers and in less elaborate forms. In his 1765 design book, *The Cabinet and Chair-maker's Real Friend and Companion*, for example, Robert Manwaring claimed that his designs were "calculated for all People in different stations" and, whether executed plainly or grandly, would still be elegant. Although mahogany was his clear preference for his designs, however, he did suggest other choices, such as walnut or pear, could be substituted.[51]

Likewise, cabinetmakers responded to growing demand by offering still more choices and design options at different price points. In 1754, Philadelphia cabinetmaker Francis Trumble aimed to reach a diverse clientele by advertising a long list of products: "Scrutores [desks], bureaus, sliding-presses, chests of drawers of various sorts, breakfast tables, dining tables, tea tables, and card tables; also cabin tables and stools. Chairs of all sorts; such as settees, easy chairs, arm chairs, parlour chairs, chamber chairs, and couches, carv'd or plain; bedsteads, . . . clock cases, corner cupboards, tea chests, tea boards." In each case, his customers could specify whether they wanted an article made of mahogany, walnut, cherry, or maple. But if furniture buyers splurged on materials, they could save some money by forgoing carving or opting for a simplified design.[52]

Material things were now assumed by many to be important signifiers of social status and hence possession of them was seen as an avenue of self-improvement. For middling and lower-level consumers, however, most furniture acquisitions still represented big investments and, in some cases, might be a once-in-a-lifetime expenditure. Prospective buyers were thus concerned about making informed choices, yet few knew how to evaluate furniture beyond its superficial appearance to consider the quality of its materials, construction, or design. Often, they turned to their friends, relations, neighbors, or prominent community figures for advice on what was fashionable, what they should expect to pay, and which cabinetmakers to patronize.

During this period, white women made inroads into furniture buying, which up to then had been a largely male-dominated task. Now women, too, educated themselves in matters of taste, sought council from others, and influenced their family's purchases. In 1746, for example, Brinley Sylvester, a prominent Long Island merchant and landowner, recorded in his accounts that a female neighbor had requested him to order "a Mahogany Tea Table" and "9 Chairs which [are] as our last from Boston." Although he acted mainly as her agent in this case, she apparently followed his lead in requesting the same type of chairs that he had recently acquired. In 1755, Esther Burr, daughter of Reverend Jonathan Edwards, similarly solicited furniture advice following her marriage to Aaron Burr, Sr., who had a meager salary as president of the recently founded College of New Jersey (now Princeton University). She inquired of a New England friend, "I want to know how a body may have some sorts of Household stuff—What is the price of a Mehogane Case of Drawers ... in Boston, and also a Bulow [bureau] Table and a Tea Table and plain Chairs with Leather bottoms and a Couch ... all of that wood." Esther's insistence on mahogany suggests how prominently it figured in her assessment of what constituted a respectable household, while her indication that the chairs be plain was a nod towards economy.[53]

By the 1760s, mahogany had become a familiar presence in the material lives of colonial Americans as it was incorporated into so many private and public settings. Almost everyone would have at least encountered it and would have likely become somewhat conversant with its qualities. If a person was in a position to buy furniture at all, he or she might save up to acquire a mahogany chair or table, typically mixing it with other articles of local maple, cherry, or pine. Alternatively, for those who could not afford the real article, even in a small quantity or plain form, as well as for those who just preferred not to spend large sums, cabinetmakers offered a veritable arsenal of affordable techniques to emulate mahogany's appearance with red-tinted stains, finishes, or paint. Windsor chairs, one of the most common all-purpose seating forms in colonial America (used everywhere from the gardens and porches of elegant country houses to the rowdiest backwoods taverns), were traditionally fabricated from several different woods suited to each chair element (ash, maple, poplar, hickory, and occasionally mahogany) and then painted to look uniform. They were available in a wide array of colors, including mahogany, which was not even the cheapest option since the necessary pigments of red ochre, burnt sienna, and burnt umber were imported from Europe and specially heat-treated to darken them. The artful application of mahogany-hued paint on architectural woodwork to create the illusion of finer woods was also very popular; even the fanciest houses might have interior doors or paneling adorned with wood-grained paint. This form of trompe l'oeil was not intended to deceive but to delight the eye and evoke positive associations. In his *Essays on the Nature and Principles of Taste,* Archibald Alison claimed that whereas "many indifferent things . . . of the Earth, of Stone, of Wood" excited no emotions, mahogany (and rosewood) stirred the soul. While he insisted that no imitation could be as beautiful as the precious wood itself, he conceded that even its evocative color was "in some measure significant to us of this value." Accordingly, painting "faux" mahogany became an art unto itself.[54]

Importantly, while mahogany (and its likeness) was assimilated into Americans' everyday material lives, it also developed into a meaningful, value-laden concept in their intellectual and emotional lives as well. The personal significance of these treasured objects, as well as their enduring economic value, is evident in how often they were carefully enumerated, assessed, and bequeathed by their owners. Oftentimes, when furniture was mentioned in eighteenth century documents—whether probate inventories, wills, personal letters, diaries, account books, invoices, newspaper articles, advertisements, sale notices, or period novels—items made of mahogany were highlighted as such, even when no other woods were specified. Although not everyone owned or stood to inherit mahogany, they would have recognized and understood it as a now integral part of the cultural landscape of colonial America.[55]

As mahogany became somewhat more accessible to middling Americans, however, those in the higher ranks of society sought to distinguish themselves from those they considered their inferiors by altering their own consumption habits. Where before mere possession of any mahogany connoted status, the elite now raised the ante of what was considered conspicuous consumption by splurging on an overabundance of mahogany objects. Benjamin Hallowell, a wealthy merchant and the royally appointed Comptroller of Customs for the port of Boston, exemplified this type of demonstrative extravagance. An inventory of the contents of his mansion listed fifty-three objects specifically identified as "mahogany," including (just in one room) a dining table, twelve matching silk-upholstered chairs, "a mahogany sideboard," "one large mahogany Desk and Bookcase [with] plate glass doors, elegantly carved," two mahogany cases of knives and forks, a mahogany tea tray, and "one set Mahogany drawers in the Closet."[56]

After passage of the Stamp Act in 1765, Hallowell found himself subjected to growing public resentment at the Crown's taxation policies. During the Stamp Act riots, his house was ransacked by an angry throng of protesters that concentrated their rage on wrecking much of his furniture (and emptying his wine cellar!). Whatever was left unscathed he was later forced to abandon when the English evacuated Boston in 1776. When Lieutenant Governor Thomas Hutchinson's mansion was similarly attacked, the mob protested the Stamp Act by stamping their feet upon his furniture before smashing it. They then proceeded to destroy his books and papers, rip out the wainscoting, and tear the slate tiles off the roof. In Albany, a crowd of hundreds, enraged at Henry Van Schaack's refusal to swear that he had not applied to be a stamp collector, showed up at his house demanding satisfaction. Finding that he had fled, they broke into the house, sent much of his fine mahogany furniture crashing out the windows into the street, and drew his carriage through the street in flames. In 1775, just two years after Copley painted his serene portrait of them, Jemima and Isaac Winslow, also Loyalist sympathizers, were forced to abandon their finely furnished home. When they fled to Halifax after the British army evacuated, they managed to bring the Copley portrait with them, but their house and all its contents were burned to the ground. Loyalists' mahogany furnishings were so often attacked during mob actions and the ensuing war years that these assaults do not seem random but rather a deliberate mode of performative violence.[57]

Targeting such prestige objects fundamentally represented a symbolic assault both on the status quo of the colonial social order with all the inequalities of wealth and power it entailed. The superabundance of mahogany enjoyed by Hallowell and his peers, far in excess of what average people could match, was just one of the more highly visible manifestations of hardening social and economic distinctions. In the post-Revolutionary era, as discussed in a later chapter, the social elite, who considered themselves among the discriminating few who could recognize and demand the best of the best, asserted a new hierarchy of materials in which connoisseurship rested not merely on the quantity of mahogany furnishings one owned but also on the quality of the materials and artistry invested in them. Having the ability and wherewithal to draw such discerning judgments became all-important not only in separating one class of goods from another but one class of people from another.

CHAPTER TWO

The Gold Standard of Jamaican Mahogany

O N AN EARLY NOVEMBER MORNING in 1756, a group of slaves—men, women, and children—wended their way up the craggy slope above their master's estate in west-central Jamaica. Shrouded in mist, they clambered over slick limestone outcroppings, around deep ravines, and through brambly thickets. Their daunting task was to clear a mountain pasture from the impenetrable forest and, in the process, to fell mahogany and other valuable trees for their master's benefit. On and off for three months, except for a three-day Christmas break when they received extra fish and cloth rations, they toiled under an over-seer's watchful eye, in gangs of thirty to forty, divided by age or gender, or occasionally "all hands" together. The able-bodied men felled the trees, cut a road, and hefted the giant logs by hand down the steepest slopes, separating out merchantable timber to be carted to Kingston for sale. The women dragged away heavy branches and cleared debris while the children trundled after them to bind up the brush. These "small hands" then stayed behind to set the stubble alight before racing down the mountainside, flames at their heels. In time, they would return to plant the scorched earth with guinea grass for their master's cattle.[1]

While no record exists of how these people regarded their exer-tions, their master Maynard Clarke applauded the transformation of wilderness into a cultivated landscape and coveted the resulting timber as an important source of revenue. His expectations for the latter seemed reasonable given Jamaica's standing as the world's leading exporter of West Indian mahogany and its well-established reputation for excellence. "Jamaica wood" had deeply influenced how people conceived of and evaluated mahogany. Since the trees initially exported were among the island's oldest and largest, their superlative wood made a tremendously positive first impression on consumers in England, Europe, and North America. Many insisted it was vastly preferable to the same species sourced elsewhere. Jamaican mahogany exports climbed steadily from the 1720s through the 1760s. At its height, according to Adam Bowett's estimates of British customs records, the island supplied an estimated 92.5 percent of all West Indian mahogany that entered England before 1748, dwarfing the second-place Bahamas and other smaller islands. After the Seven Years War, that percentage fell to around 78 percent, although it remained England's largest mahogany source until the early 1770s. By then, however, its reputation was already on the decline. With the bar set so high at the outset, it proved difficult to sustain the same consistent level of excellence, especially as the largest and healthiest trees were depleted. In a little over forty years, "Jamaica wood," the most sought-after cabinetmaking wood in the world, verged on commercial extinction. In many ways, the history of Jamaica's mahogany industry exemplifies how its production was inextricably linked with changing land uses; as trees were felled to make way for staple crops, expanding plantation agriculture intersected with, and ultimately undermined, the mahogany industry. This development pattern was prototypical of changes that unfolded subsequently on many Caribbean islands, igniting conflicts over remaining mahogany supplies and ravaging natural environments.[2]

During its years of prominence, Jamaican mahogany's significance to people on the island itself varied widely depending upon their status within its highly stratified society. For slaves, mahogany mainly meant hard labor, although for some, traversing the forests may have been a welcome respite from the grueling tedium of the cane fields and the boiling house. For sugar planters, mahogany was of secondary importance to their cane crops, although it gained significance with rising prices as growing consumer demand coincided with the depletion of healthy, accessible trees. For many less affluent small landholders and free Jamaicans without property, however, it was a vital economic lifeline. Whether their main livelihood or a supplement to it, mahogany cutting offered them a rare chance at autonomy and possible financial independence. These class differences were magnified by geographical trends as the locus of mahogany cutting shifted inexorably from the lowland coastal plains, where large planters monopolized prime sugar lands, to the island's central highlands and mountainous interior, where more marginal people were pushed.

Although slightly smaller than Connecticut, Jamaica, at about 4,200 square miles, was the largest of the British West Indies (almost twenty-five times the size of Barbados). Its varied topography supported many different economic activities, including logging, raising livestock for beef and draft animals, growing food for domestic consumption, and cultivating a mix of staple crops (including sugar, allspice, ginger, cotton, logwood, and coffee). The composition of the island's primeval forests likewise reflected a range of different conditions. The lowland plains (less than 500 feet above sea level) around the coastal perimeter were originally cloaked with the lush forests that so amazed and intimidated English settlers in the seventeenth century. In this richly fertile region, West Indian mahoganies grew straight and tall and were interspersed prolifically with other tree species. Most early mahogany exports originated here since this attractive land was the first to be cleared for sugar while logging was facilitated by the ease of access and transport, thanks to flat terrain and proximity to the sea.[3]

The central highlands included steep, rugged hills, sharp edged plateaus topped with natural savannahs, and craggy mountains (up to

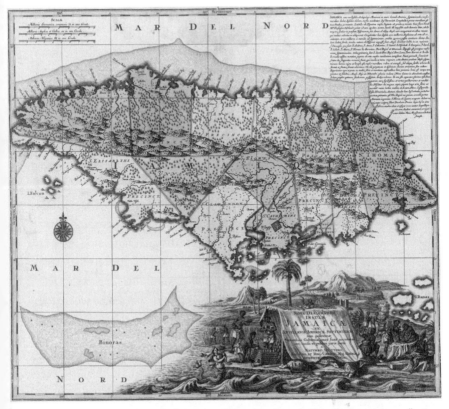

FIG. 2.1 Matthäus Seutter, Map of Jamaica, "Nova Designatio Insulae Jamaicae . . .", circa 1744, Augsburg. Hand-colored engraving. 19 × 33 in. Collection of the John Carter Brown Library. (10960).

Based on an earlier map by Nicolaes Visscher, published circa 1720 in Amsterdam, this map of Jamaica suggests the island's diverse topography. Most of the accessible mahogany trees were depleted by the mid-eighteenth century, as land was cleared for plantation agriculture. Appropriately, the map's decorative cartouche depicts African slaves harvesting and processing sugar cane.

2,000 feet above sea level). This region encompassed parts of four parishes: northern St. Elizabeth, eastern Westmoreland, southern St. James, and southern Trelawny (including the so-called Cockpit Country, a maze of erosion-chiseled limestone hills where runaway slaves often took refuge). Much of this area lay beneath a canopy of moist, evergreen forests where mahoganies stretched their heads above an understory of smaller trees, tangled vines, and epiphytes. On this "very high, broken land," mahogany trees grew somewhat smaller and more slowly than those along the coast but yielded especially hard, dense wood with highly figured grains. With few navigable rivers and almost nonexistent roads, much of this interior region was underpopulated with scattered small farms and cattle pens. Given its remoteness and treacherous terrain, extracting and transporting mahogany was extremely difficult and labor intensive. Mahogany also grew on the island's highest peaks, including the Blue Mountains (over 7,400 feet tall) that plunged to the sea along the island's northeast side where the precipitous slopes made logging still more difficult.[4]

Mahogany as a Plantation Product

As a reliable export market for mahogany developed in England during the 1720s, planters, who previously might have just burned or made shingles out of trees standing in the way of their all-important drive to clear sugar lands, began to haul the resulting timber to Kingston where local merchants and factors had it loaded onto ships bound for overseas markets. By the 1740s, thousands of trees had been extracted from Jamaica's readily accessible coastal lowlands, which were transformed from mahogany-rich forests into cane fields. Accordingly, when Charles Leslie enumerated Jamaica's produce for his English readers, he noted the "Mahogany-tree is so well known ... I need not describe it." Pointing to the "quite bare and barren" wastelands left behind by Jamaica's earlier Spanish settlers, however, he warned that the rest of the island might soon "partake of the same Fate." Another contemporary author described the few surviving lowland clusters of mahogany as "little Islands" in a sea of sugar. Given the growing demand for Jamaican mahogany, however, he assumed that any planter, with "Negroes to cut it down and saw it into Planks," would not hesitate to part with their last trees.[5]

In the coming decade, this blasé attitude changed as sugar planters began to regard their remaining mahogany trees (if they still had any) as a form of insurance and standing cash reserve; confronted with an economic setback, such as a failed sugar harvest or declining fertility of existing fields, planters could sell their mahogany trees to provide a quick capital infusion to offset losses or buy new land. Consequently, they typically felled their mahogany reserves during times of financial stress rather than as part of any long-term management strategy to sustain their timber resources. At the same time as Jamaica's native forests were rapidly disappearing, planters were forced to import increasing quantities of North American pine and oak to meet their plantations' basic timber needs.[6]

Planters' expedient approach to mahogany cutting is evident in the "Accounts Produce" records from the 1740s to the 1760s extant at the Jamaica Archives and Records Department in Spanish Town. Although these accounts are incomplete and sometimes relate to less productive periods (such as following a planter's death), they suggest how mahogany typically fit into overall patterns of plantation produce. Of several dozen plantations represented, only nineteen recorded significant amounts of mahogany (including twelve in the less-developed St. Elizabeth and Westmoreland Parishes), but those appeared only sporadically and fluctuated widely in quantity. This pattern suggests mahogany production correlated either with periods of renewed land clearance or with sugar downturns that necessitated the felling of timber reserves. In 1741, new lands were probably cleared on the Campbell family's Westmoreland plantation because it produced 7,840 feet of mahogany that year after reporting a trifling 202 feet the previous year. Meanwhile, its sugar output remained steady at around 250,000 pounds. Likewise, when William Beckford inherited his father's Westmoreland estate in 1765, it produced mainly sugar, rum, and logwood, but two years later it suddenly added 63,334 feet of mahogany. Crop failure is the more likely explanation for the brief upsurge of mahogany production in 1760 on the Dickinson family's Barton Isles Plantation; when their sugar output fell from 147 to 81 hogsheads, the decline was offset with 20,000 feet of mahogany. Two years later, however, when sugar rebounded to 278 hogsheads, they cut only 4,448 feet of mahogany, a more average amount for them. In St. Elizabeth, another Dickinson family estate recorded a major mahogany yield about every ten years as sugar fields were worn out and more virgin forest was cleared. In 1756, they thus cut over 49,000 feet but only 3,380 feet the next year. To give a sense of scale, Jamaica as a whole exported 521,300 feet of mahogany planks only three years earlier.[7]

A key factor in how quickly and intensively planters felled their mahogany was their access to labor, since most were reluctant to divert their slaves from their more profitable sugar crops. Logging was considered seasonal work and timed so as not to conflict with the cane crop—between November and late January, after the hurricane season but before the harvest rush. Aside from periodic pushes to clear more land when all hands might be pressed into service, a few male slaves were assigned to do routine woodcutting and woodworking tasks (sawing firewood, splitting shingles, making repairs, etc.) during rare breaks in the rigorous sugar routine. For more extensive logging or construction projects, most planters contracted sawyers or carpenters from England, Scotland, or Ireland as indentured servants or bought a few slaves trained in those trades. Highly valued and treated better on average than field hands, these skilled slaves, when not busy on their master's plantation, were often leased out to other landowners, gaining some autonomy, mobility, and moneymaking possibilities for themselves in the process. In one case, a slave master leaving Jamaica even allowed his enslaved carpenters to negotiate their living and working conditions with potential new masters.[8]

Large-scale commercial logging, however, was deemed by many planters to be too laborious, time consuming, and hazardous to be worth risking their valuable slaves, especially since they were essential to keeping the agro-industrial sugar complex churning at full tilt. For such enterprises, planters preferred to job out the work to independent woodcutters who brought in their own slave gangs of experienced loggers, supplemented if necessary with a few of the plantation's slaves. This became such common practice that when Edward Long, a former Jamaican planter who returned to England in 1769 and joined the West India Merchants' and Planters' Committee, calculated the costs of establishing a plantation in 1774, he assumed that any new planter would "hire laborers, for cutting down the wood, [rather] than to employ his own Negroes." Even in his day, clearing land remained expensive; virgin forest was £3 per acre but "falling and clearing" cost £5 per acre. He warned prospective planters that a "sugar-estate, settled immediately from wood-land can hardly be expected to arrive at any tolerable state of perfection in less than seven years, unless pushed on by the omnipotence of a full purse." Failing that, most planters had to carefully allocate their limited labor force.[9]

In the meantime, sugar planters' preferences for hired woodcutters created important employment opportunities for less affluent men, both white and free blacks, who worked as full- or part-time itinerant woodcutters. Their number included many former indentured servants who had completed terms as sawyers or carpenters and small landowners or tenant farmers who supplemented other economic activities with

woodcutting. Given the seasonal, short-term nature of logging, these
axes-for-hire had to be especially mobile in search of work, especially
those who owned no land and for whom woodcutting was their main
employment. As such they appear as rather shadowy figures in the
archival record and are seldom mentioned by name in plantation accounts. Nevertheless, they constituted a small but not insignificant
part of Jamaica's free labor force, a shifting roster of people characterized by transience and marginality. For example, James Gordon became a mahogany cutter after being transported to Jamaica from
Scotland as punishment for his participation in the failed 1745 Jacobite
Rebellion. Arriving as a penniless refugee, the teenager likely learned
his new trade after seeking out the only wage work he could find.[10]

Samuel Rushton, a man of modest means from St. Elizabeth Parish,
was typical of those itinerant woodcutters who supplemented their
other income sources with mahogany. His worldly estate, recorded in
1742, consisted of little more than nine head of cattle, a small plot of
"ground provisions," and 35,368 feet of mahogany plank. While this
substantial mahogany cache may have been felled in the mountainous
no-man's-land, he more likely accumulated it by cutting wood for larger
landowners. For although independent woodcutters might be paid
wages or an agreed-upon fee, their compensation was customarily in
the form of a share of the cut timber (usually a quarter or a third). In
1752, the overseer of Pepper Plantation in St. Elizabeth Parish compen-
sated the hired woodcutter with a third of the 511 mahogany planks he
and his crew cut, while the rest was consigned for sale in England to
benefit Miss Dickinson, the absentee owner. On Barton Isles Plantation the next year, the overseer recorded "258 Mahogany Planks 2/3ds
whereof on Account of Said Plantation and 1/3 upon Acco't of Edward
Fox for cuttn'g thereof." Itinerant white woodcutters were in a class
with Jamaica's other middling free whites, including overseers, low-
level managers, and hired craftsmen, who also tended to be footloose
and changed employers regularly in hopes of bettering their situations

(although ironically they often ended up working alongside or supervising enslaved Africans equally or more skilled than themselves). Not surprisingly, some of these men also supplemented their incomes by cutting mahogany surreptitiously from their employer's woodlands or moonlighting as woodcutters for neighboring planters.[11]

Maynard Clarke and his father John Clarke underscore how dramatically large planters' attitudes towards their mahogany resources changed over time as consumer demand for it took off and as the island underwent rapid economic and environmental transformations. Arriving in Jamaica in the early eighteenth century, John Clarke apparently had little interest in England's emerging tropical timber trade. When Maynard inherited his father's Jamaican lands at mid-century, by contrast, he regarded the standing trees, especially the mahogany, to be among his most important assets and crucial to his future. But just as today, those most directly involved with extracting natural resources often benefited least from their sale (as international shippers, wholesalers, processors, and retailers all add value to raw materials and receive a larger profit share of the resulting commodities). He was often disappointed with his returns and faced great frustrations realizing his ambitions.[12]

By the 1720s, John Clarke had established Fontabell Plantation, a 700-acre estate on the fertile Liguanea Plain north of Kingston in St. Andrew Parish. As he slowly bought up more land, he focused single-mindedly on clearing more acreage, planting cane, and investing in necessary infrastructure, such as an aqueduct to power his water-driven sugar mill "which doubled the value of the plantation." Although in 1724 he paid £32 for "16 months Hire of a Sawyer," no mahogany or other woods appear among the surviving records of his plantation produce. Instead, he used his slave-harvested timber to make further improvements, such 605 feet of bulletwood used for a new set of rollers to crush cane. In 1736, he hired a sawyer to go "into the woods with

the Negroes to Cutt Shingles." In 1738, he contracted an indentured
carpenter and a sawyer, both recently arrived from London, to repair
hurricane damage, again using his own timber. His goal was to integrate his operations vertically to control every aspect of sugar production, including setting up a cattle pen to provide his own draft animals.
With this in mind, Clarke purchased over 500 acres in the remote mountainous interior where he intended to establish pasturage for livestock.
This heavily forested region, long the stronghold of Maroons (runaway
slaves and their descendants) who menaced surrounding plantations
and provided a refuge for escaped slaves, had recently become of interest
to white investors after the Maroons signed a peace treaty with the colonial government in exchange for designated lands. In the meantime, all
of the timber John Clarke harvested went back into building up his small
sugar empire.[13]

Upon his father's death circa 1740, Maynard inherited Fontabell, a
profitable plantation with over 200 slaves, and the still undeveloped
mountain lands, but all were heavily mortgaged. From the start, Maynard's experiences on Jamaica differed considerably from his father's
earlier tenure. Because Maynard resided in England, he entrusted management of the estate to the Jamaican firm of Knight, Poole, and Pestell
and delegated day-to-day operations to a hired overseer, formerly one
of his father's indentured servants. Such absentee arrangements, although common on Jamaica, were notoriously unreliable and the once-
promising plantation soon ran up a large deficit. In 1749, when Samuel
Walters, his cousin and mortgage holder, demanded payment, Maynard moved to Jamaica, determined to revive his prospects by selling
off his inherited mahogany trees.[14]

Although Jamaican-born, Maynard found himself quite unpre-
pared for his new role as a West Indian planter. Arriving unannounced
in hopes of inspecting the plantation incognito, Maynard was recognized instantly by his old nurse and, according to his account, was
thronged by slaves, eager to see and touch their new, young master.

After this bewildering welcome, he was horrified at the estate's disarray. Worse still he found many of the mahogany trees were gone, poached by his hired surrogates. He fumed at "the vast Quantity they have themselves cutt & supplied others without giving me the least credit." After firing both his incompetent managers and the insolent overseer (who taunted him that "the Negroes flatter you with an empty title of Master"), Maynard described himself as "launched into a new world bereft of all friends [with] a sette of subtle Knaves to deal with." He was relieved to discover that there were still "vast Quantitys of fine & valuable timber part of which they have been kind enough to leave me." He wrote home, "[I] am clearing away some of the Stuff both for me & sale. The several Lotts all lie as it were Contiguous to the plantation which is a very great advantage . . . in the parish of St. James I have a Lott of 2,200 acres perfectly loaded with Mahogany . . . [although much] they have suffered to be cut down and destroyed."[15]

With his mahogany proceeds, he planned to pay his debts and expand the plantation. But he could not resist first ordering his slaves to build him a "Great House." Most likely, his house conformed to the typical Anglo-Jamaican Creole architectural style—combining neoclassical features with tropical adaptations (such as shutters, external staircases, porticos, and hurricane shelters) and, of course, mahogany floors, woodwork, and furnishings. At the same time, Maynard ordered the slaves to build new quarters for themselves, modest thatched-roof structures, perhaps incorporating African thatching techniques. His new overseer then directed "30 hands [in] cutting down trees abt the Negroes houses," consistent with the customary Jamaican practice of building slave housing "in strait lines, constructed with some degree of uniformity and strength, but totally divested of all trees and shrubs" to facilitate surveillance of its occupants. Aside from his stated discomfort with the vicious punishments meted out to recalcitrant slaves, Maynard largely adhered to standard Jamaican modes of slave management. Describing Jamaica as "a continual scene of pain and misery," he mainly pitied himself. "My place of property will ever be a place of plague & vexation," he wrote. "Had I been but a good Farmer's Son or ought else but a Creole [I] might have had a prospect of happiness." As the Jamaican-born son of a white planter, however, he had little choice but to grapple with that identity.[16]

In 1753, Maynard initiated a major push to clear his mountain lands and extract their mahogany trees and, in the process, fulfill his father's long-deferred plan for a cattle pen. That spring, he purchased "1 doz. broad axes," "four dozen felling axes," and twelve adzes for splitting logs. Since he opted to use his own slaves for this work, whenever they were not planting, weeding, or cutting sugar cane, they sawed, hefted, hauled, and dragged logs and tree branches. They learned to recognize mahogany, cedar, bulletwood, and other saleable woods. On the newly cleared land, they sowed Guinea grass, built fences and corrals, and tended groves of infant coffee bushes. His overseer's records included regular payments to the Maroons for returning slaves who fled into the surrounding woods to escape this relentless toil.[17]

Later that year, Maynard shipped his first mahogany to England where it quickly found buyers in London and the provincial markets of Sheffield, Newcastle, Manchester, Leeds, and Hull. Although dismayed that the price was not higher, Maynard did make some money; in Hull, for example, he netted £570 on 280 mahogany planks (21,067 feet). He was not the only Jamaican landowner disappointed by the mahogany market that year. A few months earlier, Jacob Allin of St. Elizabeth dispatched a load to the London merchant house of Lascelles and Maxwell, only to be told that he ought to have sold it to a local Jamaican merchant who could afford to wait for stronger prices. Maynard not only miscalculated the market, however, he also misjudged his agents who unscrupulously took the largest, most valuable logs for their own commission. "I am surprised you shd be so Imposed on to take such Wood," Walters complained, "for they have pick'd all the narrow out for You, the Mahogany they have is as broad again." After reproaching the agents for taking "too much advantage of Mr. Clarke's necessity," Walters advised his hapless cousin to check that future cargos were "better sorted."[18]

Nonetheless, Maynard's mahogany sales allowed him to burnish the veneer of gentility expected of someone of his social status. Widowed in 1756, he returned to England and remarried scandalously quickly. After lavishly renovating his country seat and buying land to build yet another house for his new bride, he commissioned over twenty pieces of mahogany furniture; even if they were made from his own mahogany, this was an extravagant purchase that included beds with carved pillars, several dining tables in the "Marlborough" style, and a "Solid Moho Desk [with] Brass Castors & Lifting Handles." He then splurged on "Damask curtains with crimson fringe & binding" and "Scarlett Check [wall]paper and bordering." Perhaps as a frugal afterthought, having laid out over £200 on new furniture and textiles, he updated some old chairs with fashionable bracket feet and paid four shillings for "Green Clothes" to protect his new tables. As rumors of his buying frenzy sped across the Atlantic, one of his Kingston creditors found it "astonishingly contrary" that rather than pay his bills as promised, Maynard was "building and repairing houses . . . and furnishing them at no small expense." Another of Maynard's correspondents expressed concern that London gossip predicted the "match will end your credit and complete your ruin." Before the spendthrift groom could prove the naysayers wrong, however, Jamaica's economy came to a standstill when martial law was imposed on the island for fear of an impending French attack. In the face of such uncertainty, Walters urged Maynard to "quit one of your country houses and keep that you like best." Financial necessity forced Maynard's return to Jamaica where he died in 1759. If he had lived longer, he might have prospered as the price of "Jamaica wood" soared; instead, his mountain lands, still rich in mahogany, remained undeveloped and a later appraisal dismissed some of them as "too remote to be used."[19]

Changing land uses on Jamaica meanwhile had a significant impact on mahogany consumers in England and North America. When much land was cleared simultaneously or there was a poor sugar year, planters glutted the market with West Indian mahogany, causing prices to fall on all but the choicest wood. Such was likely the case when Maynard Clarke and Jacob Allin shipped their timber in 1753 with disappointing results. When the supply constricted—whether due to hurricanes, wars, slave uprisings, or transport problems—prices spiked until the crisis subsided and market conditions normalized. Yet despite such fluctuations (and accounting for inflation), the overall price trajectory of Jamaican mahogany rose steadily over time and was consistently higher than Honduran mahogany. In the 1730s, the Gillow firm, a leading English furniture manufactory, paid £4–£8 per ton for Jamaican mahogany; by the 1740s, they paid £10–£14 per ton. By the 1750s, truly mammoth trees had become so rare that the so-called "table wood" made from them (extra-wide boards used for dining tables) had risen to £24 per ton. At that time, most lowland sugar planters, caught up in the boom-or-bust economic cycles typical of plantation societies, had felled their private mahogany reserves to weather periodic downturns or to invest in new capital projects. But as long as consumer demand remained strong, other Jamaicans sought out mahogany trees in the interior where logging proved much more challenging.[20]

Mahogany Cutting in the Central Highlands

By mid-century, mahogany cutting largely shifted away from the coast, although sporadic quantities from there still came to market as landowners eventually cut their reserves. As late as 1783, Goshen Cattle Pen, which raised 1,500 head of cattle on prime coastal land, exported "3,782 feet of mahogany plank and 600 feet of boards." For the most part, however, large sugar planters consolidated their land-holdings in the coastal region along with their political and economic power. As they created economies of scale, smaller landowners had little choice but to relocate to the more remote, undeveloped central highlands. These settlers, mostly whites and free persons of color of middling or lower status, became small farmers, cattle pen keepers, or coffee growers. Compared to establishing a sugar plantation, these activities required much less labor and land, but they still required some initial start-up capital. Since mahogany grew wild on unclaimed lands, it was one of the very few potential revenue sources available to free non-landowners.

With diligence, a farmer displaced from the lowlands or an inden-tured sawyer whose term of service expired might turn to woodcut-ting until they saved enough to buy sufficient land and slaves to start a small farm or cattle pen, which typically consisted of little more than a few basic buildings, corrals, some fields, and a provision garden. Even so, settlers in this remote, rugged region faced an enormous task merely to carve out that much from the surrounding forests. Moreover, to transport their timber or other produce to market was a daunting challenge. For every mile that lay between their inland properties and the nearest seaside wharf, the cost of transportation increased expo-nentially. Lacking the manpower and transportation infrastructure needed for large-scale commercial logging, most of these small opera-tors could extract only a few logs at a time and cleared land at a much slower pace than they might have wished. On the upside, the valuable trees were not depleted as quickly as in the lowlands, particularly as landowners learned to leave some trees standing to shade their cattle and delicate coffee bushes. By mid-century, cattle pen keepers and small farmers numbered about 1,500 and had an average work force of twenty to forty slaves.[21]

Slaves on cattle pens and small farms seem to have faced somewhat less onerous working conditions than those stuck full-time on sugar plantations. Given these operations' small scale and often isolated locations, everybody lived at close quarters, making for a more relaxed social atmosphere. Workers had considerable variety and flexibility in their assignments. The men, in particular, spent a significant amount of time out and about, often without direct supervision, while cattle droving, hauling timber or other produce to market, or on logging expeditions into the forest. These activities offered greater mobility, a broader range of human contacts, self-authorized breaks from labor, as well as the occasional opportunity to run away, at least temporarily.

The oft-cited journal of Thomas Thistlewood illuminates how mahogany cutting contributed to the economic foundations of these smaller enterprises. The second son of an English tenant farmer, Thistlewood became overseer of Florentius Vassall's Vineyard Pen in 1750. On this 1,170-acre spread of grazing lands and forests, Thistlewood supervised around twenty-four men, eighteen women, and ten children as they tended 200 cattle, harvested logwood, and raised much of their own food. On seasonal logging jaunts, the estate driver, a mulatto slave named Dick, supervised a gang of enslaved men who astounded Thistlewood with their intimate knowledge of the surrounding forest. He also permitted independent woodcutters to extract mahogany from the property, taking a share of the cut timber for his employer (and likely a cut for himself as well). By 1765, Thistlewood saved up enough to buy 160 acres, thirty slaves, and several dozen cattle. Having thus secured his autonomy, he now hired out his own logging gang to extract more mahogany from neighboring estates.[22]

Thistlewood's journal gives us a few rare glimpses at how Jamaican slaves perceived the value of the mahogany they cut. In 1760, he helped track down the perpetrators of a violent slave uprising, later known as Tacky's Rebellion, in Westmoreland Parish. He recorded that the rebel slaves had built a fortified encampment deep in the forest, fur-nished with "fine mahogany chests filled with clothes" stolen from their masters' homes. A mahogany sword, said to be "of extraordinary size and weight," elaborately carved, and decorated with red parrot feathers ("the Coromantees' Banner of war"), was purportedly used in this same uprising and later given to the naturalist, Pierre Eugène Du Simitière who exhibited it in Philadelphia. In another incident, Thistle-wood bought two mahogany chairs for "4 bits" each from a slave, who upon delivery demanded an additional "5 bitts," which the housekeeper obligingly paid out of her master's till. The slaves also collected "a Kind of worms cald Machackow's" from the bark of the mahogany tree. Ac-cording to Thistlewood, the slaves fried and ate these morsels, which were "said to look extremely well when dress'd." Thistlewood, a vora-cious autodidact, gathered many such tantalizing tidbits of ethnobo-tanical information from his slaves. Keenly interested as well in horti-culture and climatology, he eventually established a commercial nursery specializing in native trees and plants. Despite his efforts to recast himself as an enlightened gentleman, however, he was unable to infiltrate Jamaica's plantocracy; all the mahogany in the world could not polish away his rough edges.[23]

Indeed, engrained social distinctions were very difficult for small operators like Thistlewood to overcome; as long as they relied on large planters to buy their meat and other perishable produce, they remained largely trapped in a subordinate role and dependent on the island's lim-ited internal market. Moreover, as large planters established their own auxiliary cattle pens, independent pen keepers and small planters found it harder to survive, much less improve their place within Jamaica's so-cial echelons. Breaking into the export market by harvesting mahog-any or cultivating non-sugar staples (such as coffee and ginger) could make all the difference. In the 1720s, for example, colonial officials, hoping to boost Jamaica's free white population, began subsidizing

FIG. 2.2 George Robertson, "A View in the Island of Jamaica, of the Spring-head of Roaring River on the Estate of William Beckford Esqr.," engraved and published by John Boydell 1778, London. 24 × 20½ in.; Collection of the John Carter Brown Library (32881).

This engraving of William Beckford's Roaring River estate suggests the sort of rugged terrain in parts of Jamaica where mahogany was extracted, but with some difficulty.

small-scale coffee growers. They remained among the island's poorer sort until demand for their coffee exploded after the Haitian revolution destroyed St. Domingue's famed coffee plantations. New affluence soon translated into greater political influence and a commensurate rise in social status for Jamaica's coffee planters. Exporting mahogany, likewise, had the potential for similar gains but compared with staple agriculture, was harder to sustain since only limited quantities were available from the wild. Those who failed to parlay short-term timber profits into more reliable modes of wealth accumulation were almost doomed not to improve their condition.[24]

Jamaica's Last Mahogany Frontier

During the third quarter of the eighteenth century, as the negative effects of deforestation and soil depletion were manifested elsewhere, small farmers, coffee growers, and pen keepers moved into the foothills of Jamaica's high mountains, but the lack of passable roads deterred them from advancing farther up the treacherous slopes. Because the island's once bountiful mahogany was "almost exterminated . . . [except in] mountainous recesses," the center of commercial mahogany cutting was forced once again to shift—this time into the highest elevations, especially in southern Trelawny and the Blue Mountains.[25]

Up until then, few white Jamaicans had even ventured into this inhospitable territory. The occasional hunters and freelance woodcutters who traversed the mountains regarded them as an open commons, with natural resources free for the taking, but they left few permanent marks. By and large, the mountains remained the province of the autonomous Maroons who, aside for occasional market visits and dealings with planters to return runaway slaves, enjoyed a relatively isolated, subsistence mode of life that utilized many forest resources, such as lagetto tree bark from which they made cloth.[26]

The unforgiving terrain made large-scale mahogany logging exceedingly difficult. Each added mile, each additional foot of elevation exponentially increased the expense of transport, and logs had to be of sufficient size to be worth shipping. Woodcutters thus had to constantly weigh their costs versus possible returns. As these costs were passed on to consumers, Jamaica-sourced mahogany became increasingly expensive. More insidiously, however, the character of the much-touted "Jamaica wood" deteriorated as the trees coming to market were of diminished size and inferior quality compared to those harvested earlier. As buyers turned to other tropical timber sources, Jamaica's flagging mahogany industry was increasingly consolidated into the hands of a few well-financed individuals who owned large numbers of slaves and large-scale logging operations. Smaller, itinerant woodcutters, unable to compete, were squeezed out of the business.

Concerned that only those with "large capital" were still involved, Edward Long urged Parliament to impose a protectionist duty on non-English mahogany to bolster Jamaica's industry. Although eager that poor whites still be able to gain a livelihood by extracting the "fine timbers of the deep and untrodden recesses of the mountains," Long had an ulterior motive. Because loggers were "obliged to cut roads through the interior tracts of country," he believed they also could play a crucial role in opening that part of the island to new settlers who might otherwise be put off by "the arduous task of felling the woods . . . [leaving] them not a moment's respite for attending to their little plantations." Highlighting mountain regions ripe for economic development, he pointed to Clarendon, so uninhabited it was known as Siberia, yet it furnished "a vast quantity of mahogany every year, the visitors of this part being chiefly cutters." But increasingly, the mahogany cutters themselves were becoming an endangered species, particularly as labor and transport costs threatened to exceed the value of their final product. Competition from other mahogany-producing areas enlarged supplies and lowered prices on the world market, making Jamaican mahogany prohibitive by comparison. Faced with these circumstances, some Jamaican merchants and professional woodcutters dispatched slave gangs to initiate logging on adjacent islands or ordered less-expensive mahogany from suppliers in the British enclaves in Central America that they then re-exported to various overseas markets. In 1775, Governor Keith's annual report of Jamaica's exports, totaling £1,508,364 sterling, acknowledged that "part of the Mahogany [was] from the Mosquito-Shore and Honduras." Many Jamaicans tried to pass off this imported wood as their own local produce to avoid customs duties and to get a higher price. Edward Long condemned the practice because he thought that advertising Honduran wood, widely considered "sappy and very inferior," as Jamaican would only discredit the latter. Nevertheless, as long as customers were willing to pay more for what they believed was "Jamaica wood," the practice continued.[27]

In 1786, John Whitaker, one of the first white settlers to brave the mountainous interior, reported he had mahogany in "abundance on my Land . . . whilst the rest of the Island is mostly exhausted." Although his timber "had been so long preserved" because of the "difficulty in getting it out, as the rocky Precipices . . . were deemed impervious," Whitaker had recently invested over £2,000 in slave labor to build a road to his remote property, plus another £500 annually to maintain it. But even so, each rugged mile that lay between his land and local markets increased his expenses—both to haul in supplies ("salt Provisions, implements, and Clothing for the Negroes," as well as sugar-making equipment to process cane planted as his land was cleared) and to haul out any produce. Several of Whitaker's fellow pioneers, exhausted and overwhelmed, "sold off their Negroes and suffered their Estates to grow into Wilderness." Unwilling to admit defeat, Whitaker lobbied the Jamaican Assembly to subsidize interior sugar cultivation and compensate settlers for road building. In the meantime, he decided to refrain from cutting more of his precious trees until the price of Jamaican mahogany reached its apex.[28]

Unfortunately for him, Whitaker's proposal met with strong opposition from the planter elite. Many of Jamaica's large planters, including influential Assembly members, also owned mountain properties, but they were in no hurry to develop them. Moreover, since most of their established plantations were in the accessible lowland plains—at the time, 93 percent of Jamaica's 670 sugar estates were within twelve miles of the sea—they had no incentive to support interior development that might aid potential competitors. Not surprisingly, public works emphasized improving coastal infrastructure, thus reinforcing the hegemony of the planter class. As long as Jamaica's last frontier remained inaccessible, its surviving mahogany trees, clinging to steep slopes or nestled in hidden crevasses, eluded the ax.[29]

When Edward Long advocated government policies to encourage mahogany cutting in 1774, he tried to impress his readers with the value of this commodity by describing a St. Elizabeth man's sale of a single tree, twelve feet in diameter, for £500. But, in fact, he realized such triumphs were rare and that Jamaica's days as a prominent exporter of West Indian mahogany were numbered; every year, he wrote, Jamaican mahogany would "become still scarcer, and consequently dearer, unless nurseries, or plantations are formed of it in places where the carriage is more convenient for the market." From the 1780s on, sporadic quantities of Jamaica-sourced mahogany continued to come onto the international market, particularly when high prices made it worthwhile for woodcutters to extricate straggling mahogany trees from hard-to-reach niches or enticed planters who still held private reserves to part with them. Jamaican mahogany thus still experienced periodic gluts. But over the years, the overall volume of the true Jamaican article declined and the proportion of non-Jamaican mahogany passing through the hands of the island's merchants and woodcutters steadily increased.[30]

Despite its world-class reputation as a premium luxury wood and its vital economic importance to a small sector of the population, Jamaican mahogany always remained ancillary within the island's overall economy. Ultimately it was sugar, not mahogany, that cemented Jamaica's wealth and prominence within the British Empire. Moreover, since the trees were all taken from the wild, usually in the context of clearing land that would never be reforested, Jamaica's commercial mahogany industry remained fundamentally unsustainable. Inevitably, as the largest, healthiest trees were depleted, the reputation of Jamaican mahogany suffered as once loyal consumers turned to other sources. During the late eighteenth and early nineteenth centuries, as we shall see, the problems of deteriorating West Indian mahogany supplies and of tropical deforestation more generally became matters of concern in some circles within the British Empire, but they did not culminate in significant land-use changes on Jamaica. Nor was Long's beguiling notion of growing *Swietenia mahagoni* conveniently in nurseries or on plantations easily realized, although some attempted it. By 1790, William Beckford lamented that, due to waste and personal avarice, once-abundant mahogany had become "almost entirely extinct; and upon those plantations, the works of which were formerly constructed of mahogany, there is hardly a tree to be now found."[31]

Years after Jamaican mahogany had largely disappeared from international markets, many still fondly recalled the island's once-prized wood. In 1837, James Macfadyen stated, "Old Jamaica Mahogany is still considered superior to any that can be procured from any other country." Likewise, *The Cabinet-makers Assistant* (1853) recalled when the island furnished "the largest and most beautiful wood, of which we have seen several specimens in old furniture, marked by a wild irregular figuring and deep coloring." Accurately recounting how the "trees nearest the sea were cut first, those near streams capable of floating them to the sea followed, until all the mahogany which would repay the cost of its transmission had been removed," the author confided that "missionary intelligence and books of travel" suggested that some "noble trees are yet standing . . . which the difficulty of removal alone has preserved." When Philip Henry Gosse toured Jamaica in 1844 to collect botanical specimens for one of England's leading naturalia dealers, he saw only a few straggling mahogany trees left standing by the roadsides for shade, although many houses had mahogany floors, as "beautifully polished as the finest tables of our drawing rooms," buffed each morning with orange halves and coconut leaves by "sable handmaids on their knees." His tropical fantasy was complete when, high in the mountains, amidst the "most gloomy and savage scenes," he found the last survivors. In awe and wonder, he meandered among the "columnar trunks," "immense spurs and buttresses," and "fantastic roots of the huge Mahoganies . . . perhaps a thousand years old."[32]

CHAPTER THREE

Supplying the Empire with Mahogany

OVER THE COURSE of the eighteenth century, the British search for mahogany expanded throughout the circum-Caribbean, wherever the valuable trees were to be found. Restless settlers, itinerant woodcutters, sea captains, and West Indian merchants leapfrogged from island to island in the northern Antilles. Some made illicit logging forays to Spanish and French islands while others ventured to the British woodcutting enclaves in Spanish-claimed Central America. Particularly as Jamaica's mahogany industry faltered beginning in the 1760s, vicious rivalries developed among those seeking to monopolize mahogany-rich forests in other locales. Clashing timber claims, unsustainable logging methods, incompatible modes of land use, and contested national sovereignties all contributed to rising tensions over tropical timber resources.

While concerns about how to ensure future mahogany supplies might seem pertinent only to the narrow cohort of those directly involved in its production and sale, in fact, many in England and North America had come to expect it as one of their rightful rewards of Empire. Moreover, struggles over mahogany were often linked with larger disputes over land, labor, and natural resources that had serious ramifications for regional and international relations. Just as today,

spikes in oil prices caused by world events are felt acutely by American motorists at the pump, disruptions in the flow of mahogany from
the colonial periphery sent shock waves back across the Atlantic. The
cabinetmaking industries in England and North America were seriously stalled for lack of one of their most important materials.[1]

The search for a secure, reliable mahogany supply must be understood within the larger context of British strategies of colonial domination and imperial expansion. Although just one concern among many
for the Crown, the mahogany problem became a nagging consideration
in its geopolitical and diplomatic dealings. Two pivotal moments came
first in the wake of the Seven Years War and then of the American
Revolution. During both of these global conflagrations, severe wartime mahogany shortages and astronomical prices highlighted the
need to strengthen Britain's tropical timber reserves. In the first instance, following the Seven Years War, the multifaceted Treaty of Paris
(1763) realigned hemispheric power relations, significantly expanding
Britain's territorial footprint in the Atlantic. In addition, Britain reaf-
firmed Spain's sovereignty over the Bay of Honduras in exchange for
limited rights to cut logwood there, but not mahogany. Government
officials' raised awareness of the vulnerability of the nation's timber
supplies, experienced so acutely during the recent war, also indirectly
gave momentum to a remarkable governmental initiative to establish
a tropical forest preserve on the newly ceded island of Tobago, which
previously had been a French colony.[2]

Buoyed by a growing sense of self-confidence and entitlement, however, many Britons resented the agreement both for conceding too
much to their vanquished enemy and for being overly restrictive in
ways they thought would limit economic development in the newly acquired territories. In the second instance, after the American Revolution had ignited a conflict that expanded into yet another world war,
the 1783 Treaty of Versailles extended British access in the Bay of Honduras and, after it was revised in 1786, finally permitted both logwood

and mahogany cutting. Although intended to resolve Britain's long-standing disagreements with Spain over access to these much-sought-after tropical hardwoods, other provisions in the treaty fatefully enflamed the region's internal conflicts.[3]

The Search for West Indian Mahogany

As the search for West Indian mahogany advanced from one land-mass to the next—the Bahamas, the Cayman Islands, Turks and Caicos, and other smaller isles—it contributed to a steadily moving front of deforestation—spreading with wildfire speed in some places, more slowly and piecemeal in others—eventually encompassing the entire range of the species. As many of these locales were cleared for plantation agriculture, they followed a similar developmental trajectory as Jamaica; if anything, because they were so much smaller, the rate and extent of mahogany depletion, and of deforestation more generally, tended to be even more rapid, intensive, and ecologically devastating. In the early colonial period, many of the smaller islands in the northern Antilles remained heavily forested and sparsely populated. Although claimed by various European nations, they functioned more or less as an Atlantic commons, freely traversed by ships of many nations that stopped off just long enough to replenish their wood and water stores. While a ship's crew might add a few mahogany logs to their cargo, they felled only trees growing close to the shore and left few permanent traces. More invasive logging expeditions began in the late seventeenth century when residents of England's established colonies, which were already suffering from deforestation, especially Barbados and Bermuda, resorted to smaller, less developed islands to secure wood for their own needs and for export.[4]

While most such island-hopping ventures were brief, some entrepreneurs set up semipermanent logging camps on adjacent islands, where their slave gangs cut trees under an overseer's supervision for

weeks or months at a stretch. As these enterprises became more organized, persistent, and far-reaching, they impacted forests well beyond
islands' immediate shorelines. As colonization of these smaller islands intensified, however, newly-arrived settlers, claiming the trees
for themselves, sought to shut down unauthorized logging by foreign
ships and nonresidents. At the same time, these colonists remained
dependent on the larger islands' established entrepôts both for supplies and access to international shipping. Jamaican merchants and
factors, for example, profited handsomely on interisland commerce—
selling tools, provisions, and slaves to small islanders and then con-
veying their mahogany and other produce to market for a hefty commission. Some of these merchants invested in land on underdeveloped
islands with a short-term eye on extracting timber but a long-term eye
on future land speculation.

Among the most persistent seekers of fine timbers were Bermudians whose island home had suffered from severe deforestation since
the late seventeenth century. Located in the Atlantic Ocean east of the
Carolina coast, Bermuda lay just outside the native range of West Indian mahogany (although it was later successfully introduced). Finding
their island too small to sustain large-scale plantations, Bermudians
took advantage of its central location and proximity to transatlantic
sailing routes to establish a major intercolonial carrying trade, moving
goods, people, timber, and commodities throughout the greater Caribbean. The other mainstay of the island economy was a vibrant shipbuilding industry that specialized in building sleek, agile sloops out of
the native cedar, a strong, rot-resistant, aromatic wood that proved
excellent for seagoing vessels. Finding their local trees insufficient, Bermudians sustained their shipyards by buying or poaching mahogany,
cedar, and lignum vitae from surrounding islands and the Bay of Honduras, where some Bermudians eventually relocated. On their home
turf, however, the Bermuda Assembly meanwhile enacted some of the
earliest forest conservation laws in the British West Indies; in a remark-

able turnaround, inhabitants succeeded in replanting many cedar trees, eventually reforesting parts of the island. Since most free Bermudians owned land or held long-term leases, they regarded slow-growing trees as a secure investment for their grandchildren's future benefit. Their farsightedness did not, however, extend beyond their circumscribed island home, nor did it contribute to larger imperial strategies of resource management or inspire a broader conservationist ethic. If anything, as Bermudians became more nurturing of their own trees, they became even more relentless in their pursuit of timber abroad.[5]

Anglo-Bermudian settlers, although stubbornly independent where local politics and trade were concerned, eagerly followed English fashions, including the vogue for mahogany. Although some still preferred Bermudan cedar, the island's more affluent families updated their household furnishings to reflect the new taste using mahogany brought in from the Bahamas and elsewhere; by the 1770s, half of household inventories included at least one piece of mahogany furniture. As in North America, the island's cabinetmakers developed their own vernacular that, while reminiscent of English styles, included uniquely Bermudian variations in construction and design, such as ornamental dovetails, possibly derived from Moorish sources transferred by slaves. Even as Bermudians were drawn into the currents of transatlantic consumption, this synthesis gave their mahogany objects a distinctive Creole twist.[6]

The Bahamas, long one of the primary targets of Bermudians' timber forays, became an important new source of West Indian mahogany in the early eighteenth century. In 1702, Thomas Walker, a judge in the Vice-Admiralty Court in the Bahamas, sent numerous specimens of native trees and plants for presentation at the Royal Society. This show-and-tell, before an audience of England's scientific luminaries that included Hans Sloane, exhibited samples of mahogany, brazilwood, a "saffron tree," and many other "Plants . . . of Vertue." Although Walker claimed no great discoveries, he proudly saw himself as contributing to a vital British project of information gathering; some of his specimens are still extant in the Sloane Herbarium at the Natural History Museum in London. In 1705, during the War of Spanish Succession, Spain sacked New Providence, the largest of the Bahamas. Walker fled to South Carolina with only the shirt on his back. When he petitioned the Admiralty for compensation, he cited his botanizing as part of his service to the nation and promised to do more if only his property was restored. Once the war ended, however, thousands of sailors were decommissioned, some of whom became buccaneers and turned the Bahamas into a pirate haven for several years; Walker later made a name for himself attempting to prosecute these lawless miscreants. Thanks in part to his efforts, some order was achieved in 1717. Thereafter, New Providence became a center of shipbuilding, utilizing the native mahogany. But shipwrights increasingly competed for wood with other colonists who regarded it as an important export commodity, consigning large shipments to the Carolinas, the Mid-Atlantic, and New England.[7]

As the reputation of "Providence wood" became established, cabinetmakers sought it out; soon, the Bahamas were second only to Jamaica in mahogany exports. Consequently, by 1725, when naturalist Mark Catesby wrote the first formal botanical description of West Indian mahogany after visiting the Bahamas, the trees were already disappearing. Four years later, the colonial assembly, determined to protect the shipbuilding industry, enacted several forest conservation measures forbidding destruction "by Fire of all Timber Trees growing on these Islands," levying fines for damage "done by Cattle running loose," and forbidding all timber exports. Nevertheless, strong consumer demand for "Providence wood," especially in the North American colonies, prompted many islanders to ignore the export ban. The Bahamas' reputation for excellent timber became so well established that after the American Revolution many Loyalists fled there intending to take up logging and shipbuilding, only to learn that by then much of the timber utilized there actually originated on smaller, more remote islands.[8]

The Cayman Islands were the particular target of Jamaican merchants and woodcutters anticipating the demise of the accessible coastal mahogany on their home isle. Located approximately 190 miles northwest of Jamaica, the Caymans are an archipelago comprised of over thirty small islands surrounded by hundreds of tiny cays and coral atolls. Discovered by the Spanish in 1492, they initially generated little colonizing interest, serving mainly as a pirate haven and a convenient layover for ships en route farther south. Known for the sea turtles that returned every year to lay their eggs on the pristine sands, the low-lying islands supplied passing ships with hundreds of the heavy-shelled creatures, kept alive on board as a source of fresh meat or sold as a culinary delicacy. The Caymans, taken over by England in 1629, remained sparsely settled until 1735, when the English Crown awarded the first land grant on Grand Cayman to John Middleton, Daniel Campbell, and Mary Campbell. A map of their 3,000-acre claim carefully designated "hear is Timber" or "No Timber hear [sic]." Samuel Spofforth, a prominent shipowner, secured a 1000-acre grant in 1741 and initiated a regular shipping route between the Cayman Islands and Jamaica. Not surprisingly since he hailed from Bermuda, he was particularly interested in the islands' forest resources. On a typical voyage, his twenty-five-ton sloop, the *Experiment,* left Kingston for the Caymans in ballast on 21 September 1744 and returned twelve weeks later with eighty-one pieces of mahogany. It seems quite possible that at least some of this timber was cut from his own land.[9]

Kingston merchants William Foster and Benjamin Battersby formed a business partnership to prospect for timber on the Cayman Islands during this same early settlement period. In 1734, before even securing a land grant, the partners sent eight slaves—each marked "FB" upon their left shoulder—to Grand Cayman to cut mahogany. Since neither Foster nor Battersby was willing to relocate, they hired a local man to oversee their slaves and to select promising logging sites in exchange for a quarter share of the cut wood. In hopes of reducing their transport costs, the partners also chartered a sloop "to initiate a direct trade in mahogany between Grand Cayman and the mother country, in addition to trading through Jamaica." After inspecting their Grand Cayman venture two years later, Foster arranged for twenty additional slaves to be sent from Kingston and hired an experienced sawyer to "direct and instruct the said Slaves in the felling, sawing, and squareing the said timber." Since more labor was essential to extract more trees and a skilled sawyer would ensure that each tree was felled to best advantage, Foster seemed determined to transform their start-up business into a larger, more professional operation.[10]

Unfortunately, the mahogany on their claim was quickly exhausted, forcing the slaves to move constantly to new areas in search of trees. Foster personally reconnoitered deep in the interior for mahogany-rich spots, but as per local custom, the partners could only stake a claim by actually putting slaves to work on each one. Faced with rising operating costs and declining returns, Foster sued Battersby for not contributing his share to their mounting capital expenses. Battersby, in turn, accused Foster of misappropriating the slaves' labor and conspiring with the overseer and sawyer to cheat him. Whatever the truth of the matter, Grand Cayman, although still known for its lofty trees that Edward Long described as appearing "like a grove of masts emerging out of the ocean," produced less and less mahogany. As on Jamaica, the Cayman mahogany industry proved unsustainable. Although permanent settlers shifted to growing cotton, sojourning woodcutters were forced to move on in search of new mahogany sources.[11]

Beginning in 1756, Britain became embroiled in the Seven Years War, a violent contest for territorial supremacy against the allied forces of France and Spain that eventually splayed across several continents. When Britain finally prevailed and took the upper hand in peace negotiations, its diplomats had to decide what territories to keep, return, or exchange from a long list of prizes, including New France, Spanish Florida, Cuba, Guadeloupe, Martinique, and the so-called Ceded Islands of Tobago, St. Vincent, Dominica, and Grenada. As they pondered what these various places offered that Britain could not already supply to its subjects, government officials, private interest groups, planters, and colonial representatives in England and the West Indies all weighed in, giving rise to a brief, revealing moment of national introspection about the costs and benefits of their increasingly sprawling empire.

When the Treaty of Paris was concluded in 1763, Britain returned most of the established French and Spanish sugar islands (including Guadeloupe and Martinique to France and Cuba to Spain) but kept Canada, Florida, and the relatively undeveloped Ceded Islands. Many people in England and the colonies bitterly rued the decision to trade highly productive sugar islands for acres of northern snow, alligator-infested swamps, and unimproved tropical wilderness. In addition, critics felt that the negotiators' recognition of Spain's sovereignty over the Bay of Honduras in exchange for limited woodcutting privileges that excluded mahogany revealed either unforgivable ignorance or cruel indifference to the Anglo woodcutters' changing circumstances, since they increasingly relied on it as their most important line of trade.

Having sampled Cuban sugar and mahogany during Britain's wartime occupation of Havana, its restoration to Spain particularly upset English and Anglo-American merchants. During this ten-month period, they had enjoyed a flourishing trade with the island and initiated promising commercial contacts with Cuban planters and businessmen that they had hoped to expand upon. When England instead returned the island, Spain immediately re-imposed strict trade restrictions. By comparison, the decision to keep Florida, which was still largely unfamiliar to the English, seemed extremely dubious. According to one commentator: "It is said there is a great deal of Mahogany growing in the Floridas, and [if so] it will be fortunate for the first Settlers. . . . But whether [they] abound with Mahogany or not, the Island of Cuba . . . amply abounds with that Commodity; the Spaniards, perhaps, may be induced to bring large Quantities thereof to Mobile, Pensacola, and Saint Augustine." To counter such skepticism and attract potential settlers, Florida's newly appointed governor published glowing accounts of the region's rich agricultural lands and vast forests. Once loggers and shipbuilders established themselves, however, they exhausted the accessible mahogany along the Florida coast in little more than a decade. Moreover, English settlers who sought their fortunes on this frontier were later displaced when Spain temporarily regained Florida in 1784.[12]

Information about the Ceded Islands seemed more promising; earlier French sources had rhapsodized Tobago's "rich Garland" of large trees, fit not only "to ravish the Beholder's Sight, but also to employ the Carpenters, Turners, Dyers, and even the Physician['s] Skill . . . [with] the Solidity, sweet Scent, beautiful colors, and hidden Virtues of their Woods." Ironically, for all the interest in West Indian mahogany, it was likely absent from Tobago's richly diverse forests; *Swietenia mahagoni* was not a native species in the Lesser Antilles since the wide channel separating Hispaniola from Puerto Rico prevented its natural spread. It was transferred to other islands beyond that natural barrier only as a consequence of human interventions, most likely during the first half of the nineteenth century, possibly earlier on Barbados. Given the still imperfect state of knowledge about West Indian mahogany's natural history in 1763, however, many assumed that it would be found on the Ceded Islands.[13]

Nonetheless, once the decision to keep the Ceded Islands was made, public discourse shifted to *how* the newly acquired forests and lands should be developed as various interest groups promoted conflicting agendas. The ensuing debates are revealing of how concerns over managing tropical timber resources began to enter into, and at times conflict with, larger schemes of colonial development. Planters forced to move from environmentally damaged islands demanded immediate, full access to the ceded territories to establish new sugar plantations. Land speculators pushed for rapid development in hopes of snapping up cheap lands for later resale. Both argued that the revenues from expedited land sales (and the sugar duties that would follow) could help restore the nation's war-stressed treasury. Meanwhile, the powerful lobby of prosperous West Indian planters, fearful of more competition, sought to curb the expansion of sugar and to appropriate the forests for their own future use. Arguing that "the growing of Sugar must be absolutely prohibited . . . [or] the Woods would be soon destroyed," one Barbadian planter proposed admitting to Tobago only settlers (and, of course, their "servants, and slaves") who would pursue logging and nonsugar crops "consistent with the Timber Trade," such as coffee and cocoa. Even the native Caribs, he insisted, "savage as they are, understand that there can be no room for Indians to hunt, or ramble, where Canes are planted."[14]

Pointing to Jamaica as a failed model, others favored a more gradual, managed approach to land allocation and economic development that would balance agricultural expansion with forest preservation. They saw the Ceded Islands as offering a rare second chance to prove that deforestation was not an unavoidable corollary of colonization. On one level, this thinking reflected the transnational ideas of the Enlightenment that endeavored to improve the natural world for the benefit of all humankind. On another level, however, it exemplified Britain's ruthless aim to control natural resources as a matter of vital strategic interest, an approach that Richard Grove aptly termed "Green Imperialism."[15]

In 1763, the British prime minister commissioned John Campbell, a respected social commentator, to develop a plan to realize the Ceded Islands' untapped economic potential. Seeing their forests as a great asset, Campbell proposed strict regulations to ensure that they were "cut in a proper method and with discretion . . . because nothing has been more loudly exclaimed against by the sensible men in all the other islands, than the undistinguishing and destructive havoc made amongst the woods, without any regard to the general interest, or the least respect paid to that of posterity." With careful management, he insisted, they could be "properly and regularly cleared . . . [and] a succession of useful trees may be constantly maintained . . . [providing] fine woods for the use of joiners, cabinetmakers, and turners." By thus establishing a British tropical timber depot, England could reduce its dependence on foreign timber imports, support its furniture industry, and provide steady employment for its mariners. Harkening to the argument that sugar and forests were incompatible, Campbell also urged that incentives be given to new settlers to grow nonsugar crops, such as cloves, where they could take advantage of Dutch cultivation techniques developed in Ceylon and "lately published in Holland." On Tobago, he concluded, nature had done its part, now men must add art and industry to help it along.[16]

With regard to the indigenous population, Campbell advised following the French precedent of setting aside forest reservations for the Carib Indians who, before securing that agreement, fiercely resisted any colonial incursions. On Tobago, he also proposed that its native inhabitants be deputized to care for the forests, "a proper and easy employment to the Indians; in which, if bred to it, their children would certainly delight." Faced with a seemingly arbitrary change of colonial rule, the Caribs, for their part, were understandably alarmed by the demise of their previous arrangement and apprehensive about English intentions.[17]

While pro-development factions immediately rejected Campbell's plan, it attracted influential support (except for his forest-ranger scheme for the Caribs) from the Board of Trade and the Royal Society. Most importantly, Robert Melville, the Ceded Islands' new governor, embraced it. A Scottish military man who had studied medicine in Edinburgh, Melville was deeply interested in tropical agriculture, especially the cultivation of medicinal plants, and had recently established England's first West Indian botanical garden on St. Vincent. After using his own funds to clear several acres of land, he instructed its first director to seek out botanical knowledge from "practitioners of the country, natives of experience, and even old Caribs and slaves, who have dealt in cures." Melville promised further that "if at any time . . . a secret may be got at or even an improvement for small expense, I shall readily pay for it." Well-informed about emerging scientific theories linking deforestation with climate change, Melville believed in forest conservation, although he did not see it as necessarily conflicting with other land uses. To pressure Parliament to support Campbell's plan, Melville emphasized that France was gaining a future advantage over England thanks to their innovative approaches to managing tropical forestry, such as selective logging and replanting wastelands. In a major victory for Campbell and Melville, the Board of Trade announced in 1764 that, as land allocations proceeded on the Ceded Islands under the supervision of an official Land Settlement Commission, designated parts of Tobago and St. Vincent were to remain forested "to preserve the seasons so essential to the fertility of the islands and to answer all public services as may require the use and expense of timber." Accordingly, Tobago's 100,000 acres were divided up into 6,000- to 10,000-acre parishes, each with a woodland preserve, plus a larger one on the island's northeastern end.[18]

The Ceded Islands were soon inundated by immigrants from all over the British Empire, including many displaced planters who arrived with their slaves in tow. By 1771, the Land Commissioners had sold over 57,000 acres on Tobago, totaling approximately £154,058 in revenues for the governmental coffers. Despite efforts to stem land speculation and absentee ownership, many parcels were acquired by overseas investors, including bankers, merchants, and wealthy planters resident on other islands. Since a number of these same individuals were involved in the transatlantic slave trade, they accelerated the expansion of slavery on the Ceded Islands. Over the next four years, sugar production increased from 965 hogsheads to 4,550 hogsheads, while rum production increased from 411 puncheons to 3,247 puncheons; Tobagan rum became a desirable trade item at Bance Island, the large English slave factory off the coast of West Africa.[19]

In the face of such rapid expansion, well-heeled land speculators and corrupt officials made the well-intentioned attempt at a more sustainable approach to tropical forestry on the Ceded Islands difficult to implement or to enforce. Most insidiously, William Young, the head Land Commissioner, eager for rapid economic growth, cared little about conserving masses of trees which, like many at the time, he considered unhealthy. On Tobago, he opened almost the whole island to settlement, leaving only scraps of the least desirable land forested. Selecting choice acreage for himself on St. Vincent, he became one its largest landholders and owner of over 800 slaves; even Melville acquired substantial plantations on both Tobago and Grenada. Nonetheless, the experiment on the Ceded Islands set a significant precedent for future conservation initiatives elsewhere in the British Empire. For many years, however, such efforts took a back seat in the English West Indies where more influential economic and political interests remained dedicated to the expansion of the plantation complex.[20]

Arguably the more immediate impact of the forest preserves, however, was the effective alienation of the Caribs from their native lands. The new system of land tenure increasingly dispossessed them of their sacred forests and traditional ways of life. To survive, they had no choice but to trespass on newly privatized lands and official forest reserves or to retreat into the interior until threatened again by encroaching plantations. The new colonial order certainly did not offer any opportunities for the indigenous populace of the sort that Campbell rather naively envisioned. In 1765, the Land Commissioners demanded that the increasingly restive Caribs be deported to Bequia (a tiny island between Grenada and St. Vincent) because their supposedly "irregular manner" of forest subsistence interfered with agricultural expansion. Although Parliament initially rejected this request, the Caribs on St. Vincent continued to violently resist English colonization, temporarily stalling surveying and land distributions. In 1797, colonial officials received permission to deport over 5,000 Caribs to remote areas, including an isolated stretch of Belize that is still inhabited by their Garifuna descendants. At the time, however, this forced exodus resulted in tremendous suffering, disruption, and loss of life. A plan intended to protect the forests thus became one more colonial tool of domination and displacement of their traditional inhabitants.[21]

Ironically, for all the hopes placed on the Ceded Islands as a source of "fine woods for the use of joiners, cabinetmakers, and turners," they proved disappointing because non-native mahogany was not among them. Some English and American timber dealers and cabinetmakers took matters into their own hands. In the 1780s, Robert Gillow, whose cabinetmaking establishment had long relied on Jamaican mahogany, dispatched a trusted nephew to St. Kitts to personally source timber for them there. Others acquired some mahogany from Cuba, St. Domingue, Santo Domingo, and the Yucatán as part of a tenacious contraband trade, raising the hackles of colonial officials on all sides. This sampling whetted the appetites of consumers in England and North America for mahogany from these locales, laying the groundwork for its later popularity when it became more available in the early nineteenth century. Meanwhile, the search for mahogany shifted increasingly to more peripheral, contested regions, especially to the Bay of Honduras where it was a growing article of commerce and conflict.[22]

The Search for Honduran Mahogany

During the 1760s, as supplies of Jamaican mahogany became less reliable, consumer interest in the Honduran big-leaf species of mahogany *(Swietenia macrophylla)* was invigorated. Although still regarded as inferior to the West Indian article, it gained acceptability as English and American colonial cabinetmakers made more use of it as a primary wood. Growing demand sparked a mahogany gold rush, as men, dreaming of a timber bonanza, descended on the Central American coast, especially the Bay of Honduras (now Belize), where logwood cutters had made earlier inroads. In this region, many of the same tensions that affected mahogany cutters elsewhere in the Caribbean were magnified by their precarious status as English subjects on Spanish territory. Since both nations shared a common interest in regulating trade and avoiding expensive wars, they repeatedly negotiated treaties to contain woodcutting, first of logwood and then of mahogany, within agreed upon limits. Nevertheless, since their tenure remained insecure, the woodcutters developed an especially expedient attitude towards the land and its natural resources; their main objective was to extract the desired timber as quickly and ruthlessly as possible. As the search for mahogany expanded, however, diplomatic efforts to keep the peace were undermined and internal conflicts arose among the woodcutters. Although the social relations in the Bay settlement were peculiar to its geographical situation and to the specific requirements of mahogany cutting, many of the resulting problems—of imperial authority versus colonial autonomy, of local interests versus metropolitan interests—were reminiscent of those unfolding in other colonial venues in the latter half of the eighteenth century.[23]

During the seventeenth century, the first white woodcutters—or Baymen as they called themselves—descended on the Bay of Honduras in search of logwood. Although early English accounts described the region as uninhabited, remnants of the indigenous Mayan population remained, although many had been killed or displaced during the earlier Spanish conquest. To minimize contact with the newcomers and to avoid slaving raids by European ships, the Mayans moved to the interior. On the Mosquito Shore, the Miskitos engaged more extensively with the English, trading and later collaborating with them in fighting the Spanish. In both places, Anglo woodcutters established makeshift settlements that became the base of their logwood operations.[24]

In its infancy, the Bay settlement's predominantly male population numbered only a few hundred, but it was quite diverse, including Englishmen, Scots, Anglo-Americans, assorted other Europeans, enslaved (and some free) Africans, and a few multiracial Creoles. Among their ranks were former privateers, sailors, debtors, adventurers, and pirates. Captain Nathaniel Uring, shipwrecked in Belize in 1720, described them as "a rude drunken Crew," who lived in concert with "Negroes and Indian slaves which hunt for them." Like many frontier societies, the settlement was characterized less by rigid class or racial strictures than by a spirit of egalitarianism, pragmatism, and self-interest.[25]

During this early period, logwood cutting was its sole economic activity; compared with plantation agriculture, especially sugar, it required relatively little start-up capital or labor. Any free man, aided perhaps by a few Indian laborers or African slaves, could make a living by extracting the brushy dyewood from the swamps and coves where it grew wild and selling it to visiting ships that delivered it to a ready market in Europe. Since the Baymen had no property rights on Spanish territory, they customarily staked logwood claims by initiating cutting in a particular place. Because there was no recourse if a woodcutter infringed upon another's logwood claim, disputes inevitably arose which the Baymen settled among themselves on an ad hoc basis governed only by custom, informal agreements, and violence.

For many years, England and Spain engaged in an aggressive privateering campaign during which they attacked each other's ships and seized logwood shipments. The Baymen were repeatedly ousted by the

Spanish coast guard, only to return. In 1667, the rivals were finally forced to negotiate rather than escalate the violence. In the ensuing treaty, England acknowledged Spain's prior claim to the Bay of Honduras in exchange for the privilege of cutting logwood in designated areas. This agreement established two important precedents that were of major significance to the settlement's future and to the later mahogany industry: affirming Spain's sovereignty and awarding England limited usufruct rights.[26]

The English Crown, meanwhile, ordered its decommissioned privateers to seek alternate employment as woodcutters so that "these soldierly men would be kept within peaceable bounds," but still nearby, "ready to serve his Majesty in any new rupture." By leaving enforcement up to Spain, however, England tacitly condoned its subjects' defiance. In 1672, Sir William Godolphin, Ambassador to Spain, reminded his colleagues that England "had no shadow of a claim" to the logwood forests and that, in fact, Spain could "as justly pretend to make use of our [English] rivers, mountains and commons, as we can enjoy any benefit of these woods." While he advised that they should cut there surreptitiously, the incorrigible Baymen were emboldened and routinely trespassed on the treaty's limits. English officials were more annoyed, however, that they also ignored the Navigation Acts that required all ships to proceed through London. In 1682, for example, Thomas Lynch, governor of Jamaica, complained of them sending logwood to "Hamburgh, New England, Holland, etc., which injures us and the customs and trade of the nation." In another case, they sent logwood direct to Venice in exchange for glass beads.[27]

Even after Britain's accommodation with the Spanish, the Baymen's existence remained precarious during the early eighteenth century. Under the terms of the agreement, they were forbidden from establishing any permanent colonial government or judiciary; during periodic visits by British warships, naval officers provided a form of martial law, exercising police powers and trying non-civil court cases, but otherwise its residents fell under the loose jurisdiction of the governor of Jamaica, who administered various official functions from a distance. In addition, the residents convened regular public meetings and among themselves elected a board of magistrates to oversee day-to-day affairs. Another shaping factor in the Bay settlement was that the treaty still did not allow British subjects to own land on Spanish territory. In most colonial venues in the Americas, acquiring and improving land was the prime objective, and expanding agriculture was the engine of economic development. By contrast, the Bay settlement's sole *raison d'être* was to extract logwood and later mahogany, but once the trees were gone, the land itself had no long-term value to the woodcutters since they had no property rights.

During this period, the Baymen traded most extensively with English, Dutch, and Anglo-American merchants and ship captains, setting the stage for the later mahogany trade. In 1726, Nathaniel Uring reported, "The inhabitants of Boston carry on extensive trade with the Carib Islands in Jamaica. They send also several ships to the Bay of Honduras to load logwood." To cement this bond, in 1727, several Baymen donated a generous gift of logwood to fund improvements to Boston's Christ Church (now Old North Church) where several of their business contacts were prominent members. In return, church leaders reserved a special pew, "handsomely lin'd in red," next to the pulpit for "the Gentlemen of the Bay of Honduras." Although the Baymen rarely made it to church, this relationship, reinforced through gifts and symbolic expressions of appreciation, served both parties well.[28]

While the Bay settlement remained a rather rudimentary, freewheeling place, the status quo shifted dramatically in the 1760s with its shift from producing logwood to mahogany, in response to growing consumer demand for the latter. This transition was hastened by the sudden collapse of logwood prices after the Seven Years War due to the release of wartime stockpiles and a surge in cultivated logwood that glutted the market. While some woodcutters tried to make up the difference in price by cutting more logwood, most of those who could now made a full-on changeover to cutting mahogany. As the settlement's focus shifted abruptly to mahogany, however, the Baymen faced some serious challenges.[29]

First of all, England's treaty with Spain applied *only* to logwood; cutting mahogany meant breaking the law. In 1763, as Spain and Britain revisited the negotiating table at the end of the Seven Years War, the Baymen eagerly anticipated that their woodcutting rights at last would be expanded to include mahogany. To their disappointment, the Treaty of Paris merely renewed and extended the existing logwood agreement with slightly expanded boundaries. Whether this outcome resulted from a diplomatic oversight or a deeper disconnect between the metropole and the Bay is unclear, but in any event, it failed to acknowledge the region's changing economic realities. The treaty also agreed that any English fortifications on Spanish territory would be dismantled, leaving the Bay settlement defenseless. Feeling beleaguered by Spain and neglected by England, the Baymen defiantly ignored the treaty boundaries and continued cutting mahogany wherever they pleased.[30]

Secondly, mahogany extraction required a much more labor-intensive, skilled, and organized approach than was needed for logwood. Absent a large pool of indentured servants or potential wage-workers from which to draw, the Baymen turned to Jamaica's chattel markets and itinerant slave traders to meet their growing labor needs. Slavery became a defining feature of the Bay society for the first time. In this new situation, longtime Baymen, who prospered during the halcyon days of the logwood boom, gained a distinct advantage since they could afford the dozen or so slaves needed to initiate mahogany cutting; once established, they gained both social status and political clout. Most newcomers, however, lacked the necessary start-up capital, so stood little chance of emulating their predecessors' good fortunes and upward mobility. Consequently, the once relatively egalitarian population of the Bay became increasingly stratified. A small cohort of about twenty of the wealthiest, white Baymen, who controlled a disproportionate share of slaves and mahogany claims, coalesced into a powerful ruling elite. Although most came from modest or even unsavory backgrounds, their wealth enabled them to demand credit and preferential treatment from merchants in London and North America. Their mercantile connections, in turn, allowed them to control the importation of most manufactured goods and provisions into the Bay as well as access to shipping; some of the leading Baymen even acquired their own ships. Co-opted by the elite Baymen who were concerned mainly with protecting their own interests, the board of magistrates soon held sway over the settlement, strong-arming the populace into conformity with their wishes. Other people in the settlement were largely a captive market; forced to pay the elite Baymen high prices for their necessaries and stiff commissions to transport their timber to market, many small-scale woodcutters became ensnared in debt. They survived by continuing to harvest logwood and small amounts of mahogany, assisted by perhaps one or two slaves at the most. Others ended up working for the established Baymen as overseers or paid laborers. A small number of white women (mostly widows) and some free men and women of color also eked out a living from logwood claims. An underclass of poor white and racially mixed free people lived self-sufficiently by fishing or turtling and were regarded by the leading Baymen as a troublesome element.

Another major grievance of the Baymen was that the Treaty made no provision for the return of, or restitution for, runaway slaves. Controlling the enslaved population was especially challenging in a place where slaves could easily disappear into the forest or seek sanctuary in adjacent Spanish-populated areas. Moreover, in 1752, the Spanish king had renewed his long-standing offer of freedom to any fugitive slave who arrived "under the pretence of embracing the Holy Catholic Religion." Slave masters in the Bay suspected the Spanish of deviously luring their slaves away. In 1768, for example, one complained that the Spanish coast guard "kept boats constantly plying at the mouth of the River Hondo to seduce slaves." The high number of runaways was a very serious problem because a viable labor force was essential to extract any profit from the surrounding forest. Yet slaves constituted a highly mobile, unpredictable, and volatile form of capital—it was, after all, an investment physically manifested in the actual *bodies* of persons who could die, become incapacitated, or run away. By absconding, slaves could literally bankrupt their owners.[31]

One positive outcome of the Treaty of Paris was that the Baymen were granted permission to legally define the boundaries of their logwood "works" (as they called areas claimed for woodcutting) but still not to own the land outright. In 1765, the free, largely male residents drew up a set of rules that constituted an informal body of civil law known as the Burnaby Code, since it was authorized by William Burnaby, the naval commander in Jamaica who oversaw peacekeeping in the Bay. It required that "when a person finds a spot of Logwood unoccupied, and builds his hutt, that spot shall be deemed his property; and no person shall presume to cutt or fall a tree, or grub a stump within less than one thousand paces or yards." It further specified that no one could occupy multiple claims. While these de facto regulations ostensibly applied only to logwood, the Baymen quietly extended them to include their new quarry; mahogany works thereafter were bought and sold like private property even though all land remained in the hands of the Spanish king.[32]

With the Burnaby Code in place, the British Crown acknowledged the Bay residents' efforts to regularize their existence by awarding them a constitution in 1766 affirming their official status as British subjects, although living within Spanish dominions. Nevertheless, the Bay settlement remained a sphere of discord. Its residents, especially those among the powerful elite, followed the new regulations selectively as it suited them, squabbled over conflicting claims, and engaged in other illicit activities. Irritated at their continued intransigence, the Spanish commander at Bacalar ominously warned British officials that "all the results that may happen between the Sovereigns" would be blamed on the Baymen "for not executing what they are ordered." In 1768, Admiral Parry echoed his concern, describing the Baymen as "a most notorious lawless sett of Miscreants," who fled there "to avoid justice . . . [and] pursue their licentious conduct with impunity." He urged the Royal Navy to station a frigate in the Belize harbor to "prevent as much as possible Murders, Frauds, and Confusion which are notoriously practiced among the Baymen." A few years later, Spanish officials concluded that unless "the settlers are made amenable to justice they will ever be a source of contention to the two governments."[33]

On the adjacent Mosquito Shore, also claimed by Spain, the situation unfolded rather differently. Aided by the rough terrain and their military prowess, the indigenous Miskito Indians had long eluded Spanish conquest. Although fiercely independent, the Miskitos forged an alliance with the English against Spain, seeing it as their best chance to retain their autonomy. In exchange for the Miskitos' military assistance and access to the timber resources on their lands, the English provided them with arms, supplies, and manufactured goods. The Miskitos became involved in the larger Atlantic economy by trading timber products with passing ships and assisting British woodcutters with forest reconnaissance. The gigantic mahogany trees, which the Miskitos had previously used almost exclusively for canoes, became one of the region's main exports. In his later memoirs, Orlando Roberts, an English trader, recalled a Miskito leader sending a canoe to the Bay of Honduras to "convince the merchants there of the extraordinary size, and excellent quality of the timber which could be procured in his country." Indeed, the Englishmen must have been amazed as the Indians paddled up in an imposing vessel, carved from a single tree, which reportedly measured "thirty-five feet in length, nearly six feet in breadth, and above five feet in depth."[34]

With the outbreak of the American Revolution in 1776, the agreement between Britain and Spain regarding logwood access was temporarily suspended. As the conflict spread from North America to the Caribbean, the Baymen fully expected that Britain would at last put the matter to rest by seizing control of the Bay of Honduras. Several proposals to accomplish this were put forward, including a secret plan submitted to the secretary of state in 1776 to enlist the Miskito Indians in attacking the Spanish. Likely authored by Robert White (a former Baymen and the magistrates' London agent), it proposed redeploying English troops from North America on the assumption that the uprising there would be quickly squelched. In 1779, John Dalling, governor of Jamaica, reported another covert meeting with two unnamed Baymen who proposed that a force of 200 of their fellows, 500 slaves, and some Miskito Indians could easily capture the nearest Spanish garrison. Imagining their ranks would swell with "some 100,000 Indians eager for liberation from Spain," they then envisioned taking the entire Yucatán.[35]

None of these grandiose plans materialized. Instead, the Spanish surprised them all with a devastating early morning assault on St. George's Caye, where most of the Baymen's families were living at the time. On 15 September 1779, the slumbering residents were roused from their beds to see a menacing phalanx of sails as nineteen Spanish vessels swooped into the island's unprotected harbor. The Spanish forces timed their attack to coincide with the woodcutting season when most of the men "fit to bear arms" were away. By one report, there were "101 white people on the Key when it was taken & 40 of mixed Colour . . . about 200 or 250 negroes, men, women, and children, mostly House-negroes . . . the principal part that carry on the Logwood &

Mahogany cutting business were then up the River." In the resulting chaos, many slaves ran away and the defenseless settlement had no choice but to surrender. The soldiers rounded up and marched the inhabitants to the Spanish outpost of Mérida, a harrowing 300-mile trek through swamps and dense forest. Although the commander promised that if they went quietly, "great tenderness should be shown to the Ladies as well as the Mustie women and children . . . to protect them from violence," the prisoners suffered many hardships and some died. The survivors were sent to a Cuban prison where many remained for up to five years until the war's end. The Baymen sought compensation from Spain for years afterwards, claiming the "defenseless" residents were "surprised and assaulted in the most violent and hostile manner and robbed of their Negroes, property, and Effects, and many of themselves made Captives, and basely insulted in their Persons, forced to perform fatiguing and oppressive Marches up into the Country of Yucatan, and detained Prisoners there and at Havanna."[36]

Receiving belated word of the assault, the absent Baymen sought refuge on Jamaica. In 1780, many of them joined with British forces and some Miskito Indians in a counterattack, determined to end Spanish dominance in Central America. Ill-advisedly setting out during the rainy season, they seized several forts but were forced to retreat when thousands of British soldiers became ill and died; even the hardy Miskito warriors, whose misgivings about the attack went unheeded, deserted en masse. After this fiasco, Britain never again invaded Spanish strongholds in Central America. The Spanish for their part were dismayed to find that the Baymen immediately returned to mahogany cutting after the war, despite the almost five-year hiatus and their much-reduced population.[37]

In 1783, in anticipation of the Treaty of Versailles ending the American Revolution, the Baymen and their affiliated London merchants lobbied hard for the legalization of mahogany cutting. To support their case, they rather brazenly pointed out that in that year alone they had *already* exported over 70,000 linear feet of mahogany, which gave employment to an estimated 8,000 British seamen. Spain meanwhile moved to consolidate its colonial holdings. After years of ineffectual efforts to protect its territory from foreign interlopers and humiliating defeats in two major conflicts with Britain, it now sought to reassert centralized control, rein in its colonies' increasingly independent Creole population, and exert a much stronger military presence in previously neglected areas, such as the Bay of Honduras. Accordingly, in this round of diplomacy, Spain seemed to take the upper hand, reasserting its sovereignty over the Bay and insisting upon several treaty provisions intended to constrain the British subjects residing there. The new agreement revived the previous logwood cutting arrangements, even expanding the designated woodcutting areas "between the rivers Wallis or Belize and Rio-Hondo," but it still precluded mahogany. Spain also demanded that Britain enforce the agreed upon boundaries, which were to be clearly marked, and punish any Baymen who transgressed them. While the treaty was intended to remove all "causes of complaint and misunderstanding heretofore occasioned by the cutting of wood" between England and Spain, Robert White, the Baymen's London agent, immediately protested that the forests opened to logging were insufficient and that the boundaries were unfairly based upon an unknown Spanish chart.[38]

Nevertheless, Spain dispatched an engineer from the Yucatán to survey the revised boundaries. Four English delegates accompanied him as observers, namely Colonel Edward Marcus Despard (a military leader who fought in the region during the late war) and several elite Baymen, including Richard Hoare, James McAuley, and James Bartlett. "Agreeable to the Map and the instructions I received from my Sovereign," the engineer reported, "[I] placed the proper marks ... as well as executed every necessary formality required for this purpose." Indicated by blazed tree trunks and wooden columns set at intervals through the jungle, the new lines seemed annoyingly arbitrary to the Baymen. They complained, for example, of rivers divided up the middle, forcing them to travel far upstream instead of just taking trees from both sides.[39]

In 1786, the Convention of London revised the treaty to allow mahogany cutting, thanks to vociferous lobbying by the Baymen and their London supporters. This concession was conditional, however, on three requirements: first, woodcutters could not go beyond the designated boundaries; second, no further permanent improvements were permitted, including no agriculture, civic institutions, military installations, or governmental entities (apart from the existing board of magistrates); and third, Britain would reduce its regional presence by evacuating the Mosquito Shore, relocating its residents to the Bay settlement and elsewhere. This last item was especially damaging for the Miskito Indians since England's departure from their realm left them in a very vulnerable position relative to Spain.[40]

Cumulatively, these provisions amounted to a policy of containment that would deeply polarize the Bay settlement. While both Crowns hailed the Convention of London as a welcome bilateral solution to the region's chronic strife, Spain parlayed what at face value seemed a diplomacy of compromise into an advantageous position by, at least temporarily, limiting further growth and institutional development in the Bay settlement. British officials, meanwhile, expressed confidence that the Convention would both ensure the woodcutters' prosperity and security and bring them into line with imperial authority. Predictably, in a letter to King George III, the magistrates emphatically denounced the new agreement as the misguided product of ill-informed diplomats: "[While] the court of Madrid may amuse the court of London, with the number of miles and leagues [of forest] which have been ceded, . . . [and] with infinite respect to the superior Abilities and Knowledge and Wisdom of both Courts, [we] most humbly pretend to be better

Wood-cutters and better judges of the Soil, the Situation, and the Trees . . . than all the courts of Europe." This acerbic statement perfectly expressed their frustration with the feeling that their destiny was being batted back and forth like a shuttlecock between the imperial courts.[41]

The Baymen were convinced that Spanish negotiators had hoodwinked their English counterparts. They claimed that the additional acres granted in the Convention were worthless "on account of their Swamps, their Sterility, or the bad quality of their Wood . . . [since] good Wood is only profitable and bad Wood brings the Cutter into Debt." William Ryder, a Bay resident who had been a prisoner-of-war in Cuba for three years, called the agreement a "trap or snare to allure and entice British Subjects into where the Mahogany and Logwood was all principally cut." Suspecting that Spain intended to "annihilate the Settlement" by choking off their access to viable forests, another man complained that when "a stranger casts his Eyes on this newly ceded land . . . he will no doubt imagine much is granted . . . [but finding instead] an unprofitable, unoccupied wilderness, he will find very little is given by the Spaniard." After accusing the Spanish of deliberately drawing the borders along rivers to encourage runaways, he proclaimed rather melodramatically that truly it was the Baymen who were enslaved by the Convention "forming new, or more securely riveting our former shackles." The Baymen's actions soon betrayed that they had no intention of obeying the revised treaty.[42]

In 1786, Colonel Edward Marcus Despard returned to the Bay as its first royally appointed superintendent, a new position mandated by the Convention in order to oversee the settlement and enforce the treaty. The board of magistrates were initially delighted as they had long requested just such an administrator who they expected to stand up to Spain, rein in the settlement's rowdier elements, and advocate for stronger military, diplomatic, and trade protections from England. From

SUPPLYING THE EMPIRE WITH MAHOGANY

the perspective of Whitehall, however, Despard's appointment was a calculated first step toward asserting more stringent imperial control; for although the board of magistrates was permitted to remain, the new superintendent, at least on paper, had authority over it and over the Bay settlement as a whole.

Among potential royal appointees, few men could have been better prepared than Despard. A war hero who had commanded a collaborative force of English soldiers, Miskito Indians, and local woodcutters in the region, he was very familiar with the local scene and was married to a woman of African descent from the Mosquito Shore. In addition, he had recently served as an official observer during Spain's survey of the treaty boundaries. While several of the magistrates had recommended Despard for the job, he soon disabused them of any notion that he would defer to them or would serve as their personal conduit to London. His foremost intention was to carry out the orders issued to him by his superiors at the Department of State, namely to enforce the treaty, ensure order within the Bay settlement, and oversee the relocation of the Mosquito Shore evacuees.[43]

Shortly after Despard took up his new post, a Spanish official on a periodic inspection of the settlement (required under the 1786 Convention) complained that many of the Baymen were already trespassing on the boundaries and "were so imprudent as to roll out logs of Mahogany perfectly in his sight. . . . [By] the many broad and beaten roads and other marks, he could easily see that they had been employ'd there for years!" After counting twenty-six roads already cut deep into Spanish territory, his patrols confiscated the Baymen's slaves and cattle and burned the illegally cut mahogany, sending thousands of feet of valuable timber up in smoke. When the Baymen urged Despard to retaliate, he instead ordered their immediate withdrawal. They stubbornly refused and dispatched their slaves to fell as many trees as possible.[44]

Additional conflict soon arose from the Convention's controversial ban on agriculture. For although harvesting of mahogany and "fruits . . . of the earth, purely natural and uncultivated" was permitted, cultivation of crops, including even produce for local consumption, was no longer allowed; likewise, no related infrastructure, such as grist mills or sugar boilers, could be erected. Spain's clear goal was to hinder the settlement's population growth by limiting its food production and to prevent the long-term capital investments required to establish a plantation economy. However, the free residents, terrified of food shortages and possible uprisings by hungry slaves, united in opposing this restriction. In 1789, after several violent confrontations between Bay residents and Spanish guards sent to uproot illegal crops, Despard finally convinced Spain to allow free men and women to retain provision grounds to feed themselves and their slaves. While the lowlier members of the Bay settlement were grateful for his advocacy on their behalf, Despard had by then already antagonized much of the Bay elite.[45]

The third major provision of the London Convention, requiring that Britain evacuate the Mosquito Shore, caused even more significant problems. The British subjects and their slaves displaced in the process were to be relocated, mostly to the Bay of Honduras. The Shore residents, who included many poor and racially mixed individuals, were not eager to move, insisting that their home "was in every consideration to be preferred, as being inexhaustible in mahogany." Negotiating a complex situation from afar, the English ambassador offered them some modest financial incentives and guarantees of mahogany claims within the newly opened lands in the Bay. To his surprise, the elite Baymen vehemently protested this proposal, arguing that such an influx of population was unsupportable given the settlement's limited natural resources. They particularly bridled at the promises of preferential treatment in awarding mahogany claims to the evacuees. Having dominated the local political scene and woodcutting business for more than twenty years, they had no desire to accommodate people who they regarded as both unwelcome competition and socially and racially inferior. Another outspoken opponent was London merchant George Dyer who had invested heavily in mahogany claims on the Mosquito Shore and in the Bay as a hedge against eventual timber shortages elsewhere. As Despard pointed out, Dyer had "entered into so deep speculations in Mahogany" that the government's plan to evacuate the Mosquito Shore and allocate mahogany claims in the Bay to displaced woodcutters "must have been his ruin." Despard further suspected Dyer of conspiring with a few rich Baymen to corner the mahogany market, manipulate production levels, and fix prices. Charged with promoting the general good, Despard was determined to foil such self-serving schemes.[46]

Despite the opposition, in 1786 more than 2,000 refugees, three-quarters of them slaves, were relocated from the Mosquito Shore to the Bay of Honduras, resulting in a huge population increase since the settlement's residents numbered only about 700 after the war. Amidst the disruption of the evacuation, however, hundreds of slaves escaped, hiding out in the bush until British transport ships were forced to leave without them; many of their former owners thus arrived in the Bay lacking the necessary labor to start up new mahogany works. Concurrently, several hundred Loyalists fleeing from former British colonies arrived in the Bay, attracted by similar promises of government assistance. From both of these constituencies, the elite Baymen quickly co-opted the wealthiest (mostly white) few to join their ranks, strengthening their monopolistic hold over the less affluent. When Despard defied them by allocating mahogany works to the refugees by lottery without regard to their economic status or race, the white oligarchy denounced him for putting free "Negroes and Mulattoes . . . who, in all the West India Islands, were considered in a very inferior light . . . upon a footing with Gentlemen and Mahogany Cutters, who were the supporters of the land." Despard insisted that the law of England "knows no such distinction" among its subjects and that "people of color were as much entitled to places to live in as the first mahogany cutters."[47]

Warning ominously of imminent mahogany shortages caused by the unwelcome refugees, the magistrates demanded the Spanish open more land to logging, without admitting they had *already* long since stripped the recently opened areas of the best trees. To limit who could claim a mahogany works without their prior approval, the magistrates instituted a minimum property requirement of four able-bodied male slaves; to secure additional claims required a minimum of ten male slaves or indentured servants. Despard objected that this policy specifically favored "the opulent People" to the detriment of those of lesser means, "who with one or two Negroes, together with their own labour might support themselves and their families, with some degree of comfort, by cutting Mahogany." Since many of the wealthiest woodcutters got their start without any slaves, this hypocritical policy particularly rankled Despard who felt it unfairly protected the Bay's "very arbitrary aristocracy."[48]

In 1786, Despard commissioned a large map, based on an official survey by David Lamb, to record the treaty boundaries and established mahogany claims. Drawn in sepia ink with watercolor highlights, the map, at first glance, presents a serene landscape defined by the Belize and New Rivers winding like ribbons from the interior to the coast and a dense mesh of interlinked lagoons, small creeks, meandering streams, and swampy expanses of mangrove. Upon closer examination, however, the map offers clues to the actual scene on the ground that was far from placid. A handful of names appear repeatedly—Bartlett, McCauley, O'Brien, Tucker, Potts, and Hoare—indicating their claims to multiple mahogany works and vast swathes of untapped forest both inside and outside the treaty's boundaries. Symbols denoting "old works" indicate abandoned timber claims (even outside the treaty's limits) where the mahogany was already depleted. With its uneven distribu-

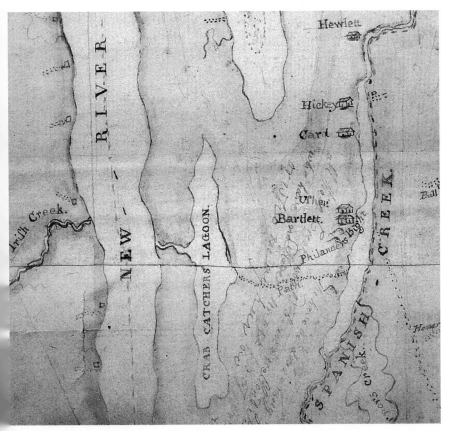

FIG. 3.1 Detail of "A Map of that Part of the Yucatan in the Bay of Honduras Allotted to Great Britain for the cutting of Logwood as specified by the sixth article of the Peace of 1783, Also the New Extended Limits Granted with the Privilege of Cutting Other Dyewoods and Mahogany . . . ," [David Lamb], Belize, 1786. Collection of the National Archives, England. (NA/CO700.)

In 1786, Spain and Britain agreed to enlarge the Spanish territory open to British wood-cutters in the Bay of Honduras (Belize) and to permit mahogany cutting. Depicted here is the northern quadrant of the revised area. On Spanish Creek (right), the house-shaped icons indicate mahogany works claimed by Jonathan Card (Chap. 4) and other Baymen; the square with dotted lines indicates an "Old Mahogany or Logwood works," abandoned because the trees were cut out. Past the New River boundary (left), the squares with dotted lines indicate "works without the limits," violating the treaty.

tion of people and forest resources, the map accurately represents the Bay settlement's fragmented social character in which a handful of elite Baymen monopolized the richest forest lands while poorer whites and free people of color, shut out of viable mahogany works, gravitated towards marginal lands or congregated in Convention Town, a residential area established by Despard for the Mosquito refugees. Annotations on the map indicate each place where Anglo woodcutters had trespassed on the treaty boundaries, running afoul of Spanish inspectors who burned their huts, provision grounds, and mahogany logs and drove their cattle into the woods. Superimposed on the paper landscape, these memorandums of violence document the strife-filled realities of the Bay.[49]

After initially agreeing more land was needed since "wood was becoming very scarce within the limits," Despard rejected the magistrates' alarmism, citing their conspiratorial machinations to usurp the remaining mahogany as the true problem. Bartlett bemoaned the fate of his "poor distressed much to be pitied brethren" from the Mosquito Shore, for example, but he single-handedly had claimed mahogany lands slated for thirty-two refugee families. In August 1787, Despard's efforts to distribute mahogany works equitably by a lottery took a nasty turn when Joshua Jones, a free black man, was awarded land informally claimed by Aaron Young, a well connected white Bayman. After attempting to take legal possession of the mahogany works, Jones was seized by an armed posse of Young's friends. When a delegation of free colored men demanded Jones's release, Young and his men barricaded themselves and their prisoner in the courthouse. Amidst this tense standoff, Despard forced his way in, placed his hand on Jones's shoulder, and proclaimed "In the King's name, I release this Man!" Grabbing their prisoner by the other arm, one of the ringleaders replied, "As a Magistrate and one of the people of Honduras, I detain him." Although Despard successfully negotiated Jones's release on a £500 bond, this tug-of-war epitomized the larger struggle over who held ultimate authority in the Bay. While the elite Baymen were determined not to cede any power, Despard was resolved to fulfill his orders in spite of the magistrates' bullying. Shortly thereafter, he disbanded the board of magistrates for acting so "independent of the King of Great Britain . . . [that] even the King's Superintendent could not make them obey."[50]

Meanwhile, the free colored population backed Despard and protested to Parliament that the magistrates denied them the "privileges of British subjects." Alarmed by Despard's growing grassroots support, the elite Baymen mobilized their merchant allies in London to oust him. With George Dyer taking a head role, the leading English mahogany merchants gathered at London Tavern in October 1789 to demand Despard's removal, citing the ill effects his enforcement of the despised London Convention was having on their commerce. Shortly thereafter, Lord Sydney, bowing to political pressure, suspended the superintendent. After acknowledging that Despard acted from "the best motives," Sydney admonished him for not preferring the affluent white settlers over "people of Colour or Free Negroes, who from the natural prejudices of the Colonies, are not . . . considered upon an equal footing." Although Despard was promptly elected to the board of magistrates thanks to enthusiastic support from "turtlers, steersmen, carpenters, color'd and free people," he was forced to return to England in a futile attempt to expose his enemies and save his career.[51]

Over the following decade, subsequent superintendants largely deferred to the white oligarchy that continued to dominate the racially divided settlement. After Britain finally wrested control of the Bay of Honduras from Spain in 1798, some residents established plantations but most continued their accustomed occupation of mahogany cutting. Since mahogany remained their main economic objective, the accessible trees were soon depleted. In 1814, the Baymen petitioned the King for trade protections, claiming their timber supply was inadequate because mahogany trees were "of extreme slow growth, but cannot be propagated." Forced to send logging crews ever farther inland and more distant from the main waterways, they faced rising labor and transport costs, growing competition for the best trees, and renewed resistance from the Mayans who attacked their camps, only to be pushed deeper into the interior. Once again, the relentless search for mahogany exemplified the imperial drive to find, expropriate, and control people, space, and nature.[52]

CHAPTER FOUR

The Bitters and the Sweets of Trade

IN 1765, *The West-India Merchant, Factor, and Supercargoes Daily Assistant* reported that "Mahogany is a never-failing Merchandize . . . if good, and bought on adequate terms; nor is there any Fear of the British market being overstocked . . . [because] beautiful Household Furniture made thereof [is] growing more and more in Fashion amongst all sorts of People." Yet, it cautioned novices to carefully ascertain "that the Wood is really Mahogany," that "the Planks or Trees are sound," and that it was all "sawed off square," since any irregularities were measured "in Favor of the first Purchaser." Although already well established, the mahogany trade clearly required accurate information, discerning judgment, constant vigilance, and a modicum of good luck.[1]

The mahogany trade functioned within the larger context of the mercantilist system that dominated British trade for most of the eighteenth century. Since it required that debts and credits often be extended over many years and miles, trust and mutual confidence were essential lubricants for the wheels of commerce. Despite improvements in business information (such as published reports of current commodity prices and of ships' arrivals and departures), most people still preferred to do business through personal connections or direct referrals from loyal friends, kinsmen, former neighbors, or coreligionists.

Although dealing with close associates could be problematic, most deemed it preferable to transactions with strangers. Given the long-distance and decentralized nature of the mahogany trade, correspondence between timber suppliers and their metropolitan associates, in both directions, resounded with pleas for candor and fair dealing, requests for favors or preferential treatment, and, when things went wrong, accusations and recriminations. As the ongoing search for mahogany expanded from the West Indies into Central America in the 1760s, the uncertainties of the trade intensified, especially on the production end where participants had to negotiate difficult conditions in an alien and, at times, hostile environment. Since prior to the 1786 Convention, mahogany cutting in the Bay of Honduras was not allowed, Anglo woodcutters operated in constant fear of the Spanish evicting them, seizing their slaves, and confiscating or burning their valuable timber. Moreover, local events and frictions between the Baymen and Spanish colonial officials often reverberated unexpectedly with significant consequences for mahogany buyers and sellers a hemisphere away.[2]

Undaunted by this challenge, some New Englanders nonetheless played an integral role in expanding the production, availability, and consumption of Honduran mahogany during this period. By examining the experiences of three participants, this chapter demonstrates that these developments emerged from a dynamic, reciprocal process of exchange among diverse peoples, interweaving threads of private and shared interest, kinship, debt, and obligation. Each one of this trio, however, offers a different perspective—from a Newport counting house, where merchant Aaron Lopez poured over his account books; from a ship's deck, where fellow Rhode Islander Captain James Card transported mahogany throughout the Atlantic region; and finally, from a frontier outpost in the Bay of Honduras (now Belize), where Jonathan Card, James's expatriate brother, supervised slaves in extracting mahogany from the rain forest. Their respective vantage points influenced how each man grappled with the myriad economic, political, social, and environmental conditions that shaped (and, in some cases, were shaped by) the mahogany trade and that made it such a slippery business. Their intertwined personal and business relationships, while at times rocky, proved vitally important to their involvement in the mahogany trade and largely influenced their timber trading patterns up until the American Revolution.

The View from the Counting House

Ever on the lookout for new opportunities, Rhode Island merchant Aaron Lopez entered the mahogany trade in the early 1760s. A savvy purveyor of luxury goods and commodities, he had built up a sizeable fortune supplying the elements of refinement to those eager to join in the emerging culture of gentility. Lopez catered to their desires by specializing in exotic products such as Bohea tea, fine wines, chocolate, powered snuff, coffee, sugar, dyewoods, and the purest spermaceti candles. Mahogany, increasingly in demand among high-end consumers, fit well into this marketing scheme. Moreover, having previously dealt in logwood, Lopez already had contacts in the Bay of Honduras with New England expatriates who were eager to supply him with mahogany as well.[3]

Even as he branched out into Honduran mahogany, Lopez continued to buy, sell, and trade a diversified mix of goods. After starting with next to nothing, Lopez had become a very successful merchant thanks to his willingness to take entrepreneurial risks and to juggle multiple simultaneous transactions. In 1752, at twenty-one years of age, Lopez, along with his wife and infant daughter, emigrated from Lisbon to Newport, joining the vibrant, small Jewish community where his older brother had already been a member for decade. In his words, by keeping his "Little trade in a Continual Circulation," Lopez gradually accumulated enough capital to invest in shipping ventures and eventually to buy his own vessels. In 1756, he invested in a candle manufactory started by Jacob Rodríguez Rivera, who innovated the use of spermaceti (a waxy substance extracted from sperm whales) to make brighter, cleaner-burning tapers. In a day when people relied on candles for artificial illumination, this business initially proved exceedingly lucrative. Their partnership was strengthened when, after his first wife's death in 1762, Lopez married Rivera's daughter.[4]

In addition to this propitious union, Lopez forged an extensive circum-Atlantic mercantile network with connections among the Jewish diaspora as well as with non-Jewish merchants. He aggressively launched new enterprises, including a shipyard, a snuff manufactory, and an Antiguan sugar plantation. Within ten years of his arrival, Lopez was a wealthy man and the largest taxpayer in thriving Newport. Enjoying the fruits of his labor, Lopez took up gentlemanly pursuits, such as drinking fine wines and playing cards, but he also made substantial charitable donations, most notably to help fund the building and furnishing of the Touro Synagogue, dedicated in 1763. His entry into the mahogany trade coincided, however, with a temporary downturn in his candle business due to growing competition and to spermaceti shortages, problems he and other New England candle makers eventually resolved through a price-fixing agreement that has been described as perhaps "the world's first energy cartel."[5]

In the meantime, Lopez sent his first mahogany cargos to London where consumer demand was highest. His close attention to his new venture was underscored in a letter to his London agent emphasizing that his latest shipment included "2 remarkable Large pieces which measured 1,200 feet & are esteem'd of much greater Value [than] the comm[on] Mahogany, therefore when you order them for Sale desire that note be taken of their particular Sizes." Although he likely did well on that sale (unusually large mahogany was always quickly snapped up by cabinetmakers), he quickly realized that because so much timber was being landed in London, it created more cutthroat competition and lower prices than he had anticipated. Figuring he might do better outside the great metropolis, he began investigating English provincial markets. Encountering these same conditions in London, some New England merchants went even farther afield, sometimes blatantly ignoring the Navigation Acts. Nicholas Boylston, one of Boston's leading merchants, tested the Baltic waters by sending ships to St. Petersburg where Francophile Russian aristocrats emulated the Parisian taste for exotic woods. In 1763, his ship, the *Wolfe*, arrived there laden with mahogany, sugar, indigo, rum, and sassafras and returned with a cargo of hemp and Russian sheeting for making sails. After repeated voyages, however, the English consul-general in St. Petersburg brought the ship's activities to the attention of the secretary of the Admiralty who ordered a British squadron "to cruize very diligently and keep a sharp look out for the said ship, in order to seize her, if you find she is employed in an illicit trade as expected." Although the sly *Wolfe* seems to have eluded capture, Lopez opted more conservatively for Bristol, one of England's main secondary ports; but, to gain a footing in this unfamiliar venue, he needed a contact.[6]

Most likely, his brother, who had lived in New York, introduced him to a merchant there named Gabriel Ludlow who, in turn, connected him with Henry Cruger, Sr., formerly of Bristol. Fortuitously, Cruger's family was politically influential—Henry, Sr. and his brother both held public office in New York—and was at the center of a broad-based trading network that included four sons—John Harris in New York, Telemon in Curaçao, Nicholas in St. Croix, and Henry, Jr. in Bristol. Upon Ludlow's recommendation, Henry Cruger, Jr. agreed to serve as Lopez's new Bristol representative, guaranteeing the same terms that Lopez received in London in exchange for exclusivity. In 1764, Lopez wrote to Ludlow, "I am greatly obliged to you for the notice you took of my request & of introducing me to a Gentleman whose conduct [I] am confident will answer for the Character you gave him."[7]

After a promising start, however, the new partners' plan to dominate Bristol's mahogany trade proved more difficult than expected. For although they faced less competition, demand in this less-populous provincial area also lagged behind that of the metropole. Moreover, as trade recovered after the recently ended Seven Years War, woodcutters shipped their stockpiles to London, glutting the market and depressing prices throughout the country. Less than a year into their new arrangement, Cruger informed Lopez that mahogany was "a mere Drugg all over the Kingdom." Although their polite epistolary exchanges teemed with conventional expressions of friendship, they were increasingly peppered with frustration and disagreement about the timing, quality, size, and sources of Lopez's mahogany shipments. Although merchants and suppliers have always wrangled over such issues to gain advantage, it boded ill when in 1766 Cruger wrote that Bristol buyers spurned Lopez's recent consignment because "the quality is not liked." Clearly aggravated, he wrote: "I am sorry so much more Mahogany is coming. . . . I have halled about a quarter of the [last shipment] away, in order to lessen the quantity in the Eyes of the Buyers, as well as to make room on our Keys. [T]he great Piles that now remain . . . get me a rap over the Knuckles every time I fall in company with our Mayor, but I laugh it off, saying it will soon be removed and so forth. [I]f you can meet with *some fine Jamaica Mahogany* of proper lengths and good breadths, it will sell." Perhaps after laughing off the mayor's reprimand once too often, Cruger informed Lopez that "no Body offer'd to buy [it, because] the quality is so soft and spungy; I found nothing to be done but at publick sale. . . . I have at least sold [it all] at one stroke. . . . It is very cheap but it would do no better keeping, such large quantitys are dayly arriving and expected." Cruger later complained, "Does not a bad piece of Wood take up the same room in a Ship as a good piece? Such Wood as cou'd not bear the Freight aught not to have been shipped." Any competitive edge the men might have enjoyed in Bristol was eroded by poor quality control and Bristol consumers' continued reflexive preference for Jamaican mahogany.[8]

This conundrum likely embarrassed Lopez who normally took pains to ensure the superiority of his goods in order to attract and retain devoted customers. Indeed, in many cases, he added considerable value to merchandise by carefully selecting, processing, and refining raw materials in New England to guarantee the excellence of his end products. Rather than just sell cocoa beans, for example, he paid by the pound for a "Negro" named Prince Updike to grind them at a nearby chocolate mill. Lopez even refused to sell an inferior grade of candles requested by a frugal customer, for although he would have profited, he did not want to tarnish his reputation. Drawing on those experiences, he now supplied choice mahogany and cedar to local Newport cabinetmakers, some of whom were close neighbors, to make furniture for him as venture cargo, which brought him a higher profit margin than if he had just sold logs. He also had mahogany objects fabricated for his own home and as gifts to beautify the synagogue.[9]

Before a splinter of mahogany arrived in Newport, however, Lopez was completely reliant on others to select the timber that ended up on his ships. Moreover, when his vessels proceeded directly to Bristol, London, or other foreign destinations, he never even saw the wood and certainly had no direct oversight of what was consigned in his name. He simply could not monitor all aspects of his supply chain. After their recent disappointment, Lopez and Cruger scrutinized changing market conditions more carefully. In one instance, Cruger advised a captain leaving the Bay of Honduras that Jamaica would "be the best market for your Mahogany, [as] tis with us almost unsaleable at present . . . there are no purchasers that can pay for it and what is worse England and Ireland are also glutted with it, and none of the foreign markets that we trade to hold that wood in any esteem equal to its value." A few months later, he more optimistically predicted a "ready and advantageous sale" for some mahogany of "extraordinary great breadth and superior good quality." Such assessments underscore that profitability required both securing excellent mahogany and accurately judging where and when it would best sell.[10]

Lopez meanwhile hedged his bets by continuing to deal in many other goods and commodities including—when the opportunity arose—people. Wherever his ships sailed in the Greater Caribbean, they engaged in casual, itinerant slaving, often involving just a few individuals at a time. Circumventing the large chattel markets in Jamaica and elsewhere, his captains and supercargos dealt directly with small-scale local slave traders, factors, and planters or acted as middlemen, buying, selling, and transporting slaves in exchange for ready cash, bills of credit, or tropical produce to make up a vessel's return cargo. In a typical transaction, Lopez received payment from "William Gray Esq. of Jamaica for half the Passage of a Negro belonging to said Gray, from the Bay to Jamaica." On another occasion, a Jamaican slave owner requested one of Lopez's captains to sell two slaves in the Bay of Honduras and send the "proceeds of my Negroes" to London in the form of merchantable timber; if they did not sell, the slaves were to be sent to Lopez to be auctioned off in New England or reconsigned on outbound vessels. If the slaves were laid over in Newport, Lopez typically leased them out or put them to work, sawing mahogany, chipping logwood, lading cargo, or repairing and outfitting ships. Exploiting such individuals as both labor and merchandise was just one more angle for a savvy merchant.[11]

Around the same time he began his mahogany trade, Lopez also initiated a much more capital-intensive form of slaving, namely the transatlantic slave trade. In November 1764, at the same time that his ship *Argus* was "ready on my wharf," pending arrival of "a Cargo of Mahogany . . . expected from Mosquito Shore which I have engaged at a reasonable rate," he was also "fitting a Brig . . . for the Coast of Africa," loading it with barrels of molasses to exchange for captive people. After the awaited ship, "proving leaky put into the Havana and there sunk in the

Harbor," Lopez anxiously awaited a new "Cargo from the Coast of Africa . . . [to] clear off our accounts." With his usual daring, Lopez launched almost simultaneously into two of the day's riskiest businesses, which on the surface had little in common. The Guinea trade dealt in people, gambling cruelly on individual suffering and capacity to endure. By contrast, the trade in "fancy woods" seems frivolous, certainly not comparable with the repugnant commerce in human souls. But from the perspective of the counting house, these two "commodities" were not so dissimilar. Both involved large, up-front, long-term capital outlays, expensive insurance, and high shipping fees, as well as many hidden costs and dangers. Like an excellent mahogany log, a prime African slave, delivered to market in good condition, promised a "ready and advantageous sale." But just as a log that proved unsound upon delivery was worthless, slaves who became sick, died, or escaped while in transit resulted in a severe loss for the merchant. Moreover, given the inherent difficulties in ascertaining the true condition of a log or a person from a superficial external inspection, many buyers demanded warranties until their new "property" proved fit; no sale was final until months after the initial transaction, leaving merchants uncertain if they would profit or face imminent ruin.[12]

One way that New England merchants, typically less well financed than their English counterparts, spread this risk was through joint ventures with one or more partners. In Rhode Island, for example, it seemed that any man or woman, including small farmers, grocers, bakers, blacksmiths, rum distillers, rope makers, mariners, boardinghouse keepers, and widows, with a little money to spare bought shares in oceangoing vessels. Likewise, much of the populace was variously involved in provisioning and outfitting ships and their crews. Hence, although slaves and mahogany were not necessarily transported on the same vessels, many of the same investors were involved, directly or indirectly, with both lines of trade.[13]

For Lopez, this combination likely extended to his dealings with one of his most important customers, Henry Laurens, a wealthy Charleston merchant, planter, and slave trader who supplied Carolina planters with both mahogany to furnish their opulent houses and enslaved Africans to work their rice fields. He also transshipped large quantities of mahogany to England and collaborated with John Knight, a major Liverpool slaver, to import slaves; in 1764, for example, Knight shipped 250 men, women, and children direct from Africa to Laurens in South Carolina. Since Lopez's ships arrived regularly from the Bay of Honduras, they may well have supplied some of the "Cedar & Bay Logs" that Laurens shipped to England aboard a "little Guinea Man," on the third leg of its triangular voyage.

Laurens, like Lopez, was himself an avid consumer of both slaves and mahogany furniture and had likewise learned through painful experience the importance of quality. In one case, Laurens declined to send a cargo to London because it consisted of "Mahogany of Providence . . . [that] is very ordinary . . . [since] it would really be picking your pocket to ship it;" in another case, he eagerly forwarded a load that according to "our best judges is as good as ever was Shipped." He generally regarded mahogany as superior to other woods. For example, he advised a friend who was building a house, "Mahogany is the thing by all means for your Stair case. (I believe you would agree . . . if you saw mine.) The expense is very little more . . . [but] it is firm, durable, & gains beauty whether you will or not with age." As the owner of a large plantation, Laurens similarly expected excellence in his human merchandise. For high-stakes players like Lopez and Laurens, these commodities represented some of their greatest gambles as well as some of their potentially most lucrative endeavors.[14]

After a few disastrous slaving voyages during which many captives died, Laurens decided in 1764 to reduce his exposure and avoid further "embarrassment" by selling only "Negroes [that were] well cho-

sen and healthy." Two years later, Lopez faced a similar setback when
one of his ships, returning from Africa with a valuable cargo of ninety-
eight human beings, was plagued by sickness and death, forcing the
captain to dispose of the survivors at a loss on St. Kitts. Whether he felt
scruples about the abhorrent loss of life or just wanted to forestall more
financial losses, Lopez temporarily suspended his Guinea trade, citing
his customers' "immense distance . . . which rendered it not only difficult to close such accounts but occasioned much writing." Lured by
tantalizingly high prices for slaves in the sugar islands during the early
1770s, however, Lopez decided that the time was ripe to revive his African trade; approximately twenty other influential Rhode Island merchant families, many of whom also dealt in mahogany, resumed or
entered the transatlantic slave trade around this same time.[15]

Meanwhile, quality control and good timing remained critical factors for success in the tropical timber trade as well. As they strived to
corner the Bristol mahogany market, Cruger and Lopez repeatedly
disagreed over issues of quality. "I wish it was in my power to give you
a favorable account of the Mahogany," Cruger wrote in 1772, "but it is
really quite the reverse. In the first place, Vessel after Vessel has been
arriving here for 6 months past. . . . Our Keys and Yards are so
crowded, that we are absolutely at a loss for room to put it. . . . [Yours]
is the worst parcell at present in Bristol. It consists of a great deal of
small, rather porous, much shaken [i.e., uneven], and in general *too
short*—especially the very large Loggs—which are four feet shorter
than they were coveted to be." Other English merchants echoed Cruger's concerns. When Thomas Frank reported the low price of Honduran mahogany in Bristol to his Philadelphia supplier Thomas Clifford in 1771, he deemed it "remarkable that we have had more of this
Article arrive in y[e] Course of 2 Months than is common . . . which I
cannot attribute to any other Cause than that most folks have encouraged its coming from the prospects . . . 5 or 6 months ago of a faire

Market here." He sold Clifford's cargo at the highest rate (43/4 d/ft.) because it was "a good one wch makes a difference." Clifford's son advocated acquiring a smaller, quicker ship that would "always be in season with her goods even if she carries less."[16]

Some problems, like cutting logs into incorrect lengths or not weeding out obviously flawed pieces, began at the source when enslaved woodcutters, who often worked with little or no supervision, were careless in the felling, squaring, or loading of the enormous tree trunks. In some cases, problems may have resulted from deliberate sabotage. Either way, it was up to the ship captain, his supercargo, or other assignee to inspect each log carefully before taking it on board and to adamantly make their preferences and standards known to their sometimes less-than-obliging suppliers. Ultimately, however, complaints about timber quality, size, and cost were inescapably linked to the disappearance of the largest, healthiest, most accessible trees. The deep irony, not lost on Cruger and Lopez, was that, although they had ready access to copious amounts of Honduran mahogany, nature yielded only grudgingly small, high-priced, hard-to-come-by quantities of the "fine Jamaica Mahogany" that most buyers still craved. Faced with the same dilemma, another of Lopez's competitors, George Boyd, the wealthiest merchant in Portsmouth, tried to promote black birch, supplied from his own New Hampshire sawmill, as a mahogany substitute in London. In 1774, he sent samples of "black birch Loggs suitable to your Cabinet makers . . . almost equal to Mahogony, [and] in a year or two after it is Work'd looks as well," promising his correspondents, "if it will Answer, I can get large Quantitys." Apparently, it did not—for there was no run on New Hampshire black birch. Nevertheless, Boyd's efforts suggest the growing awareness on the part of American merchants that, given the vagaries of the mahogany market, there might be a future demand for substitutes. In the meantime, it was cold comfort for Lopez when Cruger concluded, "these are the bitters that sometimes are mingled with the sweets of Trade."[17]

The View from the Ship's Deck

While ambitious New England merchants, such as Aaron Lopez of Newport, the Browns of Providence, the DeWolfs of Bristol, George Boyd of Portsmouth, and the Boylstons of Boston, strengthened the regional economy by expanding coastal and transatlantic trade, the increased commerce offered job opportunities to many likely youths, especially those who had useful maritime experience. James and Jonathan Card answered that description; sons of a retired ship captain and hailing from North Kingstown, a rural village a few miles from bustling Newport, Rhode Island, they went to sea at an early age, learned critical navigational skills, secured employment in the merchant marine, and eventually became involved with the emerging mahogany trade. James became a ship captain based out of Newport; after a brief stint as a small-scale merchant in Newport, Jonathan relocated to the Bay of Honduras but retained vital New England ties. Between the two, they fulfilled such varied roles as mariner, woodcutter, timber shipper, merchant, slave trader, slave master, and mahogany consumer.[18]

When the Card brothers first ventured from Rhode Island to the Bay of Honduras in the mid-eighteenth century, they landed on one of the most tumultuous frontiers in the greater Caribbean. Situated on Spanish territory along the Central American coast, the region boasted little more than a rudimentary woodcutting settlement surrounded by dense tropical rain forest that buffered it from adjacent Spanish enclaves. Its occupants included a motley assortment of English, Scottish, and American expatriates, as well as enslaved Africans and some Indians, who made their living harvesting tropical timbers, while resisting Spain's repeated attempts to expel them. These sojourners had long led a marginal, violence-filled existence as their logging activities repeatedly engendered inter-imperial conflicts. Nevertheless, throughout the late seventeenth and early eighteenth centuries, ship captains regularly made the long journey to the Bay to secure loads of logwood, the precious dyewood so in demand by Europe's textile industry. Each year, interrupted only by periodic Spanish attacks, wartime, and hurricanes, Belize City's harbor could be found crowded with sails from New England, Philadelphia, New York, and Charleston, as well as England, the Netherlands, and other nations. Although the Card brothers thus followed a well-plied channel of trade, their presence there during the 1760s coincided with the Bay settlement's transition from logwood to mahogany cutting. Since England's treaty with Spain at that time still prohibited the latter, however, geopolitical tensions were high while the small cadre of established Baymen were aggressively asserting themselves as the ruling elite. By monopolizing access to mahogany works and buying up the preponderance of slaves, they soon wielded disproportionate power and influence over the rest of the population, free and enslaved. The Card brothers, like everyone else, were forced to deal with this self-styled oligarchy, whether transacting business, competing with its members, or aspiring to join their number.[19]

The Cards were apparently introduced to the Bay settlement while serving aboard vessels commanded by Captain William Cahoone, a family relation, and Captain Oliver Ring Warner, and owned by leading Rhode Island merchants, including Aaron Lopez. In the early 1750s, Cahoone retired from the sea to become a woodcutter and shipping agent in the Bay. Given that his family back in Newport was heavily involved in the furniture-making business (his brother Elijah was a joiner and his nephew John Cahoone, an accomplished cabinetmaker), he likely had a ready outlet for his mahogany. He also served as a liaison in the Bay between local woodcutters and visiting ship captains, facilitating sales of imported slaves and mahogany exports. Providence merchant Obadiah Brown even relied on him to serve as cover for illicit trade in 1758, issuing false orders directing the sloop *Speedwell* to Cahoone in Belize when it was actually bound for French New Orleans. During his sojourns in the Bay, James Card dealt extensively with Cahoone, but Jonathan Card became his protégé and friend, serving later as his executor and sole heir.[20]

After earning enough to buy his own ships, Captain Warner retired to Rhode Island, entrusting the command of one of his vessels to James. Building on his contacts with influential woodcutters, Warner imported exotic woods to New England and sent shiploads of food-stuffs, manufactured goods, and slaves to the Bay for sale. He also served as a factor for woodcutters, transacting business on their behalf in London and New England and extending credit to tide them over be-tween logging seasons. Since some Baymen preferred to have their sons, and occasionally their daughters, educated or apprenticed overseas, he even took one young lad into his household for two years to school him in the "art of Navigation." This was a lucrative arrangement since the boy's transportation, lodging, and education were all paid for in mahogany (over 5,300 feet). Warner still managed to tag on additional expenses, such as "sundrys pd the Spanish guards for permitting us to pass out of Rio Hondo." Attuned to the opportunities and costs of business (including annoying items likes bribes for Spanish guards), Warner provided the Cards with a stellar role model of how to take full advantage of the moneymaking possibilities on both sides of the New England–Bay of Honduras connection from which they, too, hoped to prosper.[21]

Before gaining command of his own vessel, James Card advanced through the ranks of the merchant marine, serving as first mate on several ships owned by prominent Rhode Island merchants. His 1760 marriage to Sarah Rouse, the daughter of a successful merchant from Guernsey, enhanced his career prospects in the tight-knit Newport community. Seizing his chances, James signed on to a transatlantic slaving voyage, a very risky choice given that so many crewmembers died in the alien disease environment along the African coast; for those who survived, however, it could be very remunerative. James proved his mettle while serving aboard the *Adventure* in 1762, when the schooner, bound for Senegal, was attacked by a French privateer. When the captain was wounded, James brought the ship safely to the Goree slaving fort where he negotiated with local African merchants for "merchantable slaves in the amount of the cargo delivered." When the captain returned a month later, he punished James for insubordination, until the merchants vouched that he had "behaved like a careful, honest man." Although such abuse was a common aspect of maritime life, James refused to continue working under this captain; fortunately, thanks to his demonstrated grasp of the Guinea trade, James returned to Africa the next year but this time as captain of the *King of Bonney.*[22]

After weathering several years of that unsavory business, James shifted to more predictable, less perilous American coastal routes. He now sailed regularly from New England down the Eastern Seaboard to the Caribbean, as far south as the Bay of Honduras, where his brother had settled, and the Mosquito Shore. On a typical voyage in 1764, James—now at the helm of the sloop *Rising Sun,* owned by Aaron Chase and Brothers of Newport—transported mahogany from Belize City to Charleston, reloaded with rice and "Indian corn," and returned home to Rhode Island. While his employers' instructions for that trip were clear, others left it to his discretion as to where to go, in which case he generally tramped around the Greater Caribbean, gathering a variety of cargo before returning home. Other times, he delivered Honduran mahogany directly to Rhode Island for sale or transshipment to England. Entrusted with his employer's power of attorney, he acted as his proxy in a wide range of business. When retained by Oliver Ring Warner, for example, one of Captain Card's more onerous duties was collecting overdue accounts from Baymen who had failed to pay or worse, had died, so he had to dun their heirs or executors. James also supervised many transactions for Warner relating to the itinerant slave trade. In 1763, he oversaw the sale of two slaves: "a man named Nicholaw and a negro girl named Present, from Wm Cahoone to Capt. Oliver R. Warner." James also delivered one of Warner's slaves, a young African man named Newport, to Cahoone who leased him to serve as a woodcutter. As we shall see, this young man "of the Gold Coast Country" spent years toiling in the bush before finally eluding his master's long grasp. Adding a few slaves to their cargo this way required little effort for ship captains and promised easy commissions. Although the vast majority of enslaved woodcutters were imported via the large Jamaican chattel markets, New Englanders provided at least a small portion of the slave labor used to produce the mahogany they so avidly desired.[23]

During these years, James and Sarah Card established a modest household, acquired a few fancy furnishings (including a mahogany desk and tea board made by a member of Townsend family, the city's foremost cabinetmakers), and celebrated the birth of two sons. With James often away at sea, Sarah managed their affairs largely on her own assisted by a few enslaved Africans. As was typical in the northern port cities, the slave women probably performed a range of domestic labor— cooking, baking, cleaning, laundering, sewing, and gardening—while the slave men worked as stevedores, ship builders, carters, and sailors. The Cards' accounts reveal their reliance on slave labor, including receipts for leasing an extra "negro man" for ship's labor, buying shoes for their slaves, and having a coffin made for a "negro girl."[24]

As James's letters to his various employers reveal, successful involvement in the mahogany trade required strategic planning and close attention to many critical factors. A ship captain, for example, had to carefully time his arrival in the Bay to coincide with the seasonal rains when the Baymen floated their logs down river to the harbor—if too early, he wasted time on a long wait; if too late, he missed out on the best timber in the crush of ships. He had to be cognizant of the best timber sources, the comings and goings of competing ships, the monopolistic finaglings of the elite Baymen, and the ever-shifting prices of various goods and commodities. He also had to retain a solid crew of men, free and enslaved, and keep them in line with a minimum of trouble which, as was typical, meant subjecting his subordinates to the same sort of mistreatment he once experienced. In one case, he paid £50 in damages to a sailor who charged him with "striking me while in the Bay of Honduras and also for his beating me this day on Board the Sloop *Rising Sun*." Such occurrences were all part of doing business for James; each step of the way, he negotiated a wide range of relationships and secured a cargo as, one by one, each mahogany log was purchased, marked, measured, and loaded for sale in distant places.[25]

Not all ship captains, however, were as responsible as James Card seems to have been. Aaron Lopez had many reasons to rue his choice after entrusting a vessel to one Captain John Newdigate. In 1769, Lopez received word that Newdigate was neglecting his duties in the dissolute watering holes of Jamaica and Belize City. Thomas Smith, a passenger who had sailed with Newdigate, warned Lopez that the captain had become "as much a Bayman as the most abandon'd wretch living there and I assure you they are as wicked there as any people can be on this side of Hell & He has a Heart as bad as the worst of them." Accusing him of mishandling the ship, abusing the customs officials worse "than a temperamental child," and keeping "publickly a common whore," Smith concluded Newdigate was a "puffed up foolish fellow whose Head is as soft as a boiled turnip." Rather remarkably, Lopez extended credit to Newdigate's wife back in Rhode Island while her errant husband dallied for two years. After somehow scoring a load of mahogany, Newdigate at last wrote to Lopez, "if you have any charity left for me to send down a vessel and I will load her to the amount of 60 thousand [feet] . . . [and] settle every matter agreeable to your will." Although he also brazenly requested a barrel of rum and some ruffled shirts, Lopez dispatched a ship to collect the mahogany but not the hapless captain who pleaded "for God sake don't leave me hear." The last straw was when the turnip-head charged unauthorized expenses to Lopez's account and then confessed to having lost "my mahoggany waiting for your vessel." By comparison, James Card was a model of probity.[26]

The View from the Rain Forest

While James stuck to the seafaring life, Jonathan relocated to the Bay of Honduras, perhaps following Cahoone's example. Shortly after his arrival, Jonathan took the first necessary steps towards becoming a serious mahogany cutter; somehow, either with borrowed capital or some accumulated savings, he began buying slaves which, in turn, enabled him to lay claim to a mahogany works and start logging. He also forged a business partnership with his friend Captain Francis Hickey that proved to be an enduring relationship. The men took up adjacent claims on Spanish Creek, many miles upriver from Belize City, staked out according to "the laws of the country, . . . by falling a tree, building a hut, and hanging a grindstone." Since these locales existed solely to support woodcutting activities, they typically boasted few amenities beyond simple huts, a few storage sheds, and provision grounds for food. Jonathan likely resided there only during the woodcutting season, returning downriver during the rainy months with his slaves to St. George's Caye, an island situated at the mouth of the Belize River. Considered healthier than the swampy mainland, it was home to many of the Baymen's families and slaves.[27]

Jonathan's immediate family included his wife, Dorothy Taylor (known also as Dolle), a free woman of color who was formerly his housekeeper, their son (also called Jonathan), and their daughter Sarah. They also owned at least ten or twelve enslaved men, women, and children. Among them was María Pérez, a woman of mixed Spanish and Indian ancestry, who was captured and sold into slavery after an English attack on her Yucatán village in 1762. While it is unclear whether she was officially the property of Jonathan or Dorothy, who was a slave-holder in her own right, María became a dependent in the Card household. According to her testimony, when missives to "her Native place" went unanswered, she concluded her family and neighbors were all dead or scattered. Making the best of an unfortunate situation, María developed a relationship with her master's partner, Francis Hickey, who afforded her, and the children he had with her, some protection and support. Although she and the children remained the Cards' property, she reconciled herself to life within this racially mixed, extended household.[28]

Drawing on his New England connections, Jonathan found ready outlets for his timber shipments, most propitiously with Aaron Lopez who was in the midst of expanding his tropical wood trade into the London and Bristol markets. Like other novice woodcutters in the Bay, however, Jonathan would have struggled to adapt to the unfamiliar tropical environment, to avoid harassment by Spanish guards, to curry favor with the more powerful Baymen, and to prevent his slaves from running away or worse. In September 1765, the murder of another slave master by his slaves sparked a widespread slave uprising, terrifying white residents and halting all work until the culprits were captured weeks later. Although ship captains and merchants awaiting mahogany deliveries complained, they had no choice but to weather disruptions and delays or miss out on the year's timber harvest. Such were the vagaries of frontier life.[29]

After a few years of cutting mahogany and logwood, Jonathan purchased a sloop called the *Swordfish*. In a place where British subjects were precluded from land ownership because of the region's Spanish sovereignty, such a substantial piece of moveable property constituted a major asset. Moreover, by owning his own ship, Card gained independence, transporting his own produce as well as generating shipping revenues. Since only the most affluent Baymen owned or held shares in vessels, this acquisition was just the sort of necessary edge that might elevate a small-scale woodcutter into one of the powerful cadre of elite white woodcutters who dominated access to the best mahogany works and monopolized trade into and out of the settlement. Jonathan recruited his trusted brother to sail the *Swordfish*. For a while, this arrangement seemed to suit them both. For at least two years, James sailed Jonathan's sloop on many successful ventures to Honduras Bay, the Windward Islands, and in the wide-ranging coastal trade. James sailed around the Caribbean, checking in regularly with his brother for loads of mahogany, stopping elsewhere for other tropical produce, and then returning to his family in Newport. Compared with his misadventures in Africa, this may have seemed a less hazardous route for the young father, but it was not by any means uneventful. At one point, for example, Captain Card and the crew of the *Swordfish* were lauded in the newspapers for saving two men from a sinking ship which had been hit by a whale off Long Island. As the Cards prospered during the 1760s, their names appeared frequently among Lopez's accounts, buying supplies and wholesale merchandise and paying with logwood and mahogany. When at home, James indulged in small luxuries for his family and his parents. In 1768, apparently feeling confident of his financial future, he revisited Townsend's shop to order two new mahogany tables. Meanwhile, Jonathan was, by all appearances, well on his way to becoming a member of the Bay elite.[30]

In June 1769, however, disaster struck the *Swordfish*. Nine days out on a trip from Cape Fear to Jamaica, the ship encountered a vicious gale and lost its main sails, rigging, and boats. With eight feet of water swamping the hold, the crew manned the pumps around the clock for five days as waves breached over the decks. As their situation worsened, a passing ship thankfully spotted the distressed vessel. According to their rescuer, only "being loaded with Lumber . . . kept her from sinking," and the crew was "much disabled, and worn out with fatigue, when he took them all on board." The sea ran so high, however, that the *Swordfish* and all her cargo were lost. This misfortune seems to have created a rift between the Card brothers. The root of their animosity is uncertain – perhaps Jonathan blamed James for the disaster, or, perhaps, it stemmed from bitter disappointment as the elder brother saw his aspirations shattered. James later complained that he feared Jonathan "will never pay me for my three years service and my negro in his sloop."[31]

In any event, the brothers' alienation seems to have deepened when James returned to the employ of Oliver Ring Warner, the Newport merchant and former ship captain. In 1768, William Cahoone died, leaving Jonathan all of his property. Since this inheritance increased Jonathan's number of slaves to thirty, he was suddenly vaulted into a new category as a large slaveholder. Since he unfortunately became responsible as well for all of Cahoone's debts, he was forced to sell some slaves (including a few Cahoone intended to free) and was uncooperative when Warner, back in Rhode Island, commissioned James to settle the account. James was also under orders to retrieve Newport, the slave Warner had leased to Cahoone, and to invest the man's back wages in mahogany and logwood. But after weeks of trying to fulfill his instructions, James reported that he had accomplished none of his assigned business; not only had the slave eluded him, but that his own brother would "not show me any favours nor have nothing to say to me by Reason I came in Your Schooner."[32]

In trying to extract mahogany from other of Warner's debtors on the Mosquito Shore, James encountered further delays. By the time he returned to the Bay, the bulk of the season's harvest had already been shipped and he was stalled "till a flud comes in the River to get there cargo." In frustration, James purchased a pricey load of timber from William Tucker, an affluent Baymen who owned multiple mahogany works and large stockpiles of timber, and dispatched it to Warner on the *Betsey*. Deciding to stay on through the off-season, James also sent over 1,300 feet of mahogany home on the *Betsey* on his own account.

He may have intended to sell it to make up his losses, to commission more furniture for his home, or to re-export it to England or elsewhere. Meanwhile, he ferried slaves from Jamaica to the Bay, including Primrose, "a seasoned man," March, "a new Negro man," three children, and a slave "try'd for stealing and ... condemned to be transported." The following year, however, his promising maritime career abruptly ended. Jonathan was upriver cutting mahogany when word came that James had died in Belize City. Perhaps contrite after their unfortunate breach, he took charge of sending Sarah the sad news of her husband's demise, along with his personal effects. After deducting a sum to pay the doctor's bills and burial expenses, Jonathan sent the rest of his brother's funds—fifteen doubloons, some pistoles, eleven dollars, and a few bits—to Sarah by way of "Mrs. Dorothy Taylor who goes with my Children to Long Island," although he did not acknowledge that his children's chaperone was also their mother. His instructions directing his sister-in-law to go Sag Harbor and discreetly inquire there after "Dorothy (or rather where my family is)" were secretive in tone, but it is unclear why, possibly to avoid thieves or creditors.[33]

Impact of the American Revolution

Following James's death, Jonathan continued to cut mahogany but, drawing on his earlier mercantile experience in Newport, also established himself as an importer-exporter in Belize City. Most importantly, he became affiliated with Thomas Potts and Magistrate Richard Hoare, two influential, well-connected Baymen, who enlarged his business network beyond Lopez and his Rhode Island circle. Potts and Hoare most likely facilitated his introduction to Anthony Van Dam, a successful New York merchant and entrepreneur. In 1774, the trio consigned a large quantity of mahogany to Van Dam, including 19,618 feet (sixty-seven logs) from "Mr. Jonathan Card, in the said Bay

of Honduras, by the Sloop *Content*," and 63,723 feet consigned by
Hoare and Potts. Van Dam was a man of significant stature in New
York as was amply reflected in his East River estate which included a
mansion surrounded by "an ornamented Board-Rail-Fence," a garden,
an orchard, a "Rope-Walk, Hemp-House, Tar-House, Yarn-House,
Smoke-House, Barn, [and] stables." He also owned a boat, many slaves,
and a large wharf where he often handled large quantities of mahogany.
In October 1774, he advertised Jonathan's mahogany for sale: "Now
landing from on board the brig *Content* . . . from Honduras Bay, and to
be sold by Anthony Van Dam, 20,000 feet Mahogany, 30 tons Logwood,
1,500 weight Sarsaparilla." Although this connection promised to open
up a whole new regional market to the three Baymen, the venture
proved short-lived due to the onset of the American Revolution. Before
their subsequent shipments of mahogany could be sold, the British
forces in New York City requisitioned a large quantity to make "Caps,
Gun-carriages & other naval works, for the use of his Majesty's Navy."[34]

As the conflagration of war intensified, it brought strife as well to the
Bay of Honduras once Spain joined France in supporting the Americans against the British. At some point during the conflict, most likely
during Spain's 1779 attack on St. George's Caye, Jonathan Card was
killed. According to Van Dam, his Bay associates were "pillaged &
robbed of their property. Mr. Card died . . . Mr. Potts was carried into
Captivity and remained in that wretched Situation for upwards of two
years; and Mr. Hoare, having with others escaped with the loss of their
property, afterwards assisted in reducing the Fortress of Omoa." Contrary to type, he emphasized, these Baymen, although "Unfortunate &
distressed, . . . [were] the best and most Loyal of his Majesty's Subjects." For his part, Van Dam, an ardent Loyalist, also suffered a life-
changing upheaval when he was forced to flee to Bermuda at the war's
end. All of his property, plus the Baymen's remaining consignment of
mahogany (estimated to be worth £6,600), was confiscated by the new
United States government.[35]

Meanwhile, British naval forces had occupied the city of Newport for several years beginning in 1776, all but destroying its maritime economy. Aaron Lopez, suspected by some of harboring Loyalist sympathies, was alarmed to find his ships menaced by both sides. Unable to transact any normal business, he moved with his family to Massachusetts for the war's duration. As international trade was strangled, Newport's cabinetmakers suffered as well. They could not export their furniture and had to rely on their existing mahogany stocks since little made it past the naval blockades, except if a ship was captured. In September 1776, for instance, an auction in Portsmouth disposed of the English prize ship *Nelly* and her cargo, which included "120,000 feet of Mahogany, (from the Bay of Honduras) ... forfeited to the United Colonies and captors, by the court maritime for the State of New Hampshire."[36]

In England, as well, the war had negative economic consequences, including for Henry Cruger, Jr., Lopez's erstwhile mahogany-trading partner, who was elected to Parliament in 1775. His family was politically divided by the Revolution—John Harris, a Loyalist, joined his father and brother in England while Nicholas fought on the American side, becoming a confidante of George Washington. Henry, Jr. favored placating the rebellious colonists, mainly because of their importance as consumers to the British Empire. By 1780, when Bristol's international trade had fallen by over 40 percent, he urged Parliament to grant America its independence in order to restore the peace and get commerce flowing again. Whether or not he and Lopez would have revived their mahogany-dealing arrangement after the Revolution seems quite uncertain given the changed political landscape and the earlier difficulties they encountered. In any event, they never faced that decision for Lopez accidentally drowned in 1782, just months after hostilities ended. Newport never fully recovered its former economic vitality, but Aaron Lopez had no opportunity even to try.[37]

If the war wreaked havoc on people's lives in North America and England, the same was true for the woodcutters on the Central American frontier. Jonathan Card's sudden demise foreshortened what might have been the beginning of the most prosperous chapter in his life. After burnishing their reputations through their personal sacrifices and defense of the settlement, his former associates, Hoare and Potts, returned to the Bay, prospered, and solidified their place within the ranks of the restored oligarchy. Although Britain tried to restrict trade with its former colonies and Van Dam was now a bankrupt refugee, they found that other New York merchants were eager to satisfy their customers' pent-up desire for mahogany. In the postwar years, both men accumulated substantial wealth that included many slaves, mahogany works, houses, fine furniture, silver plate, and shares in ships. Their experiences as white male slaveholders, however, differed markedly from that of Jonathan Card's son, known in the Bay as "Colored Jonathan," who was a free man of mixed racial heritage.[38]

When the younger Jonathan returned to the Bay after the war, he took possession of his father's Spanish Creek mahogany works and twenty-four slaves. He also revived his father's partnership with Francis Hickey, who bought out Sarah Card's share of her deceased father's mahogany works upon her 1785 marriage to New York merchant William Roach. The 1786 treaty map (Figure 3.1) provides an excellent overview of the Bay as the younger Jonathan knew it. His mahogany works, indicated by a small icon of a house next to Hickey's works, is sandwiched between other claims which line both sides of the creek. The surrounding landscape likewise is heavily annotated with the names of the elite Baymen who monopolized the mahogany forests and the locations where they had clashed with the Spanish for transgressing the boundaries. As this suggests, the Bay settlement during this period had become a highly competitive and often tumultuous place. Nevertheless, by 1790, the younger Jonathan had acquired thirty slaves, including a logging gang of eleven men, and a boat, co-owned with Hickey. Since slaves were the foundation of wealth and social status in the Bay settlement, this placed "Colored Jonathan" among the top tier of the free colored population and on par with many of the leading white residents. Yet he found himself in a society increasingly riven by racial animosities, as the white elite sought to marginalize people of color. In this context, Jonathan's background as the son of a "Mustee" housekeeper weighed against him. While more and more Honduran mahogany made its way into English and North American homes— transformed into beautiful chairs, tables, and sideboards—in the contested forests of the Bay, it was becoming ever more the object of strife.[39]

Meanwhile, the elder Jonathan Card's demise had serious negative consequences for his slaves, especially María, her four daughters, and two grandchildren who were among the slaves inherited by his son. Whatever protection her personal relationship with Francis Hickey had afforded her family ended abruptly with his unexpected death. When her new master treated her family harshly, María filed a complaint asserting that, as a Spanish subject, she had been wrongfully enslaved. Asked why she had not filed an earlier claim, a colonial official, who vouched for her freedom, explained that "she lived happy till young Card and his Sister came, who used her Children ill, [otherwise] she could . . . [have lived] all her days with Hickey." He concluded, however, that the fact of "her not being at liberty many Years ago is her own fault owing to her happy Situation, not considering poor Creature that her Friend might die." Presented with this case shortly before he was recalled to England, Superintendent Marcus Despard was more sympathetic and officially manumitted the whole family. After twenty-five years in bondage, María was free. Cuffee, her infant grandson, born into slavery, would come of age a free man. Given the chance to be repatriated to the Spanish Yucatán, however, the Pérez family declined because they had "connections in the [Bay, and] . . . wished to remain there, provided they could be free." They moved to Convention Town, the community established by Despard to resettle many of the poor and mixed-race people displaced from the Mosquito Shore. Before the members of the Pérez family could enjoy their liberty, however, they had a terrible fright in 1789 when an accomplice of the Cards "went in the night time to Convention town where this family lived, and by force carried off the . . . children and put them on board of a vessel bound to America in Irons." At the last moment, they were rescued, sparing them a dreadful fate at some distant auction block. That "Colored Jonathan" would go so far to regain possession of the Pérez family suggests how much he felt was at stake. For although around this same time he freed two of his father's slaves (a woman named Lucretia, who he later married, and her daughter, who was likely his child), he clearly saw the loss of these other slaves as a humiliating blow. Already at a disadvantage as a man of mixed race, he likely feared it would further undermine his tenuous social status and long-term financial security.[40]

Since Despard's manumission of the Pérez family coincided with his efforts to accommodate other people of color in the Bay, his actions served only to further alienate the white elite. Claiming that his decision set an alarming precedent that might inspire other slaves to demand their freedom, the magistrates promoted a general hysteria that the sanctity of their only private property—namely their human property—was threatened. In fact, Despard took no steps towards a general emancipation and made no sweeping statements about universal rights. As a stickler to uphold the Crown's treaty with Spain, he freed the Pérez family only because they proved to his satisfaction that they were Spanish subjects and therefore exempt from slavery under its terms. Regardless, this incident further antagonized the magistrates who rallied local slave owners, including "Colored Jonathan," against Despard.[41]

Although his term as superintendent was cut short, Despard's efforts on behalf of the lowliest people of the Bay, whatever his motives, made a profound difference for many of them. Only three years after her manumission, María Pérez appeared on a list of Bay residents as the head of a household of eight free people in Convention Town, where she had applied for a provisioning garden and set up her own produce business. She thus achieved a measure of independence and economic self-sufficiency for her family even though they still resided within the oppressive constraints of a patriarchal slave society. Having faced down repeated disappointments, obstacles, and challenges, including the thwarted attempt to abduct her children, María Pérez's story highlights the frequently contingent nature of life and liberty in the Bay.[42]

Ironically, her former master found himself stuck as a second class citizen within the Bay settlement's increasingly racialized society. He continued to harvest mahogany, sometimes as few as ten logs at a time, which he consigned mainly to London through Henley Company, one of several English firms that dominated the Bay's trade after the American Revolution. But as the white elite reasserted their local hegemony, it became harder to secure new mahogany works. In rejecting Despard's progressive leadership in favor of securing his own slave property, Jonathan arguably went against his own interests by helping the "arbitrary aristocracy" to retrench. Forced to adapt, he redirected his slaves, for at least part of the year, into other economic activities, including salvaging shipwrecks, turtling, tending his fifty head of cattle, and provisioning outgoing vessels. In 1805, for example, he supplied one ship with beef, turtle meat, and eight live turtles. He eventually became quite successful, turning what had long been regarded as marginal economic activities into substantial enterprises. In 1790, in anticipation of renewed war with Spain, he was appointed commander of the colored militia, heading up a company of forty-one free people of color and serving as the main liaison between the magistrates and the free colored population. Eight years later, he and the rest of the colored militia joined in the 1798 battle, when Spain attempted to oust the Baymen once and for all. In a stunning turnaround, the British defeated Spain and, at long last, Belize became a British protectorate. Yet despite his growing wealth and his important contribution to this military victory, Jonathan was not rewarded with an equal elevation in his social or political status. A decade later, George Hyde, also the mixed-race son of a white woodcutter and known in the Bay as "Colored George," encountered very similar obstacles. His father, James Hyde, had survived and thrived in the Bay, becoming one its largest slave owners, the patriarch of a large family, and an influential magistrate. His son, although very articulate and British-educated, found his father's social and political achievements did not clear the way for him. As these sons of the Bay pioneers discovered, the white oligarchy was intent on blocking their full participation in the local government, even as the magistrates became increasingly despotic, reactionary, and insular. As late as 1827, George Hyde was still beseeching Parliament to ensure full civil rights to his "freeborn brethren of the mix'd race."[43]

As they initiated their involvement in the mahogany trade, Aaron Lopez and the Card brothers reinforced the ties between the Bay of Honduras and New England. But as they found, it was not always so easy to manage commerce between these very different worlds. For all their efforts, the mahogany trade remained risky—at times, very profitable, but at other times, a heartbreaking disappointment. Of the three, Aaron Lopez was best able to weather this volatility, since mahogany remained only one avenue of his expansive trade. While he eyed the ups and downs of the tropical timber trade from the relative comfort of his Newport counting house, the Card brothers were fully and literally exposed to the environmental and political hazards of the Central American frontier. The costs of the mahogany business proved much higher for them, as both their lives were cut short in the search for desirable trees. James Card could reasonably have expected to graduate into the ranks of prosperous New England merchants, as Captain

Warner had successfully done. Instead, after shipping home a promising load of mahogany, he succumbed to a tropical disease, leaving his widow to raise their two sons, both of whom eventually followed their father's footsteps into the merchant marine. At the time of his death, his probate inventory totaled a meager £38, including "1 Square table of Mahogany" and "1 Round Table of Mahogany." Jonathan Card as well seemed destined for a rosy future. He established himself as a large slaveholder and a rising member of white elite, only to be killed as the winds of war swept through the Bay. His son and his former slaves, on the other hand, experienced firsthand how shifting notions of social hierarchy, racial categorization, and freedom could reshape the lives of individuals, intensify conflict, and exacerbate competition for diminishing resources. For the Card Family, as for many of those involved in the mahogany trade between New England and the Bay of Honduras, however, the American Revolution and its aftermath brought a painful rupture as personal and economic ties that had long bridged the geographical and cultural distance between these two very different regions—mingling the bitters and the sweets of trade—were, at least temporarily, severed.[44]

CHAPTER FIVE

Slavery in the Rain Forest

IN 1770, Oliver Ring Warner, the Rhode Island merchant, instructed Captain James Card to retrieve "a negro man of mine named Newport" from the Mosquito Shore. As his name suggests, this young African man, "of the Gold Coast Country Aged twenty five or there abouts," was enslaved in New England before his master leased him out to William Cahoone as a woodcutter in the Bay of Honduras and then on the Mosquito Shore. When Cahoone died, Newport apparently continued to cut wood on his own until his master sought to retrieve him. When Newport got wind of Card's mission, however, he quickly made himself scarce. In searching for "your Negro man Newport," Captain Card dutifully reported back to Warner, "[I found] by Sum Negroes where his Wife Lived, but Can't Come at him . . . I believe it will not Be in my power to Git him." Anticipating this difficulty, Warner had instructed Card to sell the missing man and invest any proceeds "in good merchantable Mahogany or any other produce of the Mosquito Shore." Not surprisingly, no buyer stepped forward to purchase a slave *in absentia*. Drawing upon his local knowledge, Newport successfully hid until Card's ship set sail without him.[1]

Compared to other places where slaves enmeshed in the tangled web of the Atlantic slave trade might end up—as plantation fodder on a sugar island, up to their knees in the rice paddies or tar pits of the Carolinas, or in a sweltering tobacco field in the Chesapeake—the mahogany forests of Belize might have been one of the more tolerable outcomes. For although logging mahogany entailed hardship and danger, it offered some opportunities as well, thanks to the frontier setting that necessitated a relatively flexible form of bondage. Given how mahogany typically grew—with individual trees dispersed across vast stretches of rain forest—logging it required small groups of slaves to range widely in remote settings, often with minimal supervision. Slaves played vital (if involuntary) roles in finding and felling the coveted trees, inscribing their rough bark with their masters' marks, and then transporting them out of the forest. In the process, the enslaved Africans gained valuable knowledge of their surroundings which they deployed to their own advantage whenever possible. Unlike the West Indies where tree removal was usually the precursor to agriculture, woodcutting was the primary economic activity in the Bay of Honduras and, with the growing emphasis on mahogany (over logwood), the specific challenges of its extraction increasingly dictated the labor regimen and materially shaped the lives of everyone in the Bay, free and enslaved. Furthermore, since Baymen could not officially own land on Spanish territory, their slaves were by far their most valuable form of property, to the extent that the number of slaves they owned determined their access to mahogany works as well as their social status and political participation.[2]

Given their proximity to Spanish colonies where English runaway slaves were promised freedom, the Baymen sought to retain their slaves through an odd mixture of positive inducements, such as rewards, incentives, and concessions, and various forms of coercion and discipline, including threats, harsh punishments, and negative propaganda about the Spanish. The contingent world of the Bay was thus characterized by permissiveness, ambiguity, volatility, and violence. But on the whole, slave masters were so dependent on their slaves to extract any value from the forest that more often than not they were forced to grudgingly offer accommodations rather than risk mass desertions, especially since their efforts at control often backfired. As Newport's autonomy and apparent resourcefulness suggest, enslaved woodcutters pushed the boundaries of their bondage, sometimes to surprising degrees and, in some cases, even secured their freedom.[3]

An adequate labor force was essential because mahogany cutting could not be easily standardized. Extracting each individual tree from the forest presented a new set of challenges, depending upon its size, shape, growth pattern, location, distance from a river, and the terrain across which it had to be hauled. Unlike logwood, which grew in accessible coastal lagoons and could be shipped in easy-to-handle pieces, the colossal mahogany logs were usually taken in one piece, making proximity to a waterway essential to move them any distance. The Baymen had trouble, however, acquiring enough strong, rigorous workers. Most slaves were purchased, often at great expense, via the closest chattel markets on Jamaica, where Baymen competed with sugar planters to buy up young, fit men. Some were imported directly to Jamaica from Africa and sold after a seasoning period; others were born in the West Indies or transported from elsewhere within the broader Atlantic region. Visiting ships, like that of Captain James Card, also gathered up individual or small lots of slaves along their trading routes who found a ready market in the Bay. In its early years, the settlement also eagerly accepted individuals deemed undesirable elsewhere, such as those condemned to transportation for crimes or insurrection.

The enslaved population's uneven sex ratio, with males outnumbering females by two or three to one, meant that many men were left without partners and the birth rate remained low. Moreover, given the dearth of white women in the Bay, many white men relied on enslaved women or free women of color for sexual and domestic services. Since slave owners sometimes manumitted the children resulting from such unions, along with their mothers, these offspring contributed to a small but growing population of free people of color. Due to the gender imbalance, low birth rates, manumissions, high slave mortality, and large numbers of runways, the enslaved population never reproduced itself. To offset its erosion, masters imported new slaves whenever possible.[4]

For most of the eighteenth century, the population of the Bay remained small, composed of a white Anglo minority, a small number of free people of color, and a black majority. In 1745, approximately 120 slaves resided in the Bay, constituting 70 percent of the total population; by 1779, the slave population stood at 3,000, or 86 percent of the population. In that same year, when the Spanish seized the Bay settlement, hundreds of slaves ran away or became captives of the invaders. When the English returned five years later, the reduced population included around 2,000 slaves, 200 free whites, and 500 free people of color; up until the abolition of the slave trade, slaves in the Bay continued to comprise between 70 and 80 percent of the total population. By comparison, on nearby Jamaica, slaves increased from 45,000 in 1703 to 167,000 in 1768 and, by century's end, there were ten times more blacks than whites. Relative to those numbers, the slave-based mahogany industry in the Bay, even at its height, remained a narrow specialized market compared to the immense expansion of slavery for sugar production. This fact significantly shaped the character of daily life for woodcutters in the Bay.[5]

Daily Life for the Woodcutters

In 1776, Olaudah Equiano purchased his freedom after many years as an enslaved sailor only to be shanghaied as a mahogany cutter. This unexpected detour began when he boarded a ship supposedly bound for Jamaica only to discover that it was actually headed to a wild stretch of the Mosquito Shore. "I was compelled to assist in cutting a great deal of mahogany wood on the shore as we coasted along it," Equiano later recalled. "This fretted me much; but as I did not know how to help myself among these deceivers . . . patience was the only remedy I had left." Eventually, he jumped ship and signed on to another vessel that was "trading for turtle shells and silver." Promised a modest wage by his new captain, he "thought this much better than cutting wood for nothing." While Equiano narrowly escaped reenslavement, other men were not so lucky, and cutting wood for nothing became their destiny. Given Equiano's extensive maritime experience, however, some aspects of his short career as a woodcutter may have been familiar. According to one account, "setting out on a mahogany-cutting expedition resembles in some degree that of departing on a long voyage. The dreary time that must be passed in the woods . . . may not unaptly be compared to what is felt by many in a long confinement on shipboard." Like sailors out on the high seas, the logging gangs lived and worked within an isolated, male-dominated environment characterized by intermittent violence and constant danger. Whereas sailors kept their eyes peeled for treacherous reefs, pirate ships, and the telltale spouts of whales, the woodcutters were hunters of trees.[6]

At the beginning of the logging season, usually during the dry months from November to May, the men would set off on a long expedition upriver into the rain forest. From a rudimentary base camp, individual logging gangs would venture still deeper into the forest to find and extract the scattered mahogany trees. The minimum number of slaves required for a mahogany gang was around ten or twelve but larger operations had as many as fifty slaves divided into multiple gangs. If a master owned only a few slaves, as was typical in the earlier logwood days of the Bay settlement, he often worked alongside them, shoulder to shoulder. By the mid-eighteenth century, however, as established Baymen

FIG. 5.1 "Cutting & Trucking Mahogany in Honduras," frontispiece of *The Mahogany Tree: Its Botanical Character, Qualities and Uses . . . in the West Indies and Central America.* Chaloner & Fleming (Liverpool: Rockcliff and Son, 1850). Collection of the LuEsther T. Mertz Library of the New York Botanical Garden, Bronx, New York.

acquired more slaves and multiple mahogany works, they usually relied on white overseers or enslaved foremen to supervise the slaves' activities, although some gangs seemed to have had little to no oversight. During the logging season, the woodcutters set up base camps, usually situated on a river bank near their intended work sites; while the logging gangs set off to hunt trees, a few men "unfit for work" and perhaps a few women served as support workers at the camps. According to one description, the camps were like small rural villages, made up of huts constructed in the "different modes peculiar to the several Nations or Tribes of Africa, as also the improvement introduced by European [building] experience." They were erected by the slaves "in a single day, and with no other implement than an axe." A 1790 traveler's account described a typical hut as "a thatched roof and inclosed with . . . Pimento sticks, tyed together with small yarns."[7]

Since locating the elusive mahogany trees required considerable expertise, slave owners entrusted this important task to a skilled slave designated as the "huntsman" who headed up each logging gang. An 1811 account by George Henderson, an army officer stationed in Belize, emphasized the huntsman's vital role in searching "the woods, or, as . . . it is termed, the bush to find labor for the whole." The huntsman "cuts his way through the thickest of the woods . . . and climbs the tallest tree he finds, from which he minutely surveys the surrounding country. . . . [An] eye accustomed to this kind of exercise can discover, at a great distance, the places where the wood is most abundant. He now descends . . . and without compass, or other guide than what observation has imprinted on his recollection, he never fails to reach the exact point to which he aims."[8]

Once a sharp-eyed huntsman led the slave gang to one of his finds, the other men built a high platform alongside the towering tree's trunk to reach above the wide buttresses at its base. Precariously balanced on this scaffold, skilled axmen, wielding long-handled axes, attacked the wall-like trunk. Once they laid low the tree, men on the ground stripped off its branches with machetes and roughly squared its edges. Before it could be moved, however, they had to clear a serviceable pathway, often several miles, through thick undergrowth to the nearest river tributary, a task that could take weeks. Often working at night by torchlight to avoid the heat, the men rolled or skidded each log to the closest waterway and returned to the forest for another one. By the early nineteenth century, the remaining trees grew too far inland to haul by hand, so oxen became an indispensable mode of transport. By whatever means the logs were moved, they had to be extracted within a set window of opportunity. If not hauled to the closest waterway before the onset of the rainy season, they might be-

FIG. 5.2 "Felling Mahogany in Honduras" in *The Mahogany Tree: Its Botanical Character, Qualities and Uses . . . in the West Indies and Central America.* Chaloner & Fleming (Liverpool: Rockcliff and Son, 1850). Collection of the LuEsther T. Mertz Library of the New York Botanical Garden, Bronx, New York.

come hopelessly mired in mud. In the meantime, if they were not kept damp, they might split and crack, making the mahogany worthless before it was ever shipped. With proper timing, however, the logs would be ready and waiting at the riverside when the torrential rains began around June or July.

After scoring each log with their master's mark, designating them as his property, the slaves then floated the logs downstream where other workers caught them at the river's mouth before they were washed out to sea. Another nineteenth-century innovation was the installation of iron-chain booms which effectively corralled the logs at the coast. Slaves then sorted the bucking logs into rafts of 200 or more, according to each owner's mark. In a last Herculean effort, they loaded

the cumbersome logs onto awaiting ships. Jacob Nagle, a sailor on the
Liverpool vessel *Brilliant,* "bound for Jameca and from thence to the
Bay of Hundoras for mahoganey," vividly recalled kedging (throwing
out a rope with a light anchor and pulling up to it using iron clamps
called "dogs") their small boats out to the larger ship and then loading
the heavy blocks of mahogany aboard, all while avoiding hungry
sharks and sharp reefs:

> When the ship was [moored] we cleared away to take in mahogany and
> logwood. We had to tow off the [mahogany] blocks with iron dogs . . .
> with two boats and kedges. While hauling up to one kedge, the other
> run out the other kedge ahead till we reached the ship . . . nearly two
> miles. In that manner they have to bring the blocks along side, then
> sling them one by one and heave them in by the capstan . . . [With] all
> hands at work, I had charge of the deck, hoisting in the blocks from
> alongside, and the capt[ain] and chief mate in the hold giving direc-
> tions in . . . stowing the blocks according to the size and measurement
> which must be done and then the vacancies fill'd up with logwood.

After this laborious winching process, the last step of inserting logwood padding was essential to prevent the huge logs or blocks of mahogany from shifting dangerously in stormy seas. When the heavily
laden ships at last weighed anchor, the woodcutters took a well-deserved
holiday break in Belize City before preparing for the next season.[9]

This work was no doubt very arduous; however, compared to the
strict discipline and regimented routines aboard a naval vessel or on a
typical sugar plantation, a woodcutter's life allowed for a relatively less
structured, more flexible, and, at times, more autonomous existence.
Moreover, as the woodcutters traversed the rain forest and maneuvered
back and forth between the boundaries of the English settlement and
the surrounding Spanish territory, they experienced a high degree of
mobility and greater possibilities for flight. Thrown together in makeshift camps, the woodcutters experienced both the camaraderie and

the inevitable conflicts of shared work and close quarters. And, just as sailors sometimes seized opportunities to mutiny or jump ship, enslaved woodcutters had the option of wielding their machetes against a despised authority or just slipping away into the surrounding forest.[10]

For enslaved workers who spent long stretches out in the bush, learning about its hazards and natural resources was the key to survival. To supplement whatever provisions their master allocated to them, they foraged and hunted in the surrounding woods for such things as fruits, nuts, and monkeys, which woodcutters, black and white, considered among "the foremost delicacies the woods afford." Some evidence suggests that they adopted hunting and foraging practices used by the local indigenous people. Some who came from similar climate zones in Africa may have had previous familiarity with tropical settings to draw upon; but for those without such backgrounds, such as the few New England transplants, the alien environment may have caused profound culture shock. Whatever their individual backgrounds or abilities, they had to find ways to adapt to this new world. Logging also presented many serious occupational hazards. A glancing saw blade or a wayward log could easily kill or maim an inattentive worker. Woodcutters also faced ever-present dangers from poisonous snakes and insects, heat stroke, dehydration, infectious diseases, and, in swampy areas, an affliction called *bay sore,* which caused painful lesions curable only through the use of strong corrosives.[11]

Huntsmen, in particular, developed sophisticated knowledge of the forest and valuable skills, such as tracking and tree climbing, that required stamina, speed, and agility. Since there existed no "patents for discovery," a savvy huntsman also developed stealth and discretion to carefully conceal his footsteps and keep his own counsel so others could not retrace his path or get clues about where to find the best trees. Given that a single mature mahogany tree might be worth upwards of

£1,000, an accomplished huntsman was by far a master's most valuable slave, which in turn gave him status among the other slaves. This elite corps became accomplished information brokers because once a huntsman identified "a large body of wood in some remote corner . . . it becomes a contest with his conscience whether he shall disclose the matter to his master or sell it to his master's neighbor." They thus made their masters compete (often unwittingly) with each other for advantageous intelligence. Acknowledging the huntsmen' critical importance to the whole logging enterprise, Baymen rewarded them with extra rations and time off in an effort to cultivate loyalty. Skilled axmen were also considered very valuable by their masters because their job, too, required experience and judgment to fell trees without imperiling other workers on the ground and to get the best cuts of timber. For example, since the widest part of a tree's base often contained richly figured grains, axmen who invested more labor in cutting a tree lower on the trunk, with an eye towards how it translated into timber, delivered a more valuable product.[12]

During the logging season, most enslaved women, children, and men "unfit for work" remained behind in the English settlement and worked at least part-time as agricultural laborers on "plantations" (as Bay residents called their provisioning gardens). Since their masters had to import all other supplies at great expense, their labor supplied essential foodstuffs to the whole settlement and to the woodcutters in the bush. Many women also worked as domestic servants in the Baymen's households located either in Belize City, St. George's Caye, or in more isolated enclaves upriver. Compared with the male woodcutters, these women experienced much closer supervision and discipline from their masters and mistresses. Although enslaved women had fewer opportunities to run away, some did so nonetheless, usually escaping as part of a group. Some male slaves (especially those no longer serviceable on a woodcutting gang) engaged in blacksmithing, coopering, chipping logwood, fishing, and pickling turtle meat. Others

served as drovers tending their master's livestock (used as draft animals and for beef) which wandered along grassy riverbanks or clear-
ings where the trees had been previously felled. Many of the slaves,
who were not directly involved with logging, performed tasks that
brought them from the settlement into the bush—gathering firewood,
delivering supplies to the woodcutters' base camps, and collecting useful natural materials such as medicinal plants. Circumventing their
masters, some even found ways to profit from their knowledge of the
natural surroundings. Slaves salvaged mahogany scraps or collected
logwood, grew vegetables, or caught fish and sea turtles, which they
sold in the local marketplace or directly to ship captains. Slaves familiar with the rivers and coastal waters provided essential services as
river guides or pilots, steering visiting ships around dangerous shoals.
Some slaves made and sold canoes (called pitpans) hollowed out of
tree trunks. Although the local magistrates ordered unattended boats
confiscated and destroyed to prevent runaways, this law was largely
unenforceable in a land where boats served as a major means of transport, and slaves had both the skills and the materials with which to
build them. An unknown number of slaves paddled their way to freedom in self-fashioned vessels.[13]

Another less tangible aspect of the slaves' engagement with their
natural surroundings was in the realm of spiritual beliefs. Historical
sources and anthropological studies both suggest that enslaved Africans may have experienced and valued their natural surroundings in
very different ways than their English masters. In many African religious traditions, various components of the natural world were highly
venerated and were believed to connect with powerful spiritual forces.
Living trees in particular held symbolic significance in many African
traditions. Likewise, objects, items of dress, or ornaments fashioned
from the bark, wood, or seeds of trees were believed to contain the
potency of their living source. Amidst the oppression of colonial settings, the retention (or revival) of such beliefs may have reinforced

important aspects of personal and shared cultural identity among enslaved people.[14]

In addition, when the woodcutters converged on Belize City during their breaks, especially for the Christmas holiday, the slaves celebrated with dances, *gumbays* (drum-playing events), and other revelries that reflected their diverse African and West Indian Creole backgrounds. Such events were not only an important time for returned slaves to reconnect with their families but also to reinforce a larger sense of community and solidarity. Although in the Bay, as in many slave societies, the white minority sought to restrict or eliminate such forms of expression, which they deemed potentially subversive. African cultural practices and belief systems nonetheless survived or influenced slaves' songs, drumming, dances, storytelling, and oral history traditions. As enslaved Africans participated in the local economy, developed family and social networks, and shared in the vibrant street life and festivities, such as late-night dances, they forged a sense of belonging within the slave community. These interpersonal ties served as a powerful binding agent, motivating enslaved woodcutters to return to the Bay settlement and encouraging those already there to remain. Nevertheless, some people still found the slave system so oppressive that they sought out alternatives which usually involved running away. For others, just knowing they could potentially escape, even temporarily, from the settlement if conditions warranted may have made their lives more tolerable.[15]

Alternatives to the Bay Settlement

Throughout the eighteenth and early nineteenth centuries in the Bay settlement, the Baymen's greatest fear, aside from the constant danger of Spanish invasion, was of slaves choosing to run away and, in essence, liberate themselves. The many swamps, lagoons, and winding waterways provided fugitive slaves with endless hiding places and secret passages, often quite close to the heart of the settlement. But even for experienced woodsmen, marronage meant a difficult existence of danger and deprivation out in the bush. Seeking asylum among the Spanish may have seemed tempting but also uncertain. The majority of slaves who ran away permanently were woodcutters who worked at large in the rain forest; sometimes whole logging gangs simply did not return—a dozen or more workers deserting at a time. Men accustomed to the solidarity of working together as a unit acted together to change their situation. One Bayman complained that thirty of his slaves escaped like this over a four-month period. Over time, as nearby trees were exhausted, woodcutting crews ventured farther and farther from the settlement, increasing the temptation to escape. While some fugitive slaves formed independent Maroon communities hidden in the interior, many made their way beyond the treaty boundaries into Spanish territory, taking advantage of the Spanish Crown's long-standing policy to free other nations' fugitive slaves if they converted to Catholicism. In 1765, the magistrates' annual register claimed, "numbers of the Baymen's slaves desert daily to the Spaniards . . . [yet] all the wood in the old tracts . . . being cut down, their labour is wanted more than ever." One slaveholder complained that no Bayman "however well disposed he may consider his Negroes, can think his property safe for a single Night. It is but a Week ago, since a whole gang of about Twelve . . . deserted in a Body to the Spaniards . . . even those Negroes who never had the least disposition to quit their masters, . . . from motives of curiosity and . . . [Spaniards'] holding out freedom, . . . [are] led not only to desert themselves but induce others to do likewise."[16]

Usually, the Spanish denied such charges or insisted that runaways were motivated by their desire to embrace the true faith. In one case, a slaveholder claimed to have lost a "very valuable and favorite domestic servant . . . under the fraudulent pretext of Religion." When he demanded the return of his property, Spanish officials replied that the man had gone voluntarily to Bacalar for baptism. In 1765, John Christopher was dispatched from the Mosquito Shore to meet with Don Francisco Aybar, commander of St. Fernando de Omoa, to demand the return of five slaves named Jacques, Augustine, Lepere, Peg, and Chloe, as well as two slaves from a naval vessel, Pompey and Blow, "said to belong to the King." After weeks of travelling in small boats and on horseback over muddy roads through the bush, traversing from one Spanish village or guard post to the next, Christopher arrived in Omoa only to be detained as a spy. When he finally was granted an audience with the Spanish commander, Don Aybar declared with wonderful audacity that since the Mosquito Shore settlement was on Spanish territory, there could not be any English slaves and therefore no runaways. Furthermore, he proclaimed that if any poor wayward slaves came "to seek Christianity . . . he had sent them away to Guatimala [sic] to be instructed in the Christian principles." Adding insult to injury, he stated that the escaped "negroes were no Rogues, but that every body [else] upon the Mosquito Shore were nothing but Harborers of Robbers and Villains." After this acrimonious exchange, Christopher returned home empty-handed. From the Spanish perspective, the modest expense of harboring runaways was a satisfying means of both tweaking their imperial rival and curbing expansion of the Anglo woodcutting settlements by draining away their human capital.[17]

Given the seeming ease with which slaves on the woodcutting gangs could escape, a pertinent question is why *more* slaves did not take advantage of this option. The answer partly lies in the Baymen's somewhat effective campaign of deterrence through which slave masters sought both to placate slaves *and* to instill fear in hopes of keeping them anchored within the predictability and security of the known. Incentives for enslaved workers included, for example, extra provisions and leisure time during the rainy season. Slaveholders in the Bay regarded these concessions as a necessary cost of doing business and a worthwhile investment if they proved even minimally effective in reducing the number of runaways.[18]

In addition to such inducements, slave masters employed various forms of coercion to physically and psychologically control their slaves. Horrific measures were sometimes used to terrorize slaves into compliance, such as in 1785 when the magistrates ordered that the chained body of a slave, hung for murdering a white man, be publicly displayed because "an example is wanting among the negroes, who have of late acted as if they thought it impossible for the Country to punish them." The Baymen also generated a constant stream of anti-Spanish propaganda, which may have been at least partially internalized by their slaves. While officially offering freedom to English slaves, Spanish settlers in the Yucatán, in fact, still owned human property themselves and did not hesitate to capture slaves from the English during wartime. In 1745, a group of sixty Spaniards went up the New River and "burn'd and destroy'd all before 'em, and took several Negroes." During their 1779 attack on St. George's Caye, they captured over 200 slaves, most of whom ended up on Cuban plantations. Some former slaves may have communicated back to those still in the Bay, but others, spirited away by the Spanish supposedly to receive religious instruction, were never heard from again. At the very least, the Spanish may have seemed dangerously unpredictable; escaping to an uncertain reception among the Spanish or remaining enslaved among the English may have seemed a choice between two evils.[19]

Another highly effective means that the Baymen used to prevent enslaved woodcutters from absconding was to control their wives and children back in the settlement. In 1797, for example, amidst renewed hostilities with Spain, the Baymen sent their own families out of harm's way but did not evacuate the enslaved women and children, figuring that the enslaved men, drafted as soldiers, might be more motivated to stay and fight in order to protect their families. Without them, the Bay-men, who were aided by only one British warship, would have been hard-pressed to defeat the Spanish, in what proved to be the last deci-sive battle over the territory. Ironically, once the region's security was assured as a British protectorate, the Baymen later rewarded their "loyal" slaves for their military service, citing their defense of the set-tlement as proof of their devotion. Of course, the slaves had no choice but to fight or to see their families become spoils of war.[20]

Given the relative ease of running away from the Bay, one colonial official remarked "Slaves, in this Settlement . . . [are] so by choice only." In other words, those who stayed did so of their free will because they were contented with their situation. Indeed, some early accounts per-petuated the myth that slavery in the Bay was a significantly kinder, gentler institution than in the West Indies or the American South. Slave owners in the Bay viewed themselves as benevolent patriarchs and rationalized that runaways were actually stolen or lured away, like im-pressionable children, by the Spanish. Yet the Baymen's constant com-plaints of slaves absconding and their use of violence to quell resistance belie those notions. In truth, as more recent historians have shown, the institution of slavery remained grounded in repression. Slaves' margin-ally better living conditions and somewhat wider scope for mobility and negotiation did not necessarily translate into contentment or pas-sivity. If anything, slavery in the Bay seemed to be a minefield of shift-ing power relations between slaves and masters.[21]

Negotiating Slave-Master Relationships

Enslaved workers in remote logging camps seemed to have been very aware of their critical importance to the whole mahogany enterprise. Accordingly, they developed expectations regarding their working hours, living conditions, provisions, and, most important, their holi-days. In their eyes, customary practices often carried contractual weight that, if violated, would bring immediate reactions in the form of strikes, protests, or work slowdowns. Living within the microcosm of the Bay settlement, the slaves also seemed to have understood the local and international politics of their masters' precarious situation on Spanish territory very well. While many slaves quietly resisted, such as by entering into the marketplace for themselves or by subtly manipulating their masters, others took a more confrontational approach, forcing concessions from their masters and local magistrates by threatening to abscond or simply by defying their authority. And yet, as the following examples demonstrate, slaves' scope of action in a particular dispute or negotiation varied, depending their status and gender and whether the event occurred out in the bush, within the settlement, or in the bosom of their owner's household.

One revealing case involved William Cahoone's slaves who—less fortunate than his leased slave Newport who gained his freedom—were sold upon their master's death to pay his debts, in spite of his explicit intention to manumit them. As part of his estate settlement, a few ended up in the temporary custody of Mansfield Bowen because their new owners were minors. An affluent magistrate, Bowen was apparently notorious for abusing his slaves. When the slaves later complained of mistreatment, their owners' guardian pressed charges against Bowen for cruelty and misuse of the estate's assets. The recorded testimony from this court case included three incidents involving confrontations between this would-be master and the slaves under his command. In the first incident which occurred circa 1768, Mansfield Bowen deputized his brother, Frederick Bowen, to inspect one of his mahogany works where the slaves "had refused to do their duty for some time past, and [had] other frivolous grievances." After attempting to compel the slaves back to work, Frederick reported a tense encounter in which, "the Gang surrounded me, with this Man Robert at the Head of them, swearing that unless I granted him, and all Hands, liberty to go to Belize, they would take to the Bush." Infuriated by this impertinence, Frederick restrained Robert, declaring him to be "an unfit character to appear on such a mutinous occasion, he having either been sick or skulking for a great length of time." At that point, "the whole of the Gang entered my House and swore unless I released him from Chains, I should also put all of them in." Intimidated by their united stance, Frederick "gave the Negroes one and all permission to take the crafts for the purpose of proceeding to Belize." Although Robert was later punished, the woodcutters, standing together, achieved their goal of returning to Belize City. Whereas they could easily have killed Frederick and fled, they chose to avoid such drastic actions; their emotional bonds to their friends and family seemed to tie them to the settlement as much or more than their condition as slaves.[22]

In the second incident, Mansfield Bowen purchased a slave named Guy for £275 at a courthouse auction. But according to an eyewitness, Guy "said he would not belong to him, and if he did not sell him to somebody else, he would lose his money, or that he [Guy] would go into the bush." Bowen indignantly replied that Guy "ought to have said that sooner, that if he had known [Guy] did not want to belong to him, he would not have bid £5 for him." Angry and humiliated, Bowen threw his recalcitrant property in prison until another buyer could be found. In a remarkable test of wills and a very public setting, Guy took a calculated risk in hopes of improving his situation. The embarrassment that Bowen experienced as a result of Guy's actions was a direct blow to his ego, undermining his self-confidence in his mastery over others.[23]

A third incident involving a young enslaved African woman named Peggy, who was a domestic within Bowen's household, highlights the contrast between male woodcutters, like Robert and Guy who had considerable leverage over their master, and the enslaved women who had much less leeway. Returning from the marketplace after a day of vending colorful handkerchiefs for her master, Peggy could not account for all of her merchandise. Accused of theft, she was whipped and, after briefly running away, was confined in chains for ten days in a dank basement. While imprisoned, she received covert aid from her fellow slave women, and it was likely one of them who secretly brought Bowen's cruelty to light. During the subsequent trial against him, three of the women, Sarah, Thisbe, and Nancy, suddenly declared that they were wrongfully enslaved. Bowen insisted they had "no claim whatever to their Freedom, in consequence of their original owner [Cahoone] dying so much in debt, that the whole of his Estate was obliged to be sold." The women produced a certificate signed by Cahoone and officially filed and recorded in 1774 that manumitted their grandfather and his family. Intrigued with the women's story, the then superintendent wrote to the Jamaican court clerk inquiring about "A very large Family of poor slaves . . . [who claim] they were free'd from Slavery by their Master previous to his Death; and that the Manumission of their Grandmother named Rose, or Rosetta, is on the record in Jamaica." In a twist reminiscent of María Pérez, who escaped slavery by proving herself to be a Spanish subject, the reply from Jamaica confirmed that not only had their grandmother been manumitted, she was an "Indian" and therefore exempt from slavery. Nevertheless, the women were not allowed to testify against Bowen nor were they immediately freed. Acquitted of all charges by a jury of his peers, Bowen was reelected as a magistrate over the superintendent's objections that he set a bad example for other slave masters. To protest this blatant reassertion of white hegemony, a large number of slaves took "to the Woods."[24]

Slaves also found ways to take advantage of the tense relationship between the Spanish and the English. Indeed, for those living and working along this contested frontier, tensions between the two countries would have been impossible to overlook; everyone knew that their existence in the Bay was supposed to remain confined within treaty-designated imperial boundaries. In reality, however, these invisible lines were ones that could be transgressed at times without ill effect, but that at other times, mattered (or could be made to matter) quite significantly for slaves and their owners. Indeed, masters may have seemed less than awe-inspiring when scolded by the Spanish commander at Bacalar that "by their disobedience they [could] lose their Negroes and find themselves under a violent arrest." In 1789, Spanish soldiers seized three enslaved cattlemen (owned by the elite Baymen, Richard O'Brien and James Bartlett) on Spanish territory. The slaves, named Scotland, George, and James, initially claimed that they merely followed their cattle without any awareness of where they wandered. On a second interrogation, however, the men asserted that they had acted upon their masters' instructions to trespass onto "land clearly being no part of the land allowed to the English." As soon as the slaves made this statement, the Spanish inspector confiscated them and sent them to Bacalar. Although it is impossible to know if their statements were freely given or coerced, the three may have offered a calculated confession, fully grasping the consequences of violating the treaty. If so, they essentially "traded in" their current owners and took their chances as slaves among the Spanish. If their confession was forced, on the other hand, they may have unwillingly severed connections in the Bay. Pleading ignorance would have been their least risky option. By laying claim to their own knowledge, demonstrating comprehension of abstract geopolitical boundaries, they involved themselves instead in a complicated interimperial chess game—whether they played the part of sacrificial pawns or shrewd knights was a matter of perspective.[25]

Sometimes whole groups of slaves were left in legal limbo following their owner's death. In one case, the Flowers, an extended slave family sent from the Bay to cut wood on the Mosquito Shore, continued to live and work freely as mahogany cutters there for over thirty years, long after their master had died. Their situation changed abruptly, however, when their deceased owner's heir sold them to Richard O'Brien, a powerful Bayman, who attempted to retrieve them on the eve of the 1786 British evacuation of the Mosquito Shore. The Flowers fled into the forest and convinced many other slaves to join them in a mass desertion. When the evacuation (which involved hundreds of people, military personnel, and dozens of ships) ground to a halt, Spanish officials accused the British of intentionally stalling and the white population was thrown into a panic. In desperation, the Shoremen's elected council, considering the danger "of a family so numerous and so generally connected with other families, flying to the woods ... [in] general desertion and open rebellion ... [and] the state of Freedom in which this family have lived," resolved to manumit the Flowers if they agreed to return and move to the Bay. When the Flowers accepted this amnesty, the evacuation proceeded. What might have remained a private standoff between the Flowers and their would-be owner thus culminated in a region-wide geopolitical crisis wherein an interimperial agreement trumped the property rights of a private individual. That the Flowers ultimately decided to move to the Bay settlement suggests how closely their livelihood as mahogany cutters kept them enmeshed within the larger Atlantic economy. Many other Mosquito Shore slaves who ran away, however, did not return. Dozens of slaves (including men, women, and children) paddled off together in large groups, opting for freedom rather than accompanying their refugee masters to the Bay.[26]

In another case, the death of a slave owner again precipitated a personal crisis that expanded to involve the whole settlement. When a female slaveholder died intestate in the Bay around 1814, the magistrates assigned two of their cronies to oversee her estate, causing the superintendent to accuse them of corruption. In the midst of this disagreement, according to the superintendent, "The Negroes of this large Property were enticed to ... [leave] their works in the interior of the Country, come down in a Body to the Town of Belize to dictate who should be their Masters." Suspecting that some self-interested slaveholders incited the slaves to trouble, he reported that when the magistrates perceived "the mischief that they had produced [they] flew to me for assistance." Although the forthright demand to "dictate who should be their masters" might seem astonishing in most slave societies, it reflects the ability of slaves in the Bay to use internal divisions within the free population to their advantage. In this instance, the superintendent put a quick end to the slaves' demonstration by calling out the militia. "Precedents of this sort are full of danger!" he warned the fractious Baymen, so they had better give "additional attention to [keep the slaves] quiet and peaceable and certainly not to give them just grounds for discontent." Such occurrences, however, gave substance to slave owners' fears that the settlement's defenses were "very inadequate to oppose any combination among the several Thousand Slaves."[27]

Slave Uprisings

Compared with other colonial frontier settlements, such as Demerara or Surinam, relatively few serious slave uprisings occurred in the English woodcutting settlements. The very fragmented character of mahogany cutting—with small gangs working scattered in the forest, remote from each other and from Belize City—minimized slaves' ability to organize concerted acts of resistance outside their own immediate gang. Yet given the high proportion of slaves deported to the Bay for involvement in rebellions elsewhere, the risk of slave revolts loomed large for slaveholders, and even short-lived uprisings kept the settlement on edge. The most dramatic example of a concerted slave rebellion occurred in June 1773 when an altercation over food shortages between some disgruntled slaves and their master escalated into an apparently unplanned revolt that left six white men dead. According to the Baymen's later testimony, the instigators were "join'd by several others, the whole about fifty armed with sixteen Musquets, Cuttlasses, etc. Our people attacked them . . . but the Rebels after discharging their Pieces retired into the Woods. . . ." The Baymen appealed to the British Admiralty in Jamaica to track down the participants, fearing that if the rebels succeeded in creating a Maroon stronghold, their remaining slaves would be "exposed to their incursions and there will be an Asylum for all the Negroes who choose to run away from their masters." In mid-October, the rebellion essentially was crushed, but nineteen of the rebels remained at large and were presumed to be heading for Spanish territory. Of the relatively few slave uprisings in the Bay, most appear, like this event, to have been spontaneous outbursts, precipitated by a specific clash between slaves and slaveholders.[28]

In 1790, on the eve of renewed war between England and Spain, some of the Baymen became convinced that Spain plotted to incite a slave rebellion. During one of the Spanish commissioner's regular inspection tours of the settlement, his translator, Peter González, was arrested for "walking in the Negro section without good reason" after dark; purportedly disguised as a sailor, "in a Blue seaman's Jacket with a check or striped Shirt," he supposedly attempted to encourage slaves to run away to Spanish territory. According to testimony elicited from a man named Cudjoe, described as "a sensible and intelligent slave," González offered to "make him and his family free and guarantee a happy and comfortable situation in Spanish country." In addition to naming others as suspects, Cudjoe reported that González claimed to have already recruited a hundred slaves to set fire to the town; the rising smoke was to be the signal to waiting Spanish vessels to "come on boldly" and participating slaves were to identify themselves by placing pieces of white paper on their hats and flee to the Spanish ships. If this plot had any substance, which seems unlikely, Cudjoe may have confessed in order to avoid punishment, out of fear at the prospect of a Spanish invasion, or in hopes of a reward. The Baymen were horrified to even contemplate the possibility of their slaves collaborating with Spanish forces; such an alliance could indeed have been the undoing of the settlement.[29]

Another source of labor unrest was the importation of prisoners, including white men convicted of serious crimes and rebellious or troublesome slaves sentenced to deportation from other locales. In 1784, during Superintendent Despard's tenure, the magistrates sought to curtail the practice of admitting English convict ships to sell their cargos as indentured servants; Robert White, the Baymen's London agent, specifically objected that the *Hercules* had recently sailed to the Bay "with upwards of a hundred Felons, to be sold . . . for as much Mahogany or Logwood as they will fetch . . . a Continuation of this Impure and Infectious Commodity will necessarily establish a colony of Out-laws in the Bay." For many years, the Baymen had regarded convicts as an attractively cheap workforce, making the settlement, in Despard's words, "the mart for every black villain that is transported from the British Islands." In 1762, for example, slaves found guilty (but not executed) after a major slave rebellion on Jamaica were shipped off to the Bay of Honduras where they were quickly bought up, including by some of the same Baymen who were now complaining. Several of these slaves later purportedly participated in a revolt that left sixteen white people dead and resulted in the execution of its leaders "by burning, gibbeting, and other methods of torture." One Bayman knowingly purchased a slave that had been found guilty of theft after breaking into his previous owner's iron chest and a second slave that was the convicted "ringleader of a very dangerous conspiracy in Jamaica against his Master and family." Another Baymen, who owned a slave who had been "publickly whipped at Black River on a conviction of theft before the Court there, . . . [had] no difficulty in importing this same Negro to England when he himself came home in the year 1789."[30]

The magistrates' sudden claims to disapprove of such persons on the grounds that they might corrupt the morals of the populace seemed disingenuous. In fact, they moved to curtail this notorious labor market mainly to prevent potential competitors from taking advantage of this cheap labor source. Once again the internal divisions among different classes of slaveholders came into play as the elite Baymen sought to protect their own advantages. In addition, they aimed to exclude white convicts who might reasonably expect to secure mahogany claims after completing their sentences. Efforts to restrict immigration gained more credibility as a security measure in the context of the escalating Maroon wars in Jamaica (1794–1796) when the magistrates, concerned that the Bay was becoming "a depot of the most dangerous characters in the West Indies," prohibited the importation of any slaves from there or elsewhere that were suspected of involvement in a rebellion.[31]

Likewise, when the Haitian Revolution broke out, the Baymen feared that its reverberations would send waves of slave unrest sweeping throughout the Atlantic region. Fleeing white refugees, often bringing slaves with them, fanned out across the region, bringing word of the violent transformations that resulted in the world's first black republic. Terrified that their settlement would face a similar fate, the magistrates further restricted the importation of slaves who were of suspect or unknown origins in a desperate effort to exclude any person tainted with a revolutionary contagion. Slave owners importing enslaved persons had to attest to how long they had owned incoming slaves and certify each one's place of origin, unless they were "new negroes" arriving directly from Africa. The ability to move and trade enslaved individuals, once carried on with little oversight, was now monitored and restricted.[32]

In addition, the magistrates passed laws limiting slave gatherings and instituted extra patrols during Christmas to prevent slaves' unrest during customary holiday revelries. In addition, they forbade *obeah,* a Creolized African religion practiced by some slaves, because it seemed subversive and threatening. Nevertheless, many of the slaves, when not off cutting wood, resided together in a segregated quarter known as "Eboe Town." In the absence of any police force, the magistrates exercised little control over activities there. Especially after dark, all sorts of transient people, including some of the poorer, white residents, sailors, stray soldiers, and occasional Spanish visitors (who were by definition considered suspicious) wandered the quarter and attended the slaves' dances. Uninhabitable areas surrounding Belize City also provided illicit spaces for slaves to carve out their own social existence away from their masters' scrutiny. In 1806, the Baymen sought to curb slaves' lively nightlife, claiming that "a very large assemblage of Negroes, either free or Slaves, together with persons of various descriptions [gathered in] Huts situated in different parts of the Swamp . . . [near] Town whose apparent motive . . . is Dancing. Whatever may be their real motive for such meetings, certain it is these nightly revels are productive of much noise and disturbance in the Neighborhood."[33]

For all the Baymen's anxieties, however, when some slaves were detained for breaking curfew, their masters furiously demanded their workers be returned; their main concern was for the slaves to keep up the flow of mahogany. Unable to enforce any meaningful discipline over the Baymen or their slaves, the military commander blasted the magistrates: "You must be fully aware Gentlemen that there is not in this Settlement even the Shadow of a Civil Police. The Pestilential Filth of your Shores, the dirty conditions of, and irregularities permitted in your Streets, & the Constant passing and repassing of People of Color of every description during the whole of the Night speak so strongly to this fact, that . . . no Man who pays the least regard to truth will attempt to deny it." So even though the early nineteenth century brought increased legal restrictions, the freewheeling frontier atmosphere and the type of labor organization that mahogany cutting required continued de facto to shape the unusual character of slavery in the Bay of Honduras.[34]

Through information brokering, mastery over their environment, and taking advantage of personal, political, and military upheavals in the Bay, slaves pushed the boundaries of the slave system wherever they could. Even the misguided observer who claimed that slaves remained in bondage "by choice only" acknowledged that the enslaved harkened to any "encouragement held out to seek *freedom*." As much as they resented it, perhaps the Baymen, many of whom had themselves sought out a more latitudinous existence as woodcutters, could identify with their slaves' desire for self-determination. It is telling that, when given the choice to stay in the Bay or begin life anew somewhere else, the Flowers and Pérez families both opted to stay but only "provided they could be free."[35]

CHAPTER SIX

Redefining Mahogany in the Early Republic

*I*N 1780, when Benjamin Franklin commissioned a mahogany object from a London artisan, he urged the man to "recollect, if you can, the species of mahogany of which you made my [previous] box, for you know there is a great deal of difference in woods that go under that name." Failing that, he requested the "finest grained [mahogany] that you can meet with." Franklin's suspicions about what passed for mahogany were indicative of a growing problem in the last quarter of the eighteenth century as the size and quality of available mahogany from established sources became increasingly inconsistent and unpredictable. The already complex mahogany business required ever greater attention and expertise to find, evaluate, and select fine woods. While American merchants and cabinetmakers had become accustomed to occasionally getting stuck with a rotten log, such losses had been insignificant relative to the quantities of large, excellent mahogany they routinely handled. But as problems of sourcing and quality control became more pronounced, they, as well as their customers, had to recalibrate their sense of what constituted quality in mahogany in terms of its purported place of origin as well as its size, color, texture, and figure. In many cases, this required that they let go of set preferences, biases, and preconceptions.[1]

These changes stemmed fundamentally from the harsh environmental realities and shifting economic and social conditions in mahogany-producing regions. Although Jamaican and Bahamian mahogany were still very much in demand and fetched premium prices, increasingly what little was available came from immature or inferior trees previously passed over by woodcutters. Compared with earlier exports, this generation of island mahogany was often much reduced in size, suitable only for making diminutive objects, small pieces of veneer, or discrete furniture parts, such as chair rails. In 1777, for example, Thomas Bowen offered his customers "a quantity of good seasoned Jamaica Mahogany Planks of an exceeding hard quality . . . very suitable for fifes, drum sticks, etc." Amidst the wartime mahogany shortages, it seems unlikely that he would have emphasized those particular uses if the wood was not too small for anything more substantial. A more insidious problem was that some suppliers deliberately mixed poor-quality wood into larger shipments or misrepresented its actual source. Given these circumstances, the excellent reputation of established West Indian mahogany producers began to erode, adding another element of uncertainty into the mahogany market. Cabinetmakers adjusted their wood-buying practices accordingly, making more use of Honduran mahogany for large-scale objects and West Indian mahogany from previously inaccessible French and Spanish islands, especially Cuba and Hispaniola. Over the coming decades, mahogany from each of these geographical sources achieved periods of dominance in the American marketplace, setting the new gold standard of excellence as Jamaican mahogany had once done. In each of these locales, however, the particular social, political, and environmental contexts were critically important in shaping their mahogany exports, which in turn had consequences for American craftsmen and furniture buyers.[2]

To ensure more knowledgeable and trustworthy timber sourcing agents, some cabinetmakers sent family members or former journeymen to serve as their liaisons in the West Indies. As early as 1760, the

Gillows Company, a leading English cabinetmaking firm with premises in Lancaster and London, reminded their buying agent that "as there is a good deal of Deception in this article, we need not advise you to procure some good Judge to make choice of Right Jamaica Wood, & see that proper allowance in Measure is made for defficiency [sic]." By the 1780s, they sought to remedy such problems by engaging an experienced cabinetmaker to oversee their timber buying in Kingston, Jamaica which had become a major hub of transshipment for mahogany from many locales. When a customer complained of the high cost of a dining table in 1786, Richard Gillow explained that this was due to his firm's insistence on using only "fine hard mahogany," rather than soft mahogany or "baywood." Since a dining table depended "on the quality of the wood more than any other furniture—as these may be made of inferior kind of mahogany," he claimed that a Gillows product would last exceptionally well, "the tops are fine old mahogany that have been sawn up nearly five years and will improve with use." Not all cabinetmaking firms, however, had the wherewithal to install a representative on site with the necessary expertise and trustworthiness to ensure the quality of their wood supply.[3]

In many North American seaports, the issue of quality control came to the fore as mahogany was off-loaded from arriving ships. In addition to regular wood surveyors who measured and graded all kinds of timber, many cities began appointing specialized "mahogany surveyors." In Boston, for example, John Cogswell, a well-established cabinetmaker, had supplemented his income by serving as "surveyor of boards and shingles" for over ten years before also becoming the "surveyor of mahogany" in 1799, a title he held for another two decades. With every shipment, he measured and labeled each individual log, calculating how much useable wood it contained. Even with such controls in place, merchants, cabinetmakers, and furniture buyers alike had to bring new vigilance to their mahogany selections. Careful buying agents and sharp-eyed surveyors could not solve the more fundamental problem that the mahogany market was inexorably changing as the trees from previously favored sources were exhausted.[4]

The shrinking widths of available mahogany boards also contributed to changes in furniture design in the late eighteenth century as cabinetmakers were forced to modify how they utilized raw materials. Dining tables, for example, were reconfigured with narrower leaves. Although so-called "table wood" was still available, as the Gillows example underscores, it had become exceedingly expensive. As Adam Bowett points out, the thirty-inch-wide boards typical in an eighteenth-century mahogany table required a mature tree of at least three to four feet in diameter. Perhaps the greatest design transformation was the increased reliance on veneering which, although not a new technique, began to be used much more widely during this period. This technique involved gluing thin slices of a fine wood, often a high-quality figured mahogany, onto a plain base made of a secondary wood, such as low-grade mahogany, pine, maple, or tulipwood. Sawing logs by hand into paper-thin sheets required great precision and skill, so veneer cutting was generally undertaken by professional sawyers (including some who specialized in mahogany), often working in pairs to wield long, two-handled saws. The veneers then had to be artfully matched and carefully adhered onto the wood base to create sound, aesthetically pleasing objects. Given all these labor-intensive steps, veneered furniture was not inexpensive to make or buy. But by reducing the use of solid mahogany, it brought cabinetmakers a considerable savings on their most expensive material.[5]

During this period, consumers regarded veneers (which later came into disrepute) as beautiful and marvelous in their own right, particularly as they adorned an array of innovative furniture types. Inspired by the rediscovery of the Roman sites of Pompeii and Herculaneum, European furniture makers began to create neoclassical objects that emphasized perfect symmetry, abstract geometrical forms, and delicate, airy ornamentation. Very different from the robust rococo (so-called Chippendale) style that it superseded and that had been so well suited to the use of solid mahogany, the neoclassical style of furniture was lighter, less ponderous, and emphasized the use of thin veneers. This stylistic change, however, continued and, if anything, increased, the earlier emphasis on smoothness and polish; hence, the refined surface qualities that people had long appreciated about mahogany continued to be very important.[6]

Popular new furniture forms included diminutive ladies' sewing tables and writing desks; designed to be lightweight and portable, they typically had slender tapered legs, cleverly outfitted interiors, and exteriors adorned with highly polished, geometrically-patterned veneers. At the other end of the spectrum, objects regarded as more masculine—desks, bookcases, and case clocks—remained large in scale but became more restrained, symmetrical, and rationally geometrical in design. In the post-Revolutionary years in the United States, objects in the neoclassical style (or Federal style as it has come to be called) were often further distinguished by the decorative use of patriotic emblems such as eagles, stars, shields, arrows, swags, and the "chain of unity" representing the thirteen original states. New materials, new craft techniques, and a new republican iconography came together with the self-reflective quality of mahogany to reinforce in Americans a stronger sense of shared national identity.

Educating Mahogany Buyers

In Franklin's case, his anxiety about ordering the correct "species of mahogany" had more to do with scientific and practical concerns than with aesthetics or nationalism. His acute awareness of the "difference in woods that go under that name" was both that of an Enlightenment man keenly attentive to the material properties of the natural world and a well-informed consumer. Even while suffering from painful gout and hobbling about Versailles fulfilling his diplomatic duties, Franklin was still observing, analyzing, and reassessing his understanding of his physical surroundings. Since there was no reliable way at the time to measure changes in the humidity of the atmosphere, his latest brain-storm was to build a hygrometer made out of mahogany wood. For al-though he had previously been of the "opinion that good mahogany was not affected by moisture so as to change its dimensions, and that it was always to be found as the tools of the workman left it," he realized his mistake after bringing a London-made set of magnets in a mahog-any case home with him to Philadelphia, only to discover that the mag-nets were suddenly difficult to remove because their wooden housing had contracted slightly in the drier environment. Likewise, on some English furniture that he had also shipped home, the veneers immedi-ately began to "get loose and come off . . . [and] were forever cracking and flying." From this evidence, he concluded that mahogany did in-deed react to atmospheric changes, shrinking and swelling as the mois-ture levels in the air vacillated. With his typical droll humor, he attrib-uted London's higher humidity to the profusion of dyers, brewers, and teakettles. Although he apparently never perfected a prototype, Frank-lin theorized that an instrument to measure these fluctuations could be outfitted with thinly planed, carefully-calibrated pieces of mahogany to indicate minute changes in humidity with "much less trouble than by any hygrometer hitherto in use."[7]

As the above examples suggest, Franklin was drawing on his cumu-lative experience with mahogany in his daily life, gleaned from years of selecting and using it for many different purposes. During an extended stay in England, beginning in 1757, he patronized some of London's foremost cabinetmakers to order furnishings for his elegant Philadel-phia townhouse, shipping home a hefty new mahogany desk and other fine furnishings. (Hence his understandable annoyance when the veneers later popped off his expensive acquisitions.) In addition, he paid close attention to his wife's furniture acquisitions even while he was away. In 1765, for example, Deborah updated him on her recent purchases, including "a verey hansom mohoganey Stand for the tee kittel." After returning to Philadelphia, he continued to combine innovation and fashion in his domestic surroundings, personally designing several mahogany objects and supervising their fabrication by local cabinetmakers. These creations included a four-sided music stand, a library chair with built-in folding steps, and a custom-made case for a glass armonica, his improved version of an unusual musical instrument he had admired in Europe. Franklin's choice of mahogany for his printing presses, "made under his own Inspection [with] Improvements," likely reflected somewhat different considerations as the wood used in their construction had to be particularly heavy-duty.[8]

Compared with his intrepid father, Benjamin's son William Franklin seems to have been a more typical consumer. Although appointed to the post of Royal Governor of New Jersey while still in his early thirties, he seemed less than secure when it came to ordering new furniture. Rather than become directly involved in designing his furniture or selecting the precise mahogany to be used, he looked to see what fashionable Philadelphians were buying and followed their lead. In 1772, for example, William wrote to his father in London that he coveted a set of mahogany chairs that "Capt. Williams brought over with him from England . . . which cost him about 22s. Sterling a Piece." After approaching several local cabinetmakers to copy these chairs, young Franklin turned to his father for assistance. "I wanted the Workmen here to make me a Dozen like them, but tho' Mahogany is considerably cheaper here than in England, I could not get anyone to undertake to make them under 55s. Currency a Piece, and they would probably not be so well finished," he wrote, "I shall therefore be obliged to you if you would send me a dozen of such kind of Chairs, made in a fashionable Taste." After much anxiety, William did finally find a local cabinetmaker willing to make the chairs at an acceptable price.[9]

Despite their sometimes thorny relationship, the Franklin men regularly conferred on such matters of daily life. Corresponding about

furniture must have been one of the few neutral topics of shared interest where they could at least hope for a meeting of the minds. Such
diversions were entirely subsumed by their serious political differences,
however, when the Boston Tea Party in 1773 provoked a confrontation
between the colonies and the Crown. Forced to choose between king
and country, William remained a Loyalist. In 1776, he was imprisoned
by the Patriots and his property confiscated; the few furnishings his
wife retained were subsequently destroyed in a fire, including very
likely the once-debated chairs. After the war, William moved to England but, although he received partial compensation for his lost possessions, the painful rift with his father was never healed.[10]

As furniture buyers slowly became more aware of the variability of
mahogany, cabinetmakers found themselves thrust into a difficult, at
times contentious, role as arbiters of what constituted excellence in
mahogany. As their informed eyes selected or spurned lots of timber,
they set the market standards and influenced consumer choices. But,
of course, there was still much room for error. Moreover, when unscrupulous cabinetmakers passed off inferior wood to their customers, buyers' trust in the material (as well as in the men who sold it) was further
eroded. In such cases, it was up to furniture buyers to beware lest they
overpay or end up with disappointing products.

In many cases, cabinetmakers played an active role in influencing
their customers' choices. In Woburn, Massachusetts, for example,
Leammi Baldwin displayed finished goods in his cabinetmaking shop,
which served as an informal educational venue. In September 1773,
Jonathan Green ordered a chest of "Drawers like those I see in your
shop . . . Please to put on large brasses and please to make for me a
charry [cherry] table and don't put the sap of the board into it but let it
be like yourn that your wife shoed me both as to color of the leaf and
largeness of it, and please make for me a square black walnut table with
leaves as large as the late fashen [fashion]." Unwilling or unable to afford

pricey imported wood, Green specified precisely what materials he desired but otherwise deferred to his cabinetmaker's taste and awareness
of fashion.[11]

At times, however, misunderstandings and differences of opinion
arose between cabinetmakers and their clientele about what constituted quality. In Philadelphia in 1786, the merchant Tench Coxe sued
cabinetmaker David Evans, claiming he was "by no means entitled to
the price of well-made furniture" because he had used mahogany with
"a great deal of sappy stuff in it, that it is very slight and thin . . . that it
is patched in places much exposed to View, [and] that it was made of
unseasoned wood and badly put together." Coxe's dispute with Evans
dated back to 1782 when the cabinetmaker purchased a piece of land
from him for £260, half to be paid in cash and half to be paid in furniture. In anticipation of his impending marriage, Coxe demanded that
Evans deliver the first installment of thirty-four pieces of furniture in
only two months. What happened next is difficult to fathom because
Evans had a well-established reputation and a solid clientele that included leading Philadelphians. But in the aftermath of the Revolution,
Evans was struggling with financial problems and was having difficulty
finding skilled journeymen or high-quality, well-seasoned mahogany.
Before he could even begin work, he had to borrow money from Coxe to
purchase the necessary materials. Without adequate help, Evans apparently took shortcuts to make the furniture on time; if he expected this
large commission to improve his situation, he grossly miscalculated the
time and resources it required as well as the fierce indignation his shortcuts would elicit from his client.[12]

When Evans delivered the first load of furniture, Coxe was dis-
gusted with the poor-quality mahogany and the faulty workmanship.
The fact that the chairs' slats and crosspieces kept falling out was proof
that Evans had used unseasoned wood, a clear case of negligence. At
this point, Coxe requested Francis Trumble and Thomas Affleck, both
well-respected local cabinetmakers, to appraise the objects; they con-

curred "several articles are not merchantable qualities." By calling on
Evans's professional peers, Coxe probably intended to pressure him to
rectify the problems and improve on the furniture still to be made.
This tactic apparently failed because in 1786, Evans delivered more
shoddy goods. This time, Coxe complained to the Society of Friends in
Philadelphia where Evans was a devoted member. To avert a lawsuit,
the Quakers reprimanded Evans and referred the case to a binding ar-
bitration committee for resolution. Once again, two local cabinetmakers, George Claypoole and Jesse Williams (Evans's former journey-
man), were entrusted to evaluate his products. When they too found in
favor of Coxe, Evans scrambled to pay off his outstanding debt in cash.
Evans ultimately specialized in making venetian blinds and coffins,
which were less labor intensive and required less expensive materials
than large case pieces; although some of the coffins he fabricated were
mahogany, he probably could get away with using less than the finest
wood.[13]

Another revealing dispute over the quality of mahogany, also in
1786, involved James Monroe, then a delegate to the Continental Congress in New York. Amidst trying to shape the federal government
and resolve disputes among the various states, Monroe married Elizabeth Kortright, the daughter of a former British army officer who
amassed a fortune through privateering in the West Indies. Although
her father suffered financial reverses during the late war, she had grown
up in elegant surroundings in New York City and apparently had quite
sophisticated tastes. After residing for a time with his in-laws, Monroe
became determined to improve his financial situation and reluctantly
resigned from Congress to set up his own law practice in Fredericks-
burg, Virginia. Judge Joseph Jones, his trusted uncle, advised the young
couple to furnish their first home modestly with "Mahogany Tables of
middling size" and "neat & strong Mahogany chairs." Skeptical of finding furniture as "well made and as cheap" in a big city, he suggested
they patronize a rural craftsman who was known to him. Ignoring

that sage advice, Monroe instead visited a random cabinetmaking shop just before he left the city and ordered a whole suite of furniture, specifying it was to be "of the best kind." Determining what exactly those words meant again nearly led to a lawsuit.[14]

After Monroe moved to Virginia, his sister-in-law inspected the completed furniture for him in New York and declared it all to be "vile." Alarmed by this response, he requested James Madison to give a second opinion: "You will examine it & if so [vile], reject it. Tell him [the cabinetmaker], I decline taking it, for if it is not of the best kind I had rather have none. You will proceed regularly so as to prevent his suing me." For moral support, Madison rounded up William Grayson, Monroe's cousin and also a Virginia delegate, and their friend William Bingham, a wealthy Philadelphia merchant just back from a grand tour of Europe, to accompany him. Although claiming to have "little confidence in my own judgment of Cabinet workmanship," Madison, backed up by his well-informed friends, pronounced that, although "the aspect of the furniture does *not* . . . entirely please my eye . . . [the cabinetmaker] says the taste of it is conformable to instructions, and no particular defect appears in the workmanship." The cabinetmaker also insisted that it must "be considered too that Mahogany is one of the few things which appears worst when New." For comparison, the men visited Thomas Burling's nearby shop and deemed his furniture "certainly superior to that of your workman."[15]

After insisting the cabinetmaker exchange the worst card table for a better one, Madison advised Monroe to accept the other objects rather than risk legal action. If Mrs. Monroe was still unhappy, he could always "dispose of them . . . and send us a commission to replace them. I think we can please you both; and on terms not dearer than those of your purchase." In this case, the very subjective question of what constituted quality was resolved through comparison of different cabinetmakers' products, negotiation between individual patrons and artisans, and by the consensus of interested consumers. That the "vile" furniture failed to please, despite its maker having competently executed the requested design, suggests the main defect was with his choice of materials. The cabinetmaker's defensive comment that mahogany appeared "worst when new" seems akin to the "trust me" assurances of a shady used-car salesman. High-quality mahogany, like a fine wine, might improve with age and polishing, achieving a richer color and sensual depths, but to suggest that a patina would eventually rectify the appearance of mahogany that was inferior from the outset was at best disingenuous. This painful experience stood the Monroes in good stead, however, because they became more educated consumers. In 1817, after several years as ambassador to France, James Monroe became President of the United States. Elizabeth made a splash the next year by updating the White House in the bombastic new Napoleonic (or Empire) style that she had admired in Paris—combining American-made mahogany furnishings with flamboyant French chairs topped with gilded eagles. This time, however, she enjoyed the luxury of spending someone else's money, since Congress appropriated the then exorbitant sum of $20,000 for her redecorating project.[16]

Changing Mahogany Sources

Following the American Revolution, there was a renewed influx to North America of *Swietenia mahagoni,* coming this time from two key islands: Spanish Cuba and Hispaniola, which was divided between French St. Domingue (now Haiti) and Spanish Santo Domingo (now the Dominican Republic). Although cabinetmakers debated the relative merits of these islands' mahogany, the size and quality of timber each one exported varied according to localized growing conditions, the logging methods used, and the available modes of transport. Some mahogany from both islands had arrived in American seaports previously, mostly through smuggling, privateering, or, in the case of Cuba, through a flurry of trade over the course of Britain's ten-month occupation of Havana during the Seven Years War. More substantial exports became possible only after France and Spain liberalized their colonial trade policies in the last quarter of the eighteenth century.

Mahogany from St. Domingue was the first of the newly available sources of West Indian mahogany to make a major impression on the American marketplace after France opened its ports to free trade in 1784. Although by then already the world's leading sugar producer, it retained significant forests, mainly in the east-central part of the colony, especially along the mountainous frontier with the Spanish side of the island. The French in St. Domingue had long used mahogany for their furnishings and exported significant quantities to Paris. But even more than on Jamaica, local planters were focused on developing their plantations. Stephen Girard, a French émigré who had lived in St. Domingue and had quietly maintained his contacts there after moving to Philadelphia, jumped at the opportunity to begin importing mahogany as well as large quantities of sugar and coffee from the island. Other Americans followed suit, and for a brief period, St. Domingue seemed poised to blossom into a major trading partner with the United States. This propitious but still fledgling relationship was disrupted, however, when violent slave uprisings and then a full-on revolution burned across St. Domingue, eventually engulfing much of Hispaniola. As vying imperial armies and slave insurgents battled it out across the island, trade and production came to a near halt. By the end of the conflagration, the entire infrastructure of the plantation system was destroyed.[17]

In an amazing rout, the former slaves at last seized power and declared independence, making Haiti the world's first free black republic. As the smoke cleared, Jean-Jacques Dessalines, Haiti's authoritarian new leader, faced the enormous task of raising the country up from the ashes. After declaring himself emperor in 1804, one of his first objectives was to restore the plantation system by forcing workers back to the sugar fields, but the former slaves understandably resisted. Instead they turned to subsistence farming or independent wood-cutting, autonomous modes of existence that some historians have characterized as a neo-peasantry that drew on African and European influences. Since most of the forests were in the mountainous interior, former slaves, working on their own or in small groups, usually could extract only a few logs at a time, hand-carrying them out of the forest. When this trickle of timber made its way to Port-au-Prince for eventual sale and export, the men who actually wielded the axes likely made little on the transaction. Nonetheless, as the only valuable commodity or product to which they had access, mahogany was a vital lifeline.

Unfortunately, for the same reason, access to the island's mahogany became the object of a major power struggle between the state, desperate for revenues, and the citizenry, desperate for mere survival. Recognizing the untapped potential of the island's forests, Dessalines was very interested in initiating large-scale commercial mahogany production, but that was impossible until he could organize logging gangs and acquire large numbers of oxen. In the meanwhile, to preserve the mahogany, he banned timber exports and prohibited further independent woodcutting. When merchants and woodcutters flouted the law, he burned all their wood stocks. After these and other more serious provocations, Dessalines was overthrown. But there continued to be an ongoing tug-of-war over control of the mahogany trees among subsequent rulers, landowners, and former slaves. Some mahogany still continued to be exported, but since the United States refused to recognize Haiti's nationhood, most of the timber exported from Haiti during the first quarter of the nineteenth century was sent to France.[18]

Meanwhile, in Santo Domingo, on the eastern side of the island, the situation was even worse. Years of slave uprisings, warfare, and repeated occupations by various imperial powers had scoured the land, which was already less populated and less developed than the

western half. Cattle ranching and mahogany cutting, although much
diminished, were the only economic activities. During the years of
conflict, mahogany was sought after by all the warring parties; when
France occupied the whole island from 1804 to 1808, for example, colonial officials planned to cement their political control by filling their
coffers with earnings from mahogany exports. At the same time, Don
Juan Sánchez Ramírez, a Dominican who before the years of war
had made a fortune on mahogany and cattle, financed local resistance
against France by smuggling mahogany to Puerto Rico. When his
scrappy forces, with help from the British, ousted the French in 1808,
Ramírez subsidized his new government by requisitioning all the mahogany and curtailing independent woodcutting. Consequently, the
trees that were readily accessible along the island's few navigable waterways were quickly exhausted. Those that remained were in hard-to-
reach places, especially along the contested border between Haiti and
Santo Domingo. Extracting the remaining mahogany from this rugged
frontier was exceedingly difficult. Woodcutters thus often resorted to
hacking big logs into smaller pieces that could be hand-carried down
the steepest slopes or packed out on mules. According to a later traveler's
account, it was "no uncommon sight to see, in the woods or on the road,
trains of these diminutive animals each with a small square piece of
mahogany in the straw panniers carried on each side." Although workers cut up the mahogany out of necessity, in the process they destroyed much of its potential value. Except for pieces with exceptionally
fine-figured grain, which were desirable even in tiny pieces as veneers,
the price of mahogany was often in direct proportion to its size—the
smaller the timber, the less it was worth.[19]

Rather than deal with the continued social upheavals and political
turmoil on Hispaniola, many American merchants, including Stephen
Girard and the Rhode Island slave trader James DeWolf, redirected
their vessels and their economic ambitions to Cuba. The largest island
in the Caribbean, it was richly endowed with natural resources, in-

cluding rich forests. With the elimination of smoldering Hispaniola as a competitor, Cuba's sugar plantations rapidly expanded, resulting in a major economic boom. Unable to supply its colonies while at war with England, Spain had reluctantly opened Havana and other key ports to neutral ships in 1797. As flocks of American sails alighted alongside their wharves, Cuba's free Creole population was more than eager to acquire the incoming cargos of foodstuffs, manufactured goods, and slaves and to send off their sugar, rum, and mahogany to expanding northern markets.[20]

The main reason so many mahogany trees remained on Cuba in the late eighteenth century was due to the Spanish Crown's long-standing restrictions on logging, designed to bolster its imperial supremacy by reserving many forest tracts for the exclusive use of the Royal Navy. Vast quantities of Cuban mahogany, cedar, and other woods had gone to build warships and to benefit the Royal Treasury, but everyone else (including private landowners) was prohibited from cutting down trees without a government-issued license. Along the southern coast, however, landowners did smuggle some clandestinely-cut mahogany to nearby Jamaica (where it was likely relabeled "Jamaica wood" for sale in England and the United States). Cuban settlers deeply resented the Crown's restrictive policy because it not only hindered their timber exports, it severely retarded their ability to clear land for agricultural expansion. It had, however, effectively preserved much of Cuba's expansive forests; in the late eighteenth century, little deforestation was evident except in the heavily settled urban area around Havana. In the 1790s, however, reform-minded members of Cuba's Creole elite began to push for both liberalization of the timber regulations and for greater innovation in the island's sugar industry. In particular, they emphasized the need for scientific and technological improvements to tackle what they saw as the island's backwardness and deep-seated inefficiencies. Mahogany production was a case in point since, even when a logging license could be procured, there were few sawmills and

inadequate roads. Whole logs could only be transported via a few rapidly flowing rivers but, in the process, much timber sank, got mired in
mud, or was washed out to sea. In years when seasonal rains were
meager and the rivers remained low, large logs moldered away on the
ground. A later account estimated this "absurd method" succeeded in
bringing only a fraction of the merchantable timber that was felled to
market.[21]

In 1815, the Spanish king was persuaded to "put his seal on the royal
edict giving private property owners the perpetual right to fell their
trees with complete freedom." In short order, Cuba went from having
the most rigid forest regulations in the Caribbean to having none at
all. Cuban landowners who expected, at long last, to profit from their
timber holdings were annoyed when American ships saturated the local
market with North American pine and oak, while taking "from our own
forests the wood that they then sell us manufactured." In the decade after the Haitian Revolution, as Cuba's sugar industry boomed, many of its
planters, flush with new wealth, did indeed import fine furniture made
in the United States. Several exquisite mahogany tables, for example,
survive in Cuba that are attributed to Charles-Honoré Lannuier, the illustrious Parisian émigré who was New York City's most fashionable
cabinetmaker at the time and who very likely used Cuban mahogany.
Nevertheless, the United States offered such a large market that it became an important outlet for Cuban planters as well, many of whom
used the proceeds from their timber to update their sugar works and to
expand their slave holdings. With more labor and greater productive
capacity, they cleared vast areas of forest and doubled sugar exports in
little more than a decade. Whereas previously on other islands, such
rapid development resulted in much timber being wasted—burned or
left to rot in the fields—this was not the case in Cuba because there was
already an established market for West Indian mahogany.[22]

For mahogany buyers on the receiving end in the United States or
Europe, it was not always clear where exactly this new influx of West

Indian mahogany originated. To many people, it did not much matter, except insofar as various place names connoted levels of quality. "St. Domingo wood," for example, gained a reputation for excellence and deservedly so. Much of this wood, harvested in mountainous areas, was hard and dense with vivid colors and figures that rivaled Jamaica's best. Cuban mahogany initially was regarded as inferior to this new favorite even though it had many of the same characteristics. Given that black-market Cuban mahogany had previously infiltrated the Jamaican timber market, such prejudices had little foundation in reality. Another more legitimate complaint was that incoming shipments of West Indian mahogany were often comprised mainly of unsatisfactorily small logs, to the extent that when large ones did come to market they fetched extraordinarily high prices. From the outset, this generation of island mahogany was considered useful mainly for veneering wherein small pieces could be joined together.[23]

Despite this limitation, government officials in Haiti and Santo Domingo were determined to strengthen their tropical timber exports. Mahogany, and the revenues it would generate, were key to their dreams of rebuilding their nations' devastated economies in the wake of the Haitian Revolution. They resolved to invest in the infrastructure that commercial logging required and, through coercion if necessary, to revive a structured labor regime. In Cuba, by contrast, the mahogany trade was increasingly in the hands of self-interested planters who, although mainly focused on increasing sugar production, recognized the island's precious timber resources as a means of jump-starting Cuba's modernization. Eventually, Cuban mahogany came to dominate the world market and its reputation was elevated within the pantheon of mahogany until it surpassed all other sources. To achieve that goal, however, Cuba too needed to improve its infrastructure in order to increase production and extract larger trees.

Meanwhile, Honduran mahogany, long regarded as a secondary wood suitable mainly for hidden structural elements, began to be considered as a show-worthy primary wood in its own right. Its impressively large sizes also made it the only option for many large-scale woodworking projects. Long over-shadowed in the marketplace by Jamaican mahogany, its particular qualities began to be more appreciated, like the plainer of two sisters who shines more brightly when on her own.

Consequently, in the Bay of Honduras, mahogany extraction intensified after 1798 when Britain seized Belize from Spain allowing the Baymen to push their slaves far beyond the old treaty boundaries where untapped mahogany remained abundant. With the use of multiple teams of long-horned oxen, acquired from adjacent Spanish settlements, the distance that the great logs could be hauled increased from half a mile, with mere manpower, to an average of ten miles. But the woodcutters still relied on the annual rains to flood the waterways so logs could be floated out of the forest, which limited them to a seasonal logging schedule.

In the years immediately after the American Revolution, Britain attempted to exclude American ships from the Bay to ensure that Honduran mahogany was sent directly to England. But that policy proved impossible to enforce in the face of growing demand for Honduran mahogany in the United States. Although the war disrupted some long-standing trade relationships, as happened with the Card family, other Americans soon found their way to the Bay of Honduras, although their ships were generally smaller than their English counterparts. William Rysam, a merchant from Sag Harbor, New York, even acquired his own mahogany works. In 1794, he ordered a set of nine solid mahogany Windsor chairs from Nathaniel Dominy, Jr., whose family ran a successful clock and cabinetmaking business in East Hampton on Long Island. Signed and dated by their maker, these chairs were almost certainly made from Rysam's own trees. In 1798, Rysam placed an order for a "double geared sawmill" from Dominy, who had fabricated many of the windmills on Eastern Long Island. After testing its works in the

Atlantic breezes, Dominy dismantled the structure and its machinery and shipped the whole lot to "the Bay of Honduras to saw mahogany" aboard Rysam's 200-ton brig *Merchant*. With this new power source, the workers at his mahogany works could transform unwieldy logs into more manageable boards on site for ease of transport. Rysam's investment in this technology would have given him a significant competitive edge over other woodcutters in the Bay as well as over other North American merchants interested in mahogany.[24]

New Modes of Mahogany Distribution

As mahogany from multiple sources permeated the American market, the way in which it was distributed changed during the last quarter of the eighteenth century. During this period, as David Hancock has argued, the proliferation of more specialized commercial services had an immense effect on the distribution of almost all consumer goods. In the case of wine, he traces a shift away from general dry goods merchants (who imported wine, along with many other goods, for resale to lesser wholesalers, storekeepers, tavern owners, and individuals) to a more organized, narrowly-focused system of wine importers who sold only wine but offered a larger, more diverse selection. Many merchants on the Eastern Seaboard continued to handle mahogany periodically alongside other goods, such as Henry Drinker who in 1791, sold 1,127 feet of Bay mahogany to cabinetmaker Daniel Trotter. Around the same time, Stephen Girard sold Trotter a load of Cuban mahogany. In both cases, Trotter bought whole logs and then hired local sawyers to cut them into planks. As with wine, however, the timber trade, and mahogany dealing in particular, were becoming increasingly specialized. While some merchants focused more on the timber trade, they faced growing competition from another group of men who already possessed considerable knowledge and experience in judging wood—namely, cabinetmakers.

Cabinetmakers' dissatisfaction with relying on merchants to meet their timber needs or to profit from them was exemplified by an initiative in Salem, Massachusetts by furniture makers to coordinate their timber buying in the 1790s. A vibrant seaport at the time, Salem boasted over twenty cabinetmaking workshops that turned out large quantities of fine furniture, most of which was destined for export. Wherever outbound ships were headed, Salem-made mahogany furniture was sent, from the Carolinas and Surinam to the East Indies. Finding themselves each at the mercy of the powerful merchant class to supply their wood and ship their manufactures, however, the cabinetmakers agreed to collaborate in order to cut their costs for raw materials and shipping. In 1795, several of them went in together on a large bulk order of mahogany logs and shared in the cost of having it sawed into planks; the next year, they acquired a ship. In 1801, they formed a society to fix prices and manage labor disputes. This initiative proved short lived, however, because as Dean Lahikainen has argued, the cabinetmakers' unity was undermined by both internal and external competition. By 1803, when a group of nine cabinetmakers shipped fifty cases of mahogany furniture to Brazil, their arrangement was unraveling as individual participants secretly sought to undersell the others.[25]

More typically, as the furniture-making industry shifted towards more modular modes of production, the larger cabinetmaking firms, especially those in urban areas, stockpiled larger and larger quantities of precut lumber for use by their journeymen and subcontractors. When they began re-selling stock as well to other cabinetmakers, joiners, and carpenters, dealing in timber became a natural extension of their business model. Large lumberyards sprang up offering an enormous selection of wood, including mahogany from a variety of places. For their customers, especially smaller cabinetmaking shops that lacked either storage space or capital for large outlays on materials, relying on large timber wholesalers allowed them to buy seasoned wood on an as-needed basis. Economical, efficient, and convenient, this new approach also reduced cabinetmakers' risks because they could readily inspect wood before laying out any money.

Alongside his Philadelphia cabinetmaking shop, for example, Samuel Williams ran a "joiners board-yard" in the 1770s. From his convenient location near Market Street, he offered a variety of seasoned lumber including ready-to-use furniture parts in mahogany and walnut, such as pre-cut coffin boards, tea table columns, and pieces "suitable for chair-making or gun stocks." In 1774, New York cabinetmaker Thomas Burling announced the opening of "a yard of all kinds of stuff for country Joiners." He advertised both furniture "of the best mahogany, which he proposes to sell at the lowest rate good work sells at" and seasoned mahogany wood, "ready sawed, fit for carpenters in staircase building and all other kinds of stuff suitable for . . . the joiners business." In 1804, Elbert Anderson likewise sought to expand from New York City to a broader regional clientele by advertising, "Wood of every description suitable for city and country Cabinet Makers, viz. Mahogany in Boards and Planks; ditto in Veniers [sic]." Their attention to serving rural markets reflects the growing demand for mahogany even remote from the metropolitan style centers of the major port cities. In 1801, Julius Barnard, a New Hampshire cabinetmaker, offered both local woods (like cherry) and imported mahogany but, as he warned a customer, if the latter was desired, he would "need time to get it from Boston."[26]

After circa 1785, "mahogany dealers" began to appear in many city directories, along with other tradesmen, lumber dealers, and merchants, indicating the emergence of a new category of luxury wood imports handled apart from the more generalized timber trade. As this niche market developed, some cabinetmakers, taking advantage of their wood expertise, made mahogany sales their main business and a number of them gave up furniture making altogether. In 1801, Andrew Gifford, for example, advertised: "Mahogany. The Subscriber has on Hand, Sixty Logs, of the first quality. He intends dealing in this article alone, and to have always on hand an assortment (ready sawed) to suit all purposes, at his Yard . . . in Greenwich-street. Logs can be floated to and from his Yard." Others opened mahogany yards that remained closely affiliated with established cabinetmakers. Michael Phyfe, the youngest son of the famous cabinetmaker Duncan Phyfe, branched off from his family's successful furniture-making business to run a mahogany yard. George Allison, the son of Michael Allison, one of Phyfe's main competitors, did the same (although he handled other types of woods as well). Both young men apprenticed as cabinetmakers before launching their own semi-independent careers, riding the coattails of their fathers' established reputations and drawing on wood identification skills learned at their fathers' knees.[27]

As the tropical timber distribution system became more specialized, mahogany dealers needed ever more expertise because of the complexity of their main product. The range of quality and sizes was becoming both more varied and more unpredictable, especially with regard to the bewildering proliferation of geographical labels. In 1793, for example, Samuel Williams offered some Jamaican mahogany as well as Bay, and "Providence" (Bahamian) mahogany for sale in Philadelphia. Each of these different types of mahogany fetched a different price, suggesting their relative popularity and availability at the time, while especially choice wood of any kind could command premium prices. In 1798, the price current in Boston and New York listed Bay mahogany at ten shillings per foot while Santo Domingo mahogany (a term used generically for any mahogany from Hispaniola) was twelve shillings per foot. In addition, mahogany dealers oversaw all aspects of processing their raw material before it was saleable—from seasoning the wood to sawing logs into planks, precutting standardized lumber, and hand slicing veneers. Most used a combination of in-house labor and subcontractors, such as sawmills and professional sawyers, all of whom were experienced specifically in handling mahogany; by 1829, the New York City directory listed eleven "mahogany yards," a "mahogany mill," and seven "mahogany sawyers."[28]

George Shipley offers a good example of an entrepreneur who developed both a more specialized approach and a larger economy of scale. From 1801 to 1803, Shipley's advertisements highlighted that he had "on hand a large stock of mahogany of the very first quality and the choicest of materials for manufacturing Cabinet Furniture." Conveniently situated in the heart of New York City's booming seaport, his cabinetmaking workshop and lumber yard occupied a building that stretched the block from Water Street to Front Street. It featured a furniture showroom, ample warehouse space, and a large gangway for moving furniture and materials in and out. Taking advantage of his proximity to the docks, he stockpiled enormous quantities of mahogany. In 1801, he offered 30,000 feet of Santo Domingo and Honduran mahogany for sale "in logs of the first quality, to be sold very low for cash or approved notes, at a short date; also a large quantity of seasoned plank . . . and verniers, all of which will be sold very low." Thomas Burling and Sons likewise expanded their lumber business, long ancillary to their well-established cabinetmaking shop, into a large, specialized "Mahogany-yard." In 1802, the firm advertised the availability of "St. Domingo, Cuba, Bay Mahogany, in Logs, Plank, and Boards." Notably absent from the list was the now increasingly rare Jamaican mahogany.[29]

In their newspaper advertisements, cabinetmakers and timber dealers also wreathed their offerings of timber for sale in reassurances of quality. In 1805, Elbert Anderson advertised "sixty logs of an excellent quality and very sound St. Domingo mahogany for sale." When the New York firm of W. F. Pell and Co. advertised the sale of a mahogany shipment in 1811, they specifically reassured customers that "a competent judge was sent from this place, and employed six months in the woods of St. Domingo, selecting the most approved sticks." The

advertisements of I. M. M. Labatut, another New York cabinetmaker-
turned-mahogany dealer, likewise emphasized his firm's care in selecting mahogany. In March 1809, he advertised "about 25,000 feet
choice St. Domingo Mahogany, allowed by the best judges to be of a
very superior quality, and best in the city." In June, he advertised
"40,000 feet, choice and very large St. Domingo Mahogany of superior
quality, picked out of different cargoes for exportation." While official
wood measurers would have evaluated and graded incoming mahogany, Labatut most likely saw himself and his trusted journeymen as the
best judges of superior quality. In 1819, when Charles-Honoré Lannuier
died in New York, Labatut served as his executor. As might be expected
of a cabinetmaking outfit owned by an artisan of his stature, Lannuier
had accumulated a large store of fine mahogany which he drew on to
make his stylish neoclassical furniture. In addition to auctioning off the
completed furniture in Lannuier's shop, as well as a shipment recently
dispatched for sale in Cuba, Labatut sold off the stockpile of seasoned
mahogany. Other cabinetmakers were no doubt eager to buy timber
vetted by one of New York's finest workshops, which had an excellent
reputation for quality and whose exquisite creations had dazzled New
York society. Indeed, many of the objects marked with Lannuier's
name have stood the test of time and are still considered among the
finest furniture ever made in America.[30]

For those who could not get their hands on timber with such an illustrious provenance, however, mahogany must have seemed a slippery substance. Not coincidentally, as the sourcing of timber became
more complex during the early nineteenth century, furniture makers
began to label their manufactures more consistently, using paper labels,
brands, or ink signatures. With the exception of clock makers, few
American cabinetmakers prior to this period had bothered marking
their furniture unless it was intended for export. Increasingly, labels not
only identified who made an object and where but served also as a war-
ranty and a form of advertising. Labels reassured potential buyers that a

known fabricator stood behind a product and, of course, satisfied customers were more likely to purchase additional furniture.[31]

Cabinetmakers and mahogany dealers had to be constantly vigilant to keep up with the rapidly changing tropical timber market and to accurately judge the innumerable variables of what constituted quality in their raw materials. If this was difficult for experienced judges of wood, it proved even more daunting for novice furniture buyers. To fulfill their desire for mahogany, they could do their best to seek out a reputable cabinetmaker, but ultimately they had to trust that the timber buyers and craftsmen had done due diligence. In many cases, only time would tell the integrity of an object—whether the mahogany and other woods used were sound and well seasoned, the joints were tight and the structure solid, the veneers were correctly cut and properly adhered. In the meantime, customers warily handed over their money, held onto their warranties, and hoped for the best. In the forty years since Franklin complained that there was "a great deal of difference in woods that go under that name," the challenges of defining mahogany had only become more formidable.

CHAPTER SEVEN

Mastering Nature and the Challenge of Mahogany

*U*PON FIRST ENCOUNTERING the massive mahoganies of the West Indies, Europeans, awed by their primeval appearance, speculated wildly about their possible age. Although no one was quite certain, it seemed self-evident that their lives must span hundreds if not thousands of years, far exceeding human memory or imagination. Attempting to cultivate such trees seemed ludicrous, sheer hubris in the face of God's wondrous creation. In 1708, John Oldmixon, although worried that tropical deforestation posed a serious problem for the British Empire, concluded that "the time required for the growing of those hard Woods, in the room of such as are cut down, is . . . so many Hundreds of Years, that . . . proposing to plant them, would be rather a proof of Madness than Foresight." Most West Indian planters agreed; fixated on immediate, short-term gains, they were loath to divert their slaves from the cane fields to nurture slow-growing trees.[1]

By the latter half of the eighteenth century, however, such views changed in some quarters as deforestation gained the upper hand on many Caribbean islands. In particular, the depletion of West Indian mahogany on Jamaica and elsewhere, as well as the proliferating conflicts over remaining supplies, raised concerns about the future of this important line of trade and gave new impetus to the idea of growing replacement trees. In 1756, Patrick Browne reprimanded Jamaican planters for the "destitute" state of the island's forests, emphasizing that mahogany's scarcity was "not to be admired," nor that "the culture of the tree has been so wholly neglected." He concluded, "It is a pity that it is not cultivated in the more convenient waste lands of that Island." While conceding "the difficulty to conjecture the age of some of these trees . . . [that did] not attain to their full growth and dimensions in less than a century," Edward Long in 1774 likewise urged Jamaican planters to establish nurseries or plantations of the increasingly scarce and expensive trees to "produce a future fortune for their younger children." Attempting to grow mahogany no longer seemed delusional but eminently reasonable; indeed, possibly the *only* alternative to heightening conflicts, future shortages, and the trees' ultimate extinction. Faced with such dire prospects, people began to recalibrate their deeply subjective perceptions of time. If wild mahogany could be transformed into a plantation-grown commodity (as had been done successfully with other valuable species), a reliable, renewable supply would at last be guaranteed in less-contentious places under British colonial rule, either within the trees' native range or beyond. As the oldest mahogany trees disappeared, cabinetmakers grudgingly adapted their furniture designs to the reduced wood dimensions of more juvenile trees—perhaps a mere eighty to a hundred years old—a foreshortened timeline that made cultivation seem still more feasible. Clearly, in the decades since Oldmixon's pessimistic pronouncement, the distance between madness and foresight narrowed considerably.[2]

Serious efforts to learn about the natural history of West Indian (and later Honduran) mahogany thus began only decades *after* it was well established as an important article of commerce. By then, planters, woodcutters, ship captains, merchants, and cabinetmakers all claimed knowledge of mahogany based on their own experiences with it. Planters and woodcutters, and more aptly their slaves, learned to identify and extricate the trees from amidst dense forests; ship captains and

merchants learned to evaluate and select merchantable logs, albeit
still with much trial and error; cabinetmakers, in turn, gained profi-
ciency with manipulating mahogany's dense fibers to achieve pleasing
results. But like the proverbial blind men describing an elephant, their
discreet spheres of expertise were circumscribed, fragmentary, and
colored by their various expectations and assumptions about mahogany as a commodity and as a raw material. None of their respective
slices of know-how were particularly helpful, however, in understanding the trees as living organisms.

In his history of Jamaica, first published in Edinburgh in 1739,
Charles Leslie asserted that the "Mahogany-tree is so well known, that
I need not describe it." While his readers may certainly have been familiar with the wood by then, accurate information about the actual
trees—such as their modes of reproduction, growth patterns, and preferred growing conditions—was, in fact, quite limited. Investigations
into the natural history of New World mahoganies made slow, incremental progress—from the first formal description and botanical illustration of West Indian mahogany by a professional naturalist, completed by Marc Catesby in 1725, to the formal classifications of New
World mahoganies as separate species and the assignment of their official Latin names, thirty-five years later in the case of West Indian
mahogany and over 160 years later in the case of Honduran mahogany. Additional research and experimentation meanwhile focused on
studying their respective life cycles and preferred habitats—a term first
coined in 1762 to connote a species' "natural place of growth"—with an
eye toward cultivating them in a variety of settings. In spite of these
knowledge production efforts, however, most would-be growers continued to be confounded by the trees' complexity as repeated attempts
to plant them proved less than fruitful. Consequently, efforts were also
directed towards discovering viable mahogany substitutes, using other
kinds of trees or wood treatments that were faster, easier, and cheaper
to grow or manufacture than the genuine article. Meanwhile, the long,

frustrating struggle to unlock the secrets of mahogany growing revealed the limits of man's ability to master nature.[3]

The burgeoning interest in mahogany's natural history must be understood within the larger context of the Enlightenment. This philosophical movement, which had its roots in the sixteenth century but blossomed in the eighteenth century, emphasized knowledge production as both a virtue in its own right to elevate mankind and as a means toward an end—namely controlling, manipulating, and improving the natural world. During this period, the study of natural history developed into a vibrant realm of intellectual inquiry and exchange of information about the properties and potential uses of unfamiliar flora and fauna. At the same time, this growing body of knowledge was recognized as a matter of major strategic importance by European imperial powers jockeying for international supremacy; accurate intelligence was vital to their schemes of exploiting the natural resources of colonized areas and of dominating the world. To comprehend an expanding natural world that seemed bewilderingly profuse and chaotic, they sought to compile a comprehensive catalog of all the marvelous plants and creatures that European explorers were discovering, especially in the Americas and the Far East. By observing, collecting, illustrating, dissecting, naming, and organizing endless specimens, naturalists attempted to organize each new type into a logical, systematic taxonomy of life forms. Although this process gave rise to differing ideas about the shape of nature's family tree, their shared goal was "to stabilize and naturalize a network of power relationships through particular forms of classification and representation."[4]

In France, the Netherlands, Spain, and Britain, government agencies, private trading companies, and scientific organizations financed efforts to investigate, cultivate, and redistribute valuable species across their colonial spheres. Medals, monetary prizes, and other incentives were offered to encourage investigation and innovation in natural history, horticulture, silviculture, and scientific agriculture. Faced with severe deforestation on Martinique, the French took an early lead in developing and applying more sustainable forestry methods in their West Indian colonies, including selective logging and replanting. They also established the first botanical garden in the Caribbean which was dedicated to researching tropical agriculture. The Dutch likewise encouraged the development of horticultural expertise and were instrumental in transferring the cultivation of precious spices from the East to the West Indies. In England and its colonies, a diverse group of people—including amateur and professional naturalists, physicians, private investors, progressive planters, military men, and government officials—supported or participated in various natural history pursuits. Among their number were members of the Royal Society of London for Improving Natural Knowledge (officially founded in 1660), which during this period emerged as one of the world's foremost promoters of scientific investigation and an influential promulgator of new knowledge. Through its library, lectures, and publications, the Society compiled and disseminated all manner of new research, including in the arena of natural history. Whether motivated primarily by intellectual curiosity, economic self-interest, or national chauvinism, those involved in natural history investigations, whether directly or indirectly, largely shared the belief that learning more about the colonies' natural assets would enhance Britain's wealth, power, and influence.[5]

Thanks in part to such initiatives, many notable advances were made in botany, horticulture, and scientific agriculture, adding significantly to Europeans' growing encyclopedia of natural knowledge. Compelling accounts of these learning efforts appeared in newspapers, private correspondence, and official colonial reports that circulated widely within England and its colonies. Innovative sugar planters, for example, tested different cane varieties, fertilizers, and cultivation methods to reduce the detrimental aspects of growing cane. Others experimented with domesticating other novel species, both native and introduced, on their plantations in hopes of finding new sources of profit. Many optimistically anticipated that, with enough investigation and experimentation, *any* tree or plant could be induced to produce more abundantly, more efficiently, and more conveniently—with the added benefit of allowing planters to diversify away from their mono-cultural emphasis on sugar. An impressive array of tropical trees and plants, once found only in limited quantities in the wild, were indeed converted into economically important, mass-produced staple crops. During the eighteenth century, the rate and extent of transplanting and naturalizing flora increased exponentially as thousands of species were transferred far beyond their originally circumscribed native ranges. Continuing a trend that began with the very first European encounters with the New World, this Columbian Exchange resulted in the unprecedented global movement of flora and fauna.[6]

Some critics of this phenomenon objected that England would be better served by centering natural history investigations closer to home in order to regain national self-sufficiency by weaning the pop-ulace from its growing dependence on imported commodities. In 1758, Reverend William Hanbury, for one, called on his countrymen to use only English trees as a matter of patriotism, national security, and moral good, noting there was no "more genteel" or "more rational Amusement" for gentlemen than tree planting. While proffering his own nursery stock for sale, he touted his lovingly tended trees as more virtuous than wild ones because "as with Men; care and culture refine both. The Nursery is a Sort of Education and the Tree transplanted from thence" will exceed all others. His stubborn insistence on native stock, at a time when imported mahogany was the height of fashion in England, was decidedly out of step with popular opinion. Most Brit-ish people, especially those involved in pursuing, sponsoring, or pro-moting natural history investigations, saw extending knowledge pro-duction abroad as essential to the nation's future. Moreover, they believed that, with sufficient "care and culture"—not just at home but around the world—everything from wild trees to savage peoples could be tamed, harnessed, and improved in the service of Empire.[7]

In the British West Indies, the urgency to subdue untamed jungles into restrained, well-ordered agricultural landscapes, as well as to domesticate wild trees and plants into managed cultivars, reflected the continued deep ambivalence that many Englishmen had long harbored towards nature in the tropics. In the mid-eighteenth century, this sentiment was still influenced by discussions about tropical forests' possible effects on human health, climate, and natural environments. Charles Leslie, for example, claimed that Jamaica's rainfall had declined due "to the cutting of the Woods . . . [that] retained large Quantities of Vapours . . . [which] diffused in Dews and Showers." Yet he still exhorted against the abundant acreage that remained "overgrown with Woods and Shrubs, of no manner of Use, but to afford a sure Shelter to the Runaways." Most West Indian planters agreed that reducing wilderness was a net positive since cleared land had more productive potential, as well as facilitating the control of slaves. Although a few voices advocated tree conservation and managed forestry, such as on Tobago, most held fast to the dominant belief that the road to sustainable wealth in the West Indies required clearing as much land as possible for plantation agriculture.[8]

As some valuable trees consequently became scarce in the wild, the first attempts to cultivate them on plantations were made during the late seventeenth and early eighteenth centuries, although not yet the largest hardwoods like mahogany. On Jamaica, for example, the accomplished naturalist Hans Sloane observed in 1687 that because nearly all the fustic trees ("one of the Commodities this Island naturally affords") had been cut down for use as a dye, a few landowners had begun replanting them "for Shade in their clear'd Fields . . . and [to] make Profit of the Wood." This fast-growing species could be harvested for use in as little as seven years. On Barbados, Richard Ligon reported that settlers were also cultivating fast-growing native species but adapting them to traditional English hedging practices to fence their fields. Slaves collected seeds or seedlings from the wild, planted them close together in straight lines, and then pruned them into wall-like shapes as they grew. Ligon admired the pleasing effect produced by a physick nut hedge, which although only four years old, was eighteen feet high and resembled "so much green Sattin hang'd on a rail or line." By the early eighteenth century, many West Indian islands were crisscrossed by these living architectural features. By manipulating the indigenous flora in such ways, settlers transformed what they perceived as alien, hostile wilderness into more familiar, wholesome, and unthreatening pastoral landscapes.[9]

Two indigenous American species—pimento (or allspice) and logwood—were initially presumed to be prototypical for mahogany cultivation because they were endemic to the same geographical regions and climate zones as Honduran mahogany. Both pimento and logwood verged on extinction in the late seventeenth century due to overharvesting by Europeans, only to be transformed into highly productive staple crops during the mid-eighteenth century. Eventually it became clear, however, that they were not very useful exemplars where mahogany was concerned because they required completely different cultivation methods.

Tiny pimento berries, described as "very aromatical, and of a curious gusto, having a mixt taste of diverse Spices," gained favor with Europeans for culinary uses; Jamaica's earlier Spanish occupants had "set a high esteem thereon, and exported it as a very choice commodity." While the spice was available "in great plenty, wild in the mountains" when the English took over the island, it was common practice for planters to "go with their Slaves into the Woods, where 'tis plenty, and cutting down the Trees, pick it off the branches. Thus no Pimentoe comes into Europe twice from one Tree." Not surprisingly, pimento quickly became extremely scarce, which in Oldmixon's words meant that it could not be "rely'd upon as a National Advantage." This unwelcome fact put tremendous pressure on planters to preserve the trees or grow replacements. Planters tried several incremental approaches to isolate pimento from the wild, but they could not figure out how to grow it from seed. Some regarded it as "purely a child of nature . . . mock[ing] all the labors of man, in his efforts to extend or improve its growth." Pimento plantations, or "walks" as they were called on Jamaica, had become common by the 1750s, but they were all established by either selectively clearing forest patches to leave only the pimento or by transplanting wild pimento seedlings from surrounding forests into segregated plots. In 1774, Edward Long still feared pimento would be "soon exhausted . . . without hopes of replanting . . . [although] the visible scarcity of the trees taught the settlers a better economy, by gathering the berries, without felling them." Fortunately, shortly thereafter, planters figured out that the seeds had to be fermented before planting—just as in nature, the forest birds softened the berries in their stomachs and then dispersed the digested seeds through their droppings. With this breakthrough, pimento at last became a viable staple crop; by the early nineteenth century, most Jamaican plantations produced some quantities of it for export.[10]

In the case of logwood, its transformation into a plantation-grown commodity was widely credited to one individual—Henry Barham, an intellectually rigorous English doctor who lived on Jamaica and took a great interest in studying and experimenting with the island's native flora. Determined to overcome Britain's intractable difficulties securing logwood from Spanish territories (especially since it was also nearly depleted in many places), Barham later recalled, "I had an Indian slave . . . sent down to the Bay of Campeche to cut logwood, whom I ordered to send me up some of the seed of it, which he did." Barham often credited Indians and African slaves who assisted him. In another instance, after a carpenter showed him an unusual wood, Barham reported that he sent a "negro that I employed to get some of it, [who] when he brought it to me, said the same sort grew with them in Africa where they called it *columba*." Likewise, when a local doctor refused to share the source of a medicinal bark, Barham learned from "a Negro that used to gather it for him, what tree it was." In the case of logwood, Barham probably figured that sending an Indian worker to sneak the seeds out of Spanish territory would be least apt to arouse suspicion.[11]

As these examples attest, Native Americans and enslaved Africans, while ostensibly the recipients of European efforts at improvement and control, actually served as invaluable (if not necessarily voluntary) teachers, guides, and informants in Europeans' learning process, proffering information about plants and the natural environment derived from their own experiences, traditions, or beliefs. In many cases, they also provided much of the necessary labor to undertake natural history explorations, investigations, and experiments. While some European beneficiaries of such assistance simply appropriated Indian and African expertise and labor without acknowledgment, others, such as Barham, readily credited them, sometimes to enhance their own credibility through the supposed veracity and authenticity of their informants. With the assistance of the Indian spy who smuggled out the precious seeds and the enslaved Africans who planted and tended them, Barham found that logwood grew "admirably well, even in the worst of the lands; so that there are now seed-bearing trees enough to stock the whole island." Logwood hedges, "so thick and prickly that nothing can pass through them . . . [and so] evergreen, you can hardly see through them," became a familiar sight.[12]

Barham's "care in bringing over the Seed" was hailed by Hans Sloane and others as a great achievement of national significance because all conflicts over logwood would "for the future be prevented." When Mark Catesby later observed logwood cultivation on the Bahamas, he too emphasized that it alleviated "bloody Disputes which this useful Tree has occasioned" between the English and the Spanish. Another major benefit was that slaves no longer had to collect the dyewood from swamps and lagoons, which entailed "standing up to the knees in water, with the mosquitoes lancing and tearing their flesh, by which many thousands die." Now they just pruned the hedgerows, conveniently situated alongside roads and fields. But most advantageous was that this costly luxury item was suddenly transformed into an inexpensive, readily available commodity, which was a great boon to the English textile industry and to consumers. Logwood cultivation had a serious downside, however, for those who made their living collecting it from the wild or who grew it as their only staple crop. The increased supply contributed to its price collapse in the mid-1760s. Planters were forced to make up the difference through vastly increasing their volume of production. But many logwood cutters in the Bay of Honduras suffered financially, except for those who had accumulated enough capital to upgrade to mahogany logging by importing large numbers of enslaved Africans. Barham's pursuit of knowledge and his admirable intention of ending interimperial conflict thus inadvertently caused distress in the lives of many colonial subjects and contributed to the expansion of slavery.[13]

At least from the English metropolitan perspective, the positives were seen as outweighing the negatives. To encourage others to follow Barham's example, the Crown, the Royal Society for Improving Natural Knowledge, and the Royal Society for the Encouragement of Arts, Manufactures, and Commerce (founded in 1754 by William Shipley) offered incentives to stimulate new research towards similarly worthy goals. Under one government incentive plan, for example, Charles Price, a politically influential Jamaican planter, secured a 5,000-acre land grant by promising to grow logwood to further obviate England's "dependence on the troublesome Honduras Shore," although he never actually produced much and his true motive seemed to have been land speculation. In 1758, the Royal Society of Arts offered a prize to whoever planted "the greatest quantity of Logwood, in any of our plantations." On 7 February 1765, the *Maryland Gazette* reported, "Mr. Lloyd, an eminent Merchant in Georgia, has lately imported several Thousand Plants of the Logwood Trees from Honduras, in order for Cultivation on the River Savannah. Those already planted thrive well . . . [I]n a few years Great Britain may be supplied with this useful Dye from her own Colonies, in sufficient Quantities to answer all the Purposes of Manufacture." In 1785, Robert Pringle, a South Carolina planter who saw himself as part of a transnational circle of intellectuals, wrote to the Royal Society detailing his efforts in transplanting and growing logwood on his plantation.[14]

The fantastic turnarounds of pimento and logwood seemed proof that the reproductive and geographical limits of any rare and desirable tree or plant could be similarly overcome with enough knowledge and experimentation; scarcity of any wild flora (whether natural or man-made) was no longer an unavoidable fate but just another botanical puzzle to solve. Within this context, the dream of growing tropical hardwoods began to seem more attainable. As Edward Long reminded his readers, many valuable tropical plants might have been lost to Europeans "had not some knowledge in natural history revealed them." He and others hoped the same ingenuity would be applied to learn about and grow Jamaica's "most noble woods."[15]

Learning about Mahogany

To prepare for his American tree-finding mission, Pehr Kalm, Linnaeus's protégé, spent six months in London in 1747 at the Royal Society, reading in the extensive library, honing his language skills, and consulting with naturalists who had completed similar botanical surveys. One of his advisors was Mark Catesby, the first professional naturalist to explore parts of both North America and the Caribbean. Another personage Kalm would have been eager to meet was Hans Sloane, a regular fixture at the Royal Society, who published one of the first natural histories of the West Indies, after a fifteen month sojourn in Jamaica. Up until his death in 1753, Sloane continued to be an avid supporter of all kinds of natural history investigations. In fact, he was among the first to underwrite Catesby's expedition and he solicited additional support for the venture from his wealthy friends and Royal Society colleagues, including William Sherard, an avid collector of naturalia.

Whereas Kalm was well acquainted with mahogany objects, Catesby had actually encountered the living trees when he visited New Providence and several of the smaller islands of the Bahamas in 1725. Fascinated with the diverse flora and fauna, he painted images of colorful birds, vibrant tropical fish, and crustaceans, as well as many trees and plants. He devoted more time than he wished, however, to collecting natural curiosities to send home to his rather demanding sponsors who eagerly awaited his offerings; many of these specimens still survive, including those collected by Hans Sloane (now at the Natural History Museum in London) and William Sherard (now at Oxford University). During his travels, Catesby documented many botanical marvels for the first time, but he also observed that some of the most useful trees and plants were already "much exhausted." While he did not specifically mention mahogany among these early casualties of over-harvesting, he noted that its excellence "for all Domestik Uses is now sufficiently known in England" and that in the Bahamas and elsewhere it was preferred for shipbuilding, surpassing "Oak and all other Wood, viz. Durableness, resisting Gunshots, and burying the Shot without Splintering." For these very reasons, in fact, the trees already were disappearing from the Bahamas at an alarming rate.[16]

Upon first encountering the West Indian mahoganies, the islands' largest trees, he was duly impressed by their "stupendious" height and girth, which averaged four feet in diameter. More astounding was that they seemed to grow right out of the cliffs; in his words, "No one would imagine, that Trees of this Magnitude should grow on solid Rocks. . . ." In almost anthropomorphic terms, he described their fingerlike roots creeping along this unforgiving surface, insinuating themselves into tiny crevasses and scraping into hollows to find enough water and nourishment to support their enormous trunks and branches. Based on his limited observations, he surmised incorrectly that such rocky terrain was their sole habitat. On the other hand, his botanical illustration of the tree was quite accurate and beautifully rendered in his graceful, naturalistic style. The hand-tinted print, based on his original watercolor, depicts feathery pinnate leaves, oval seedpods (shown in various stages of maturation), and tiny, star-shaped flowers, which are all readily recognizable. Likewise, he carefully described the bark, leaves, flowers, and "the curious Structure of the Seed-Vessel," which was "a very hard smooth Cone, in Size and Form of a Goose's Egg" that opened when ripe to release winged seeds that were dispersed by the wind.[17]

After returning to England, Catesby spent many years preparing his work for publication, which required engraving all the plates of his paintings himself since he lacked funds to hire a professional engraver. *The Natural History of Carolina, Florida and the Bahama Islands* finally appeared in installments over several years and he presented a copy of each one to the Royal Society. Since his first volume was published just before Linnaeus's *Systema Natura* (1735), which introduced the classification system of binomial nomenclature still in use, Catesby referred to mahogany only by its common name. Although well aware of Linnaeus's work, which was the subject of keen interest among English botanists and natural historians, Catesby opted not to adopt the new nomenclature in his subsequent volumes for consistency's sake, although later revised editions of his work incorporated the new system.[18]

In 1756, when Patrick Browne published his natural history of Jamaica, he assumed more confidently than Catesby that everyone would be familiar with this "now universally esteemed" wood. Closely paraphrasing Catesby's prior text, Browne stated that the West Indian

mahogany tree's trunk grew "very tall and streight [sic], . . . the flowers are of a reddish or saffron colour," but he claimed the seed pod was
rather "the size of a turkey's egg." In an age before copyright, his description also reappeared, often verbatim or only slightly modified, in
numerous encyclopedias, travel books, botanical and horticultural
reference books, popular gardening books, and cabinetmakers' guides
published both in England and North America into the nineteenth
and early twentieth centuries. Usually copied without attribution, it
was always stated with an authoritative air and always with mention
of the "turkey's egg," an analogy perhaps more familiar to earlier generations of readers. Contrary to Catesby's account, Browne explained
correctly that West Indian mahogany trees could thrive in various
settings and that the color, texture, and density of their wood depended on whether they grew in "low and richer lands," in the mountains "among the rocks," or in "mixed soils." His anecdotal account
was likely based on a composite of information gathered from Jamaican woodcutters, cabinetmakers, and planters. In his 1759 edition of
Systema Natura, Linnaeus, citing both Catesby and Browne as references, grouped West Indian mahogany in with the cedars, anointing
it "Cedrela mahagoni," a designation that proved short-lived.[19]

The following year, Nicolai Jacquin, a Leiden botanist who was recently returned from a four-year expedition to the West Indies, published his natural history observations. In his book, entitled *Enumeratio systematica plantarum quas in insulis Caribaeis vicinaque Americes
continente . . .* (1760), he separated mahogany out for the first time as a
distinct genus which he called *Swietenia*. He then christened the particular island species he had encountered: *Swietenia mahagoni.* As was
already common practice among botanists during this period, Jacquin named the tree after his friend and patron, Gerard van Swieten,
a Leiden doctor who became the court physician in Vienna in 1745. A
towering figure in European intellectual circles, he had sponsored
important botanical investigations and helped develop the magnifi-

cent gardens at Schönbrunn Palace (although he is perhaps best remembered for his efforts to debunk myths about vampires). Jacquin
felt a personal debt of gratitude to van Swieten for recommending
him to participate when a royally-sponsored botanical expedition to
the Caribbean was proposed. Part of Jacquin's duties during the trip
was to gather exotic West Indian plants to send back to the gardens in
Vienna. While van Swieten never went to America and likely never
saw a living specimen of his namesake, he was certainly worthy of such
an honor. For Jacquin's part, the expedition was the chance of a lifetime; his research, and subsequent publications, made his reputation
as a promising academic. While his scholarship was almost universally
well received, Jacquin must have blushed when Linnaeus coyly pronounced him "the ambassador of Flora," because, after reading the
young botanist's new book during the evening, he said, "[I] could not
sleep at night because I dreamed of your beautiful plants."[20]

Upon his return to Europe, Jacquin became a professor at the University of Hamburg (and later at the University of Vienna) and in 1763
published a more comprehensive account of his American findings,
entitled *Selectarum Stirpium Americanarum Historia*, citing both
Catesby and Browne among his sources. The frontispiece in volume
two of Jacquin's *Selectarum* includes a depiction of a tiny lizard astride
a mahogany bough, both based on Catesby's earlier images, a small
homage perhaps to the man who first illustrated the tree to which
Jacquin now affixed an official label.[21]

Despite the efforts of Catesby, Browne, Jacquin, and others to compile information about *Swietenia,* however, knowledge about the living trees remained as abstract and fragmentary as the snippets of
dried leaves, turkey-egg seed pods, and shriveled flowers they shipped
home to fill the drawers of European cabinets of curiosities. Neither
could botanical prints, howsoever naturalistically rendered, convey
the true stature, antiquity, and vitality of a mature mahogany tree
within the still mysterious realm of the American rain forests.

FIG. 7.1 Frontispiece, Nicolai Jacquin, *Selectarum Stirpium Americanarum Historia* (1763), vol. 2. Collection of the John Carter Brown Library.

In his book's frontispiece, Jacquin included a branch of the mahogany species he named, *Swietenia mahagoni* and a small lizard, based on Mark Catesby's earlier botanical images (top right, see Plate 1 for comparison).

Attempting to Cultivate Mahogany

One of the earliest documented attempts to grow a mahogany tree outside its native habitat was in 1739 by Phillip Miller at the Company
of Apothecaries' Physic Garden (founded in 1673, but revived by
Sloane in 1722) in Chelsea, England. Miller was interested in mahogany less for its known virtues as timber, than for its potential medicinal value. Mahogany bark, often of unknown origin and species, had
long been imported in small quantities to Europe for use as a medicine
based on colonial accounts that native peoples in Central America ingested it for a variety of maladies. Published inventories of *materia
medica* at the time generally included it among the valuable botanicals
of the West Indies, however, little systematic study had been done to assess its particular properties, efficacy, or safety. Miller hoped to learn
more about its purported curative powers by studying a living specimen. Most significantly, he hoped to ascertain if, as rumored, it might
be akin to cinchona (also known as Peruvian Bark or Jesuit's Bark),
a natural source of quinine, which was a lifesaving antimalarial and
fever medicine. This possibility was tantalizing because, although the
English were introduced to cinchona in 1677, the Spanish closely
guarded its sources in South America and enforced a complete mo-
nopoly on its export. Numerous English and French explorers risked
their lives or even died trying to smuggle cinchona plants or seeds out
of Spanish territories. In 1735, the French scientist Charles-Marie de
La Condamine famously succeeded in spiriting some cinchona seedlings out of Spanish Peru with the help of Indian guides; it was a devastating blow to him and the French officials who funded his expedition
when all the plants shriveled and died. From the West Indies to the
Indian subcontinent, meanwhile, European explorers, naturalists, and
doctors (especially military surgeons concerned with combating the
malaria epidemics that plagued troops stationed in the tropics) all
hotly pursued possible cinchona substitutes.[22]

If anyone at the time had the ability and experience to attempt the cultivation of a tropical hardwood in England, it was Miller. As reflected in his remarkable work in building the nation's foremost apothecary collection of medicinal plants, Miller was an accomplished horticulturalist, skilled at coaxing even persnickety exotics to grow. He had successfully introduced innumerable imported species to England, in spite of its dank, often inhospitable clime. An enthusiastic and influential promoter of his own horticultural triumphs, he authored several very popular, widely read gardening encyclopedias and instruction manuals, some of which went through multiple editions from the 1720s to the 1830s. He was particularly passionate about encouraging amateur horticulturists to experiment with novel plants and innovative techniques in their own gardens. With his advice and guidance, English men and women successfully grew everything from North American tulip trees and magnolias to Indian figs, Arabian jasmine, Peruvian heliotrope, and African marigolds. While he acknowledged mahogany as so "generally fashionable" that it had displaced other native English trees for furniture making, his attempts to grow it were apparently less than satisfactory. He certainly did not make any breakthroughs in the cinchona market; nor did he encourage his readers to emulate him in cultivating tropical hardwoods as he usually did with his success stories.[23]

More concerted investigations into the growth and reproduction of the genus *Swietenia* did not really take off until the 1770s when West Indian mahogany was already seriously depleted and demand for Honduran mahogany was intensifying. These efforts were initiated both within and outside of their native ranges. Among the latter, one of the most high-profile venues was again in England, at the Royal Botanic Gardens at Kew. Located about ten miles from London, the Garden had simultaneously become a living laboratory of experimental horticulture, a vast repository of living botanical specimens, and a central clearinghouse for the international exchange of botanical in-

formation and plant materials. In this intellectually conducive setting, professional gardeners confidently set about trying to grow a
variety of tropical hardwoods within the artificial environs of large
greenhouses.[24]

Despite the staff's dedication, however, these slow-growing trees,
intensely nurtured but distorted within their glass habitat, offered
little useful data as to their real-world habits or growth patterns, and
they stubbornly refused to set seeds. According to a later English account, for example, a lignum vitae tree (a wood widely used in shipbuilding and industry) had, for years, been "reared by artificial heat in
this country; but, as it grows slowly even in the West Indies, its growth
here must of course be slower, and therefore it does not admit of being
cultivated, except in botanical collections, or as a curiosity." The results of their efforts to grow mahogany were doubtless similar.

Nonetheless, throughout England and North America, professional
horticulturalists and naturalists, gentlemen-farmers, amateur garden
enthusiasts, and many others followed reports of such horticultural
activities with interest, and some even attempted to grow these exciting
exotics themselves. By 1809, for example, William Hamilton's Woodlands estate near Philadelphia boasted multiple greenhouses, including one that was 140 feet long. In his personal quest to secure rare
species from every continent, acquired through much expense and international correspondence (including with the new director of the St.
Vincent Botanical Garden), he had created a mini jungle where visitors
agreed, "the beauty and rich variety of its exotics, surpasses any thing
of the kind on this continent." Among his more than 5,000 plant species were a mahogany tree (although what kind is unknown), cinnamon, pepper, Bengali and Arabian coffee, Bohea tea, and several varieties of sugar cane. Within their steamy glass home, these plants
comprised a veritable shopping list of tropical products that Americans had integrated into their daily lives; but while most people were
content to buy sugar or tea in brown paper wrappings, ignorant of

their organic sources, visitors to the Woodlands gained a new perspective on these botanicals as part of a living world beyond themselves. They could admire mahogany furniture in any of Philadelphia's finer houses, but to see a living mahogany tree was truly exceptional.[25]

Given the exorbitant heating, labor, and maintenance costs required to sustain delicate tropical plants through cold, dark winters, whether in England or Philadelphia, mahogany growing in northerly realms remained strictly a novelty, limited to scientists thirsting for new knowledge or wealthy hobbyists feeding their fascination with natural curiosities. Although such experiments proved that, if sufficiently coddled, lone mahogany specimens could survive in captivity, no one succeeded in getting them to grow normally, much less make them grow faster, reliably procreate, or achieve their full potential size.

Efforts to cultivate *Swietenia mahagoni* within its native West Indian range had a much more serious aspect, given the negative economic and environmental consequences of its depletion. Initially, many assumed that growing mahogany within its natural range would certainly be much easier and more successful than attempts elsewhere; surely, replanting the trees would be merely a matter of helping nature along. As would-be mahogany growers discovered over time, however, outcomes differed widely depending on the soil, light, water, and exposure. Moreover, their efforts were stymied by many critical how-to questions: Where were the best mahogany seeds to be found? How should the seeds be transported, and how long could they be stored? How did one get the seeds to sprout before they rotted in the ground? Failing that, could one transplant saplings from the wild to proper tree plantations? Could they be planted on the islands' wastelands to restore lost forests? Was there a way to speed the growth of a young tree or to improve the color and texture of its wood? Finding answers to these myriad unknowns was imperative, but they could only be addressed through slow, painstaking experimentation.

Developing a reliable formula for how to grow mahogany was thus not a straightforward matter. In 1774, John Dovaston, a retired Jamaican planter and nurseryman, attempted to compile step-by-step directions for how to grow tropical trees, as part of a larger treatise, entitled *Agricultura Americana, or Improvements in West-India Husbandry Considered*; although never published, the manuscript was apparently intended to be a helpful instruction manual for planters. It is also revealing of the fluid state of knowledge about tropical hardwoods at the time. Dovaston was atypical among West Indian planters in that he emphasized the aesthetic and practical benefits of living trees as much or more than their economic value as timber. When planters cleared new land, he thus advised them to leave some trees as windbreaks and shade for livestock and slaves as well as for the "beauty arising from them around the estate." His perspective reflected as well an awareness of the new theory that deforestation might diminish local rainfalls with deleterious climatic effects.[26]

Dovaston also touched on contemporary debates over the health effects of tropical trees. For while he did not completely reject the still prevalent belief that clearing forests prevented miasmas, he seemed aware that some thinkers had recently begun to question this theory and to reassess the nature of disease. Joseph Priestley's "Observations on Different Kinds of Air," published by the Royal Society in 1772, for example, documented a series of experiments that involved placing mint plants together with dead mice into glass jars. He effectively demonstrated that the foul air surrounding the putrefying rodent corpses could be restored by the fresh greenery. By extension, he theorized that on Earth, as dead organic matter decayed, the air was purified by "the immense profusion of vegetables . . . inhaling and exhaling." In other words, trees served as nature's air freshener. Benjamin Franklin, after observing Priestley's experiments, hoped they would "give some check to the rage of destroying trees that . . . has accompanied our

late improvements in gardening, from an opinion of their being un-
wholesome." He, at least, was convinced "there is nothing unhealthy
in the air of woods, for we Americans have every where our country
habitations in the midst of woods, and no people on earth enjoy better
health."[27]

Franklin's ringing endorsement notwithstanding, a lot of confusion surrounded this topic as many people still harbored deep-seated
fears about the health risks of tropical forests. Edward Long, for example, claimed that overexposure to bad air could be injurious since
noxious fumes lingered even after "the dense veil of wood is removed."
Yet, he noted, Indians and slaves, both "fond of living among trees,"
seemed to suffer no ill effects; this puzzled him because, despite his
ingrained racial prejudice, he had assumed that all human beings
would react similarly to something so fundamental as air quality. Citing Priestley as his authority, he concluded that "congregations of trees
are, in their growing state, far more friendly than inimical in the alterations which they produce on our atmosphere." Dovaston, too, refer-
enced Priestley's expertise on air quality but seemed more circumspect
in his conclusions. Attributing Jamaicans' improved health to the re-
duction of dense forests, he concluded that a moderate number of trees
posed no significant health risks. He thus advised planters to plant cedar, ironwood, lignum vitae, and, of course, mahogany to "adorn their
Estates . . . [and] sell to the Merchant."[28]

Having resolved this dilemma to his satisfaction, Dovaston offered
silvicultural tips to planters based on his own experience. He prag-
matically advised that, if at all possible, promising seedlings be left in
situ wherever they happened to sprout. If left in peace, they required
only occasional care, such as weeding, "until they can defend themselves." Recognizing perhaps that his naturalistic approach ran counter
to the standard emphasis on reconfiguring landscapes into conformity,
he also gave instructions on transplanting trees for those who insisted
on moving them into specific arrangements. He warned, however, that

most seedlings died of stress when transplanted, and starting them from seed was quite difficult. For those determined to try, he explained for most trees, "seeds must be sown in moist weather on rich soils in Gardens without dung; and when they come up must be defended from Weeds for the first year; the second year in a rainy season about November, I would advise you to transplant . . . [the seedlings] in two rows in your Garden or Nursery." Tropical hardwoods, however, required considerably more care, including staking, daily watering, mulching with "large leaves or cane tops," and regular weeding. Once they reached seven to nine feet tall, he claimed, they could be transplanted to the desired location, but great care had to be taken so as not to damage their taproots. Even then, many more years were needed for them to reach even a modest merchantable size.[29]

In spite of general skepticism and resistance to investing in such long-term ventures, some intrepid planters did experiment with re-planting trees on their estates, usually with an eye toward restoring wastelands. Typically, once cultivation ceased, former agricultural lands were quickly overrun with weeds that multiplied "like the hydra's heads," scrubby bushes, and fast-growing trees, such as cottonwoods that resprouted "like a phoenix" from ragged stumps left behind after clear-cutting. If the land was not completely worn out, secondary forest would eventually grow. Unfortunately, the more desirable tropical hardwoods, such as mahogany and lignum vitae, most often did not naturally re-generate in this spontaneous fashion.[30]

Although admitting that growing tropical hardwoods to produce merchantable timber required a very long-term commitment, Edward Long emphasized that *Swietenia* was "easily propagated from the seeds" in hopes of encouraging planters to attempt it. Although such claims lent weight to popular expectations that breakthroughs in mahogany cultivation were imminent, that proved not to be the case. For although Long was correct that, if conditions were right and the soil was not too degraded, mahogany seeds would sprout readily in man-made clear cuts and abandoned fields, the young trees proved extremely vulnerable. Since they remain unbranched until they are about twenty feet tall, they had to be carefully protected from weeds and other trees for several years or they would be choked to death. In addition to that problem, cultivating mahogany on a large scale turned out to be unexpectedly difficulty because of two major challenges—maintaining a viable seed supply and avoiding killer pests and diseases.[31]

Access to seeds was a decisive factor in whether or not mahogany cultivation or reforestation could succeed. Unfortunately, *Swietenia* seeds proved to be extremely perishable. Whereas many seed types can sprout after years of dormancy, mahogany seeds do not retain their vitality beyond a few months and thus could not be easily stored for future use. Furthermore, since mature, healthy trees were being felled faster than they were able to replace themselves, demand for seeds often exceeded the supply. But it was extremely difficult to determine what minimum number of seed-bearing trees was needed or what might be a sustainable rate of logging, because oftentimes the tipping point— beyond which the species' reproductive capacity was permanently destroyed—had long passed before people realized it. This became a persistent, recurring, and baffling problem. On the surface, it might seem like a simple corollary—extraction cannot outpace replacement lest young trees be cut before they can mature and reproduce—but in the case of *Swietenia*, as with many other trees adapted to tropical rain forest environments, there were also a multitude of complex, interconnected variables that contributed to what we would recognize today as healthy ecosystems.[32]

Another stumbling block to growing mahogany was that whenever the trees were concentrated in homogenous stands, as typical on farms, plantations, or replanted clear cuts, they became highly susceptible to endemic pests and diseases. In their natural habitat, mahogany trees were seldom afflicted in large numbers because they tended to grow apart from each other and dispersed among less susceptible species,

creating a sort of herd immunity. Once planters began cultivating mahogany trees in concentrated numbers, however, this natural protection broke down, enabling epidemics and pestilential swarms to kill or
maim entire stands of trees. The worst plague was of mahogany shoot
borers (*Hypsipyla grandella*), the larvae of a moth that lays its eggs on
the leaves and stems of young mahogany trees; when the eggs hatched,
the larvae would gnaw into tender mahogany shoots, killing or permanently stunting their host tree. No longer held in check within the
natural rain forest setting, these voracious insects feasted and multiplied wherever mahogany trees grew in concentrated plantings. By the
early nineteenth century, mahogany shoot borers had ravaged man-
made mahogany groves throughout the northern Antilles.[33]

Long after Jamaica's reputation for producing the world's best mahogany had faded, and after its logging industry was largely defunct,
efforts to revive *Swietenia mahagoni* through cultivation continued.
In 1806, for example, the Jamaican Agricultural Society, as part of
its mission to promote "improvements on plantations" (that included
rewards for the largest natural increase of a plantation's slave population and the best new method of cane cultivation), offered a gold
medal to "the person who shall most properly plant out not less than
one thousand mahogany . . . and other timber trees." Unfortunately,
what constituted a proper planting during that period often undermined the trees' long-term survival. In retrospect, the difficulties of
cultivating New World mahogany trees within their native ranges
appear directly attributable to a lack of accurate information about
the species and their habitats.[34]

By the late eighteenth century, a strong push began to introduce New
World mahoganies to new regions within the British Empire and, following American independence, to the United States as well. These
efforts reflected changing ideas about the nature of climate and the
mutability of species which emphasized incremental strategies of

seasoning people, animals, and plants to facilitate their adaptation to new environments. To what degree non-natives could be conditioned to survive in alien places without adverse effects had been the subject of intense speculation since the earliest days of European colonization. In the case of mahogany, this remained a very pertinent issue since efforts to grow it, even just within its own native habitat, had proved so singularly disappointing.

The first attempts to transplant Honduran and West Indian mahogany beyond their natural habitats, however, were relatively close by—namely to the Lesser Antilles. Although these islands, including the Virgin Islands, Trinidad, Tobago, and Puerto Rico, were all climatically suitable for *Swietenia*, it had never spread there naturally because they were effectively isolated from its native range by expanses of ocean. As development of the less-populated of these islands accelerated in the mid- to late eighteenth century, however, settlers easily overcame that age-old geographical barrier by deliberately importing mahogany seeds to their new plantations to enrich their timber resources. Meanwhile, on the older island colonies, such as Bermuda and Barbados, mahogany was introduced as a means of combating deforestation which was undermining their economic viability. Transplanting valuable sylvan species was a priority in Barbados, for example, because, as one 1750 account explained, the few trees that remained were "planted near Dwelling-Houses, generally more for Ornament than Use," while all other timber was imported "at a great expense, chiefly from the Island of St. Lucia and Tobago." In 1798, however, an inventory from Belle Plantation in Barbados enumerated over 300 mahogany trees growing on the estate. Since some of them were reportedly "big enough to square to the largest furniture," that suggests they must have been planted approximately forty years earlier. If so, that would make this one of the earliest documented records of a successful mahogany plantation in the British West Indies. Eventually, mahogany was successfully planted elsewhere on Barbados as windbreaks, in tree-lined *alleés,* and on wastelands with "virtually non-existent soil." On this ecologically-devastated island, such a transformation had significant positive effects, and not just for humans who planned to eventually fell the trees. As small mahogany woodlots matured, they also sheltered shorter trees, shrubs, and plants, creating small oases of biodiversity amidst an otherwise homogenous landscape, over 80 percent of which was devoted to sugar cane. According to John Francis, the first documented mentions of *Swietenia mahagoni* on the Virgin Islands were in 1790; *Swietenia macrophylla* was introduced in Puerto Rico circa 1904, where regular nursery production of the trees began in the 1920s to 1940s, although mostly for use as ornamentals.[35]

The successful transplantation of mahogany to the Lesser Antilles (and Bermuda) is directly attributable to the fact that they initially had the virtue of being relatively free of the pests and diseases endemic to *Swietenia* species in their native range. Wherever mahogany trees were transplanted, however, their invasive enemies were not far behind. Mahogany shoot borers spread throughout the Caribbean, from the Greater to the Lesser Antilles as well as to parts of Central America. By the late nineteenth century, they had wiped out or severely damaged almost every mahogany plantation in the western hemisphere; mahogany plantations renewed in the region during the twentieth century mostly suffered the same fate. Rather remarkably, a few nineteenth- and early twentieth century remnants of planted mahogany stands survive, including on Barbados. There has also been a major push to integrate mahogany into the surviving forests of the Lesser Antilles, most notably on Puerto Rico. But they were insufficient to support any significant or sustained commercial logging operations. Ironically, on many of islands where *Swietenia* species were introduced, they are now often assumed to be indigenous.

Another region initially considered a promising venue for mahogany transplantation during the mid- to late-eighteenth century was the southern coast of North America, especially since small quantities of *Swietenia mahagoni* grew naturally around the tip of southern Florida. Many gardeners and planters in adjacent colonies assumed that they would be able to transplant it quite readily to their estates. In 1758, for example, Robert Pringle reported his success with logwood in South Carolina to the Royal Society, but his concurrent efforts to grow mahogany proved unsatisfactory. Apparently, the delicate seedlings he imported from the Greater Antilles could not withstand even the relatively mild Carolina winters.[36]

At Mount Vernon that same year, George Washington planted forty-eight mahogany seeds which his nephew had brought for him from the West Indies. Since Washington's elegant home was already well outfitted with expensive mahogany furnishings (many of which he had personally ordered from London), he was clearly appreciative of this material's special qualities and aware of its economic value. His interest in growing mahogany trees, however, seemed focused primarily on their beauty and novelty as ornamentals inasmuch as he was intent on developing Mount Vernon's gardens into a showcase of botanical delights. He had already planted a wide variety of exotic trees and was excited to add mahogany to his collection. A prolonged drought persisted throughout that summer, however, so it seems unlikely that the finicky mahogany seeds sprouted. As many of his other delicate trees perished, Washington did a lot of hand-wringing and blamed his horticultural losses on his slaves' failure to water enough.[37]

While extending mahogany cultivation into the North American colonies was seen as both a cost savings and a means of reducing international strife, it became an even more compelling object of nationalist interest following their independence. The vulnerability of the former colonies' mahogany supplies had been highlighted during and immediately after the American Revolution, when shipping was interrupted by wartime hostilities and then by English attempts to curtail trade between its former and remaining colonies. While some American ships found ways around these trade barriers, others sought

out alternative mahogany sources, especially among the newly accessible islands of French St. Domingue and Spanish Cuba. All the recent
upheavals and trade disruptions, however, strengthened the popular
sentiment in the United States that the fledgling nation needed to become more self-sufficient. Just as Reverend Hanbury had earlier done
in England, ardent nationalists called for reduced dependency on imported commodities, especially such luxuries as tropical produce. But
whereas Hanbury had advocated a return to native English woods,
these voices favored a redoubling of efforts to naturalize valuable West
Indian plants and trees, thus transforming them into homegrown
products. In one 1789 editorial, for example, the author insisted, "We
generally fancy that exotic plants . . . will not thrive in our climate, but
we too suddenly make this conclusion. . . . Experience must determine
this matter." Citing the example of a tropical tamarind tree that had
survived several killing frosts in Providence, Rhode Island (no doubt
in some sheltered garden corner), he asked, "why then may not . . . the
lignum vitae, mahogany, logwood, or other trees and shrubs of West-
India [origins], be propagated here . . . which requires no longer term
of hot or warm weather, than our summers afford? Let us then make
further experiments, produce what we [now] import, and save our
money." Although this writer's ignorance of silviculture was evident
in his naive expectation that tropical hardwoods could thrive during
brief New England summers or survive the bitter winters, he clearly
aimed to push the envelope beyond people's assumptions about nature's limits.[38]

Interest in naturalizing mahogany to new venues extended even
farther than North America to Europe and beyond. Also in 1789, a
gardener in Bordeaux requested Humphry Marshall, a Quaker nurseryman based in Philadelphia, to ship him fifty-seven American tree
species, including the mahogany tree "which makes such beautiful
furniture." The Frenchman had undoubtedly read Marshall's popular
book, *Arbustrum Americanum: The American Grove* (1785), recently

translated into French, which proclaimed the author's intention to "make a contribution to the sum of natural knowledge" and to assist the "foreigner, curious in American collections" to select appropriate trees for ornamental as well as "economical purposes." Marshall's primary motivation, however, was patriotic as he felt the United States could not be fully independent if it was reliant on foreign imports; he believed that through "observation and research to increase knowledge of Botany," American planters, especially in the southern states, could learn how to grow tea, dyestuffs, and many other imported crops.[39]

In Marshall's nursery business, his biggest sellers were not tropical exotics but temperate American species that he stocked and sold in the thousands, both domestically and abroad. As an active participant in the lively transatlantic botanical exchange, he traded plants, seeds, and botanical information with correspondents throughout the Caribbean and Europe. So, although he did not specifically include mahogany in his book and likely did not stock it in his nursery, he may well have been able to fulfill his French customer's request through his extensive network of botanical enthusiasts. Unfortunately, there is no record of whether a mahogany tree ever grew in Bordeaux.

The French government, meanwhile, funded its own natural history investigations to assess what American trees might be introduced to the Continent in hopes of reviving their own stressed forests, supplying their navy with timber, and introducing adaptable new species that might take root on worn-out land where native species no longer would grow. In 1785, the French ministry dispatched the naturalist and explorer André Michaux to undertake an ambitious government-sponsored survey of American sylvan resources. Surpassing the earlier adventures of Catesby or Kalm, Michaux traveled widely in the United States and, during what turned into an eleven-year sojourn, gathered thousands of specimens, and corresponded with Thomas Jefferson and other influential Americans who shared his botanical interests. He also established an extensive tree nursery to grow stock from his most promising finds. Although in Florida, he gathered samples of semitropical species (likely including *Swietenia mahagoni*), officials back in Paris deemed them suitable only as ornamentals and decided against acquiring any. Nonetheless, Michaux sent over 6,000 other America trees from his nursery to France, many of which reportedly were destroyed during the French Revolution.[40]

As Britain's colonial presence shifted eastward, it too sought to expand its tropical timber supply globally by transplanting American mahogany species to India. When William Roxburgh was appointed superintendent of the Calcutta Royal Botanical Garden in 1793, one of his first projects was to plant mahogany seeds sent to him by the West India Company. A doctor for the East India Company and a passionate botanist, Roxburgh specialized in naturalizing introduced plants as well as in cultivating wild species indigenous to India. Given his medical training, he was especially interested in finding new medicinal plants. He is credited, in fact, with discovering a new, distantly-related member of the mahogany family that was an effective antidote for fevers. Naming it *Swietenia febrifuga*, he successfully promoted it as a cinchona substitute and the directors of the East India Company, always attuned to new possibilities for profit, sent packets of the bark to the Royal Colleges of Physicians in London and Edinburgh to "make trial of its effects and to communicate to the Company their opinion of its virtues," noting that if it proved effective it would be of great benefit to the British in India because Peruvian bark was scarce and expensive.[41]

Alarmed by India's severe drought problems, he was particularly committed to planting trees as a means of combating desertification. Realizing that the English had already overharvested India's wild teak trees to the point of scarcity, he was instrumental in transforming that species into a plantation crop. Relying heavily on the skills and advice of local Indian people, he undertook extensive experimentation and overcame numerous setbacks before formulating a reliable agricultural protocol for growing teak. He subsequently raised thousands of teak seedlings for distribution, facilitating the establishment of vast teak plantations all over the subcontinent. By comparison, his effort to naturalize American mahoganies—absent, of course, any local expertise—was only a very qualified success. The vast majority of the delicate mahogany seeds he imported from Jamaica and Central America were damaged on arrival, failed to germinate, or withered soon after sprouting. He managed to establish a handful of specimen trees in the botanical garden but, even with careful nurturing, they grew very slowly and produced no seeds; he thus never repeated with *Swietenia* the tremendous horticultural success that he had had with teak.[42]

During the late-nineteenth century, cultivating useful trees became a high priority for colonial officials because severe deforestation and drought were spreading in many parts of India. To conserve the remaining trees, especially for their own needs and those of the government, they sought to regulate and restrict access to forests. The local populaces that relied on these woods for subsistence and fuel angrily resisted such measures. These tensions spurred further investment in new methods of scientific forestry and silviculture. In 1878, Dietrich Brandis, the inspector-general of forests in India, reported that of "the exotic trees which are cultivated by way of experiment, mahogany is the most important, and its success seems not improbable, though it is too early yet to form final conclusions on the subject." Apparently tone deaf to Brandis's hesitancy, Sir Joseph Hooker, director of the Royal Botanic Gardens at Kew, seized on this statement as validation of his institution's long-term support for this attempted botanical transfer.[43]

An 1885 government survey of India's professional horticulturalists and official forest managers, however, presented a much less rosy assessment, concluding that mahogany trees "planted in regular forest plantations have not usually succeeded." Survey respondents voiced universal frustration that the few trees that they had managed to grow were confined mostly to regional botanical gardens and a few private

Plate 1: "The Mahogony Tree," hand-colored botanical engraving of leaf, flower, and seed of specimen (shown with mistletoe at bottom), from Mark Catesby, *The Natural History of Carolina, Florida, and the Bahama Islands . . .* , (London: for the author, 1743), Vol.2: Plate 81. Courtesy of The Library Company of Philadelphia.

Plate 2: Mahogany Tree (*Swietenia macrophylla*), Honduras, 2005. Photo courtesy of the Environmental Investigation Agency-Global; Photograph © D. Sims/EIA/CIP.

Plate 3: High Chest, unattributed, Philadelphia, circa 1769. Mahogany with white pine, tulipwood, and maple secondary woods 102 ½ × 46 ⅛ × 24 ⅝ in. Collection of Winterthur Museum, Wilmington, Delaware; gift of Henry Francis du Pont. (1957.506)

This object was originally owned by the family of Miriam and Michael Gratz of Philadelphia.

Plate 4a: *John and Elizabeth Lloyd Cadwalader and Daughter Anne,* Charles Willson Peale, American, 1772. Oil on canvas. 51½ × 41¼ in. Collection of the Philadelphia Museum of Art; purchased with funds contributed by the Mabel Pew Myrin Trust and the gift of an anonymous donor, 1983. (1983.90.3)

Plate 4b: Card Table, Workshop of Thomas Affleck, American, circa 1770. Mahogany, yellow pine, yellow poplar, oak. 28 7/8 × 39 × 19¾ in. Collection of the Philadelphia Museum of Art; purchased with funds contributed by the Mabel Pew Myrin Trust and with the gift of an anonymous donor, 1984. (1984.6.1)

This card table, one of a matching pair, has a provenance as part of a large group of furnishings made by Thomas Affleck and others for John Cadwalader of Philadelphia. One of these tables is likely depicted in Peale's 1772 portrait of the Cadwalader family.

Plate 5a: *Jeremiah Platt,* John Mare, New York, 1767. Oil on canvas. 48½ × 38½ in. Collection of The Metropolitan Museum of Art Victor Wilbour Memorial Fund, 1955 (55.55). (Photo Credit: Art Resource, New York.)

Plate 5b: Side Chair, attributed to Thomas Affleck, Philadelphia, circa 1770. Mahogany. 36 × 24 × 23 in. Collection of Winterthur Museum, Wilmington, Delaware. (1958.2290). This chair, one of a matching set, has a provenance as part of a large group of furnishings made by Thomas Affleck for John Cadwalader of Philadelphia.

Plate 6: *Mr. and Mrs. Isaac Winslow (Jemima Debuke),* John Singleton Copley, Boston, 1773. Oil on canvas. 40 × 49¾ in. Collection of the Museum of Fine Arts, Boston; M. and M. Karolik Collection of Eighteenth-Century American Arts (39.250). Photograph © Museum of Fine Arts, Boston.

Plate 7a: Federal-style Side Board with Knife Boxes, detail of Du Pont Dining Room (period room installation). Collection of the Winterthur Museum.

Plate 7b: Federal-style Dining Table, detail of Du Pont Dining Room (period room installation). Collection of the Winterthur Museum.

Plate 8: Secretary, attributed to Isaac Miles and Joel Lyons, Greenfield, MA, circa 1840. Mahogany and mahogany veneers, with butternut, yellow poplar, white pine, glass, and fragments of green silk. 68½ × 42 × 12⅛ in. Collection of Historic Deerfield, Deerfield, MA, purchased with funds contributed by Michael and Ruth Swanson. (88.092)

gardens and these stragglers, despite constant attention, remained stunted and "rarely if ever yield perfect seeds." The heartiest mahogany specimens to be found were, in fact, Roxburgh's original trees that still graced the Royal Botanical Garden in Calcutta. Although there were not yet any reports of diseases or the dreaded mahogany shoot borers, why the trees refused to produce seeds was both a riddle and a serious problem. Imported West Indian mahogany seeds, however, were rarely available at any price and Honduran mahogany seeds were becoming so scarce in Central America that people there were reluctant to export them. Colonial officials were nonetheless bound and determined to see mahogany established as a viable commodity in India. As one exasperated horticulturalist pointedly stated in the survey, without healthy mahogany seeds, he and his colleagues could never meet this expectation or ever hope "to rival the teak plantations." Although colonial officials prevailed upon Hooker to facilitate shipments of some of the distinctive turkey-egg pods from Belize to India via Kew's centralized botanical exchange network, the global demand for seeds vastly exceeded supplies.[44]

Nonetheless, thanks to these dogged efforts, the center of mahogany cultivation slowly shifted away from the Atlantic region to the other side of the globe; aside from on-going difficulties in procuring seeds, Honduran mahogany eventually flourished in places like India, Ceylon, and Singapore, although once again its old nemesis, the mahogany shoot borer, was not far behind. Ironically, it was in India, far from the trees' native home, that they were finally officially classified as a separate species. Quite serendipitously, in 1886, George King, then superintendent of the Calcutta Botanical Garden, received a handful of unlabeled seeds that he planted alongside some previously introduced *Swietenia mahagoni Jacquin*. As the new trees began to emerge from the anonymous seeds, he observed that they were different from their neighbors. As he later explained, although they appeared to be "closely allied" with "true mahogany," they had slightly larger leaves, flowers, and seedpods; recognizing the cumulative import of these subtle distinctions, he declared the trees to be of a previously unidentified species, which he named after himself, *Swietenia macrophylla King.*[45]

Inventing a Better Mahogany

While would-be mahogany growers faced unexpected challenges in the late eighteenth and early nineteenth centuries, other people focused instead on finding convincing mahogany imitations or substitutes. While the scientific interest in this goal was new, the motivation was not. Almost from the outset of its introduction in Europe and North America, cabinetmakers had sought to simulate mahogany in order to satisfy customers' demand for less expensive versions. Their techniques ranged from finishing red-hued woods, like cherry, to enhance their natural color to treating dissimilar woods, like pine, birch, or maple, with paints, stains, or finishes to create the appearance of mahogany. Eighteenth-century cabinetmakers' manuals, housekeeping guides, and even cookbooks often included recipes for mahogany finishes and polishes that involved such ingredients as iron ore, ox blood, cochineal, logwood, and dragon's blood, a toxic, dark-red resin obtained from several species of trees found in Asia and America. In southern New Hampshire, for example, cabinetmaker John Dunlap relied on a recipe, possibly of his own devising, "To stain wood to Resemble Mehogany," that called for a mixture of logwood, ginger root, and dragon's blood. While such concoctions all purported to duplicate the rich color or sublime polish of mahogany on any piece of wooden furniture, their results were never entirely believable.[46]

During the latter half of the eighteenth century, the search for mahogany look-alikes extended as well into the realm of scientific inquiry. In 1763, for example, a correspondent to the Society of Arts in London summarized his extensive but futile attempts to imitate mahogany using a convoluted process of soaking wood samples in pond water and injecting them with various red vegetable dyes and minerals. His motivation sprang from his awareness that people "had been, for some years past, running mad after mahogany furniture . . . [until the wood] is grown scarce in our West Indian islands so that a great deal of French mahogany is yearly imported" and the price is "very much risen." Furthermore, he expressed concern that recent importations of Cuban mahogany lacked the deep color associated with Jamaican mahogany, a problem he had hoped in vain to make irrelevant. No doubt damp and frustrated, he urged the society to offer a prize to inspire others to join in his quest.[47]

Chemists also joined the search for mahogany imitations, experimenting with all manner of substances to emulate its distinctive physical properties. In 1805, enthusiastic reports circulated in the English newspapers of a new method of producing "Artificial Mahogany," invented in France during the Napoleonic Wars when mahogany was scarce. According to the *Lancaster Gazette*, due to "the difficulty of procuring Mahogany . . . and the consequent exorbitant cost demanded for the ordinary articles of family convenience," French chemists had developed a process to "render any species of wood, of a close grain, so nearly to resemble mahogany . . . that the most accurate judges are incapable of distinguishing it. . . ." French polishing, as the technique came to be known, was greeted as a marvel of modern chemistry and set a new standard for furniture finishes. But conceptually, it merely added to the existing repertoire of methods to dress up lesser woods that cabinetmakers had improvised and refined over many years. Many of these methods were also used to improve the color of mahogany that was deemed too pale or lacking a vivid enough red hue. During this same period, chemists attempted to replicate mahogany's durability in less expensive woods by impregnating them with various preservatives, including salt, arsenic, and mercury. Others focused on using heat and chemical treatments to reduce the seasoning time required before mahogany and other woods could be used; one experimenter, for example, claimed to have reduced the seasoning time of mahogany from a minimum of two years to a mere two months.[48]

While most attempts to imitate mahogany similarly treated wood as an inert material, a more radical approach focused on manipulating living trees. Significantly, this strategy sought to take advantage of new knowledge about the circulatory and digestive systems of organisms, much of which was derived from experiments that injected dyes into plants and animals to observe how they moved through living bodies. When a few of these dyes were discovered to permanently tint plant fibers and creatures' internal organs, bones, and bodily fluids, some theorized that this technique could be used to artificially produce desired color effects in other natural substances. In 1757, for example, Dr. Alexander Garden, a South Carolina physician, investigated the effects of the "Prickly Pear . . . in Colouring the Juices of Living Animals." He hoped to discover what caused the exquisite scarlet color derived from the crushed bodies of cochineal bugs, which was a valuable and highly coveted dye; since cochineal bugs fed exclusively on prickly pears, he theorized that perhaps their extraordinary red tincture originated somehow with this foodstuff. His report, read aloud to the Royal Society, explained that this peculiar fleshy plant grew "in great abundance about Carolina; and . . . the cochineal insects are found upon it; but hitherto no attempts have been made to cure them as the Spaniards do." Instead of focusing on the parasitic bugs themselves as earlier researchers had done, he focused on testing whether "some rich dye may be produced from the plant itself." Using his own slave as a test subject, he "gave six pears to a Negroe wench . . . and strictly forbad her suckling her child for six or eight hours; and then taking some of her milk in a tea-cup . . . [found] the cream had a reddish lustre, tho it was very faint." Apparently unmoved by the cries of a hungry baby, he conducted this experiment after learning that some cows that grazed in an indigo field later produced cream "of a most beautiful blue color."[49]

Such accounts inspired efforts to apply this knowledge to more commercial applications, including producing other forms of artificial mahogany. Very similar experiments were conducted on fast-growing trees, adding red colorants to the soil to be absorbed through their roots, in hopes of tinting their interior wood. One investigator in 1788 reported his high hopes for the use of a common weed called *madderroot* for that purpose because he had read reports of cattle whose bones were permanently dyed red after eating it. In his words, just "as the tubes, by which trees derive nourishment from the earth are analogous to the mouths of animals, it is not unlikely that the curious naturalist . . . [could] convey colored juices into the bodies of trees through this channel." The article outlining his technique, reprinted in 1823, described the results as "a happy imitation" of the "natural produce." Whether experimentation was confined to controlled laboratory settings or carried out in the field using living subjects, people resorted to science to find mahogany substitutes, with the intention of improving natural processes.[50]

During the eighteenth century, the Enlightenment fascination with nature that resulted in the transplantation and naturalization of thousands of new species in Europe, the Americas, Africa, and Asia, benefitted vast numbers of people. One of the most important outcomes of this activity, according to J. H. Plumb, was the psychological impact of "the sense of modernity and novelty generated. . . . People no longer expected flowers, vegetables, and trees to be static objects in the field of creation, but constantly changing, constantly improving, the change and the improvement due to the experimental activity of man." The global transfer of valuable species was widely celebrated and scientific agriculture embraced as the best avenue for refining and elevating both nature and humanity.[51]

At the same time, many investigative breakthroughs and promising innovations never found their way into practicable real-world applications or precipitated unwanted side effects. For example, some

Jamaican planters introduced fast-growing bamboo to help curb erosion only to see it become an invasive nuisance as it dispersed across the island. Likewise, the lack of communication about unsuccessful efforts and failed projects resulted in pointless duplications and missed opportunities for information sharing and collaboration, particularly due to the often rigid boundaries between different spheres of knowledge compartmentalizing the worlds of science, natural history, and artisanship. So while cabinetmakers, scientists, naturalists, and horticulturalists all simultaneously sought to address the problem of sustaining an affordable, abundant mahogany supply (or, at least, viable substitutes), they did not necessarily have much correspondence with each other. In 1830, for example, William Hooker, the senior professor of botany at Glasgow University, noted that, where *Swietenia mahagani* and *Swietenia macrophylla* were concerned, although "workmen make an important distinction between the two woods," it was "much to be lamented that [their] botanical characters are not yet known to us." A botanical text published the same year by the Society for the Diffusion of Useful Knowledge also bemoaned the continued lack of knowledge about *Swietenia*, for even its "precise period of . . . growth is not accurately known; but as, when large, it changes but little during the lifetime of a man, the time of its arriving at maturity is probably not less than two hundred years." Nonetheless, advancing knowledge about *Swietenia*—including about its natural habitat and its co-evolved enemies—remained an important goal. Compared to many other American species, however, that learning curve was—and continues to be—unusually long, steep, and bumpy.[52]

Consequently, despite the growing urgency to replace the majestic trees as they vanished from the Greater Caribbean, mahogany eluded large-scale conversion to plantation agriculture and former mahogany-rich forests proved difficult to restore. The earlier vision of regiments of young nursery-grown mahogany trees deployed to green the wastelands of the West Indies remained largely unfulfilled and hopes of producing an artificial bounty dimmed. Moreover, repeated attempts to manipulate young mahogany trees to speed their growth, elicit desired qualities, or increase their rates of reproduction also largely foundered. These cumulative failures tempered the seductive notion that—given the correct application of empirical study and science-based agricultural practices—climate, geography, and time could all be subjugated. The fact that *Swietenia* grew better in alien environments than within its native range seemed counterintuitive and somewhat perverse, confounding well-established assumptions about indigenousness. Mahogany in many ways thus defied the Enlightenment idea that humans could master the living world. Confronted with the limits of their natural knowledge, people were forced to admit that they could *not* always unlock nature's secrets to find the antidote to human-made scarcity.

CHAPTER EIGHT

Democratizing Mahogany and the Advent of Steam

_D_URING THE 1820S AND 1830S, Americans once again redefined their conceptions of mahogany as the advent of steam power transformed how it was produced, transported, manufactured, and consumed. On the production end, steam trains and steam-powered portable sawmills significantly expanded the geographical areas accessible for logging and increased the rate and number of trees felled. On the manufacturing end, steam-driven saws and furniture-making machinery increased outputs and lowered costs, allowing raw materials to be processed into finished objects faster, more precisely, and in greater volume than ever before. Many at the time hailed the advent of steam as the solution to the declining quality, size, and availability of mahogany. Steam-powered veneer saws, for example, were touted for conserving valuable mahogany by squeezing more useable wood out of each log. After all the concerns and conflicts over diminishing mahogany stocks during the eighteenth century, technology seemed to have opened a limitless new vista.[1]

Another aspect of this technological development was that mahogany furniture, made with machine-cut veneers, became more widely available in a range of price points; this once-rarified material came into reach for more people than ever before. To many Americans, this fact seemed proof positive of the nation's rising standard of living and growing equality, a shining exemplar of the benefits of democratization. Some in the upper tier of society, however, resisted what they saw as a dangerous leveling trend, a complaint that harkened back to similar concerns raised during the eighteenth century when non-elite people first began to acquire mahogany (although not even close to the current extent). Reluctant to see its aura of exclusivity further erode, those in the upper classes sought to redraw distinctions among different types of the wood as well as among those who consumed them. Consequently, a new hierarchy of mahogany developed, but one that was increasingly divorced from any geographical reality. At the same time, where mahogany was produced (as well as how and by whom) continued to determine the size and quality of what was available to consumers at any given moment. Over the long term, steam power, and the mass consumption it helped make possible, contributed to the extentsification and intensification of mahogany exploitation in ways that ultimately undermined its sustainability as a commercial commodity.

The Impact of Steam on Mahogany Producers

Beginning in the early 1830s, plans to expand and modernize mahogany production began to be pursued, with varying degrees of success, in Cuba, Hispaniola, and the Bay of Honduras, which was now a British protectorate. During this period, logging remained (as it is still today) an extremely dangerous occupation but steam power promised to alleviate some of the most backbreaking labor once done by men and beasts. Whereas previously, the difficulty and expense of transport had always limited woodcutters' range to areas adjacent to waterways, steam trains, although precluded from the most rugged terrain, chugged right over natural obstacles and across long distances that were impossible or extremely onerous to negotiate with only men or draught animals. Wherever rails could be laid and trees were to be found, steam trains delivered workers, equipment, and supplies to new logging sites and hauled out the massive logs. In addition, woodcutters were liberated from their former strict adherence to a seasonal logging schedule since they no longer had to wait until the rainy season to float logs out of the forests. With the introduction of portable steam-powered sawmills, large logs could be cut on-site into more manageable boards. As a global network of steam shipping also developed, mahogany from the Caribbean and Central America began to be exported to markets as distant as Australia.

This new technology was not without its difficulties; keeping steam engines operational required skilled engineers, regular maintenance, and replacement parts, which were often unavailable. When machinery broke or malfunctioned, slave masters typically complained that their slaves were simply incapable of understanding complex technology. More likely, coerced workers felt little incentive to keep the sawmill blade whirring since it was they who had to feed its relentless appetite for logs. In most cases, successful industrial logging ventures required some governmental support to create essential infrastructure as well as infusions of foreign capital from American, British, or, in the case of Haiti, French private investors or companies. To mahogany-producing nations, the potential benefits of industrializing the logging sector were compelling, particularly as steam power had already revolutionized the sugar industry throughout much of the Caribbean.

On Cuba, steam technology spurred a major surge of economic development, which, although centered on sugar, also significantly expanded mahogany production. The first steam engine was imported to Cuba from England by a progressive Spanish planter in 1797 to power his sugar mill. Other planters followed suit until by the 1820s, steam-powered sugar mills and sawmills had become quite prevalent, although older style mills (powered by water, wind, or cattle) remained in use. The island's first railroad (and the first in the greater Caribbean) was built in 1837 with British financing and American equipment to connect established plantation regions with the main seaport in Havana.[2]

Efforts to establish large-scale logging enterprises on Cuba were somewhat hampered, however, precisely because so much of the infrastructure was designed to service the sugar industry. Wherever railroads were extended, they precipitated a brief upsurge of mahogany production along their routes that quickly ended as adjacent lands were cleared for sugar cane. More mountainous areas, including some of the richest forests, were among the last to be linked to the coast by rail. In the meantime, independent woodcutters and logging companies still relied on slaves to chop logs into pieces to be hand-carried, packed out on mules, or floated out on rivers during the rainy months.

As the search for mahogany shifted to Cuba, some wealthy Cuban and American investors became interested in industrializing the island's logging industry. In 1832, the DeWolfs of Bristol, Rhode Island underwrote the construction of a steam-powered sawmill as part of a larger initiative to expand their already significant property holdings on the island and to build on established trade relationships that dated back to at least the turn of the century. Between them, Senator James DeWolf, his son Mark Antony DeWolf, and his nephew George De-Wolf owned five large plantations. The family's wealth came in large part from their involvement in the transatlantic slave trade. When it was banned in the United States in 1808, James DeWolf continued to ship human cargo to Cuba where the rapid expansion of sugar created a voracious demand for labor among neighboring plantations as well as on his own estates. On one of his properties, for example, the Senator owned over a hundred slaves. Largely absentee owners, the family visited Cuba (and Mark Antony married the daughter of a local planter) but relied largely on hired managers and trusted kinfolk to manage day-to-day operations.

FIG. 8.1 "Clearing Mahogany Down the Rapids in Cuba" in *The Mahogany Tree: Its Botanical Character, Qualities and Uses . . . in the West Indies and Central America*. Chaloner & Fleming (Liverpool: Rockcliff and Son, 1850). Collection of the LuEsther T. Mertz Library of the New York Botanical Garden, Bronx, New York.

FIG. 8.2 "Cart of the Country Loaded with Mahogany in Cuba" in *The Mahogany Tree: Its Botanical Character, Qualities and Uses . . . in the West Indies and Central America*. Chaloner & Fleming (Liverpool: Rockcliff and Son, 1850). Collection of the LuEsther T. Mertz Library of the New York Botanical Garden, Bronx, New York.

In the meantime, the DeWolfs also diversified their profits into other financial sectors, including New England textile mills, banking, insurance, whaling, and the China trade. As their wealth grew, they built impressive mansions and enjoyed a lavish lifestyle back in Rhode Island. Prominently situated in the center of Bristol, George DeWolf's Linden Place was a large white confection with elaborate woodwork and elegantly furnished interiors; built in 1810, its cost was purportedly equivalent to the "profits from a single year of the outlawed [slave] trade." In 1825, however, George's sugar crop failed, causing him to default on a large loan. His business interests proved so intertwined with those of his extended family and the Bristol townspeople that when he declared bankruptcy and creditors called in his notes, the banks failed, and the entire local economy collapsed. Hounded by creditors and suddenly a social pariah, George DeWolf fled to Cuba, sneaking out in the middle of the night with his wife and children. Before Linden Place could be sold, its entire contents—from its fine mahogany furnishings to the crystal chandeliers—were seized by creditors or looted by enraged neighbors.[3]

The DeWolf family spent the next decade trying to salvage their reputation and regain their fortune. By 1832, they had recovered sufficiently that James and Mark Antony DeWolf gambled on a new Cuban venture, acquiring 200 acres located 150 miles east of Havana. They hired George Howe, James DeWolf's nephew, to supervise construction of a new plantation, wishfully named New Hope. Howe's brief but well documented tenure as its manager offers a rare look at the introduction of steam power and its impact on mahogany production during this period.

Leaving his young family in Rhode Island, Howe arrived in Cuba in the spring of 1832. After a rough journey out to the remote site, he disconsolately described it as little more than a clearing surrounded by "almost impenetrable forests, amidst whose dark solitudes . . . the eye in vain may seek a vista to the clear blue sky." To his chagrin, he observed that "many of the larger trees, particularly of Cedar and

Mahogany, have been cut down and carried off," most likely by free-lance woodcutters. Nonetheless, he was amazed by the abundance of enormous trees that remained, describing them as "the giant offspring of untamed Nature . . . [that] magnificently rear their huge trunks, and reach aloft in [the] air their awful arms—high as those hills." He immediately sent wood samples home to his employers for evaluation.

Howe's first assignment was to supervise construction of a steam-powered sawmill so, as the slaves cleared the land, the resulting timber could be cut up for export. Since his uncle had already invested almost $40,000 dollars in New Hope "without the jingling of one Iota in reimbursement," Howe was anxious to get the sawmill running since they expected it to quickly "defray all the expenses of the Estate, and at the same time yield a handsome dividend." Howe confidently predicted that "this one Mill will drive many [competitors'] vessels from the Market. . . . [W]ho can say that we have no material in these extensive forests that may supersede the Mahogany of St. Doming[o]? . . . Who can say that the operations of this Mill may not develop resources as yet undreamt of? This is indeed a New Hope!"[4]

When the steam boiler was at last installed over the summer, the newly-hired engineer stoked the fire while Howe stood by. As the pistons, wheels, and cogs whirred to life, the chattering blade began chomping ferociously through piles of logs. Howe celebrated the occasion by penning a tongue-in-cheek "Stump Speech at the Raising of the New Hope Sawmill":

> You have this day reared in the land of imbecility and ignorance, a proud monument to American skill, industry, and enterprise. . . . The passing Spaniard shall here rein up his jaded pony and gaze in wonder and amazement on this edifice, which but for Yankee enterprise, had forever slumbered . . . amidst the dark solitudes of the forest. . . . [P]etrified with astonishment, he shall see the awful elements of Fire and Water—harnessed by Science. . . . [T]he triumph of Genius over untamed Nature!

FIG. 8.3 "Steam Sawmill on the New Hope Sugar Estate, Cuba," George Howe, circa 1832, Watercolor in his Diary and Letterbook, Collection of the Bristol Historical and Preservation Society, Bristol, Rhode Island.

George Howe painted this watercolor in his journal to commemorate the dedication of the new steam-powered sawmill on New Hope Plantation in Cuba.

Whether or not Howe literally gathered the slaves together to hear his oration before the bellowing sawmill (that they, of course, had built), one can only wonder what they thought of his claims to have harnessed the forces of nature "to subserve the purposes of man." In any event, his speech was a remarkable display of self-congratulation and nationalistic chauvinism.[5]

After this auspicious launch, events quickly soured at New Hope. By August, Howe reported to his employer that the man in charge of the sawmill made out "tolerably in sawing timber and plank, but it requires more art than he possesses to saw boards well . . . He may however improve with practice—[or] he may spoil the saw." Howe insisted that many more slaves were needed to fell trees, run the sawmill, and start construction on the planned sugar works. By early December, Howe reported that few logs had been sawn, the only road was in "desperate condition," food was running short after a gale destroyed their crops, and the engineer was threatening to quit unless he got a substantial raise. Eight days later, the sawmill broke, apparently because a critical part was made of unseasoned wood. Far worse, on Christmas Day, a ship that was carrying four mechanics bound for New Hope was lost at sea. By then, the sawmill's steam engine, after repeated stalls, adjustments, and repairs, was out of commission entirely for want of a leather belt. Moreover, the slaves were "destitute of blankets and clothing." The outlook seemed to improve in the new year, when the sawmill was repaired, but then Howe had trouble with his labor force. He had to punish several of his hungry men for killing another planter's pigs that they caught in the woods. Several other slaves were ill, with "one negro apparent near his end." After attempting to bleed a sick man with a dull lancet, Howe inquired after a doctor willing to make the long journey from Havana, only to learn that the city was beset by a deadly cholera epidemic. Throughout these travails, Howe complained that James DeWolf and his son were unresponsive and slow to fulfill his requests. Clearly depressed, he asked his diary, "Do Labor-saving machines conduce to the general happiness of mankind?" Despite his earlier enthusiasm, he may well have answered in the negative.[6]

In April 1833, while fifty to sixty Havanans were still dying of cholera every day, Howe, having fulfilled his year-long commitment, returned to Rhode Island. One of his concluding remarks about his Cuban sojourn was that, without more supplies and attention from the absentee owners, "New Hope will be converted to No Hope." While Howe's experience illuminates some of the significant challenges of integrating first-generation technology into an undeveloped region using slave labor, the DeWolfs' investment in steam power eventually paid off. Despite labor problems and technical difficulties, perhaps some the result of deliberate sabotage, they revived their fortunes with sugar, mahogany, and slaves. Although the disgraced George De-Wolf remained an outcast from Bristol, the rest of the family regained their social prominence and diversified their slave-derived assets into more respectable and highly remunerative American businesses and industries.

For Cuba as a whole, steam power brought great wealth to the ruling Creole elite who were the leading landowners. Since its sugar boom came later than elsewhere in the Caribbean, Cuban planters benefitted from state-of-the-art technologies that catapulted them into the forefront of world sugar production. This transformation resulted in a very similar pattern of land clearance and deforestation as occurred earlier on Jamaica and other sugar islands but, thanks to the infusion of steam power, the scale and speed of change was unprecedented. Not least, steam trains proved especially destructive of the island's forests as enormous quantities of wood were consumed to fuel their engines and to make railroad ties. While cheaper wood and coal soon began to be imported from the United States for these purposes, the pressure to stoke the boilers of every steam engine on the island meant that sometimes even valuable tropical hardwoods ended up in the fireboxes. In 1831, Ramón de la Sagra, the Spanish naturalist, already alarmed at the rapid diminishment of Cuba's forests, denounced this practice of burning for fuel "the most costly trees, which cannot be recovered in four generations." But the biggest consumer of Cuba's mahogany was the export market. Thousands of the island's trees ended up in the lumberyards of North America where cabinetmaking firms, large and small, urban and rural, provided a ready market. During the 1840s, for example, the D. C. & W. Pell Company of New York regularly advertised auctions of mahogany logs from Cuba (as well as highly coveted Cuban cigars). While a few concerned individuals on the island sought to restore some balance between the private rights of landowners to exploit their timber as they wished and the communal good of maintaining forests for the future, attempts to re-regulate logging on Cuba went nowhere. From the late eighteenth century to the end of the nineteenth century, Cuba went from having around 80 percent forest cover to less than 15 percent.[7]

Compared with Cuba, the exploitation of mahogany resources on Hispaniola proceeded more slowly because, after the conflagration of the Haitian Revolution, almost no infrastructure survived and much of the island's remaining capital had fled with the exodus of its French and Spanish residents. After years of war, the island's economy was completely shattered and the former prosperity of St. Domingue was but a memory. In 1822, Haiti's new president, Jean-Pierre Boyer, took over Santo Domingo in an effort to unite the island. As in Haiti, he instituted a new system of land tenure (which included confiscating the abandoned estates and redistributing them to his supporters) and freed the remaining slaves. He then sought to placate the few remaining large proprietors and to resuscital the economy.[8]

The terrible conditions in Haiti were exacerbated by the United States' refusal to recognize it as a new addition to the world family of nations. Since 1806, the United States had also imposed a trade embargo on Haiti that hindered its recovery, even as it renewed economic ties with France, its former colonial occupier. Any thaw in American relations with Haiti, however, was loudly opposed by white Southern slave owners, especially after the 1822 Denmark Vesey slave conspiracy which was allegedly inspired by the revolutionary example of Haiti. These policies had serious, long-term negative consequences for the island economy. Boyer regularly appealed to the U.S. government to soften its hard position towards Haiti, but to no avail, although some minor trade did revive during the 1820s.

Catalogue of 305 Logs

CUBA MAHOGANY,

PER BRIG FALCONER,

TO BE SOLD AT AUCTION,

On TUESDAY, October 12th, 1847,

AT 3 O'CLOCK, IN RUTGERS' SLIP, E. R.

BY D. C. & W. PELL & CO.

TERMS.—Four Months, over $100, approved endorsed Notes.

	1	255	0	R,	8	207	2	R,	3	262	6	R,	5	383	2
R,	2	276	8		9	168	0		4	143	0		6	311	8
	3	262	10	R,	10	192	6		5	160	0	R,	7	275	6
	4	181	4	R,	1	213	10		6	303	4		8	168	9
				R,	2	235	0		7	105	0		9	157	6
		975	10	R,	3	190	0		8	154	0	R,	40	128	11
R off		138	4		4	165	0			1127	10			1425	6
nett		837	6	R,	5	250	2	R off		131	3	R off		893	9
				R,	6	123	8								
R,	5	596	0			1745	4	nett		996	7	nett		1031	9
	6	227	6	R off		706	2								
		823	6	nett		1039	2	R,	9	228	8		1	184	0
R off		298	0					R,	30	222	10		2	223	8
				R,	7	350	0	R,	1	169	0		3	155	10
nett		525	6		8	140	0	R,	2	238	0		4	270	4
				R,	9	146	8	R,	3	247	10		5	232	6
R,	7	624	0		20	205	4	R,	4	154	0		6	176	0
R off		312	0	R,	1	134	0			1260	4			1242	4
nett		312	0		2	97	6	R off		630	2	R off		621	2
						1073	6	nett		630	2	nett		621	2
				R off		315	4								
				nett		758	2								

FIG. 8.4 "Catalogue of 305 Logs, Cuba Mahogany ... to be Sold at Auction," D. C. & W. Pell & Co., New York, NY, 12 October 1847. Collection of Winterthur Museum Library; Joseph Downs Collection of Manuscripts and Printed Ephemera.

This annotated auction catalog itemizes each Cuban mahogany log to be sold, indicating the estimated board feet and refuse in each, officially measured inspected by Thomas Constantine, a mahogany surveyor and experienced cabinetmaker.

After agreeing to pay a huge indemnity to France in exchange for its recognition of Haiti's independence, Boyer became desperate to generate revenues for the state. As others had done during the Revolution, he recognized that mahogany was the only natural resource on the island of immediate value so he fixated on monopolizing it. Although previously much less significant to the island's economy than sugar, mahogany briefly became the most important commodity as Boyer sought to overcome the current crisis.

His first step towards reserving mahogany for the sole benefit of the state was to prohibit all unlicensed mahogany cutting on private as well as public lands. This decision instantly alienated many islanders, both propertied and unpropertied, who were relying on mahogany to sustain themselves. Boyer faced protests from large landowners whose support he had hoped to elicit, especially those on the east side of the island where mahogany and cattle hides were their sole produce. His decree was even more devastating, however, for freed slaves who relied on woodcutting to survive. For them, hauling a few merchantable logs down from the no mans land of the mountains was an essential supplement to their meager subsistence.

To extract any value from Haiti's rich forests, Boyer realized that he needed both a viable work force and a significant infusion of capital to establish large-scale logging operations. Having only recently achieved their freedom, however, the former slaves had no desire to give up their new-found autonomy to work for others, whether cutting mahogany at the president's behest or returning to the sugar plantations. To address the resulting labor shortage, President Boyer instituted the infamous 1826 *Code Rural* that dictated a coercive new set of labor laws. While mainly designed to force former slaves back to the cane fields, it also precluded "those whose profession it is to cut timber for exportation" from being self-employed; they now had to sign on to six-month contracts with large landowners who were licensed to cut mahogany for the state. Across the board, these laws met with intense resistance from freed slaves who were unwilling to return to the scenes of their former oppression.[9]

To attract more motivated laborers, Boyer sought assistance from the American Colonization Society, a controversial organization in the United States that advocated and funded the voluntary immigration of free blacks and recently manumitted slaves to Africa and other foreign destinations. Boyer proposed that some of their recruits should be encouraged to move to Haiti, where he hoped that they would inject new vitality into the workforce and perhaps bring useful contacts that would be "an infallible means of augmenting the commerce of the United States [and Haiti]." He was particularly eager to attract men who were skilled as wood sawyers, cabinetmakers, carpenters, and those "capable of working in a timber-yard." As incentives he offered land grants and the guarantee of full citizenship, free from "the degrading yoke of prejudice." Approximately 6,000 African Americans took President Boyer up on his offer. Their idealized vision of the black republic was soon undermined, however, when they confronted the language barrier, unexpected cultural alienation, conflicts over the promised land grants, and harassment from hostile neighbors who resented their preferential treatment. As persons of African ancestry, the newcomers were automatically eligible for Haitian citizenship, but in reality the government's oppressive policies severely limited their political rights. The *Code Rural* was particularly galling to them since it severely restricted workers' rights to move or change jobs. While some of the Americans stayed and made new lives in Haiti, the vast majority, unable to reconcile the promise of Haiti with the reality of widespread poverty and dictatorial governance, ultimately returned home, convinced that they could enlarge their freedom more effectively in the United States, despite continued slavery in the south.[10]

As a black market for Haitian mahogany began to develop, Boyer finally modified the woodcutting ban in 1830 to allow landowners to fell the trees on their own private lands, but mahogany exports were still closely regulated and taxed. Production continued to be limited by the lack of sawmills and economical modes of transport. According to a later account, residents on the formerly Spanish side of the island claimed that the first steam engine to run a sawmill was "brought out from the United States by the village priest, Padre Moya, who had it put up; and [hired] an American . . . to run it. Logs from the neighboring hills were sawn and afterwards floated down the Camou River. . . ." But after years of war, "the Spaniards left the mill ruined, as they did everything when they departed the island."[11]

In 1834, President Boyer succeeded in reestablishing a steam-powered mahogany sawmill. With help from a few wealthy individuals, he set up a public-private partnership to finance the purchase of $20,000 worth of equipment imported from France. But the enterprise quickly failed due to a lack of experienced engineers to train operators and to maintain the sophisticated machinery. Thereafter efforts to attract additional capital proved exceedingly difficult. American investors, in particular, were skittish because the United States still refused to extend formal trade and diplomatic relations to the fledgling nation.[12]

In the absence of adequate investments of foreign capital, the methods of cutting and transporting mahogany remained, by and large, quite primitive. Most logging continued to be done by "black and poor colored people, who live isolated upon small farms of one family, scattered within the rich, uncut forests." In addition to doing subsistence agriculture, these independent men felled a few logs at a time, taking only those that they could move by hand with a few men or that they could cut up into manageable pieces. Larger logs were often abandoned by workers when the paths proved too muddy to traverse. Years later, a visitor reported seeing "the country people . . . in their strange boats, a canoe dug out of huge trees, which, propelled by its one man occupant, probably comes forty or fifty miles" to bring to market "two or three bits of mahogany the average size of which is about three feet long." According to this observer, "all of this cutting is done with the rudest of implements, no saw whatever being used, and the pieces being simply hewn into rough logs of a size suitable for transportation." The lack of railroads or passable roads also hindered Haiti's mahogany industry from reaching the level of productivity that President Boyer envisioned, especially once the more accessible mahogany trees were depleted. The first steam railroads were not built until the 1870s and then the routes were laid out to service the still struggling plantation sector.[13]

In the meantime, landowners supplemented their incomes with mahogany exports. Since timber was typically sold through foreign agents, however, the majority of revenues generated did not end up with the landowners or stay on the island. By the late nineteenth century, most landowners, having felled their merchantable trees, shifted to growing tobacco and other crops. Independent woodcutters fared worse, receiving a mere pittance for all their exertions, after middlemen and mahogany dealers took their shares. In one backwoods community, for example, the main outlet for their timber was through a "South Carolina mulatto" who had settled there and traded "with the country people for mahogany and other woods." In addition to the export market, there was also some demand for mahogany on the island. According to Benjamin Hunt, a white man who lived in Haiti for many years, cabinetmaking was "carried on sufficiently to supply nearly all the furniture of this sort used in the island. . . . An elaborate armoire or clothespress, . . . some high-post bedsteads, washstands, a few simple tables, and a dozen or two of gaily painted cane-seat chairs from Boston, comprise the cabinet furniture of the average city house." He also noted that for some years, "the proprietor of one of the best cabinet-making establishments at Port-au-Prince was a colored man from Philadelphia; but the unsettled state of the country caused him to remove to Jamaica." Both the South Carolina timber trader and the

Philadelphia cabinetmaker may quite possibly have been among the Americans who came to Haiti under the auspices of the American Colonization Society.[14]

One American who invested in Haiti during the 1830s was Zephaniah Kingsley, a white planter and the patriarch of a large mixed-race family from East Florida. Despite owning several large plantations near St. Augustine, Zephaniah resolved to move his clan to Haiti a decade after Spanish Florida became a territory of the United States. Formerly Spanish subjects, the Kingsleys were very disturbed by a growing hostility towards free people of color on the part of other white planters, many of whom moved to Florida from Georgia and South Carolina after the change of sovereignty in 1822. Although slavery was already prevalent in Florida before then, race relations under Spanish rule had been somewhat relaxed, and there had been a thriving free black population. Under the new political regime, increasingly prejudicial laws were enacted aimed at controlling slaves, discriminating against free people of color, and undermining free black communities.

Having amassed considerable wealth in the slave trade, Zephaniah feared that his children might be prevented from inheriting his property. His extended family included his wife Anna Madgigine Jai Kingsley, a Senegalese woman he bought when she was a young girl and who was now a propertied slaveholder in her own right, his grown children (by several slave mothers) and their families, and large numbers of slaves and former slaves, some of whom he had permitted to buy their freedom for half their assessed value. After trying unsuccessfully to promote the establishment of a caste system based on people's legal status (slave or free) rather than their skin color, Zephaniah decided his children would have greater security and opportunity in the independent black republic than in the United States. Since slavery had been abolished on Haiti, he was officially required to manumit any slaves he moved there; instead of freeing them outright, he forced them to sign on to nine-year indentures in what amounted to his own personal apprenticeship system. He also retained numerous slaves on his Florida plantations where their labor subsidized his Haitian settlement. Although he saw Haiti as a haven for his own progeny, Zephaniah remained ruthlessly proslavery.[15]

To resettle this group of about sixty persons, Zephaniah scouted out a valley on the northeast side of Hispaniola near Porte Place (now the Dominican Republic) that was surrounded by mahogany-rich forests and bisected by the narrow Yasico River, which flowed down to the open ocean. Since white men were no longer allowed to own land on Haiti, Zephaniah applied directly to President Boyer to secure title to this land in the name of his eldest son, George Kingsley, who he described as "a healthy colored man of uncorrupted morals, about thirty years of age, tolerable well educated, of very industrious habits, and a native of Florida." Leaving his son in charge, Zephaniah returned to Florida and sent six "prime African men, my own slaves, liberated for that express purpose" to clear the land which was "thickly timbered with lofty woods." A year later, the rest of the family relocated to Haiti, settling into freshly built whitewashed log cabins with an adjacent provisions ground. The men also built a sawmill and began to export mahogany and other timber. The indentured men received parcels of land to cultivate for themselves, but they were also required to work the Kingsleys' land. Some Kingsley family members eventually returned to Florida (including two sisters, who both married Scotsmen, one a shipbuilder and the other a sawmill operator), but George stayed, cleared the land, and established a viable plantation.[16]

Zephaniah meanwhile actively promoted Haiti in the United States, publishing pamphlets describing its natural resources and economic potential, soliciting American capital to invest in its agricultural and industrial development, and encouraging the American Colonization Society to sponsor further immigration of free blacks to the island. He lobbied Congress to normalize diplomatic and trade relations with Haiti. To Southern slave masters he recommended it as a preferred destination for free blacks who might otherwise become troublesome. Despite his efforts, however, the United States still refused to recognize Haiti. Some French capital flowed into Haiti, but most American companies and private investors remained reluctant to sink substantial money into projects as long as Haiti's status remained in limbo. Haiti's independence was not formally recognized by the United States until 1862 when Lincoln initiated diplomatic relations, with an eye towards possibly sending former slaves there.

After years of political isolation and economic struggles, Hispaniola's development was seriously stunted and industrialization lagged far behind that of Cuba. In 1871, Philadelphia publisher Samuel Hazard travelled to the island as part of President Grant's commission to assess whether the United States should annex Santo Domingo. While generally dismayed by the island's lack of modernization, he was especially appalled by the inefficiency of the logging industry, observing later that "hardy lumbermen from the Middle and New England States, with their experience and sawmills, would find a mine of gold in all these timbered lands . . . [since] the present mode of getting out this timber is very rude." At one point during his journey, he stumbled upon an abandoned steam engine that once powered a mahogany mill, lying on the banks of a river, "utterly useless and broken." Darkly eyeing this rusted hulk, Hazard pronounced it "a fitting emblem of dead progress."[17]

Meanwhile, demand for Honduran mahogany increased during the 1830s as it became more popular in the United States, although it was still mainly exported to England. Even surrounded by political turmoil as much of Central America pursued independence from Spain, tiny Belize—now a British protectorate—remained little changed since the days of the Card brothers. For all intents and purposes, it was still dominated by a handful of powerful Baymen. When slavery was abolished in 1834, a four-year apprenticeship was instituted to bridge the transition to a free labor market; even after it ended in 1838, however, the formerly enslaved woodcutters were not truly "freed from the very real constraints of persistent power structures." In fact, they had few options other than continuing to work for their former masters, who still effectively monopolized the forests and controlled access to land, thus limiting freelance woodcutting and subsistence agriculture. Moreover, in the face of entrenched social relations and the one-dimensional economy, the Baymen were not very interested in innovation; mahogany continued to be harvested using the same old methods, although competition for trees was fiercer than ever.[18]

In neighboring Guatemala, Francisco Morazán, president of the short-lived Central American Federation, sought to monopolize the land's mahogany trees to fund his new government, but he needed assistance to extract the valuable timber. Marshall Bennett, one of the more entrepreneurial (or one might say, cagier) Baymen, successfully ingratiated himself with Morazán, offering his logging expertise and overseas trade connections in exchange for an exclusive woodcutting contract. Along with a few friends to whom he leased woodcutting concessions, Bennett sent logging crews from Belize into Guatemala. In true Baymen's style, they ignored orders from British officials to desist from private dealings with an unrecognized foreign government. Although Bennett died in 1839, others succeeded him, sparking another rush on the region's mahogany. Land, labor, and capital became increasingly concentrated in the hands of a small number of logging companies.[19]

Within twenty years, the negative effects of years of intense mahogany extraction were evident. While large tracts of untapped forest remained in the interior, maps of the Bay of Honduras from the early nineteenth century reveal a proliferation of areas designated as "cut out," especially along the main waterways and coastal lowlands. The general consensus was that "Mahogany woods, once cut out, are gone for ever, as the growing of mahogany is impossible" and abandoned mahogany works were considered "forever after useless." Although a few Baymen cited "instances of abandoned works recently reopened and providing a plentiful supply" and others optimistically claimed cut-out areas could be re-logged in a mere thirty years or so, in reality, once woodcutters had taken all the mature mahogany trees and moved on, the ravaged forests seldom recovered. In 1835, local leaders, conceding that some regulations were needed to protect future seed-bearing trees, banned the export of undersized wood and, three years later, enacted "a Law for the preservation of the young mahogany." The restrictions were too late, however, to reverse the general trend of mahogany depletion in much of the country.[20]

The faltering mahogany industry in the Bay of Honduras received a major boost in the 1850s when the first steam railroad was built. As was the case on Cuba decades earlier, the combination of new technology and infrastructure allowed logging to expand into remote areas that had been previously uneconomical to reach. During the 1880s to 1910s, government officials in Belize solicited several large American and British timber companies to invest in steam-powered sawmills, steam launches, and additional rail lines to penetrate still deeper into the interior. While these new modes of production and transport gave Belize's mahogany industry a reprieve, it never regained its former prominence. The once all-powerful oligarchy weakened and became increasingly irrelevant. Left with nothing but expanses of sun-scorched land, many residents either migrated elsewhere or refashioned themselves as planters or ranchers. For wageworkers, however, conditions worsened as they lost what little negotiating power they once had. Restrictive patterns of land and labor use kept many freed woodcutters enmeshed in the logging industry, even as it contracted.[21]

The Impact of Steam on Furniture Makers and Buyers

Coinciding with other trends of democratization in the United States during the antebellum period, mahogany became more accessible to a broader segment of the American populace than ever before, thanks to the revolutionary impact of steam power. With this technological innovation, the American lumber and furniture industries were increasingly reoriented towards high-volume production. Most dramatic was the invention of steam-powered veneer saws that could cut razor-thin veneers at a fraction of the former cost in labor, time, and materials. In 1806, Marc Isambard Brunel, a brilliant French engineer who worked at the Chatham Dockyards in England, patented the first steam-powered veneer saw. After developing several other steam-powered saws for use in shipbuilding for the British Navy, he set up a veneer sawmill as a private venture. Finding his invention's horizontal knife-like blade could negotiate only smooth-grained woods, such as Honduran mahogany, he continued to experiment and developed a more versatile circular-saw that could delicately fillet any wood with speed, precision, and consistency. When one London observer first witnessed the human sawyers' mechanical replacement huffing along in 1814, he was astonished that it almost instantly sliced "veneers 1/16 of an inch thick, with a precision and grandeur of action that was really sublime . . . so even and so uniform that it appeared more like a perfect work of nature than one of human art." He was equally impressed that it "converted the whole of the wood into veneers, without waste." Revolving sixty-five times a minute, it reportedly could cut a ten-foot veneer sheet in ten minutes; an average machine-cut log yielded over 3,000 feet of veneer whereas a pit saw, drawn steadily by two men, yielded only about ninety feet, and it took much longer.[22]

In America, from the 1820s on, patents proliferated for all manner of innovative wood-processing machinery—all powered by steam—

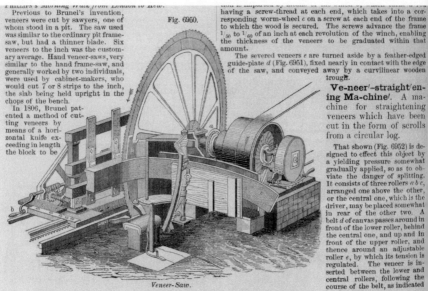

Previous to Brunel's invention, veneers were cut by sawyers, one of whom stood in a pit. The saw used was similar to the ordinary pit frame-saw, but had a thinner blade. Six veneers to the inch was the customary average. Hand veneer-saws, very similar to the hand frame-saw, and generally worked by two individuals, were used by cabinet-makers, who would cut 7 or 8 strips to the inch, the slab being held upright in the chops of the bench.

In 1806, Brunel patented a method of cutting veneers by means of a horizontal knife exceeding in length the block to be

Fig. 6950.

having a screw-thread at each end, which takes into a corresponding worm-wheel c on a screw at each end of the frame to which the wood is secured. The screws advance the frame $\frac{1}{50}$ to $\frac{1}{60}$ of an inch at each revolution of the winch, enabling the thickness of the veneers to be graduated within that amount.

The severed veneers e are turned aside by a feather-edged guide-plate d (Fig. 6951), fixed nearly in contact with the edge of the saw, and conveyed away by a curvilinear wooden trough.

Ve-neer'-straight'en-ing Ma-chine'. A machine for straightening veneers which have been cut in the form of scrolls from a circular log.

That shown (Fig. 6952) is designed to effect this object by a yielding pressure somewhat gradually applied, so as to obviate the danger of splitting. It consists of three rollers $a b c$, arranged one above the other, or the central one, which is the driver, may be placed somewhat in rear of the other two. A belt d of canvas passes around in front of the lower roller, behind the central one, and up and in front of the upper roller, and thence around an adjustable roller e, by which its tension is regulated. The veneer is inserted between the lower and central rollers, following the course of the belt, as indicated by the arrows.

Veneer-Saw.

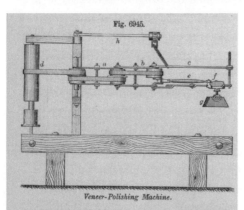

Fig. 6945.

Veneer-Polishing Machine.

and through the pitman e reciprocates the carriage f, from which the rubber g depends. The whole arrangement has sufficient flexibility to permit the rubber to be traversed laterally by the hand, while the polishing is effected in right lines by its reciprocating motion. The arm c, from which the rubber depends, is supported by a cord or chain from the stationary arm h above.

Smith's machine (Fig. 6946) comprises a band a having its exterior surface covered with an abradant, and passing around

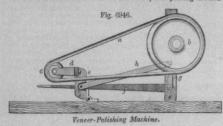

Fig. 6946.

Veneer-Polishing Machine.

FIG. 8.5 Steam-powered Veneering Saw and Veneer Polishing Machines in *Knight's American Mechanical Dictionary.* Edward H. Knight, vol. 3 (New York: Hurd and Houghton, 1876). Collection of the American Antiquarian Society.

that included numerous designs for veneer saws, sanders, and polishing machines. Some of Philadelphia's very first steam engines were used to run giant saws to cut veneers, which had always been a laborious task. In 1825, a newspaper advertisement announced that Richardson and Company's "Steam Saw Mill and Mahogany Yard . . . [having] recently put in operation their Improved Patent Rotary Veneer Cutters, propelled by steam power, are prepared to cut Veneers of any given dimension . . . Fine Veneers, cut to convenient sizes, can be supplied for shipping, on the shortest notice . . . [to] any part of the United States." By 1838, there were ten steam-powered sawmills churning out lumber and veneers in the Philadelphia vicinity; a cabinetmaker had "only to purchase a log of the wood which suits his purpose, send it to the saw mill, and he has it returned cut up to the thickness that he wishes, in a very short time, and at a trifling expense." A lithograph of the Keyser and Foxe's Mahogany Steam Sawmill, circa 1854, depicts what would have been a typical scene during this earlier period as well. Brawny workmen using block and tackle, ropes, and skiffs, heft large squared-off mahogany blocks from a hand cart into the three-story brick mill to meet the saw blades. A contemporaneous view of the Price and Harper's Steam Saw Mill, which advertised "all kinds of plain and fancy sawing," shows the "after" scene: heaps of mahogany and other types of milled woods piled high in the lumber yard, awaiting buyers while sooty black smoke from the steam engine billows out of the tall chimney.[23]

Inventors and manufacturers promoted these new technological wonders for their virtues both as labor-saving and wood-conservation devices. As one report proclaimed, the value now extracted from "a single log of fine timber . . . by means of the improved sawing machinery, is really incredible." In 1836, an article in the *Franklin Institute Journal* endorsed another new veneer saw, not only for its "cheapness and expedition, but . . . [for its] smaller waste of wood in saw dust" as compared with common saws. The author was also enthusiastic that

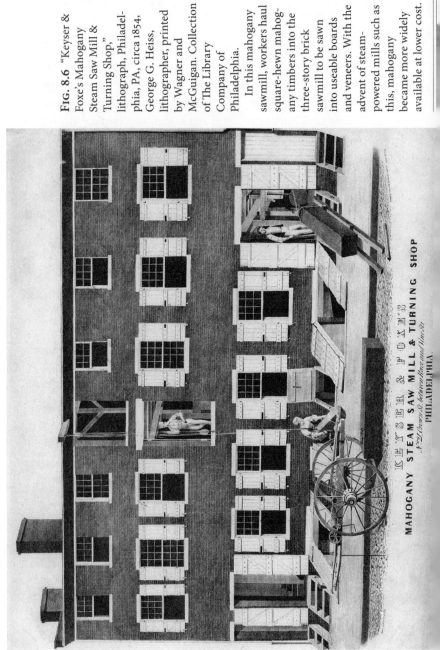

FIG. 8.6 "Keyser & Foxe's Mahogany Steam Saw Mill & Turning Shop," lithograph, Philadelphia, PA, circa 1854, George G. Heiss, lithographer, printed by Wagner and McGuigan. Collection of The Library Company of Philadelphia.

In this mahogany sawmill, workers haul square-hewn mahogany timbers into the three-story brick sawmill to be sawn into useable boards and veneers. With the advent of steam-powered mills such as this, mahogany became more widely available at lower cost.

FIG. 8.7 "Price & Harper's Steam Saw Mill, Fancy Chair Manufactory and Lumber Yard," color lithograph, Philadelphia, PA, 1855, William H. Rease, lithographer, printed by Wagner and McGuigan. Collection of The Library Company of Philadelphia.

This large-scale lumberyard, with its vast stockpiles of timber, highlights the exponential increase in mahogany consumption during the nineteenth century. Mahogany is advertised here alongside other locally-harvested woods, such as walnut, cherry, and maple.

the device could be "worked by a single man, with the aid of a boy to gather the leaves as they are taken off . . . a thousand leaves may be cut in an hour from hard wood." As the price of veneers subsequently came down, cabinetmakers dressed up all sorts of plain wooden furniture frames with a thin decorative layer of mahogany at a fraction of the expense and effort that would have been required to fabricate the same object out of solid mahogany or with thicker hand-cut veneers.[24]

One entrepreneur who catered to the demand for inexpensive veneers was John Copcott, who expanded his father's mahogany yard into one of the largest veneer-cutting enterprises in the country. Years of experience in dealing with tropical hardwoods gave him a discerning eye for the quality of timber. According to one contemporary, Copcott "could see right through a log." In 1835, he established a veneer-cutting mill in the Bronx. After it burned, he moved his enterprise up the Hudson River to Yonkers where he converted a former gristmill on the Neperhan River into a veneer-cutting sawmill and eventually became one of the city's wealthiest residents.[25]

Thomas Williams, the son of a New Jersey farmer and part-time cabinetmaker, exemplified the profits to be had by harnessing the new technologies. After learning his father's woodworking craft and perhaps growing bored with rural life, Williams moved to New York City in the early 1820s where he established his own cabinetmaking shop. After a few years, however, he followed the example of the New York cabinetmakers who capitalized on their craft knowledge of wood to transition from furniture making to timber dealing. Setting aside his tools, Williams opened a large lumberyard on Wall Street, just down the street from the booming workshops of Duncan Phyfe and several other leading New York cabinetmakers.[26]

Thanks to a propitious marriage, he built his business into a small empire that seemed to grow in size along with the city itself. What set him apart from many of his peers was that he immediately invested in all the newest, most innovative wood-processing technologies. He was quick, for example, to install a lumber-drying facility that seasoned wood in a fraction of the time once required. Every few years, he expanded to ever-larger waterfront premises, improving and streamlining his supply and distribution networks by connecting with steamship lines and nearby rail links. His firm imported huge quantities of Honduran mahogany and, by the mid-nineteenth century, it was also in the forefront of importing other exotic woods from India, Australia, Burma, Java, Ceylon, and Africa. In many of these locales, the firm hired its own agents to select and cut woods according to company specifications.

Despite the growth of large-scale urban lumberyards, however, cabinetmakers, especially in provincial or rural areas, still operated with a high degree of uncertainty as to what mahogany would be available to them at any given moment. In western Massachusetts, for example, information about the latest fashions, consumer products, and inventions reached the general populace quickly through newspapers, periodicals, visiting lecturers, and other media, yet maintaining a reliable mahogany supply proved difficult at times. In May of 1847, Edward Carpenter, a cabinetmaker's apprentice, recorded in his journal that his master, Isaac Miles, had traveled from the town of Greenfield, Massachusetts, to Hartford, Connecticut, the closest city, to buy a supply of mahogany veneers. In the following months, Carpenter carefully glued them over the butternut cases of bureaus and secretaries, which flew out of his master's shop to the parlors and dining rooms of local residents. Miles soon returned to Hartford for more veneers but came home empty-handed; he was forced to "send to New York after veneers, for there was none to buy in Hartford that was good for anything."[27]

Moreover, since each mahogany log was to some degree unique, it could be difficult to maintain consistency and, at times, impossible to match woods. In 1837, for example, Joseph Willoughby, a New York mahogany dealer, explained to a Providence cabinetmaker: "You wish me to send you 400 feet of the same kind of Veneers of which you had

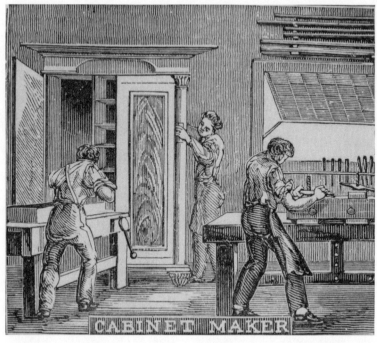

FIG. 8.8 "The Cabinet-maker, and The Upholsterer," engraved illustration, *The Panorama of Professions and Trades, or Every Man's Book*. Edward Hazen (Philadelphia: Uriah Hunt, 1836). Collection of the American Antiquarian Society.

some . . . I had much rather send the remainder of the Log, it is what you never will get of me again . . . there is in all probability [no chance] of me ever having the like again."[28]

While many variables might account for the temporary unavailability of mahogany veneers in provincial New England cities, one important contributing factor was the reverberating effect of tropical deforestation. Yet, the constant influx of mahogany from new locales as older ones were depleted, the proliferation of large urban lumberyards, and increasingly industrialized furniture production gave most

Americans the illusion of limitless mahogany supplies. But quite contrary to the early conservationist promises made about steam technologies, industrialization led instead to vastly increased consumption of precious woods. Demand for inexpensive furnishings exploded and their manufacturers were understandably intent on selling more parlor sets as long as consumers were eager to buy them. Hence, although manufacturers indeed sliced each log thinner and thinner—stretching their raw materials—they ultimately used more trees.

Mahogany for the Masses

The mechanization of the furniture industry in the nineteenth century is sometimes cited as having contributed to a degradation in the quality of craftsmanship, a misconception that has been termed the "myth of technological decadence." In fact, skilled artisans in England and America continued to turn out much excellent furniture that was well designed, carefully constructed, exquisitely ornamented, and meticulously finished and polished. Although some were custom made, many of these objects, destined for the upscale market, were made for stock out of machine-milled lumber and pre-fabricated parts, but reputable cabinetmakers sought out the finest available mahogany (solid or veneers as needed) and still did considerable handwork such as carving and hand-finishing. By definition, such high-end goods were expensive, both in terms of labor and materials, but they certainly were available to those willing and able to pay for that level of quality.[29]

At the same time, however, with the introduction of inexpensive steam-cut veneers, mahogany objects of lesser quality also proliferated. Consequently, this once rarified material (or at least a superficial version of it) became a truly mass-produced, mass-marketed product. Almost anyone could now boast of a mahogany desk or table enhanced with a razor-thin layer of fancy wood. Most average Americans were wildly enthusiastic about the democratization of mahogany that veneers made possible. An 1830 book on domestic economy approvingly reported that, "the comparative cheapness of furniture made . . . of this beautiful material . . . [has] introduced a more elegant description of furniture even into the commonest of houses. In this, there is a great national benefit."

Not everyone was so sanguine about the social effects of this new level of consumer spending on household goods. Touring rural England in 1825, William Cobbett, an English reformer and advocate for the poor, was startled to find many a farmer's cottage, "formerly the scene of plain manners," updated with a "mahogany table, and the fine chairs, and the fine glass." While he believed that "abundant living amongst the people at large . . . [was] the surest basis of national greatness and security," he feared that the accessibility of such nonessential consumer goods was tempting people to live beyond their means and station in life, transmuting them into "a species of mock gentle folk." In his *Advice Book for Young Men,* reprinted in the United States in 1833, Cobbett warned of the ruinous "consequences of a want of frugality in the middle and lower ranks," especially among young women "full of admiration of the trappings of the rich and of desire to be able to imitate them." While Cobbett was somewhat sympathetic to the strivings of humble folk within bounds, others roundly condemned the mass consumption of mahogany among the lower and middling orders as crass, inappropriate displays of indulgence and vanity. Rather paradoxically, even as mahogany became more commonplace, in the form of inexpensive veneers, its powerful cultural associations with gentility and refinement remained strong, resonating far beyond their elite white origins. Indeed, one of the main reasons that the democratization of mahogany was so objectionable to some was that this material still *mattered* as a marker of social status. Even as the social elite sought to exclude others by emphasizing the quality and quantity of their mahogany over mere possession of it, more humble people sought it out and regarded its acquisition as a legitimate avenue of self-improvement.[30]

During the antebellum period, the high regard for mahogany was particularly evident among free African Americans in northern cities. Furnishing their homes with mahogany objects bespoke both their modest economic gains and desire for respectability. It also asserted their right to join in the dominant culture of consumption, partaking of all the trappings and rituals of domesticity. In New York, Boston, and Philadelphia, free black communities established their own institutions—including churches, schools, literary groups, abolitionist societies, mutual aid associations, and newspapers—many of which were geared towards promoting education, morality, and social reform. The churches played a particularly important role as centers of community life. Accordingly, their congregations stretched themselves financially to construct substantial buildings with sumptuous sanctuaries, often outfitted with mahogany pews and pulpits. These dignified edifices confidently announced their presence as an integral part of the urban landscape. To their members, the lofty spaces and beautiful interiors were intended to be inspiring and spiritually uplifting places, especially for those whose daily lives permitted few material indulgences.[31]

As African American communities strived to improve their situation, mahogany seemed to align with their aspirations because of its literal and metaphorical associations with refinement. In 1837, for example, *The Colored American,* one of New York City's first black newspapers, published a heated debate sparked by a used-clothing drive. Sponsored by a society dedicated to "the Moral Elevation" of black youth, the drive was intended to outfit children with proper attire and thus encourage their regular school attendance. After someone complained that the event over-emphasized the superficialities of dress, another writer responded that for African American children to succeed in the dominant white culture, they had to cultivate *both* a respectable outward appearance and a solid inner character: "Our children should be taught that a decent exterior does not destroy merit, but greatly adds to its lustre; just as the brush and varnish does to the mahogany furniture. The value of furniture is not destroyed by the brightness of the polish it receives, but rather enhanced, by being brought more fully to view." Furthermore, the writer insisted, "the inward and outward man should correspond. . . . [If] the intellect be cultivated, polished, and refined, so should our dress and manners be also." For better or worse, appearances mattered in the United States; as Ralph Waldo Emerson phrased it, there remained "a strict relation between the class of power, and the exclusive and polished circles." To many in the free black communities of the North, acquisitions of polished mahogany symbolized both their accomplishments and their hopes for future advancement.[32]

Some in the African American communities, however, feared that consumption of nonessentials was part of a frivolous trend that might undermine the economic foundations and the moral rectitude of their communities. One critic, for example, expressed concern that the increasingly elegant churches might intimidate poor people and discourage them from attending if they found everything "polished and cushioned above [their] level." An 1841 article in *The Colored Freeman* scolded a poor mother for insisting on burying her young son in "a beautiful mahogany coffin," rather than a more affordable and more appropriate "common stained coffin." Reminiscent of William Cobbett's comments about the "mock gentle folk," the author complained that such conceits set a bad example for the working poor.[33]

African Americans' new consumption patterns attracted unwelcome negative attention from outside their own number as well. Amidst the growing racial animus that troubled many northern cities during the antebellum period, blacks' acquisition of highly visible consumer goods aroused particular resentment on the part of their white, mostly working class, neighbors. In August 1834, a riot broke out in Philadelphia in which white mobs viciously attacked African American churches, homes, and businesses. Sparked by an altercation between white and black youths, the angry crowd was comprised mainly of young, white men, including laborers, apprentices, Irish immigrants, and "a class of mechanics of whom better things are expected," including at least one cabinetmaker, a carpenter, and a blacksmith. When the police finally quelled the chaos in the "city of brotherly love" three days later, one black man had been killed and many injured, two black churches had been burned, and over thirty houses lay in ruins. In a typical incident, later reported in the *U.S. Gazette,* a substantial three-story brick house "owned by a black man named Mr. Moor, was assailed . . . and every article of furniture destroyed . . . the mahogany sideboard hewed to pieces . . . the bedsteads and mahogany banisters, cut up into small particles, as for kindling wood." The *Commercial Herald* reported that the rioters' major target seemed to be "negroes of property and substance." During the 1830s to 1840s, numerous similar attacks took place, including some directed against abolitionists, black and white; in those instances, their participants (and possibly their instigators) included elite whites who were proslavery.[34]

To understand the significance of these disturbing events—in which, amidst generalized violence, African Americans' treasured mahogany objects were apparently deliberately targeted for destruction—they must be considered in light of the period's popular literature in which people of color were increasingly described as "mahogany." Mahogany objects thus seemed to serve provocatively as stand-ins for absent black bodies. Moreover, the dramatic destruction of African Americans' most personal household possessions—beds, cradles, chairs, and dining tables—acted out in the public streets, functioned as a form of psychological terrorism, a deliberately humiliating campaign

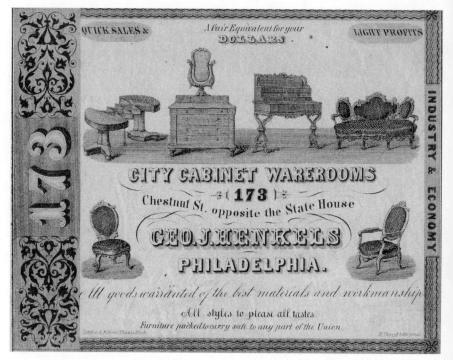

FIG. 8.9 Trade Card, George J. Henkels, Cabinetmaker, Philadelphia, PA, circa 1850, Augustus Kollner, lithographer, printed by H. Camp. Collection of The Library Company of Philadelphia.

George J. Henkels advertised and warranted furniture stock readily available in his City Cabinet Warerooms, emphasizing his "Industry and Economy" and "Quick Sales & Light Profits." Notable here is the image of an innovative expandable dining table.

of intimidation aimed at people's fundamental sense of security, belonging, and self-worth. While the perpetrators may or may not have been self-conscious about their actions, the emotional impact for their victims was the same. These acts revealed the fault lines of class and racial tensions as alienated, mostly working-class, white citizens, disgruntled with their own situations in life, sought to puncture what they perceived as their black neighbors' unacceptable social pretensions.[35]

FIG. 8.10 "George Mecke's Northern Cabinet Ware-Rooms." Lithograph, Philadelphia, PA, circa 1847. Published by W. H. Rease, Wagner and McGuigan. Courtesy of the Library Company of Philadelphia.

George Mecke, a Philadelphia cabinetmaker and upholsterer, established his furniture warerooms in a central location so his clients could conveniently see samples of his work or purchase ready stock.

Veneers of Deceit

By the mid-nineteenth century, the character and sourcing of mahogany had changed considerably, resulting in a new hierarchy of materials that looked quite different from what an eighteenth-century cabinetmaker would have been familiar with. In 1860, the *Journal of the Society of Arts* laid out this revised line up: St. Domingan mahogany is "only used for cabinet makers' work of the best description, and generally in the form of veneers. The Cuba mahogany is frequently as good as the second class Spanish, and, in these days of fraud and adulteration, it is no doubt often made to pass muster under the name of the better kind." What little Jamaican mahogany still occasionally came to market was dismissed as so "inferior even to the Honduras wood that [it is] practically unknown to wood buyers." This revised mahogany hierarchy, and the persistent concerns about quality and fraud that pervaded it, reflect how changing environmental and economic conditions forced people to reassess their perceptions.[36]

Only seven years later, Philadelphia furniture maker George Henkels expressed regret that he could no longer supply his customers with the famed Santo Domingan mahogany. "The best wood has been cut off," he explained. "After the depletion of the wood on this island, Cuba mahogany [is] the best to be had." Had Henkels traveled to either island, he would have seen landscapes dominated by fields of sugar cane and dotted with tall tree stumps. The mahogany trees once grew so abundantly that woodcutters had sawn out only their most ornamental parts, leaving the rest to rot. Keenly aware that his most important raw material was disappearing on a growing list of West Indian islands, he anxiously scouted out other sources to fulfill the orders of his fashionable customers. Henkels's dilemma, of course, stemmed from the intensive drive to meet consumers' demand for exotic timbers (and clearing the way for sugar that they also desired) that culminated in the near extinction of West Indian mahogany.[37]

Amidst the ongoing globalization of timber sourcing in the nineteenth century, however, cabinetmakers' hierarchy of woods was constantly changing as they encountered and experimented with new timber imports, some of which were falsely labeled as mahogany. So-called "African mahogany" enjoyed brief popularity when it was introduced from Gambia to England and America in the mid-nineteenth century. Once "its true character was known," however, this imposter was quickly deemed unsatisfactory. Objects made from it could not be trusted because they changed color, deepening "into a dirty purple, of a most disagreeable appearance ... inferior to genuine mahogany." The resulting scandal seriously damaged the reputations of several cabinetmakers who used it "in ignorance of its qualities." At the same time, the "celebrity attained by the exports from St. Domingo" encouraged timber dealers to falsely label wood from other locales by that name, as was once done with Jamaican wood during its earlier reign.[38]

The changes in the mahogany market and the industrialization of furniture production had some unexpected side effects, which consumers had to learn to negotiate. In particular, some unscrupulous furniture makers cut corners by using flimsy veneers and lower grades of mahogany that previous generations of cabinetmakers would have spurned. Clad in a miniscule layer of mahogany veneer, their productions often looked beautiful in the showroom, only to warp, chip, or delaminate once an unsuspecting customer brought them home. Astute consumers learned to recognize substance and quality beyond an object's superficial appearance, but many people expressed anxiety that they could no longer trust in an object's external appearance to assess its integrity. The earlier appreciation for the artistic finesse of veneers began to be tinged with suspicion. During this same period, some consumers were wary of the new technique of silver plating, in which a microscopic silver layer was applied onto a base metal (such as copper), because the polished surfaces seemed similarly deceptive.[39]

Advice books laid out some of the pitfalls for ill-informed furniture buyers. In 1838, for example, one popular women's magazine featured a long article about the hazards of veneers, warning of cabinetmakers who "from press of business, or lack of principle," used poor-quality timber or took shortcuts by not seasoning wood long enough. Cautioning that one should buy only high-quality furniture from retailers "of known probity," it distinguished between coarse Honduran mahogany objects, that "rarely fail to crack," and superior Spanish mahogany, that "though much more expensive . . . is far more certain, hard, rich-colored, and durable." American merchants, it warned, were swamping the market with Honduran mahogany in "vast quantities of that open-grained, ugly, inferior kind, that . . . is so cheap that purchasers are continually deceived by unprincipled tradesmen, by the substitution of the one for the other." Just as cabinetmakers mistrusted wood dealers who might sell them a log that appeared outwardly sound but was rotten within, furniture consumers had to be on guard against swindlers who sought to pass off cheap imitations as the genuine article.[40]

Qualms about possible deceptions in the marketplace reflected deeper apprehension about eroding social relations, particularly in light of the unprecedented migration of people into urban areas in England and the United States. During the first quarter of the nineteenth century, many traditional indicators of social hierarchy began to break down. Consequently, as daily life was increasingly "characterized by frequent face-to-face contact with strangers, the fleeting impressions made by surface appearances . . . [became] of great importance." As formerly clear, well-understood markers of kinship, social class, and economic status eroded, an individual's background, prospects, or intentions could no longer be easily evaluated. These changes gave rise to a crisis of confidence in people's ability to perceive or accurately judge others by external appearances. As early as 1817, William Wordsworth remarked with consternation that as society's "moral cement is dissolved, habits and prejudices are broken and rooted up, nothing being substituted in their place but a quickened self-interest." In anonymous cities, where callow young men and innocent young women might fall prey to all manner of devious persons, learning to distinguish false fronts from honest substance became a necessary survival skill. In such settings, sociologist Robert Park explained, an unknown person's status and character by default had to be evaluated "to a considerable degree by conventional signs—by fashion and 'front'—and the art of life is largely reduced to skating on thin surfaces and a scrupulous study of style and manners."[41]

Social commentators at the time, however, worried about the break-down of honesty and trust that seemed to characterize urban life. They emphasized the importance of assiduously cultivating a solid, sincere character. Distinguishing surface from substance also became a recurring theme in the popular literature and theater of the day. In *The Evil Genius* (1850), the protagonist was a man of "selfish deception . . . a mere veneer of good taste on a surface of wormwood." Another writer told the tale of a confidence man, known to be "a mere piece of surface—of simple veneer," who nevertheless achieved social prominence through flattery and guile. In a more serious context, in 1853, a critic reproached Gerritt Smith, the radical white antislavery organizer, for his involvement in the fractious Liberty Party, claiming he was using the abolitionist banner to "veneer the political aspects of the movement with a kind of moral mahogany, which ought . . . never to be thrown over it as a flimsy disguise. Honest politics have no more need to wear a mask than has virtue herself!" The harsh accusation that Smith hid his true motives behind a flimsy mask of "moral mahogany" likely struck contemporary readers as a disturbing image.[42]

Among the upper (mostly white) echelons of society in America, differences in materials served as an apt metaphor as well for class differences. The same 1830 book that celebrated the national benefit of the popularization of mahogany, as it was "universally diffused throughout society," also observed that the wealthy had responded by becoming "desirous of procuring articles not so accessible to the many." While the affluent predictably sought out more exclusive materials (such as rosewood and ebony) and indulged in still more extravagant conspicuous consumption, they did not abandon mahogany. Instead, they placed a greater emphasis on its quality and substance. Literally and metaphorically, they regarded solid mahogany and high-quality mahogany veneered objects as having greater substance and virtue than the thin veneers of their flimsy, morally suspect counterparts. Hence, the upper-crust social establishment became synonymous with the former while the nouveau riche and grasping lower orders with the latter. Charles Dickens, whose popular novels were often published serially in periodicals and widely read by Americans, thus satirized a community where on the affluent side of town all was "mahogany and French-polished," while on the other side of the tracks, all was cheap woods, "entirely changed in grain and character." In *The Mystery of Edwin Drood,* he differentiated between shops that sold elegant French-polished objects to the rich but offered everyone else "groves of deceitful, showy-looking furniture." Adapted "to the taste, or rather the means, of cheap purchasers," the latter included "the most beautiful *looking* Pembroke tables that were ever beheld: the wood as green as the trees in the Park, and the leaves almost as certain to fall off in the course of a year." In another novel, Dickens spoofed the nouveau riche with his appropriately named characters, "Mr. and Mrs. Veneering" who were:

> Bran-new people in a bran-new house in a bran-new quarter of London. . . . All their furniture was new, all their friends were new, all their servants were new . . . if they had set up a great-grandfather, he would have come home . . . French polished to the crown of his head . . . all things were in a state of high varnish and polish. And what was observable in the furniture was observable in the Veneerings—the surface smelt a little too much of the workshop and was a trifle sticky.

T. S. Arthur's *Trials and Confessions of a Housekeeper*, an advice book published in Philadelphia in 1854, offered a humorous fable of a young housewife who tried to persuade her parsimonious but impressionable husband to buy substantial mahogany furniture. Instead he was seduced by a cheaper, flashier veneered parlor suite that looked fabulous in the showroom. In just a few months, its true character was revealed when a shoddily-made chair collapsed under the weight of a hefty visitor, who tumbled over, upset the shaky center table, and sent the oil lamp crashing to the floor. As the family scrambled to find a light, their mortified guest scuttled out under cover of darkness. At last, the husband admitted the folly of his vanity and false economy. The implicit moral of the story was that a wise and virtuous person, a person of quality and substance, would not to be taken in by "common material and common workmanship."[43]

Trepidation about possible fraudulence in the external appearances of people, materials, and things were symptomatic of the rapid social and class changes underway in nineteenth-century America. But at the same time, mass consumption also served as an important democratizing current that offered individuals the chance to craft and polish their own identity. Although they were perhaps less beguiled by "mahogany" than formerly and some wealthy consumers eschewed it, American furniture buyers continued to purchase veneered furnishings, despite the risk of deception, because they were affordable, available, useful, and, hopefully, attractive.

Overall, the technological advances that made this level of consumption possible and that transformed how mahogany was produced, transported, and manufactured had mixed results. Steam engines increased the rate and geographical scope of mahogany extraction, resulting in short-term gains for mahogany logging companies but putting freelance woodcutters at a disadvantage. In the furniture industry, steam-powered veneer saws and other machinery increased output and saved on labor and wood but insulated Americans from engagement with the negative effects of their voracious consumption of a nonrenewable natural resource. People in former mahogany-producing regions, like Haiti, were left to grapple, sometimes for generations, with the often irreversible ecological destruction of their fragile environments. American timber merchants and logging companies meanwhile set their sights on new horizons in the seemingly boundless forests of Brazil, Africa, and the Far East. The notion that technology could overcome nature's limits, while still a popular American gospel, proved a false doctrine where New World mahogany was concerned.

CHAPTER NINE

An Old Species of Elegance

*T*HE AGE OF MAHOGANY waned in the latter half of the nineteenth century as the Atlantic tropical timber industry faltered
and global competition introduced such novelties as Indian rosewood, African ebony, Burmese teak, and Hawaiian koa (dubbed "the
mahogany of the Pacific"). While increasingly just one among many
consumer options, mahogany nonetheless still held powerful cultural
connotations for many Americans. The meanings and values that they
attached to it, however, shifted over time like a slow-moving kaleido-
scope. Since the late eighteenth century, references to "mahogany" had
multiplied in popular print sources—newspapers, periodicals, prescrip-
tive literature, novels, and plays—helping to generate, reinforce, and
spread its various cultural associations. "Mahogany" could evoke very
different, at times conflicting, concepts. In addition to the tensions between refinement/coarseness and solidity/superficiality discussed in
previous chapters, its new meanings included racialized exoticism,
romanticized nature, and historical nostalgia. As "mahogany" entered
the common parlance, it paralleled the actual material's assimilation
into English and later American material culture. As with many raw
materials transformed through manufacturing, however, most consumers became intimately familiar with mahogany only in its more

refined state, as finished objects in whatever shape they were given. Furthermore, as people incorporated these objects into their everyday lives, the presence of mahogany was normalized and taken for granted. But for most people, their experience with this substance was largely disconnected from the natural resources and labor invested in its production. "Mahogany" became an abstract concept that, while ostensibly signifying the wood, correlated more powerfully with the various racialized, romanticized, or elegiac *ideas* about it.[1]

Mahogany as People

In *Oroonoko: or, The Royal Slave* (1688), Aphra Behn described the heroic African prince in her play as having "a face of polished ebony." Similar uses of "mahogany" as an adjective to describe human skin color entered into the common parlance in Europe and North America during the eighteenth century, on the heels of the introduction and popularization of the wood itself. The addition of this new hue to the color vocabulary used to describe people merely added to an existing linguistic palette that linked the colors of various natural substances (such as ebony, ivory, and coal) to seemingly similar skin pigments. Initially the meanings of such terms were variable and, depending on the context, could be neutral or racially-charged descriptors. Such terminology entered into usage in Europe during the late sixteenth century (and possibly earlier), when transoceanic exploration revealed the diversity of humankind. By the seventeenth and early eighteenth centuries, material associations with skin color, although still inconsistent, became more codified into racial categories, assigned symbolic meanings, and organized into a hierarchical lexicon in which whiteness was the ideal. Humanity's rainbow now included people of ivory (pure and clean), ebony (savage and noble), oak (solid and English), and coal (base and servile). Mahogany was gradually incorporated into this descriptive vocabulary, but in very particular, and often racially charged, ways.

Outside the peculiar timber-based economy of the Bay of Honduras, where enslaved Africans were literally equated with "merchantable mahogany," the word was used metaphorically, often with racist overtones, to describe and categorize nonwhite people. Although sometimes applied generically to persons of African descent regardless of their actual appearance, the term "mahogany" more typically became a convenient label applied to persons who did not fit within a strict black-white racial binary, namely light-skinned Africans and persons of mixed race. In Thackeray's *Vanity Fair* (1847), for example, a mulatto heiress, a "Belle Savage" made of "diamonds and mahogany," was disdained for her lack of polish by her husband's white family, who nonetheless coveted her fortune. Not coincidentally, such racialized references to mahogany multiplied in the popular press during the same period that more nonwhite consumers began to acquire mahogany veneered furnishings.[2]

In comparing people to a material used to make furniture, such usages underscore the powerful role of language in the objectification of Africans—as commodities to be bought, sold, displayed, and used—reflected in the curiosity, suspicion, and fascination with which white people gazed upon nonwhite bodies. Mahogany people were to be exoticized, colonized, and set apart from white Anglo society. In another twist of this same process, Jane Austen famously compared her novels to the art of ivory painting, a popular pastime among the genteel that involved painting miniature portraits of loved ones onto luminous small slices of elephant tusk. Pale English faces were disconcertingly superimposed onto a ghostly African substrate; although a product of dead elephants and slave labor, ivory was nonetheless reinterpreted as the epitome of whiteness and purity. Although Austen's personal attitude toward slavery became more critical over time, especially as her family's West Indian ties frayed, her charming depictions of English provincial life took for granted the presence of colonial products. John Mee argues that Austen's choice of metaphor is thus significant because her novels presented a world dependent on exotic commodities but obscured "its own relations to a world of war, trade, and Empire."[3]

By the mid-nineteenth century, as the abolitionist movement gathered steam, it became harder for some people to hold mahogany in high esteem while ignoring its unsavory origins. During his 1842 celebrity book tour of the United States, Charles Dickens was served by a slave for the first time—at a Baltimore dining table—and felt a troubling "sense of shame and self-reproach." Many of his stories thereafter overtly linked mahogany with slavery. A story set in Lancaster, formerly a booming center of England's slave trade, featured staid mansions, "fitted with old Honduras mahogany, which has grown so dark with time ... [its] retrospective mirror-quality ... [reveals] in the depth of its grain, through all its polish, the hue of the wretched slaves." Since Dickens's serialized books circulated widely in both England and America, such reproaches may have pricked many consciences. By shining a revealing spotlight on treasured objects, he forced his readers to recognize that the distinctive color of mahogany was really the "hue of the wretched slaves."[4]

Given its racial associations and the circumstances of its production, however, mahogany was the target of surprisingly little abolitionist criticism, even when many other slave-produced products were boycotted. Many abolitionists seemed to have drawn a dubious distinction—as William Spence did when he proclaimed that mahogany was more lasting and worthwhile than sugar or rum—between it and other more ephemeral slave-produced commodities. More ardent abolitionists were quick to ridicule those who signed petitions against sugar on a mahogany table or desk. Likewise, slavery proponents, always eager to highlight hypocrisy in the antislavery movement, seized on this contradiction; after pointing out the plight of impoverished English orphans, a Southern planter mockingly insisted his slaves were "as carefully looked after and as cleanly kept as your mahogany tables. . . . [It is pure] impudence to compare your white vermin of children . . . to my fat, glossy, comfortable little Sambos." On the whole, however, consumers enjoyed their mahogany unburdened by any scruples about, or even much awareness of, the human costs of its production.[5]

For subaltern peoples on the receiving end of imperial domination, however, mahogany, so fetishized in England and America as the epitome of refinement, became a symbol of the perverted values and ill-gotten gains of their oppressors. Just as we saw during the American Revolution and the race riots of the 1830s, mahogany objects again became targets for violent protests and resistance when social resentments boiled over. During the 1857 Sepoy Mutiny, for example, when Indian soldiers serving in the British army revolted and sought to overthrow colonial rule, *Harper's Weekly* histrionically published an unsubstantiated account that the rebels had crucified an English banker on his own mahogany dining table. Tales of such a stunningly theatrical act of violence lit up Europeans' fears because they understood the intention behind it, namely to strike terror into the very heart of Western pretensions of civilization and racial superiority.[6]

English and American examples also abound of "mahogany" being applied to persons of alien, indeterminate, or ambiguous origins, such as Arabs, Turks, Indians, and creolized Europeans, usually in tropical climes (including travelers, sailors, expatriates, or wayfaring strangers). Omai, a Polynesian passenger on Captain Cook's return voyage in 1774, became a public sensation in London after exhibiting his tattooed body, described at the time as "veneer inlaid in mahogany." But in 1786, Matthew Consent also described the unfamiliar Sami people of Lapland as having "complexions of a mahogany hue" and speaking a "harsh and unintelligible jargon." *Montgomery,* a popular play that debuted in Boston in 1825, depicted Native Americans as "mahogany men, with their Tommy-hawks and scull-ping knives!" The same year, Paulding's *John*

Bull in America featured a "mahogany-faced foreigner." In *Legends of the West* (1832), a French Acadian family had the "mahogany tinge of complexion which belongs to this region."[7]

When "mahogany" was used specifically to describe *white* people, the implication was that they had in some way transgressed racial boundaries, compromising, and in some cases forfeiting, any entitlement to "whiteness." This prejudice emerged from long-held fears within European culture about the mutability of race and identity; the fact that white people in tropical environs became deeply tanned or sunburned seemed to suggest that perhaps a person's skin color was not a fixed, God-given condition. Even after years of colonizing experience, deep-seated social anxiety remained that, just as environmental factors could darken a white person's complexion, it might corrupt his or her moral character as well. In 1751, for example, Smollett described a group of white men, who when provoked to anger, "degenerated into a mahogany tint . . . like so many swarthy Moors." In a memoir of Surinam in the 1770s, a white slave master, "already the colour of mahogany," suffered physical and moral dissipation. Jane Austen's *Persuasion* (1818) featured an upright English naval officer who made a "deplorable" first impression because his visage, "the colour of mahogany, rough and rugged to the last degree," stood out among the pale faces of polite society. Seamen in particular fit this stereotype; they were immediately recognizable with their foreign tattoos, distinctive clothing, odd physiques, and weathered skin. In one 1839 novel, a sailor developed "long ape-like arms as brown as a piece of old mahogany" after years in the ship's rigging. Charles Dickens's *The Uncommercial Traveller* (1860) featured "a mahogany-faced Old Salt" while in Mark Twain's *Roughing It* (1871), a seaman, colorfully tattooed and clad in "semi-sailor toggery of blue navy flannel," peered out from his "weather beaten mask of mahogany." Regarded as a marginal subculture categorically different from that of landlubbers, the cliché of "mahogany" sailors offered disturbing evidence of the instability of race as well as culture. Whether highlighting, racial differences, expressing class anxieties, or, in extraordinary circumstances, venting revolutionary rage, when people projected such meanings onto polished mahogany, its "retrospective mirror-quality" reflected back all the complexity of human relations.[8]

Mahogany as Nature

From the 1830s to 1850s, mahogany, although now produced with steam power, began to be invested with a new meaning that centered on its associations with Nature (with a capital N). Reflecting the influence of the Romantic movement, this reification of the natural world developed in the United States as a reaction against the period's rapid industrialization, aggressive westward expansion, and voracious consumerism. During this period, American wilderness was being destroyed at an unprecedented rate, a fact that most Americans regarded as the march of progress. Frances Trollope evoked the zeitgeist when she described a thriving factory town on the Erie Canal; in this formerly sleepy countryside, it seemed "as if the demon of machinery, having invaded the peaceful realms of nature, had . . . [chosen it] as the battleground on which they should strive for mastery." Likewise, in the West Indies, Central America, and Brazil, tropical forests were also under attack; massive amounts of steam-cut Honduran mahogany, for example, were sent to the United States for use in paneling the thousands of railcars that traversed North America.[9]

In some circles, however, enthusiasm for progress, and the destruction of nature it appeared to entail, began to be tempered by a shadow of regret at the resulting violence and loss. Mahogany seemed a case in point, as the destruction of living trees was required to make inanimate objects. Using mahogany as a metaphor for man's integral place within nature, Dr. Edward Johnson, an advocate of holistic medicine, asked, when you cut down a tree, "[have] you committed no injury upon that tree? Have you abstracted nothing from the beauty of that scene in which that tree made a prominent object? . . . Or will you choose rather to suppose that nature planted mahogany trees for the express purpose of veneering side-boards and dining tables? . . . No one can deny that a tree, which has been cut down and cut up piecemeal . . . has had the integrity of its perfection, as a tree, destroyed." Reflecting what we might call today an ecological sensibility, he concluded that the natural world functioned as an organic whole that was diminished by the destruction of any part of it; hence, the notion that man was somehow separate from Nature or could gain control over it was a dangerous delusion.[10]

The influence of romanticism during the mid-nineteenth century is especially evident in the works of American and European painters and writers, some of whom ventured to the equatorial region during this period. Like earlier European adventurers in the Americas, they were overwhelmed by the diversity, luxuriance, and abundance of tropical forests. But whereas their predecessors found wilderness discomfiting and sought to cut it down to human scale, this new generation sought it out precisely because they *wanted* to be enthralled, satiated, and awestruck. Alexander Von Humboldt explained that part of the fascination of the South American forests was that when "a traveler newly arrived from Europe penetrates [them] for the first time . . . [he] feels at every step that he is . . . *not* in one of the West India Islands, but on a vast continent where every thing is gigantic—the mountains, the rivers, and the mass of vegetation." Only in such moments, could humans hope to experience the sublime.[11]

Nineteenth century writers and authors typically described the American tropics as a Paradise, Elysium, or Eden in which the magnificent mahoganies were the natural nobility. Returning home, they poured these vivid images of the natural world into their creative works. Yet they often interspersed symbolic references to death and destruction. Many artists, such as Thomas Cole included a ragged tree stump or two in their landscape paintings in silent testimony to the ravages of progress. In literature, "mahogany" was often conjoined with natural imagery evoking mortality. Such morbid references include both literal mentions of mahogany coffins and more subtle allusions to enigmatic, dark, subsuming surfaces. In *Dombey and Son* (1848), Dickens described Dombey looking "down into the cold depths of the dead sea of mahogany on which the fruit dishes and decanters lay at anchor." In *A Tale of Two Cities* (1859), a "large, dark room, furnished in a funereal manner," was illuminated by candles that "gloomily reflected on every [table] leaf, as if they were buried, in deep graves of black mahogany." Elsewhere he depicted a house where "mystery lurk[ed] in the depth of the old mahogany panels, as if they were so many deep pools of dark water—such, indeed, as they had been much among when they were trees." Another author's 1854 gothic romance was set in a castle furnished with solid mahogany of "a cold, funereal magnificence." In an 1857 *Harper's Weekly* story, a chamber was furnished with a "mahogany bedstead . . . crested with dingy plumes that gave it the cheerful look of a hearse." Life imitated art in a later account from the Bay of Honduras that invoked similar gothic imagery to describe mahogany cutters at work:

> [Amidst] the dense, tropical foliage, the torches carried by the workmen make a flickering . . . by whose light their dusky forms, naked to the waist, are made phantasmagorically visible, moving round the huge inert mass of timber as it lies on what may readily be mistaken for a gigantic catafalque, while the patient oxen wait for the crack of the driver's whip, and the shouts of the gang break the deathlike stillness of the surrounding forest.[12]

Other writers were more direct in their critique of the destruction of the natural world that global capitalism and modern industrialization seemed to demand. In *Moby-Dick* (1851), Melville both marveled at and abhorred the factories-at-sea that rendered colossal whales into lamp oil. In a remarkably efficient, systematized process, the whales' potent life force was extinguished to light American homes. Although the book was widely panned by critics at the time, at least one reviewer, although somewhat sarcastic, nonetheless seemed impressed that: "Leviathan is here in full amplitude. Not one of your museum affairs, but the real, living whale. . . . We are made guests at his fire-side; we set our mental legs under his mahogany and become members of his interesting social circle. . . . We have his history, natural and social, living and dead." Entering the imaginary parlor of the "mystic-marked whale," this reader seemed to easily juxtapose those opposites. Melville, however, depicted humankind caught in an insidious struggle between life-sustaining and life-consuming forces. In his words, the world's bright colors that seemed so vivid and real were really only a veneer of "subtle deceits, not actually inherent in substances, but only laid on from without . . . allurements [that] cover nothing but the charnel house within." When people sat around their lamp-lit mahogany parlor tables in the evening, the reconstituted flayed carcasses of whales and trees were brought disconcertingly into domestic settings, perhaps the last harbingers of lost Eden. Yet as Ahab's fate revealed, man's destruction of nature was ultimately self-destruction.[13]

People's attitudes toward such complex dualities as life and death, honesty and deception, innocence and corruption, were not, however, always clear, consistent, or coherent. In an 1848 essay entitled "Trees," for example, the author exclaimed: "There is no more beautiful object in the vegetable world than the mahogany tree . . . as it rustles its heavy plumes in the midnight sky, [it] presents a solemn and mysterious appearance." But contrarily, he concluded, it had a "spirit destined to live beyond it . . . [as] the *leaves* of a table." In almost erotic terms, he described the masochistic tree longing for the ax, until "wreathing its old arms high in the air, its leaves palpitating . . . we can almost trace numberless fancy-streaked cupboards and stout-limbed tables." While that author indulged in a convenient fantasy in which the tree fulfilled its destiny by willingly sacrificing itself for human use, Von Humboldt was less charitable in his assessment of humans' impact on "the primitive world with its innocence and felicity." In his view, "the golden age has ceased; and in this Paradise of the American forests, as well as everywhere else, sad and long experience has taught . . . that benignity is seldom found in alliance with strength."[14]

Mahogany as History

In this tumultuous period of rapid economic and social changes, people fearful of eroding social distinctions expressed a growing appreciation for "old mahogany" (in the sense of "old money") because it seemed to embody the vanishing virtues of personal substance, reliability, and honesty. References specifically to "old mahogany" began to appear in the early nineteenth century. In 1837, for example, one report noted that "Old Jamaica Mahogany is still considered superior to any that can now be procured from any other country." Such references proliferated in the 1850s; their intended meanings varied, however, depending on the context. For fashion-conscious people who fancied themselves modern, "old mahogany" was derogatory, suggestive of the dusty, tedious remnants of a stultifying past. But more conservative consumers embraced "old mahogany" with a warm sense of nostalgia. Ironically, given its earlier history, they did so in reaction against what they saw as a déclassé trend in popular culture towards novelty, exoticism, and garish Victorian excess. In their eyes, antique mahogany objects, preferably made of solid wood and darkened with the tincture of age, exemplified the supposed virtues of an earlier time—traditional designs, solid construction, and honest craftsmanship—the very antithesis of shoddy, newfangled, mass-produced goods.[15]

Well-worn pieces, some of which had been relegated for years to back halls and attics, were dragged out and buffed up. Admiring a colonial tall chest in his Concord apartment, Nathaniel Hawthorne announced that "the moderns have invented nothing better ... than these chests of drawers, which stand on four slender legs, and rear an absolute tower of mahogany to the ceiling, the whole terminating in a fantastically carved summit." Along with their sentimental value, such objects, in many cases, also gained monetary and historical value as antiquities, particularly if they had illustrious provenances. These survivors seemed comfortingly indifferent to changing fashions, above the fray of an increasingly hectic, industrialized society.[16]

As furniture conservators today can attest, it is exceedingly difficult to convincingly reproduce the nuances of depth and color achieved on an object patinated by generations of wear and polish. Precisely because old mahogany objects could not be easily faked or imitated, their owners regarded them as having a special authenticity. Indeed, since the ancient trees from which these weathered objects had been wrought were all but gone, there was a kernel of truth to this sentiment. The chairs, tables, and sideboards that genuinely survived from the colonial period were all that ever would or ever could exist. In a very real way, they had become a limited, nonrenewable resource that would never be accessible to everyone. The patina of age emerged as the new measure differentiating one class of artifacts, and their owners, from another.[17]

Accordingly, American and English fiction from this period often featured scenes set in ancestral homes, weighted down with immovable pedigreed objects, to demarcate the established social elite from others. In Charlotte Brontë's *Jane Eyre* (1847), for example, the self-effacing heroine avoided "the spectacle" of innovation by redecorating "entirely with old mahogany." John Neal's *The Down-Easters* (1833) described an antique-filled mansion that displayed "wealth of the better kind ... that would never trust to fashion for the style or shape of its familiar household things." Such settings and their specific contents mattered in the mid-nineteenth century because many believed that one's material surroundings had a direct formative effect on one's moral character and personality. An 1857 article in *Harper's Weekly* played on this idea, dividing people into two classes: the "shop window order" whose taste for flashy new furniture "vulgarized . . . [their] mental qualities" and the "sarcophagus order," whose preference for the "funeral gloom" of old mahogany made them taciturn and dyspeptic.[18]

In the United States, antiquarian interest in "old mahogany" was part of a larger social and cultural phenomenon now termed the Colonial Revival. Beginning in the 1850s and intensifying in the years surrounding the 1876 Centennial, the nation's formative early years began to be idealized as a time of particular significance to its identity. Hagiographic tales of the people and events during the colonial and early national periods were widely circulated; although the Colonial Revival was initially promulgated by descendants of the former political elite, and arguably geared toward their self-promotion and social retrenchment, Americans of all stripes laid claim to the increasingly mythologized narrative of the nation's founding. Objects that survived from that period became historical relics, supposedly imbued with the virtues of the Founding Fathers and Mothers who once owned them. As patriotic talismans, they also served as useful object lessons in a process of Americanization aimed at inculcating patriotism in children and new immigrants. "Old mahogany" seemed to embody the solidity, strength and durability of the Founders' unifying vision, despite (or in some cases precisely *because* of) its elitist connotations.

Ironically, by the late nineteenth (and early twentieth) century, veneration of all things colonial actually helped to create a market for early American furniture that had not previously existed. Consumer demand for colonial styles, in fact, became so great that furniture manufacturers obligingly fabricated reproductions and even some deliberate fakes. To the great annoyance of those who owned or inherited authentic colonial artifacts, anyone could now purchase freshly minted heirlooms. To reassert exclusivity, connoisseurs were quick to make claims of specialized knowledge to distinguish between the true articles and what they saw as rude imposters.[19]

Among the most influential proponents of the Colonial Revival were Henry Wadsworth Longfellow and his wife who shared an antiquarian fervor for collecting colonial artifacts, preferably those associated with famous Americans. They even lived in a house where George Washington headquartered for part of the American Revolution; hoping for inspiration, the poet placed his own writing desk in the room where the general once slept. In his writings as well, Longfellow expressed sentimental regard for historical relics; in "The Old Clock on the Stairs" (1845), one of his most well-known and beloved poems, he memorialized an imposing timepiece, that through "every swift vicissitude of changeful time, unchanged it has stood." Inspired by an actual timepiece in his wife's family home, the poetic version symbolized the steadfastness and strength of the nation's guardian ancestors. The poem became very popular and was widely circulated, inspiring a song and an oft-reproduced painting by Edward Lamson Henry. Longfellow struck such a chord with his fellow Americans that his eulogists practically enrolled him with the Founders because, in the words of one, his poetic creations had "helped to *refine* a world." Appropriately enough, Walt Whitman later remembered the old poet as "reminiscent, polish'd, elegant."[20]

Herman Melville, for all his discomfort with the commodification of nature, held "old mahogany" in especially high regard. In one 1855 essay, for example, he equated a man's preference for antique furniture with his virtuous character because he was so, "wonderfully unpretending, old, and snug. No new shining mahogany, sticky with undried varnish [about him]." He concluded that every sensible American should learn the same, "that glare and glitter . . . are not indispensible to domestic solacement." Melville's appreciation for mahogany heirlooms perhaps stemmed from his own longing for a sense of stability after a peripatetic childhood. Forced to move repeatedly just ahead of the debt collectors, his family had no permanent abode. Only a set of mahogany furniture, purchased in Paris during better days, and his mother's piano followed the family from place to place, providing a veneer of respectability.[21]

Throughout his childhood, Melville found refuge at his maternal grandparents' Albany mansion. Inherited from General Gansevoot, a Revolutionary War hero and patriarch of one of New York's indomitable old Dutch families, the house was a local landmark that had witnessed many significant events, most notably a visit from the Marquis de Lafayette during his triumphal 1825 tour of America. As further reminders of the family's more prestigious past, it was filled with treasures, including the "Hero's mahogany four-poster bed," a Sheraton sideboard, elegant mirrors, a Gilbert Stuart portrait, and two towering grandfather clocks (one of which Melville later inherited). Melville was exposed to more colonial grandeur at his paternal grandfather's substantial mansion in Boston. As a young man, he also summered in Rhode Island where he visited the illustrious DeWolf family, who had long since redirected their slave-derived profits into more respectable enterprises. In 1865, Theodora DeWolf Colt, who had been forced to flee to Cuba as a child with her disgraced father, even managed to buy back and restore Linden Place (with financial help from her robber baron son). With the indignities of the past forgotten, or at least polished over, the family mansion once again perched like a large, well-iced wedding cake in the center of Bristol, refurnished, of course, with "old mahogany" made by Newport's famed cabinetmakers.[22]

Americans reinterpreted "old mahogany" as native stock to furnish the nation's sacred past. In the process, however, they obscured both its organic, existential connection to the Earth as well as its historical connections to slavery. This dissonance was exemplified by an 1857 *Harper's Weekly* story that objectified a black man (typecast as a cheerful, domesticated "old negro") as "polished and brown like our grandmother's mahogany furniture." In a country soon to be torn asunder by the Civil War, however, such nostalgic sentiments could not fully conceal the fractures in the national psyche over the issue of slavery. Nor could they salve the harsh environmental realities that came with industrialization and deforestation. Nonetheless, in the United States, as Edith Wharton later wrote, the "solid lines and deep lustre of old mahogany" furnished its citizens "with the historic scenery against which a young imagination constructs its vision of the past." Such constructed visions of the past became, and continue to be, an important component of the American national imaginary.[23]

Mahogany Redefined Once Again

Through all the vagaries of the tropical timber trade, the availability, quality, and size of mahogany at any given time remained inextricably linked with the specific local economic, political, social, and environmental conditions in the very real places where the trees grew. How aware those on the receiving end of this trade were of these factors depended entirely on the conditions of the marketplace and their particular perspective—as policy makers, mahogany surveyors, timber dealers, cabinetmakers, furniture retailers, or furniture buyers. But over time, custom, usage, language, and eventually law all converged to uncouple mahogany from any actual geographical framework, further alienating it from its natural origins and the exploited labor involved in its production. As the end of the nineteenth century neared, the geographic labels that had long been applied loosely (and often deceptively) to mahogany became increasingly abstract.

This trend was codified in a precedent-setting legal case that stemmed from a dispute between an unhappy client and his building contractor over the semantics of mahogany. In 1896, Mr. Moynihan, a wealthy midwestern businessman, commissioned an extravagant mansion to be built in the booming city of St. Louis. Wanting only the best for his showplace home, he demanded that the architect's plan specify "San

Domingo mahogany" paneling be installed in the main reception hall. Finding none available in the region, however, the contractor proffered instead a sample of Mexican mahogany, which Moynihan rejected after he and his sisters compared it with their mahogany furniture. Furious to later learn that his architect had nevertheless approved the substitution, Moynihan had all the newly-installed paneling ripped out and replaced with mahogany specially ordered from a Boston lumberyard. He then sued the contractor for damages. For over seven years, this lawsuit and its appeals sought to adjudicate what constituted quality in mahogany and the significance of geography in defining its value. For Moynihan, the term "San Domingo mahogany" clearly held special significance; his insistence on it for the front hall of his house—the first thing any visitor would see—suggests its importance to his self-presentation. Yet although he posited himself as a sophisticated consumer, his choices were highly subjective, based on his expectations of what mahogany was *supposed* to be, even if those ideas were not necessarily accurate or rational. Indeed, sworn witnesses confirmed that the replacement mahogany that he selected and approved was, in fact, the very same type of wood as that which he had torn out.[24]

The architect, for his part, testified that his former client was unreasonable and misinformed since it was common knowledge that "San Domingo mahogany" was rare, expensive, and "impossible to get" in St. Louis (although, he conceded, some was still available back east). More tellingly, he stated that, in his professional experience, geographical designations were seldom, if ever, intended literally. To fulfill the letter of Moynihan's specifications, he claimed, the mahogany did not need to be "actually the product of the island of San Domingo. [It] may be grown elsewhere, [if it] is substantially to the eye, of texture and color, as if actually grown there. . . . Color and texture is what is required. [I] don't care whether it grows on the island of San Domingo or in Central America or tropical America." Several other St. Louis contractors, merchants, and lumber dealers likewise testified that this terminology derived from "a style and language peculiar to themselves of which usage and custom are the legitimate interpreters." In 1903, the court concurred, ruling that the term "San Domingo mahogany," when used in a trade context, "does not mean mahogany that was grown on the island of San Domingo but . . . a good figured mahogany, equal in density to that."[25]

This court decision, cited as precedent in later cases, established a foundation in law for a process that had already been going on for many years—the redefining of mahogany as separate and apart from the realities of place, or for that matter from the realities of the people and natural environments in those places. Increasingly, Americans regarded the tropics as far away, seemingly imaginary places, disconnected from the forest of mahogany objects and other tropical commodities that surrounded them in daily life. The same year that the court ruled that "San Domingo mahogany" could come from anywhere in "tropical America," another author held an imaginary séance to summon the spirit of her antique dining table from this fantastical realm:

> Mahogany, when will you be fashionable again? Did not your sap rise warm and vigorous under the eye of a tropic sun long ago, in some . . . orchid-haunted West Indian forest. . . . Surely some of that warmth and light are your hidden treasure still, mysteriously hinted at when . . . a sunbeam makes your heart glow like the blush on the face of a dusky beauty in the . . . land of your growth.[26]

In 1992, Hurricane Andrew roared through southern Florida leaving a massive trail of destruction. Lives were lost, homes and businesses destroyed, cars washed away, fishing boats tossed ashore like confetti. The storm's forceful winds also sheared off thousands of trees. Among the casualties were scores of ancient mahogany trees. Hearing of this singular salvage opportunity, professional cabinetmakers and amateur woodworkers from around the United States headed south with chainsaws to help clear the debris and, in the process, to retrieve some of this storm-felled wood. Most of Florida's mahogany giants were long gone, felled by early settlers determined to carve new plantations out of the rich forests, where according to legend Ponce de León once sought the fountain of youth. The salvage loggers' abhorrence to see this rare wood go to waste and their determination to lay in stores for future projects is understandable considering mahogany's long-standing reputation as one of the world's most favored cabinetmaking woods.[27]

In recent years, major public relations campaigns have educated Americans to some degree about the dire state of the world's rain forests as well as the exploitation of workers that the production and consumption of tropical hardwoods still entails. New World mahoganies are now widely understood to be threatened species at risk of extinction. Logging of them is banned or closely regulated throughout their native ranges, although significant quantities are still exported illegally. But the onus of enforcement currently rests largely on the exporting nations; once mahogany has arrived in the United States, it is often difficult to ascertain where it originated. Knowledge of these facts, however, does not always translate into changes in consumer behavior. While some furniture manufacturers conscientiously seek out sustainable wood sources, it is difficult to ensure suppliers' compliance. Others place orders for mahogany and never inquire where, how, or by whom the wood was produced. Likewise, when most furniture buyers visit a showroom or department store, they often have little insight to the actual places where materials are sourced (or even if an object purporting to be mahogany is "true mahogany" or a mahogany-colored varnish). Some responsible cabinetmakers and timber dealers today are seeking to encourage sustainable mahogany harvesting and have launched initiatives advocating for mahogany producers and sellers to certify, on a voluntary basis, that timber has been legally felled, but again verification is difficult.[28]

Although much more is now known about the New World mahogany species, many aspects of their biology and ecology are not fully understood and continue to be the subject of extensive research. According to the 2004 *Encyclopedia of Forest Sciences*, "the three species are rather poorly defined." Likewise, the optimal conditions for their natural regeneration or their cultivation—whether on plantations or as part of reforestation programs—remain uncertain, although theories abound. A great deal of debate and disagreement persists among scientists over even such basic questions as how *Swietenia* species are pollinated, how they respond to environmental disturbances, and how exactly their life cycles are interconnected with their larger rain forest habitats.[29]

Extensive DNA analysis is underway to better delineate the genetic relationships among the various mahoganies and the differences underlying their speciation, although initial reports have only compounded the confusion by revealing considerable genetic diversity among geographically separate populations. Medical researchers, noting *Swietenia*'s long history of use in traditional medicine, are currently investigating its complex chemistry in search of possible new treatments, such as for cancer, diabetes, and hypertension. Meanwhile, mahogany silviculture continues to be studied intensively at tropical forestry research institutes around the world, yet many of the same problems and challenges continue to undermine efforts to grow the trees on a large scale.[30]

Although some major advances have been made, professional opinions among ecologists and forestry specialists vary as to how to best facilitate seed production, germination and growth. Efforts to revive mahogany populations (especially *Swietenia mahagoni)* in areas where they were once endemic have been particularly disappointing. On Haiti, for example, ambitious plans to replant valuable native species have faltered because of extreme soil depletion and unregulated woodcutting for timber, cooking charcoal, and slash-and-burn agriculture—all symptoms of desperate poverty. In the few remaining areas in the western hemisphere, such as Belize, Peru, Bolivia, and Brazil, where some mahogany is still extracted from the wild, logging often creates conflicts with forest preservation efforts, competing land uses, the rights of indigenous Indian populations, as well as with exploited workers. Furthermore, to what degree regulated logging is effective as a means of conservation is questioned by some because there is no solid consensus as to what constitutes appropriate cutting cycles to sustain natural forests and to maintain their genetic diversity.[31]

Mahogany was not successfully plantation grown on a large scale until the twentieth century, and then almost entirely outside its native range. During the 1930s, for example, the United States Forestry Service's International Institute of Tropical Forestry established a research station in Puerto Rico, which remains influential in promoting mahogany cultivation and in investigating all aspects of tropical ecology. More significant to the international marketplace have been exports of *Swietenia macrophylla,* the most commonly cultivated species, raised on plantations in Southeast Asia and the Pacific. Commercially-grown trees are usually harvested after approximately forty years. Cut off well before they achieve their maximum size potential, these relatively youthful trees are of much smaller dimensions than was the average for those felled during the mid-eighteenth century. Moreover, their timber is generally more bland, even-grained, and homogenous than that of their wild counterparts. As such their wood would likely not have compared favorably with the mature wild mahogany trees, often hundreds of years old, that colonial cabinetmakers and consumers initially took for granted.[32]

Most frustratingly, the expansion of mahogany cultivation has been limited by the long-standing problems of maintaining viable seed supplies and avoiding the ravages of insects and diseases. Until the twentieth century, mahogany planting initiatives depended solely on seeds harvested from the wild where they were increasingly scarce.

Consequently, the quantities of plantation-grown timber produced today remain insufficient to relieve the logging pressures on the rain forests. Moreover, many of the deadly pests and blights associated with mahogany species in their native ranges have since migrated into areas where they were not previously found. With the exception of a few isolated Pacific islands, for example, mahogany shoot borers have spread to tree plantations around the globe but there is still no effective control. There is an impressive list of other pests and diseases that are now associated with *Swietenia* as well, including an Asian variant of the mahogany shoot borer, appropriately named *Hypsipyla robusta*, that has proven as much of a menace for trees growers as its American cousin. Great hopes rest on hybridized mahogany varieties that have developed in places where both *Swietenia mahagoni* and *Swietenia macrophylla* were introduced, allowing them to cross-fertilize (sometimes naturally and sometimes with human help). Drawing on the desirable qualities of both species, their offspring seem to be hardier, more adaptable, and more pest resistant than either of their parents. These biological innovations have been one of the unexpected benefits of the global movement of transplanted species. Ongoing research into the DNA of *Swietenia* speices may shed new light as well on their genetic history and aid in the further development of more sustainable hybridized cultivars.[33]

In the meantime, government-sponsored efforts at conservation and reforestation continue in many places to conflict with competing land uses. In other contexts, mahogany trees have been largely reconceptualized as ornamentals rather than as future timber. In Florida, for example, *Swietenia mahagoni* trees have been successfully replanted, but they are used mainly to adorn suburban gardens and streetscapes. A 1994 Department of Agriculture publication described them as nine to twelve feet tall, "not particularly showy" or "outstanding," but "recommended for buffer strips around parking lots." Regularly pruned to allow clearance "for vehicular traffic," these young, slender trees bear little resemblance to the large, primeval trees that colonial cabinetmakers once had at their disposal.[34]

As for mahogany objects—aside from collectors, antique dealers, high-end auctioneers, and fine woodworkers—few people today own much mahogany or even have much first-hand familiarity with it, except perhaps in the context of a museum or historic site or in the form of a rare family heirloom. Yet for most Americans, if they have an image of the colonial past at all, it is furnished with imaginary mahogany objects conjured up, along with spinning wheels and three-cornered hats, like so many Hollywood props. Many eighteenth- and nineteenth-century mahogany furnishings are now highly regarded and valued as antiques. Although their beauty and substance remain a testament to human creativity and initiative, it bears remembering that they also recall a story of destruction and suffering. All that remains of much human endeavor and of majestic trees felled long ago, these objects of desire are also objects of memory.

Abbreviations

Archives

AAS	American Antiquarian Society, Worcester, MA
BHPS	Bristol Historical and Preservation Society, Bristol, RI
BNA	Belize National Archives, Belmopan, Belize
EHFL	East Hampton Free Library, East Hampton, NY
HSP	Historical Society of Pennsylvania, Philadelphia, PA
JCB	John Carter Brown Library, Providence, RI
JNA	Jamaica Archives and Records Department, Spanish Town, Jamaica
MHS	Massachusetts Historical Society, Boston, MA
NA	National Archives, London:
	Admiralty Records (Adm)
	Audit Office (AO)
	Board of Trade (BT)
	Chancery Court (C)
	Colonial Office (CO)
	Foreign State Papers (FSP)
	Map Collection (CO 700)
	Probate Records (Prob)
NHHS	New Hampshire Historical Society, Concord, NH
NHS	Newport Historical Society, Newport, RI
NMM	National Maritime Museum, Greenwich, England
NYHS	New-York Historical Society, Manuscript Division
RBG	Archives, Royal Botanic Gardens, Kew, England
RIHS	Rhode Island Historical Society, Providence, RI

Periodicals

AB	*The Art Bulletin*
ABH	*Archives of British Honduras,* ed. John A. Burdon (London: Siftan, Praed, 1931).
AF	*American Furniture* (University of New England Press for Chipstone Foundation)
AHR	*American Historical Review*
BJLS	*Botanical Journal of the Linnean Society*
CHLA	*Cambridge History of Latin America*
EcHR	*Economic History Review*
EHR	*English Historical Review*
FEM	*Forest Ecology and Management*
FH	*Furniture History*
HAHR	*Hispanic American Historical Review*
JCH	*Journal of Caribbean History*
JEH	*Journal of Economic History*
MLN	*Modern Language Notes*
NEQ	*The New England Quarterly*
ODNB	*Oxford Dictionary of National Biography*
PP	*Past and Present*
THJ	*The Historical Journal*
WMQ	*William and Mary Quarterly*
WP	*Winterthur Portfolio*

Notes

Introduction

1. Peter Kalm, *Travels into North America . . . ,* 2nd ed., trans. John R. Forster (London: T. Lowndes, 1772), 1: 33. The first edition was published in three volumes from 1753–1761 in Stockholm by Lars Salvii; the first English edition was published in 1770.

2. Chaela Pastore, "Mahogany as Status Symbol: Race and Luxury in Saint Domingue at the End of the Eighteenth Century," in Dena Goodman and Kathryn Norberg, eds., *Furnishing the Eighteenth Century: What Furniture Can Tell Us about the European and American Past* (New York: Routledge, 2007), 37–47.

3. Benjamin Franklin, "On Hygrometers," *Transactions of the American Philosophical Society,* (Philadelphia: Robert Aiken, [1786]), 2: 56.

4. F. Bruce Lamb, *Mahogany of Tropical America: Its Ecology and Management* (Ann Arbor: University of Michigan Press, 1966), 52–53; J. P. Cornelius, K. E. Wightman, J. E. Grogan, and S. E. Ward, "Tropical Ecosystems—Swietenia (American Mahogany)" in *Encyclopedia of Forest Science,* J. Burley, et al. (Amsterdam: Elsevier, 2004), 1720–1726; J. E. Mayhew and A. C. Newton, *The Silviculture of Mahogany* (Wallingford, Oxon: CABI Publishing, 1998).

5. Samuel Bridgewater, *A Natural History of Belize: Inside the Maya Forest* (Austin, TX: University of Texas Press, 2012), 164–167; Laura K. Snook, "Sustaining Harvests of Mahogany *(Swietenia Macrophylla King)* from Mexico's Yucatán Forests: Past, Present, and Future," in

Timber, Tourists, and Temples: Conservation and Development in the Maya Forest of Belize, Guatemala, and Mexico, ed. Richard B. Primack (Covelo, CA: Island Press, 1997), chap. 5; Laura K. Snook, "Catastrophic Disturbance, Logging, and the Ecology of Mahogany *(Swietenia Macrophylla King):* Grounds for Listing a Major Tropical Timber Species in CITES," *BJLS* 122, no. 1 (1996): 35–46; Monte Basgall, "Logging Creating 'Mahogany Deserts' in Tropics," *Albion Monitor* (15 January 2006); Philip M. Fearnside, "Protection of Mahogany: A Catalytic Species in the Destruction of Rain Forests in the American Tropics," *Environmental Conservation* 24, no. 4 (1997): 303–306; Terrence D. Pennington, "Mahogany Carving a Future," *Biologist* 49, no. 5 (2002): 204–208; James Grogan and Jurandir Galvão, "Factors Limiting Post-Logging Seedling Regeneration by Big-Leaf Mahogany (Swietenia macrophylla) in Southeastern Amazonia, Brazil, and Implications for Sustainable Management," *Biotropica* 38, no. 2 (March 2006): 219–228.

6. Other examples of commodity studies include Marcy Norton, *Sacred Gifts, Profane Pleasures: A History of Tobacco and Chocolate in the Atlantic World* (Cornell, NY: Cornell University Press, 2008); Sidney Mintz, *Sweetness and Power: The Place of Sugar in Modern History* (New York: Viking, 1985); Steve Striffler and Mark Moberg, *Banana Wars: Power, Production and History in the Americas* (Durham, NC: Duke University Press, 2003); Mark Prendergrast, *Uncommon Grounds: The History of Coffee and How it Transformed our World* (New York: Basic Books, 2010); John Tully, *The Devil's Milk: A Social History of Rubber* (New York: Monthly Review Press, 2011); "Plunder for Pianos," in Anne Farrow, Joel Lang, and Jenifer Frank, *Complicity: How the North Promoted, Prolonged, and Profited from Slavery* (New York: Ballantine Books, Random House, 2006); and John Frederick Walker, *Ivory's Ghosts: The White Gold of History and the Fate of Elephants* (New York: Atlantic Monthly Press, 2009).

7. William Spence, *The Radical Cause of the Present Distresses of the West-India Planters . . .* (London: T. Cadell and W. Davies, 1807), 91. On commodification theories, see Arjun Appadurai, ed., *The Social Life of Things: Commodities in Cultural Perspective* (Cambridge: Cambridge University Press, 1986), 4; Chandra Mukerji, *From Graven Images: Patterns of Modern Materialism* (New York: Columbia University Press, 1983); David Harvey, *Justice, Nature, and the Geography of Difference*

(Cambridge, MA: Blackwell, 1996); Mary Douglas and Baron Isherwood, *The World of Goods: Towards an Anthropology of Consumption* (London: Routledge, 1996); Mihlay Csikszentmihalyi and Eugene Rochberg-Halton, *The Meaning of Things: Domestic Symbols and the Self* (New York: Cambridge University Press, 1981).

8. Lamb, *Mahogany of Tropical America*, 52–53; Mayhew and Newton, *The Silviculture of Mahogany.*

9. Peter Klein, "The Use of Wood in Rembrandt's Workshop" in *The Learned Eye: Regarding Art, Theory, and the Artist's Reputation,* ed. Marieke van den Doel (Amsterdam: Amsterdam University Press, 2005), 29–31; Madeleine Dobie, *Trading Places: Colonization and Slavery in Eighteenth-Century French Culture* (Cornell, NY: Cornell University Press, 2010), 64–68.

10. R. Bruce Hoadley, *Understanding Wood: A Craftsman's Guide to Wood Technology* (Newtown, CT: Taunton Press, 2000), 11, 265.

11. D. T. Jenkins, *Cambridge History of Western Textiles,* (Cambridge: Cambridge University Press, 2003), 1: 864; P. Thomson, *The Cabinetmaker's Assistant: A Series of Original Designs for Modern Furniture* (Glasgow and New York: Blackie and Son, 1853), 33.

12. On the concept of refinement, see J. G. A. Pocock, *Virtue, Commerce, and History: Essays on Political Thought and History Chiefly in the Eighteenth Century* (Cambridge: Cambridge University Press, 1985), 70, 115; Richard Bushman, *The Refinement of America* (New York: Vintage Books, 1993), xviii.

13. R. Bruce Hoadley, *Identifying Wood* (Newtown, CT: Taunton Press, 1990), 4, 171; Thomas Sheraton, *The Cabinet Dictionary* (London: W. Smith, 1803), 120.

14. Karl Marx, "The Fetishism of the Commodity and Its Secret," in *Capital* (London: Verso, 1976), 1: 163–177.

15. Mahogany Working Group, Convention on International Trade in Endangered Species of Flora and Fauna (CITES), accessed May 25, 2011, http://www.cites.org/eng/prog/mwg.shtml; Sheila E. Ward, David Boshier, and James Grogan, "Sustainable Management of High-value Timber Species of the Meliaceae," *FEM*, 255, no. 2 (March 2008): 265–268.

16. Percy Macquoid divided English furniture into four historical periods based on dominant woods then in use: Oak (1500–1660), Walnut

(1660–1720), Mahogany (1720–1770), and Satinwood/Composite (1770–1820). Mahogany, however, remained an important furniture wood long after 1770. Percy Macquoid, *A History of English Furniture* (London: Lawrence and Bullen, 1904), preface.

1. A New Species of Elegance

1. Jonathan Dickinson's Letterbook (1698–1701) and Ledger (1699–1701), 15 and 25 February 1698, HSP, cited in Cathryn J. McElroy, "Furniture in Philadelphia, The First Fifty Years," *WP* 13 (1979): 72; Evangeline Walker Andrews, *Jonathan Dickinson's Journal . . . of a Journey from Port Royal in Jamaica to Philadelphia*, ed. Charles McLean Andrews (New Haven, CT: Yale University Press, 1945), 130; "Inventory of the Goods and Chattels of Jonathan Dickinson . . . taken this twentieth day of Fifth Month Anno Domini 1722," cited in Harrold E. Gillingham, "Notes and Documents: The Estate of Jonathan Dickinson (1663–1722)," *The Pennsylvania Magazine of History and Biography* 59, no. 4 (October 1935): 420–429; Frederick B. Tolles, *Meeting House and Counting House: The Quaker Merchants of Colonial Philadelphia, 1682–1763* (Chapel Hill: University of North Carolina Press, 1948), 43, 128.

2. *The Times* (London), 6 December 1787.

3. Christopher Columbus, *The Four Voyages of Columbus,* trans. and ed. J. M. Cohen (New York: Penguin, 1969), 56, 64, 66, 69; Ramón Dacal Moure and Manuel Rivero de la Calle, *Art and Archaeology of Pre-Columbian Cuba*, trans. Daniel H. Sandweiss and David R. Watters (Pittsburg: University of Pittsburgh Press, 1996), 44–45; Fatima Bercht, ed. *Taino: Pre-Columbian Art and Culture from the Caribbean* (New York: El Museo del Barrio, 1997), 64–66.

4. Reinaldo Funes Monzote, *From Rainforest to Cane Field in Cuba: An Environmental History since 1492,* trans. Alex Martin (Chapel Hill: University of North Carolina Press, 2008), 19; José de Acosta, *Natural and Moral History of the Indies,* ed. Jane E. Mangan, trans. Frances López-Morillas (Durham, NC: Duke University Press, 2002), 225.

5. Pierre Ramond, *Marquetry*, trans. Jaqueline Derenne (New York: Oxford Univ. Press, 2003).

6. James Macfadyen, *The Flora of Jamaica* (London: Longman, Orme, Brown, Green, & Longman, 1837), 177; F. Bruce Lamb, *Mahogany of Trop-*

ical America: Its Ecology and Management (Ann Arbor: University of Michigan Press, 1966), 34, 69.

7.   Michael Williams, *Deforesting the Earth: From Prehistory to Global Crisis* (Chicago: University of Chicago Press, 2003), chap. 7; Robert Greenhalgh Albion, *Forests and Sea Power: The Timber Problem of the Royal Navy, 1652–1862* (Cambridge: Harvard University Press, 1926); Keith Thomas, *Man and the Natural World: A History of the Modern Sensibility* (New York: Pantheon, 1983), chap. 5.

8.   Monzote, *Rainforest to Cane Field,* 19–24; John McNeill, *Atlantic Empires of France and Spain: Louisbourg and Havana, 1700–1763* (Chapel Hill: University of North Carolina Press, 1985), 31, 136.

9.   Nuala Zahedieh, "The Merchants of Port Royal, Jamaica, and the Spanish Contraband Trade," *WMQ* 43, no. 4 (October 1986): 570–593; "Deposition of Caspar La Cantor, Skipper of *Amity*" and "Deposition of Lawrence Ver Maes, Boatswain of the *Amity,*" 15 February 1654, NA/ CO1/66, 7, fol. 31. On the Western Design, see Murdo MacLeod, "Spain and America: The Atlantic Trade, 1492–1720" in *The Cambridge History of Latin America,* ed. Leslie Bethell (New York: Cambridge University Press, 1986), 378; Karen Ordahl Kupperman, "Errand to the Indies: Puritan Colonization from Providence Island through the Western Design," *WMQ* 45, no. 1 (January 1988): 70–99; James Robertson, "Rewriting the English Conquest of Jamaica in the Late Seventeenth Century," *EHR* 117, no. 473 (September 2002): 813–839.

10.   James Robertson, "'Stories' and 'Histories' in Late-Seventeenth-Century Jamaica," in *Jamaica in Slavery and Freedom*, ed. Kathleen E. A. Montieth and Glen Richards (Mona, Jamaica: University of the West Indies Press, 2002), 33; Richard Blome, *A Description of the Island of Jamaica with the other Isles and Territories in America to which the English are Related* (London: Dorman Newman, 1678), 5.

11.   David Watts, "Biogeographical Variation in the Mahogany (Swietenia Mahagoni (L.) Jacq.) Woodlots of Barbados, West Indies," *Journal of Biogeography* 5, no. 4 (1978): 347; David Watts, *The West Indies: Patterns of Development, Culture, and Environmental Change since 1492* (Cambridge: Cambridge University Press, 1987), chaps. 5, 9, 10; Richard Grove, *Green Imperialism: Colonial Expansion, Tropical Island Edens and the Origins of Environmentalism, 1600–1860* (New York: Cambridge University Press, 1995), 65–69, 276–277; Richard S. Dunn, *Sugar and Slaves:*

The Rise of the Planter Class in the English West Indies, 1624–1713 (Chapel Hill: University of North Carolina, 1972), 27–28; Richard B. Sheridan, *Sugar and Slavery: An Economic History of the British West Indies, 1623–1775* (Baltimore: Johns Hopkins University Press, 1974), 378–379; B. W. Higman, "The Sugar Revolution," *EcHR* 53, no. 2 (May 2000): 213–236; Jack P. Greene, *Pursuits of Happiness: The Social Development of Early Modern British Colonies and the Formation of American Culture* (Chapel Hill: University of North Carolina Press, 1988), chap. 7; James Robertson, "Jamaican Architectures before Georgian," *WP* 38, no. 2 (2001): 73–95; James Robertson, "Re-writing the English Conquest," 828–831; Blome, *Description of Jamaica*, 7, 24–25. Author's emphasis added.

12.   On the concept of improvement , see Anthony Pagden, *Lords of All the Worlds: Ideologies of Empire in Spain, Britain, and France, c. 1500–c. 1800* (New Haven, CT: Yale University Press, 1995), 76–77; Robert P. Marzec, "Enclosures, Colonization, and the Robinson Crusoe Syndrome: A Genealogy of Land in a Global Context," *Boundary* 29, no. 2 (2002): 131; Joan Thirsk, *Economic Policy and Projects: The Development of a Consumer Society in Early Modern England* (Oxford: Clarendon Press, 1978); Thomas, *Man and the Natural World*, chap. 6; Verene A. Shepherd, ed., *Slavery Without Sugar: Diversity in Caribbean Economy and Society Since the 17th Century* (Gainesville: University of Florida Press, 2002); John F. Richards, *The Unending Frontier: An Environmental History of the Early Modern World* (Berkeley: University of California, 2003); B. W. Higman, *Jamaica Surveyed: Plantation Maps and Plans of the Eighteenth and Nineteenth Centuries* (Mona, Jamaica: University of West Indies Press, 2001), 6; David Armitage, *Ideological Origins of the British Empire* (Cambridge: Cambridge University Press, 2000), 97–99; Richard Drayton, *Nature's Government: Science, Imperial Britain, and the Improvement of the World* (New Haven, CT: Yale University Press, 2000), 50–66.

13.   Richard Ligon, *A True and Exact History of the Island of Barbadoes* (London: Humphrey Moseley, 1657), 20–21, 66, 79, 101–106; Blome, *Description of Jamaica*, 7, 24–25; John Oldmixon, *The British Empire in America . . .* (London: John Nicholson, Benjamin Tooke, Richard Parker, and Ralph Smith, 1708), 85; Grove, *Green Imperialism*, chaps.1 and 6; Watts, *The West Indies*, chaps. 5, 9, and 10.

14. Rita J. Adrosko, *Natural Dyes and Home Dyeing* (New York: Dover, 1971), 45–47; Alan K. Craig, "Logwood as a Factor in the Settlement of British Honduras," *Caribbean Studies* 9, no. 1 (April 1969): 53–62.

15. "An Act to Explain an Act . . . Giving Further Encouragement for the Importation of Naval Stores . . . as Relates to the Importation of Unmanufactured Wood of the Growth and Product of America," (London: Charles Eyre and William Strahan, 1771), 999–1002; *Great Britain. Laws, statutes, etc., 1760–1820* (George III); Adam Bowett, "The Commercial Introduction of Mahogany and the Naval Stores Act of 1721," *FH* 30 (1994): 43–56; Kenneth Ingram, "The West Indian Trade of an English Furniture Firm in the 18th Century," *Jamaica Historical Review* 3, no. 3 (March 1962): 22–37; John M. Cross, "The Changing Role of the Timber Merchant in Early Eighteenth Century London," *FH* 30 (1994): 57–64; John M. Cross, "Mahogany in Jamaica was like Gold in the Reign of Solomon," in *The Meeting of East and West in the Furniture Trade*, eds. Paul van Duin and Hans Piena (Sixth International Symposium on Wood and Furniture Conservation, 2002), 68.

16. Henry Crouch, *A Complete View of the British Customs* (London: J. Osborn and T. Longman, 1725), 413.

17. For more on the history of consumption, see Ann Smart Martin, "Makers, Buyers, and Users: Consumerism as a Material Culture Framework," *WP* 28, no. 2/3 (Summer/Autumn 1993): 141–157; Tara Hamling and Catherine Richardson, eds., *Everyday Objects: Medieval and Early Modern Material Culture and Its Meanings* (Burlington, VT: Ashgate Publishing, 2010), 3, 136; Linda Levy Peck, *Consuming Splendor: Society and Culture in Seventeenth-Century England* (Cambridge: Cambridge University Press, 2005), 15–16, 167; Neil McKendrick, John Brewer, and J. H. Plumb, *The Birth of a Consumer Society: The Commercialization of Eighteenth Century England* (Bloomington, IN: Indiana University Press, 1982), 11; John Brewer and Ann Bermingham, eds., *The Consumption of Culture, 1600–1800: Image, Object, Text* (New York: Routledge, 1995); John Brewer and Roy Porter, *Consumption and the World of Goods* (New York: Routledge, 1993); Carole Shammas, *The Pre-Industrial Consumer in England and America* (New York: Oxford University, 1990); Carole Shammas, "The Revolutionary Impact of European Demand for Tropical Goods" in John J. McCusker and Kenneth Morgan, eds., *The Early Modern Atlantic Economy,* (Cambridge:

Cambridge University Press, 2000), chap. 7; Daniel Miller, ed., *Acknowledging Consumption: A Review of New Studies* (London: Routledge, 1995); Cary Carson, Ronald Hoffman, and Peter J. Albert, eds., *Of Consuming Interests: The Style of Life in the Eighteenth Century* (Charlottesville, VA: University Press of Virginia, 1994); Dena Goodman and Kathryn Norberg, eds., *Furnishing the Eighteenth Century: What Furniture Can Tell Us about the European and American Past* (New York: Routledge, 2007).

18. Grant McCracken, *Culture and Consumption* (Bloomington, IN: Indiana University Press, 1990), 22; *Encyclopedia Britannica* (Edinburgh: Archibald Constable, 1823), 20:159; Charles Knight, *The English Cyclopaedia: A New Dictionary of Universal Knowledge* (London: Bradbury and Evans, 1860), 5:432–433; P. Thomson, *The Cabinet-maker's Assistant: A Series of Original Designs for Modern Furniture* (Glasgow and New York: Blackie and Son, 1853), 27.

19. Barbara G. Carson, *Ambitious Appetites: Dining, Behavior, and Patterns of Consumption in Federal Washington* (Washington, DC: American Institute of Architects Press, 1990); Richard Bushman, *The Refinement of America* (New York: Vintage Books, 1993); Gerald W. R. Ward, "Avarice and Conviviality: Card Playing in Federal America," in Benjamin A. Hewitt, Patricia E. Kane, and Gerald W. R. Ward, *The Work of Many Hands: Card Tables in Federal America, 1790–1820* (New Haven, CT: Yale University Art Gallery, 1982); Rodris Roth, "Tea Drinking in Eighteenth-Century America," in Robert Blair Saint George, ed., *Material Life in America, 1600–1860* (Boston: Northeastern University Press, 1988), 445–446; Elizabeth Kowaleski-Wallace, *Consuming Subjects: Women, Shopping, and Business in the Eighteenth Century* (New York: Columbia University Press, 1997), 19–40; James Walvin, *Fruits of Empire: Exotic Produce and British Taste, 1660–1800* (New York: New York University Press, 1997); Ann Smart Martin, "Tea Tables Overturned: Rituals of Power and Place in Colonial America" in Goodman and Norberg, *Furnishing the Eighteenth Century*, 169–181; Sarah Neale Fayen, "Tilt-top Tables and Eighteenth Century Consumerism," *AF* (2003): 95–137.

20. Susan R. Stein, "Dining at Monticello: The Feast of Reason" in Damon Lee Folwer ed., *Dining at Monticello: In Good Taste and Abundance* (Charlottesville: Thomas Jefferson Foundation, 2005), 76; Margaret Visser, *The Rituals of Dinner* (New York: Grove Weidenfeld, 1991),

82–83, 156–157; Clive Edwards, *Turning Houses into Homes: A History of the Retailing and Consumption of Domestic Furnishings* (Aldershot: Ashgate Publishing, 2005), 97; Carson, *Ambitious Appetites*; Carson, Hoffman, and Albert, eds., *Of Consuming Interests,* 590–591.

21. Chaela Pastore, "Mahogany as Status Symbol: Race and Luxury in Saint Domingue at the End of the Eighteenth Century," in Goodman and Norberg, *Furnishing the Eighteenth Century,* 37–48; Diana Thornton, "The Probate Inventories of Port Royal, Jamaica," (Master's Thesis, Texas A & M University, 1992), 116–120; Michael Connors, "Spanish Colonial Furniture of the West Indies," *The Magazine Antiques* 161, no. 3 (March 2002): 74–83; Michael Connors, "Danish West Indian Furniture," *The Magazine Antiques* 156, no. 3 (September 1999): 338–347.

22. T. H. Breen, *The Marketplace of Revolution: How Consumer Politics Shaped American Independence,* (New York: Oxford University Press, 2004), chaps. 2–3.

23. James F. Shepherd and Samuel H. Williamson, "The Coastal Trade of the British North American Colonies, 1768–1772," *JEH* 32, no. 4 (December 1972): 783–810; Susan Socolow, ed., *The Atlantic Staple Trade: The Economics of Trade* (Brookfield, VT: Variorum, 1996); Daniel R. Finamore, "'Pirate Water: Sailing to Belize in the Mahogany Trade" in *Maritime Empires: British Imperial Maritime Trade in the Nineteenth Century,* ed. David Killingray, Margarette Lincoln, and Nigel Rigby (Rochester, N.Y.: Boydell Press, 2004), 31–32.

24. *Boston Gazette,* 22 and 29 August and 21/28 November 1737, and *Boston News-Letter,* 24 June/1 July 1742, in *The Arts and Crafts in New England, 1704–1775, Gleanings from Boston Newspapers,* George Francis Day, compiler (Topsfield, MA: The Wayside Press, 1927), 129–130.

25. Morrison H. Heckscher and Lori Zabar, *John Townsend: Newport Cabinetmaker* (New York: Metropolitan Museum of Art; New Haven, CT: Yale University Press, 2005), 641; George Boyd, Letter book, 1773–1775, Boyd Papers, March 1774, NHHS.

26. Phyllis W. Hunter, *Purchasing Identity in the Atlantic World, Massachusetts Merchants, 1670–1780* (Ithaca, NY: Cornell University Press, 2001); Lorinda B. R. Goodwin, *An Archaeology of Manners: The Polite World of the Merchant Elite of Colonial Massachusetts* (New York: Kluwer Academic/Plenum Publishers, 1999); Thomas M. Doerflinger, *A Vigorous Spirit of Enterprise: Merchants and Economic Development*

in Revolutionary Philadelphia (Chapel Hill: University of North Carolina, 1986); Tolles, *Meeting House*; Cathy Matson, *Merchants and Empire: Trading in Colonial New York* (Baltimore: Johns Hopkins University Press, 1998).

27. Report of the Council of Trade and Plantations, 1734, *Calendar of State
    Papers, Colonial Series, America and West Indies, 1734–35,* ed. A. P.
    Newton, (London: 1953), item 20.

28. Heckscher, *Townsend,* 64; L. H. Butterfield, Leonard C. Faber, and
    Wendell D. Garrett, eds., *Diary and Autobiography of John Adams*
    (Cambridge: Belknap Press of Harvard University, 1962), 1: 294; Hunter,
    Purchasing Identity, 149, 173.

29. Jonathan Fairbanks and Elizabeth Bidwell Bates, *American Furniture
    1620 to the Present* (New York: Richard Marek, 1981); Charles F. Mont-
    gomery, *American Furniture: The Federal Period* (NY: Viking Press,
    1966); Morrison Hecksher, *American Furniture in the Metropolitan
    Museum of Art* (New York: Random House, 1985).

30. Margaretta M. Lovell, "Such Furniture as Will Be Most Profitable: The
    Business of Cabinetmaking in Eighteenth-Century Newport," *WP* 26,
    no. 1 (1991): 27–62; Jeanne A. Vibert, "The Market Economy and the
    Furniture Trade of Newport, Rhode Island: The Career of John Ca-
    hoone, Cabinetmaker, 1745–1765," (master's thesis, University of Dela-
    ware, 1981); Morrison H. Heckscher, "English Furniture Pattern Books
    in Eighteenth-Century America," *AF* (1994): 173–206; Cross, "Mahogany
    in Jamaica," 65–69; Robert Mussey and Anne Haley, "John Cogswell
    and Boston Bombé Furniture: Thirty-Five Years of Revolution in Poli-
    tics and Design," *AF* (1994): 73–105; Brock Jobe, "The Lisle Desk-and-
    Bookcase: A Rhode Island Icon," in *AF* (2001): 120–151.

31. David Pye, *The Nature and Art of Workmanship* (Cambridge: Cam-
    bridge University Press, 1968), chap. 2; *Pennsylvania Gazette,* 18 May
    1738, cited in McElroy, "Furniture in Philadelphia: The First Fifty
    Years," *WP* 13 (1979): 80.

32. Jay Robert Stiefel, "Philadelphia Cabinetmaking and Commerce, 1718–
    1753: The Account Book of John Head, Joiner," *American Philosophical
    Society Library Bulletin* 1, no. 1 (Winter 2001): Section 10.

33. Samuel Grant, Account Book, 1737–1760, 1 and 26 June 1739, 1 August
    1739, 26 April 1743, 11 July 1751, 1 February 1753, 29 May 1760, AAS;
    Brock Jobe, "The Boston Furniture Industry 1720–1740," *Boston Furni-*

ture of the Eighteenth Century (Charlottesville: Univ. of Virginia Press, 1986), 3–48.

34. Lovell, "Such Furniture," 33, 49; Margaretta M. Lovell, *Art in a Season of Revolution: Painters, Artisans, and Patrons in Early America* (Philadelphia: University of Pennsylvania Press, 2005), chap. 7.

35. John Cahoone, Account book, 1749–1760, 11, NHS.

36. Cahoone, Account book, 28, 35–37, 44, 69, 72, 85; Job Townsend Ledger, 1–2, ms. 504, NHS; Lovell, "Such Furniture," 44.

37. Stiefel, "Philadelphia Cabinetmaking," Section 10; Cahoone, Account book, 31; see also "Excerpts from the Day-Books of David Evans, Cabinetmaker, 1774–1811," *Pennsylvania Magazine for History and Biography* 27, no. 1 (1903): 49–55; Martha H. Willoughby, "The Accounts of Job Townsend, Jr.," *AF* (1999): 109–161.

38. Breen, *Marketplace of Revolution,* chaps. 2–3.

39. Morrison H. Heckscher and Leslie Greene Bowman, *American Rococo, 1750–1775: Elegance in Ornament* (New York: Metropolitan Museum of Art and Harry N. Abrams, Inc., 1992); Heckscher, "English Furniture Pattern Books," 173–206.

40. Mark J. Anderson, Gregory J. Landrey, and Philip D. Zimmerman, *Cadwalader Study* (Winterthur, DE: Winterthur Museum, 1995), 8–13; Philip D. Zimmerman, "A Methodological Study in the Identification of Some Important Philadelphia Chippendale Furniture," *WP* 13 (1979): 193–208; Heckscher, *American Furniture,* 107, 162, 229; Nicholas B. Wainwright, *Colonial Grandeur in Philadelphia: The House and Furniture of General John Cadwalader* (Philadelphia: HSP, 1964), 118–120.

41. Jack L. Lindsey, "The Cadwalader Family: Art and Style in Early Philadelphia," *Philadelphia Museum of Art Bulletin* 41, no. 384/385 (Autumn 1996): 12, 10–23; Marla Miller, *Betsy Ross and the Making of America* (New York: Henry Holt, 2010), 4.

42. Leigh Keno and Leslie Keno, *Hidden Treasures: Searching for Masterpieces of American Furniture* (New York: Warner Books, 2000), 83–101.

43. William Gilpin, *Three Essays: On Picturesque Beauty . . . ,* 2nd ed. (London: R. Blamire, 1792, 1794), 4–5; Edmund Burke, *A Philosophical Inquiry into the Origin of Our Ideas of the Sublime and Beautiful* (London: J. Dodsley, 1757), 127.

44. Edward Long, *The History of Jamaica. Or, General Survey of the Ancient and Modern State of that Island* (London: T. Lowndes, 1774), 3: 844.

45. Sylvia Molloy, "From Serf to Self: The Autobiography of Juan Francisco Manzano," *MLN* 104, no. 2 (March 1989): 413, note 36; Robert Roberts, *The House Servant's Directory*... (Boston: Monroe and Francis, 1827; repr., Armonk, NY: M.E. Sharpe, 1998), 16.

46. Webster's definition of *refine* is "to improve or perfect by... polishing." *Webster's New Collegiate Dictionary* (Springfield, MA 1977); Richard Bushman, *Refinement of America*, xviii; J. G. A. Pocock, *Virtue, Commerce, and History: Essays on Political Thought and History Chiefly in the Eighteenth Century* (Cambridge: Cambridge University Press, 1985), 70, 115.

47. Lisa Jardine, *Worldly Goods: A New History of the Renaissance* (New York: Doubleday, 1996), 5–16, 123–124.

48. Carrie Rebora and Paul Staiti, *John Singleton Copley in America* (New York: Metropolitan Museum of Art, 1995), 103, 269, 272, 305, 313, 316.

49. Jonathan Prown, "John Singleton Copley's Furniture and the Art of Invention," *AF* (2004); Lovell, *Art in a Season of Revolution*, 54, 66, 104–105; Rebora and Staita, *John Singleton Copley*, 248, 321; Susan Rather, "Carpenter, Tailor, Shoemaker, Artist: Copley and Portrait Painting Around 1770," *AB* 79, no. 2 (June 1997): 285.

50. Rather, "Carpenter," 272; Fairbanks and Bates, *American Furniture*, 143.

51. Robert Manwaring, *The Cabinet and Chair-maker's Real Friend and Companion* (London: Henry Webley, 1765), preface, 18–20.

52. Gloria L. Main and Jackson T. Main, "Economic Growth and the Standard of Living in Southern New England, 1640–1774," *JEH* 48, no. 1 (March 1988): 27–46, 44; Lois Green Carr and Lorena S. Walsh, "Changing Lifestyles and Consumer Behavior in the Colonial Chesapeake," in Carson, Hoffman, and Albert, eds., *Of Consuming Interests*, 59–166; Breen, *Marketplace of Revolution*, chaps. 2–3; *Pennsylvania Gazette*, 8 August 1754 cited in Nancy A. Goyne, "Francis Trumble of Philadelphia: Windsor Chair and Cabinetmaker," *WP* 1 (1964): 228.

53. Brinley Sylvester Account Book, 22 April 1746, in Pennypacker Collection, 1738–1746, EHFL; Letter from Esther Edwards Burr to Sarah Price Gill, 29 September 1755, in *The Journal of Esther Edwards Burr, 1754–1757*, eds. Carol F. Karlsen and Laurie Crumpacker (New Haven, CT: Yale University Press, 1984), 318.

54. Nancy Evans, *Windsor-chair Making in America: From Craft Shop to Consumer* (Lebanon, NH: University Press of New England, 2006), 84,

148, 150, 180, 182; Archibald Alison, *Essays on the Nature and Principles of Taste* (Edinburgh: Bell and Bradfute, 1790), 210–211; David Bosse, "Economy, Elegance and Beauty: Vernacular Decoration of Wood," *Historic Deerfield* (Winter 2010): 29–31.

55. Carson, "The Consumer Revolution in Colonial British America: Why Demand?" in *Of Consuming Interests*, 619.

56. Benjamin Hallowell, "Inventory of Furniture in the Mansion House," 1776, Exhibit F, NA/AO/13/46.

57. Rebora and Staita, *John Singleton Copley*, 321; Edmund S. Morgan and Helen M. Morgan, *The Stamp Act Crisis: Prologue to Revolution* (Chapel Hill: University of North Carolina Press, 1953; repr., 1995), 133; Dirk Hoerder, *Crowd Action in Revolutionary Massachusetts, 1765–1780*, (New York: Academic Press, 1977), 2: 75; William Pencak, Matthew Dennis, and Simon P. Newman, eds., *Riot and Revelry in Early America* (University Park: Pennsylvania State University Press, 2002), 113–114, 132; Paul A. Gilje, *Rioting in America* (Bloomington, IN: Indiana University Press, 1996), 40–42; Gary Nash, "Urban Wealth and Poverty in Pre-Revolutionary America," *The Journal of Interdisciplinary History* 6, no. 4 (Spring 1976): 545–584; Benjamin L. Carp, *Rebels Rising: Cities and the American Revolution* (New York: Oxford University Press, 2009), 155–156.

2. The Gold Standard of Jamaican Mahogany

1. Based on information recorded by Maynard Clarke's overseer in "Journal of a Plantation from 2 September 1756 to 1 February 1757," Walters v. Evans, "Letters" Bundle, no. 16, NA/C104/8.

2. Adam Bowett, "The English Mahogany Trade, 1700–1793: A Commercial History," (PhD diss., Brunel University, 1996), 70–73, 82; Adam Bowett, "The Jamaica Trade: Gillow and the Use of Mahogany in the Eighteenth Century," *Regional Furniture* 12 (1998): 14–57.

3. Richard B. Sheridan, *Sugar and Slavery: An Economic History of the British West Indies, 1623–1775* (Baltimore: Johns Hopkins University Press, 1974), chap. 10; Michael Craton and James Walvin, *A Jamaican Plantation: The History of Worthy Park, 1670–1970* (Toronto: University of Toronto Press, 1970), 27, 79, 80–83; S. D. Smith, "Coffee and the Poorer Sort of People," in *Slavery Without Sugar: Diversity in Caribbean Economy and Society Since the 17th Century,* ed. Verene A.

Shepherd (Gainesville: University of Florida Press, 2002), 102, 125; Jack P. Greene, *Pursuits of Happiness: The Social Development of Early Modern British Colonies and the Formation of American Culture* (Chapel Hill: University of North Carolina Press, 1988), 159–160; David Watts, *The West Indies: Patterns of Development, Culture, and Environmental Change Since 1492* (Cambridge: Cambridge University Press, 1987), chap. 1.

4. Donald Monro, ed., *Letters and Essays on . . . the West Indies* (London: J. Murray, 1778), 26; Craton and Walvin, *Jamaican Plantation,* 1; David Buisseret, *Historic Jamaica: From the Air* (Kingston, Jamaica: Ian Randle, 1996), chap. 1; John F. Richards, *The Unending Frontier: An Environmental History of the Early Modern World* (Berkeley: University of California, 2003), chap. 12.

5. Charles Leslie, *A New History of Jamaica from the Earliest Accounts to the Taking of Porto Bello,* 2nd ed. (London: J. Hodges, 1740), 24, 327; Verene A. Shepherd, "Livestock and Sugar: Aspects of Jamaica's Agricultural Development from the Late Seventeenth to the Early Nineteenth Century," *THJ* 34, no. 3 (September 1991): 627–643; Anon., *The Importance of Jamaica to Great-Britain consider'd* (London: Printed for A. Dodd, 1741), 49.

6. Craton and Walvin, *Jamaican Plantation,* chap. 5.

7. "Accounts Produce, or Crop Accounts," 1740–1785, vols. 1–9, 1B/11/4, JNA; Richard B. Sheridan, "Planter and Historian: The Career of William Beckford of Jamaica and England, 1744–1799," *Jamaican Historical Review* 4 (1964): 38–41; Sheridan, *Sugar and Slaves,* 227–229; [Report on Timber], Her Majesty's Commissioners of Woods and Forests, Jamaica, 21 October 1874, ff. 440–441, NA/CO137/477, citing earlier figures.

8. Craton and Walvin, *Jamaican Plantation,* 100, 123; Sheridan, *Sugar and Slavery,* 112–118; Marguerite Curtin, *Orchard: A Profile of an Estate in North Western Jamaica* (Lucea, Jamaica: M. Curtin, 2001), 16.

9. Stuart B. Schwartz, ed., *Tropical Babylons: Sugar and the Making of the Atlantic World, 1450–1680* (Chapel Hill: University of North Carolina Press, 2004), 3–10; Kenneth Morgan, "Long, Edward (1739–1813)," *ODNB* (Oxford University Press, 2004); Edward Long, *The History of Jamaica. Or, General Survey of the Ancient and Modern State of that Island,* (London: T. Lowndes, 1774), 1: 391–392, 457.

10. David Dobson, *Scottish Emigration to Colonial America, 1607–1785* (Athens, GA: University of Georgia, 1994), 133; Bruce Gordon Seton and

Jean Gordon Arnot, *The Prisoners of the '45* (Edinburgh: University Press, 1929), 236–237.

11. Pepper Plantation Accounts, 23 March 1756, 3: 12, and 31 December 1752, 2: 117, Barton Isles Account, 23 March 1753, 2: 152, Accounts Produce, Crop Accounts, 1B/11/4, JNA; Craton and Walvin, *Jamaican Plantation,* 145–146.

12. John Clarke was a planter in Jamaica from the early 1720s until his death circa 1740. His son, Maynard, who inherited his father's estate, resided on Jamaica intermittently from 1749 to 1759. Letters and legal papers relating to their estates survive at the British National Archives (NA), formerly the Public Record Office (PRO).

13. Sheridan, *Sugar and Slavery,* 224–227; Buisseret, *Historic Jamaica,* 12, 48, 56–57, 66–67, 73–77; B. W. Higman, *Jamaica Surveyed: Plantation Maps and Plans of the Eighteenth and Nineteenth Centuries* (Mona, Jamaica: University of the West Indies Press, 2001), 265–266; Trevor Burnard, "European Migration to Jamaica, 1655–1780," *WMQ* 53, no. 4 (October 1996): 789; Maynard Clarke's Letterbook, 16 August 1749, no. 121, NA/C104/8; Copy of a letter to Mr. James Francis, Atty at Law, Clarke v. Knight, 22 October 1724, no. 11, NA/C107/148; "Accounts of John Clarke plantations in Jamaica, 1720–1787," no. 1, Accounts for 1720–1737 and 30 December 1741, no. 3, NAC 107/148; Accounts for 1722–1724 and 22 October 1724, "Robert Poole Accounts of the estate of J. Clarke at Leguanea," no. 11, Accounts 1737–1740, no. 2, NAC 107/148; "Accounts of the Estate of John Clarke, decd . . . from Woodcock & Goode," 31 December 1740, NAC 107/148. See also entries for 27 September, 8 November, and 20 December 1738, NAC 107/148; Copy of a letter to Rev. Mr. Blucke, Clarke's Letterbook, 20 July 1749, no. 121, NA/C104/8.

14. On absentee owners, see David Hancock, "'A World of Business to Do': William Freeman and the Foundations of England's Commercial Empire, 1645–1707," *WMQ* 57, no. 1 (January 2000): 3–34; B. W. Higman, *Plantation Jamaica, 1750–1850: Capital and Control in a Colonial Economy* (Mona, Jamaica: University of the West Indies Press, 2005), 37–39; Craton and Walvin, *Jamaican Plantation,* 168–169; and Alan L. Karras, *Sojourners in the Sun: Scottish Migrants in Jamaica and the Chesapeake, 1740–1800* (Ithaca, NY: Cornell University Press, 1992), 186–187. "Copy of letter from Daniel Marqueen on behalf of Maynard Clarke to Samuel Walters," 13 July 1751, NA/C104/248(II); "Accounts of John Clarke, decd 1743," Clarke v. Knight, no. 5, NA/C107/148.

15. Long, *History of Jamaica,* 1: 438; Clarke's Letterbook, 13 March, 20 July, and 16 August 1749, no. 121, NA/C104/8.

16. Buisseret, *Historic Jamaica,* 70–75, 86–87; Higman, *Jamaica Surveyed,* 234; James Hakewill, *A Picturesque Tour of the Island of Jamaica,* (London: Hurst and Robinson, 1825), np; "Journal of a Plantation from 2 Sept. 1756 to 1 Feb., 1757," Walters v. Evans, "Letters" Bundle, 6 January 1756, no. 16, NA/C104/8; Copy of a letter to Rev. Mr. Blucke, Letterbook [of Maynard Clarke], 20 July 1749, no. 121, NA/C104/8.

17. "Account of Contingencies with Edward Ellerington & Co. for the year 1753," 27 March 1753, "Letters" Bundle, no. 44, no. 46, NA/C104/8.

18. Samuel Walters to Maynard Clarke, [no date] circa 1753, "Letters" Bundle, no. 31, NA/C104/8; "Acct. of Sales of Sundry Goods pr the *Cato,* Abr. Remick and the *Callingburg,* Matt Foster, Comdr consigned to Saml. Walters of Hull and on acct and risque of Maynard Clarke esq of the Island of Jamaica," "Letters" Bundle, no. 47, NAC 104/8; Samuel Walters to Ellerington & Co., 15 July 1753, "Letters" Bundle 2, no. 93, NA/C104/8. Lascelles and Maxwell cited in S. D. Smith, ed., *The Lascelles and Maxwell Letter Books, 1739–1769* (Wakefield: Microform Academic Publishers, 2002).

19. Edward Ellerington to Maynard Clarke at London, 29 April 1756, No. 26 and Maynard Clarke's Account with Gale and Seabrook, 5 July 1756, No. 21, "Letters," NA/C104/8; Edward Ellerington to Maynard Clarke, 26 February 1757, No. 49 and 29 April 1757, No. 55, "Letters," Bundle 2, NA/C104/8; Maynard Clarke's will, 27 August and 8 December 1759, NA/Prob 11/851; Thomas Hibbert to Samuel Walters, Walters v. Evans, 5 September 1773, Part 2, NA/C104/248.

20. Bowett, "English Mahogany Trade," 73–74, 133–134.

21. Higman, *Jamaica Surveyed,* 199–201; Richards, *Unending Frontier,* chap. 12; Philip D. Morgan, "Slaves and Livestock in Eighteenth-Century Jamaica: Vineyard Pen," *WMQ* 52, no. 1 (January 1995): 44–76.

22. Douglas Hall, ed., *In Miserable Slavery: Thomas Thistlewood in Jamaica, 1750–86* (London: Macmillan Press, 1989; repr., Mona, Jamaica: University of the West Indies Press, 1999), 16; Trevor Burnard, *Mastery, Tyranny, and Desire: Thomas Thistlewood and His Slaves in the Anglo-Jamaican World* (Chapel Hill: University of North Carolina Press, 2004); Morgan, "Slaves and Livestock," 50, 58, 60–61.

23. Thistlewood's journal, 25 June 1751, cited in Morgan, "Slaves and Live-stock," 69; Hall, *Miserable Slavery*, 8, 101, 240; Douglas Hall, *Planters, Farmers, and Gardeners in Eighteenth-Century Jamaica* (Mona, Jamaica: University of the West Indies, 1987), 17; Burnard, *Master, Tyranny, and Desire*; Pierre Eugène Du Simitière quoted in Christopher P. Iannini, *Fatal Revolutions: Natural History, West Indian Slavery, and the Routes of American Literature* (Chapel Hill: University of North Carolina Press, 2012), 150, 170.

24. Shepherd, "Livestock and Sugar," 632; Shepherd and Montieth, "Pen-Keepers and Coffee Farmers in a Sugar-Plantation Society," 83–85 and S. D. Smith, "Coffee and the Poorer Sort of People," both in Shepherd, ed., *Slavery Without Sugar*, 102–127; James A. Delle, *An Archaeology of Social Space: Analyzing Coffee Plantations in Jamaica's Blue Mountains* (New York: Plenum Press, 1998).

25. Long, *History of Jamaica*, 1: 278 and 3: 842.

26. Steeve O. Buckridge, *The Language of Dress: Resistance and Accommodation in Jamaica, 1760–1890* (Mona, Jamaica: University of the West Indies Press, 2004), 50–53.

27. Long, *History of Jamaica*, 1: 430–431, 466–467, 497–498, footnote, and 2:91; Patrick Browne, *The Civil and Natural History of Jamaica* (London: Printed for the author, 1756), 17; Gov. Keith to the Earl of Dartmouth, 13 June 1775, f. 89, NA/CO137/70; Sheridan, *Sugar and Slaves*, 462.

28. John Whitaker to Capt. Carpenter, "Proposal for Estates settled above 12 Miles from the Sea to pay but $\frac{2}{3}$ ds of the [Sugar] Duties," ff. 301–303, NA/CO137/86; John Whitaker to Capt. Carpenter, 6 June 1786, f. 5, NA/BT6/75, also cited in Bowett, "English Mahogany Trade," 133.

29. Craton and Walvin, *A Jamaican Plantation*, 59–64.

30. Long, *History of Jamaica*, 1: 504, 3: 843.

31. Bowett, "English Mahogany Trade," 73–74, 133–134; William Beckford, *A Descriptive Account of the Island of Jamaica* (London: T. & J. Egerton, 1790), 2: 259, 260.

32. James Macfadyen, *The Flora of Jamaica* (London: Longman, Orme, Brown, Green, & Longman, 1837), 176; P. Thomson, *The Cabinetmaker's Assistant: A Series of Original Designs for Modern Furniture* (Glasgow and New York: Blackie and Son, 1853), 30; Philip Henry Gosse, *A Naturalist's Sojourn in Jamaica* (London: Brown, Green, & Longman, 1851), 156–157, 197–198; Ann Thwaite, *Glimpses of the*

Wonderful: The Life of Philip Henry Gosse, 1810–1888 (London: Faber & Faber, 2002).

3. Supplying the Empire with Mahogany

1. On wartime disruptions of mahogany supplies, see Susan E. Stuart, *Gillows of Lancaster and London, 1730–1840* (Woodbridge, Suffolk: Antique Collectors Club, 2008), 1: 130.
2. "Definitive Treaty of Peace, Paris," Article 17, 10 February 1763, NA/ FSP, *ABH*, 1: 87–88.
3. "Definitive Treaty of Peace, Versailles," 3 September 1783, *ABH*, 1: 137.
4. Michael J. Jarvis, *In the Eye of All Trade: Bermuda, Bermudians, and the Maritime Atlantic World, 1680–1783* (Chapel Hill: University of North Carolina Press, 2010), 185. For more on issues of land use and deforestation, see David Watts, *The West Indies: Patterns of Development, Culture, and Environmental Change since 1492* (Cambridge: Cambridge University Press, 1987), chaps. 5, 9, and 10; David Watts, "Biogeographical Variation in the Mahogany (Swietenia Mahagoni (L.) Jacq.) Woodlots of Barbados, West Indies," *Journal of Biogeography* 5 (1978): 347; Richard Grove, *Green Imperialism: Colonial Expansion, Tropical Island Edens and the Origins of Environmentalism, 1600–1860* (New York: Cambridge University Press, 1995), chaps. 1 and 6.
5. Jarvis, *In the Eye of All Trade,* 79–80, 129. On early efforts to address timber shortages through regulations and state-managed forestry, see Robert Greenhalgh Albion, *Forests and Sea Power: The Timber Problem of the Royal Navy, 1652–1862* (Cambridge: Harvard University Press, 1926); Karl Appuhn, "Inventing Nature: Forests, Forestry, and State Power in Renaissance Venice," *The Journal of Modern History* 72, no. 4 (December 2000): 861–889.
6. Jarvis, *In the Eye of All Trade,* 232–233.
7. Walker quoted in Raymond P. Stearns, *Science in the British Colonies of America* (Champaign, IL: University of Illinois Press, 1970), 341–342; Mark Catesby, *The Natural History of Carolina, Florida, and the Bahama Islands,* (London: n.p., 1731–1743 and Appendix, 1747), 2: 51.
8. Catesby, *The Natural History of Carolina* (London: n.p., 1731–1742), 2: 66; Michael Craton and Gail Saunders, *Islanders in the Stream: A History of the Bahamian People* (Athens, GA: University of Georgia Press, 1992), 88, 108, 135–136.

9. Michael Craton, *Founded Upon the Seas: A History of the Cayman Islands and their People* (Kingston, Jamaica: Ian Randle Publishers, 2003), 28, 34–35, 39, 50.

10. Craton, *Founded Upon the Seas,* 43–44.

11. Long, *History of Jamaica,* 1: 311–313.

12. J. R. Ward, "The British West Indies in the Age of Abolition, 1748–1815," in *The Oxford History of the British Empire,* ed. P. J. Marshall and Alaine Low (Oxford: Oxford University Press, 1998), 2:418–419; David Hancock, *Citizens of the World: London Merchants and the Integration of the British Atlantic Community* (Cambridge: University of Cambridge, 1995), 26–27; John Wright, *The West-India Merchant, Factor, and Supercargoe's Daily Assistant . . .* (London: David Steel, 1765), xxi; "East Florida, by His Excellency James Grant Esq. [Gov. of Florida] . . . A Proclamation," *The Pennsylvania Gazette,* 23 May 1765; [William Stork], *An Account of East-Florida* (London: G. Woodfall, [1766]); Bernard Romans, *A Concise Natural History of East and West Florida. . . .* (New York: printed for the author, [1775]); Charles L. Mowat, "The First Campaign of Publicity for Florida," *Mississippi Valley Historical Review* 30, no. 3 (December 1943): 359–376; Jane G. Landers, ed., *Colonial Plantations and Economy in Florida* (Gainesville, FL: University of Florida Press, 2000).

13. Anon., *Tabago: or a Geographical Description, Natural and Civil History* (London: W. Reeves, [1750]), 7–8; Kathryn Robinson, *Where Dwarfs Reign: A Tropical Rain Forest in Puerto Rico* (San Juan: University of Puerto Rico, 1997), 115–120.

14. D. H. Murdoch, "Land Policy in the Eighteenth-Century British Empire: The Sale of Crown Lands in the Ceded Islands, 1763–1783," *THJ* 27, no. 3 (September 1984): 552–553; "Reflections on the true Interest of Great Britain with Respect to the Caribbee Islands [and] . . . Neutral Islands . . . by a Planter at Barbados," 1762, Unpublished Manuscript, NA/30/47/18/3, ff. 9–11.

15. Grove, *Green Imperialism.*

16. John Campbell, *Candid and Impartial Considerations on the Nature of the Sugar Trade; The Comparative Importance of the British and French Islands . . .* (London: R. Baldwin, 1763), 128–130, 143, 154.

17. Campbell, *Candid and Impartial,* 130.

18. Quoted in Richard A. Howard, "The St. Vincent Botanic Garden— The Early Years," *Arnoldia* (Winter 1997–1998): 12; Chandra Mukerji,

Territorial Ambitions and the Gardens of Versailles (Cambridge: Cambridge University Press, 1997), 73–82; Campbell, *Candid and Impartial,* 154; "Plan for the speedy and effectual settlement of His Majesty's Islands of Grenada, the Grenadines, Dominica, St. Vincent's and Tobago . . . [by] the Board of Trade and Plantations," 3 November 1763 and proposed 1764 alterations, no. 26, NA/CO101/1; Grove, *Green Imperialism,* 269–271; D. L. Niddrie, "Eighteenth-Century Settlement in the British Caribbean," *Transactions of the Institute of British Geographers* 40 (December 1966): 67–80.

19. Hancock, *Citizens of the World,* 146, 219; David Dobson, *Scottish Emigration to Colonial America, 1607–1785* (Athens: University of Georgia, 1994), 171–172; Mark Quintanilla, "Mercantile Communities in the Ceded Islands: The Alexander Bartlet & George Campbell Company," *International Social Science Review* 79 (Spring–Summer 2004): 14–26; Land Commissioners' Report, 15 August 1768, NA/CO106/9; John Fowler, *A Summary Account of the Present Flourishing State of the Respectable Colony of Tobago in the British West Indies* (London: A. Grant, 1774), 64; Murdoch, "Land Policy," 561; Sheridan, *Sugar and Slaves,* 378–380, 457.

20. His son, William Young (1749–1815), a pro-slavery Parliament member, wrote *An Account of the Black Caribs of St. Vincent.* E. I. Carlyle, "Young, Sir William, Second Baronet (1749–1815)," rev. Richard B. Sheridan and Rory T. Cornish, "Melville, Robert (1723–1809)," *ODNB* (Oxford: Oxford University Press, 2004); Grove, *Green Imperialism,* 272.

21. Murdoch, "Land Policy," 562; Watts, *The West Indies,* 346–347; Land Commissioners' Report, 15 August 1765, NA/CO106/9; Richard Grove, "Conserving Eden: The (European) East India Companies and their Environmental Policies on St. Helena, Mauritius and in Western India, 1660–1854," *Comparative Studies in Society and History* 35, no. 2 (April 1993): 323; Land Commissioners of the Ceded Islands to the Lords Commissioners of the Treasury, 10 August 1765. Cited in Peter Hulme and Neil L. Whitehead, eds., *Wild Majesty: Encounters with Caribs from Columbus to the Present Day: An Anthology* (Oxford: Clarendon Press, 1992), 191, 228–229. Nancie L. Gonzáles, "Garifuna Traditions in Historical Perspective," in *Readings in Belizean History,* ed. Lita Hunter Krohn (Belize City: St. John's College, 1987), 77.

22. Adam Bowett, "The Jamaica Trade: Gillow and the Use of Mahogany in the Eighteenth Century," *Regional Furniture* 12 (1998): 30–31.

23. Troy S. Floyd, *The Anglo-Spanish Struggle for Mosquitia* (Albuquerque, NM: University of New Mexico, 1967); Craig Dozier, *Nicaragua's Mosquito Shore: The Years of British and American Presence* (University, AL: University of Alabama Press, 1985); Carl O. Sauer, *The Early Spanish Main* (Berkeley: University of California, 1966); Frank Griffith Dawson, "William Pitt's Settlement at Black River on the Mosquito Shore: A Challenge to Spain in Central America, 1732–87," *HAHR* 63, no. 4 (1983): 677–706; Murdo MacLeod, *Spanish Central America: A Socioeconomic History, 1520–1720* (Berkeley: University of California, 1973); E. O. Winzerling, *The Beginning of British Honduras, 1506–1765* (New York: North River Press, 1946); Robert A. Naylor, *Penny-Ante Imperialism: The Mosquito Shore and the Bay of Honduras 1600–1914* (Cranbury, NJ: Associated University Press, 1989); Narda Dobson, *A History of Belize* (London: Longman Caribbean Limited, 1973); O. Nigel Bolland, *The Formation of a Colonial Society: Belize, From Conquest to Crown Colony* (Baltimore: Johns Hopkins University Press, 1977).

24. Nancy M. Farriss, "Nucleation versus Dispersal: The Dynamics of Population Movement in Colonial Yucatán," *HAHR,* 58 (May 1978): 187–216; O. Nigel Bolland, *Colonialism and Resistance in Belize* (Mona, Jamaica: University of the West Indies Press, 2003), 112–113; Carolyn Hall and Héctor Pérez Brignoli, *Historical Atlas of Central America* (Norman, OK: University of Oklahoma Press, 2003); A. P. Andrews, *Maya Salt Production and Trade* (Tucson: University of Arizona Press, 1983).

25. Nathaniel Uring, *A History of the Voyages and Travels of Capt. Nathaniel Uring* (London: W. Wilkins, 1726), 182–183, 221–236; Bolland, *Formation of a Colonial Society,* 49; Jarvis, *In the Eye of All Trade,* 226.

26. Lawrence H. Gipson, "British Diplomacy in the Light of Anglo-Spanish New World Issues, 1750–1757," *AHR* 51, no. 4 (July 1946): 627–648.

27. Sir Thomas Modyford, Gov. of Jamaica to Lord Arlington, Secretary of State, 18 March 1670, Calendar of State Papers, *ABH*, 1:49–50; William Godolphin, British Ambassador at Madrid, to the Earl of Arlington, Secretary of State, 10/20 May 1672, Calendar of State Papers, 1669–1674, NA/CO137/48, *ABH* 1: 53; Dawson, "William Pitt's Settlement," 677–706;

Winzerling, *The Beginning of British Honduras;* O. Nigel Bolland, "The Social Structure and Social Relations in the Settlement of the Bay of Honduras (Belize) in the 18th Century," *JCH* 6 (1973): 1–42; Thomas Lynch, Governor of Jamaica to the Lords of Trade and Plantations, 29 August 1682, *ABH,* 1: 57; "Letters from His Majesty's Consul, Venice," 16 June 1699, *ABH,* 1: 58.

28. Uring, *History of the Voyages and Travels,* 111. In 1732, a "Mr. Bond & other Gentn of the Bay" proposed that the pew be reduced in size "for the benefit of the Church" and it was later removed to relieve crowding. Now restored, it bears a plaque stating, "For the Use of the Gentlemen of the Bay of Honduras, 1727." Charles K. Bolton, *Christ Church, Salem Street, Boston* (Boston: Christ Church, 1913), 42, 47; see also Ross Newton's dissertation-in-progress at Northeastern University, tentatively entitled *Patrons, Politics, and Pews: Boston Anglicans and their Transatlantic Connections, 1686–1787.*

29. Cathy Matson, *Merchants and Empire: Trading in Colonial New York* (Baltimore: Johns Hopkins University Press, 1998), 274–276, 281.

30. "Definitive Treaty of Peace, Paris," Article 17, 10 February 1763, NA/FSP, *ABH,* 1: 87–88; Petition from "Principal Inhabitants" of the Mosquito Shore, 3 May 1766, to King George III, NA/CO123/1, f. 88. See also Gordon Ireland, *Boundaries, Possessions, and Conflicts in Central and North America and the Caribbean* (New York: Octagon Books, 1971); R. A. Humphreys, *The Diplomatic History of British Honduras* (London: Oxford University Press, 1961); and Dobson, *History of Belize.*

31. Governor Knowles to Lord Holderness, "Copy of the proclamation of the King of Spain ordering Spanish Governors to free slaves who fled from the English or the Dutch," 6 and 18 November 1752, NA/CO137/59, *ABH,* 1: 79; Lord Shelburne to Sir James Gray, Ambassador to Spain, enclosed with Baymen's memorial protesting Spanish efforts to 'seduce' slaves away, 22 July 1768, NA/FSP, 180, *ABH,* 1: 115; Jane Landers, "Cimarrón Ethnicity and Cultural Adaptation in the Spanish Domains of the Circum-Caribbean, 1503–1763," in Paul E. Lovejoy, ed., *Identity in the Shadow of Slavery* (London: Continuum, 2000), 42.

32. Admiral William Burnaby to Secretary of State Stephens, Jamaica, Adm. 1/238, *ABH,* 1: 109; Bolland, *Formation of a Colonial Society,* 29.

33. 21 April 1766, NA/CO123/1, 116–128; Certified copy of orders issued by Don Joseph Rosado, Commandant of Bacalar, delivered to J. Maud, 22 February 1764, NA/FSP, *ABH*, 1: 90–92; Admiral Rodney to Secretary of State Stephens, 12 December, 1768 and 6 November, 1773, Adm. 1/238–1/239, *ABH*, 1: 116, 124.

34. Although the English regarded the Miskitos as a monolithic group, they were comprised of several loosely affiliated groups of shared ethnic heritage. For more on the Mosquito Shore, see Dozier, *Nicaragua's Mosquito Shore*, chap, 1; Nicholas Rogers, "Caribbean Borderland: Empire, Ethnicity, and the Exotic on the Mosquito Coast," *Eighteenth Century Life* 26, no. 3 (2002): 117–138; Michael D. Olien, "The Miskito Kings and the Lines of Succession," *Journal of Anthropological Research* 39 (1983): 198–241; Karl H. Offen, "The Sambo and Tawira Miskitu: The Colonial Origins and Geography of Intra-Miskitu Differentiation in Eastern Nicaragua and Honduras," *Ethnohistory* 49, no. 2 (Spring 2002): 320–372; Karen O. Kupperman, *Providence Island, 1630–1641: The Other Puritan Colony* (New York: Cambridge University Press, 1993); Orlando W. Roberts, *Narrative of the Voyage and Excursions on the East Coast and in the Interior of Central America* (Edinburgh: Constable and Co., 1827), 266; and Floyd, *The Anglo-Spanish Struggle for Mosquitia.*

35. Memorandum for the Right Honorable Lord George Germain his Majesty's Principal Secretary of State, 9 December 1776, MSS-6.6, MHS; Enclosure in Governor Dalling to Lord George Germain, 28 August 1779, NA/CO137/75, *ABH*, 1: 127.

36. Robert White, 11 December 1783, NA/CO123/2; Naylor, *Penny-Ante Imperialism,* 61; Edward Felix Hill, "An Account of the Spaniards landing at and taking St. George's Key . . . ," 1 October 1779, NA/CO137/76, *ABH*, 128–129.

37. Dozier, *Nicaragua's Mosquito Shore*, 19–25.

38. "Definitive Treaty of Peace, Versailles," 3 September 1783, *ABH*, 1: 137; Robert White to Secretary Townsend, 10 February 1783, NA/CO123/2; D. A. Brading, "Bourbon Spain and its American Empire," *CHLA* (Cambridge: 1984–1986), 1: 397; Murdo MacLeod, "Spain and America: The Atlantic Trade, 1492–1720," *CHLA*, 1: 38; Robert White, "Memorial of his Majesty's Subjects Captivated and Plundered in Yucatan and driven from the Bay of Honduras in September 1779," 8 April 1783,

NA/CO123/2, 132–140; Robert White, "Memorial of his Majesty's Subjects," 29 September 1783, f. 32, NA/CO123/3.

39. "Notice by Don Joseph Morinos Zevallez [José Merino y Ceballos], Governor . . . of the Yucatán regarding the designation of treaty boundaries," 27 May 1784, *ABH*, 1: 142; NA/CO137/48, 31 May 1784, *ABH*, 1: 143–143; NA/Adm1/238; Philipe Remirez de Estinos [Felipe Ramírez de Estenoz], Governor of Yucatán in Mérida to Joseph Maud, 29 December 1763, NA/CO137/61.

40. Article 7, "Convention of London," 4 July 1786, *ABH*, 1: 154.

41. NA/CO123/5, f. 59 Petition from his Majesty's Subjects Settled on the coast of Yucatan in the Bay of Honduras, 28 May 1787, submitted by Robert White.

42. NA/CO123/5, f. 59, 28 May 1787, Petition from his Majesty's Subjects . . . , submitted by Robert White; Edward Marcus Despard, "A Narrative of the Public Transactions in the Bay of Honduras from 1784 to 1790," 8 March 1791, NA/CO123/10; Despard, "Narrative: Appendix 12: Treaty Objections," includes copy of Bartlett's letter (pp. 35–37) to Lord Sydney from Honduras in 1786, NA/CO123/11, ff. 58–84; William Ryder's critique of treaty and compensation claim, NA/CO123/9, 94 A-B, 12 May 1790; NA/CO123/5, f. 36 Copy of a Petition by Several [London and Bristol] Merchants . . . trading to the Coast of Yucatan in the Bay of Honduras, signed 28 March and 27 April 1787.

43. Clifford D. Conner, *Colonel Despard: The Life and Times of an Anglo-Irish Rebel* (Conshohocken, PA: Combined Publishing, 2000); Mike Jay, *The Unfortunate Colonel Despard* (London: Bantam Press, 2004); Marcus Rediker and Peter Linebaugh, *The Many-Headed Hydra: Sailors, Slaves, Commoners and the Hidden History of the Revolutionary Atlantic* (Boston: Beacon Press, 2000), chap. 8.

44. Despard, "Narrative," NA/CO123/10, ff. 58–66.

45. "Convention of London," Article 3, 14 July 1786, NA/FSP, *ABH*, 1: 154–157; Robert White, 8 April 1783, NA/CO123/2, 132–140; George Dyer to "Your Grace," [recipient unknown], 28 July 1789, NA/CO123/7, 126; Richard Hoare to Robert White, 25 August 1788 [filed 1789], NA/CO123/7, 161–164.

46. Vera Lee Brown, "Chapter II. Anglo-Spanish Relations in America, 1763–1770," *HAHR* 5, no. 3 (August 1922): 351–386; Robert White to Lord Sydney, 25 November 1785, NA/CO123/3; Memorial from the Baymen, 30 September 1786, NA/CO123/4.

47. Frank Griffith Dawson, "The Evacuation of the Mosquito Shore and the English who Stayed Behind, 1786–1800," *The Americas* 55, no. 1 (July 1998): 63–89; Aaron Young, N. S. Thompson, Fras. Meany at Black River, to Col. Lawrie, 21 January 1787, f. 10, NA/CO123/6; "Affidavit of James Bannantyne respecting the proceedings of August 1787," Despard, "Narrative: Appendix 45," 224, 241 and f. 98, f. 98, NA/CO123/10.

48. 25 July 1787 and 17 August 1789, NA/CO123/8, ff. 177–179, 298; Despard, "Narrative," NA/CO123/10.

49. "Map of British Honduras," 1786, NA/CO700. See also Figure 3.1.

50. "Petition of People of Color to Col. Grimarest and Col. Despard," in Despard, "Narrative: Appendix 34," NA CO 123/11, ff. 34–37, f. 78; "List of Inhabitants," in Despard, "Narrative," NA/CO123/10, ff. 161–162; "General Return of the Inhabitants of the Bay of Honduras . . . 22nd October, 1790," NA CO 123/9, f. 248.

51. "Petition to the King in Council of the Undersigning Merchants Trading to the Coast of Yucatan in the Bay of Honduras," 28 March 1787, NA/CO123/5; Sydney to Despard, February 1788, f. 99, NA/CO123/6; James Bartlett to Dyer & Allen & Co., 12 May 1790, NA/CO123/9, 105.

52. Adam Bowett, "The English Mahogany Trade, 1700–1793: A Commercial History," (PhD diss., Brunel University, 1996), chap. 6, for estimated export figures of Honduran and West Indian mahogany; F. Bruce Lamb, *Mahogany of Tropical America: Its Ecology and Management* (Ann Arbor: University of Michigan Press, 1966); Marshall Bennett, Chairman of the Public Meeting, Memorial to his "Royal Majesty," 5 March 1814, NA/CO123/23; Bolland, *Colonialism and Resistance,* 112–113.

4. *The Bitters and the Sweets of Trade*

1. John Wright, *The West-India Merchant, Factor, and Supercargoes Daily Assistant* (London: David Steel, 1765), xxi.

2. John J. McCusker, "The Demise of Distance: The Business Press and the Origins of the Information Revolution in the Early Modern Atlantic World," *AHR* 110, no. 2 (April 2005): 295–321; Kenneth Morgan, "Robert Dinwiddie's Reports on the British American Colonies," *WMQ* 3rd Series, 65, no. 2 (April 2008): 321, 328.

3. As per Richard Sheridan, merchants are defined here as including "individuals who traded on their own account, factors who did business on

consignment, shopkeepers who bought and sold general merchandise or who specialized in one line, and men who lent money and discounted bills of exchange . . . [Many of whom] were planters and shipowners as well." Richard B. Sheridan, *Sugar and Slavery: An Economic History of the British West Indies, 1623–1775* (Baltimore: Johns Hopkins University Press, 1974), 374; Holly Snyder, "English Markets, Jewish Merchants, and Atlantic Endeavors: Jews and the Making of British Transatlantic Commercial Culture, 1650–1800," in Richard L. Kagan and Philip D. Morgan, eds., *Atlantic Diasporas: Jews, Conversos, and Crypto-Jews in the Age of Mercantilism* (Baltimore: Johns Hopkins University Press, 2009), 70–72.

4.	Aaron Lopez to Hayman Levy, 23 July 1754. Aaron Lopez Papers, Box 42, Folder 8, NHS; see also *Commerce of Rhode Island, 1726–1800,* 7th series (Boston: Massachusetts Historical Society, 1914); Holly Snyder, "A Sense of Place: Jews, Identity, and Social Status in Colonial British America, 1654–1831," (PhD diss., Brandeis University, 2000); Ellen Smith and George Goodwin, *Jews of Rhode Island* (Lebanon, NH: University Press of New England, 2004); Stanley F. Chyet, *Lopez of Newport: Colonial American Merchant Prince* (Detroit: Wayne State University, 1970); William Pencak, *Jews and Gentiles in Early America, 1654–1800* (Ann Arbor: University of Michigan Press, 2005); Noah Gelfand, "A People Within and Without: International Jewish Commerce and Community in the Seventeenth and Eighteenth Centuries Dutch Atlantic World," (PhD diss., New York University, 2008).

5.	Snyder, "A Sense of Place," 158; Peter Mathias, "Risk, Credit, and Kinship in Early Modern Enterprise," in John J. McCusker and Kenneth Morgan, eds., *The Early Modern Atlantic Economy* (Cambridge: Cambridge University Press, 2000), chap. 1; Peter Tertzakian, *A Thousand Barrels A Second: The Coming Oil Break Point and the Challenges of Facing an Energy Dependent World* (New York: McGraw Hill, 2006), 11.

6.	Aaron Lopez to William Stead, 9 November 1764, Lopez Letterbook, NHS; Norman E. Saul, "The Beginnings of the American-Russian Trade, 1763–1766," *WMQ* 26, no. 4 (October 1969): 596–600; Philip Stephens to Capt. Kennedy, 13 June 1764, 24 September 1764, copy, Sedgwick Papers, II, MHS.

7.	Aaron Lopez to Gabriel Ludlow, 20 November 1764, Lopez Letterbook, NHS; Cathy Matson, *Merchants and Empire: Trading in Colonial New York* (Baltimore: Johns Hopkins University Press, 1998), 151, 191.

8.   William Stead to Aaron Lopez, 4 October 1765, Aaron Lopez Papers, NHS; Henry Cruger, Jr. to Aaron Lopez, 9 April 1766, 20 May 1766 and 28 July 1766 in *Commerce of Rhode Island*, 153, 159, 164. Author's emphasis added. Toby L. Ditz, "Secret Selves, Credible Personas: The Problematics of Trust and Public Display in the Writing of Eighteenth-Century Philadelphia Merchants," in *Possible Pasts: Becoming Colonial in Early America*, ed. Robert Blair St. George (Ithaca, NY: Cornell University Press, 2000).

9.   Louis E. Grivetti and Howard-Yana Shapiro, eds., *Chocolate: History, Culture, and Heritage* (New York: John Wiley and Sons, 2009), 34–38; Snyder, "English Markets, Jewish Merchants," 68–69.

10.   Henry Cruger, Letterbook, 1762–68, NYHS; Henry Cruger, Jr. to Aaron Lopez, 11 October 1765, in *Commerce of Rhode Island*, 128; Kenneth Morgan, "Bristol and the Atlantic Trade in the Eighteenth Century," *EHR* 107, no. 424 (July 1992): 626–650.

11.   Eric Williams, "The British West Indian Slave Trade after its Abolition in 1807," *Journal of Negro History* 27 (1942): 175–191; David Eltis, "The Traffic in Slaves Between the British West Indian Colonies, 1807–1833," *EcHR* 25 no. 1 (February 1972): 55–64; Hilary McD. Beckles, Walter Johnson, eds., *The Chattel Principle: Internal Slave Trades in the Americas* (Yale University Press, 2004), 130–131; Aaron Lopez's Ledger 554, p. 218 and Isaac DaCosta to Captain Newdigate, 30 June 1767, Box 52, Aaron Lopez Papers, NHS.

12.   Aaron Lopez to William Stead, 9 November 1764, Aaron Lopez to Richard Alsop, 18 December 1764, Lopez Letterbook, NHS; Virginia Platt, "'And Don't Forget the Guinea Voyage': The Slave Trade of Aaron Lopez of Newport," *WMQ* 32, no. 4 (1975): 601–618; Sarah Deutsch, "The Elusive Guineamen: Newport Slavers, 1735–1774," *NEQ* 55, no. 2 (June 1982): 240–241, 248; on slave warranties, see Walter Johnson, *Soul by Soul: Life Inside the Antebellum Slave Market* (Cambridge: Harvard University Press, 1999).

13.   Rachel Chernos Lin, "The Rhode Island Slave-Traders: Butchers, Bakers, and Candlestick Makers," *Slavery and Abolition* 23, no. 3 (December 2002): 21–38.

14.   Henry Laurens to Samuel Wragg, 29 October 1764, George C. Rogers, ed., *The Papers of Henry Laurens*, vols. 1–4 (Columbia: University of South Carolina Press, 1974), 2: 518, 3: 294–296, 4: 391, 409–414, 484; Aaron Lopez to William Stead, 9 November 1764, and Aaron Lopez to

Richard Alsop, 18 December 1764, Lopez Letterbook, NHS; Platt, "Don't Forget the Guinea Voyage," 605–607; Deutsch, "Elusive Guineamen," 248.

15. Henry Laurens to John Knight, 24 August 1764; Henry Laurens to Joseph Bower, 12 September 1764; Henry Laurens to Cowles & Harford, 7 and 11 September 1764 in Rogers, ed., *The Papers of Henry Laurens*, 4: 378, 379, 417, 413.

16. Thomas Frank, Bristol to Thomas Clifford & Son, [Philadelphia], 23 December 1771 and 11 September 1772, Thomas Clifford, Jr., Warwick to Thomas Clifford, Sr., 27 January 1772, vol. 5, Clifford-Pemberton Papers, HSP.

17. George Boyd, 7 January and 1 March 1774, Letterbook, 1773–1775, Boyd Papers, NHHS; Henry Cruger, Jr. to Aaron Lopez, 1 February 1772, *Commerce of Rhode Island,* 386–387.

18. Charles H. Card, *Richard Card and Descendants* (Carrabelle, FL: n.p., 1996); *New England Historical and Genealogical Register* 69 (October 1915): 381.

19. For more on the development of an oligarchy, O. Nigel Bolland, *The Formation of a Colonial Society: Belize, From Conquest to Crown Colony* (Baltimore: Johns Hopkins University Press, 1977).

20. Jeanne A. Vibert, "The Market Economy and the Furniture Trade of Newport, Rhode Island: The Career of John Cahoone, Cabinetmaker, 1745–1765," (master's thesis, University of Delaware, 1981), 26; James B. Hedges, *The Browns of Providence Plantations: The Colonial Years* (Providence: Brown University, 1968), 8, 54–55; William Cahoone's Last Will and Testament, 15 February 1768, "Private Records," 1: 299, BNA.

21. "Estate of Richard Burrell Esq. deceas'd in Account with Oliver Ring Warner," 1764–1766, MSS 1140, RIHS.

22. Card, *Richard Card;* Certificate from Robert Gresley, Isle of Goree, 26 March 1762; James Card's complaint, 27 March 1762, Goree Bay; Receipts of *King of Bonney,* 1763, 3 and 23 March 1763, Folder 2 and Oversized Folder, MSS 1140, RIHS.

23. Sailing orders for *Rising Sun,* Aaron and Daniel Chase, 8 May 1765, Folder 4; Receipt for Nicholaw and Present, witnessed by James Card, 16 October 1763; Memo regarding the slaves' sale, 14 October 1762, Folder 3 and 4; William Cahoone to Oliver Ring Warner, 24 April 1764; Receipt, 21 April 1764, Folder 4, MSS 1140, RIHS. Trevor Burnard

and Kenneth Morgan, "The Dynamics of the Slave Market and Slave Purchasing Patterns in Jamaica, 1655–1788," *WMQ* 58: 1 (January 2001): 205–228; and Stephen D. Behrendt, "Markets, Transaction Cycles, and Profits: Merchants and Merchant Decision Making in the British Slave Trade," *WMQ* 58, 1 (January 2001): 171–204.

24. Edmund Townsend's receipt, 2 February 1761, Folder 2; Miscellaneous Receipts: 4 March 1758, 29 January 1760, 1 October 1769, Folders 1 and 4, MSS 1140, RIHS.

25. William Pearce's complaint, 28 November 1764, Folder 4, MSS 1140, RIHS.

26. Thomas Smith to Aaron Lopez, 13 February 1771, Aaron Lopez Papers, Box 168, Folder 4; NHS, Ron Potvin, "'A poor soft weak Headed puffed up foolish fellow': The John Newdigate Controversy," *Newport History* 68: 236 (1997), 137–142.

27. "Registration of Land Records," submitted by Jonathan Card [Junior], 29 June, 1810, "Private Records," BNA, 3: 290; Will of Francis Hickey, 3 October 1792, NA/Prob11/1224; Daniel R. Finamore, "Sailors and Slaves in the Wood-Cutting Frontier: Archaeology of the British Bay Settlement, Belize," (PhD diss., Boston University, 1994), 89.

28. Dorothy Taylor's will, 20 February 1788, NA/Prob11/1163; Petition signed by "Francis Hickey, Administrator of the estate of Jonathan Card and Dorothy Taylor deceased," 18 August 1783, NA/CO123/6, pp. 261–62; Col. Lawrie's account of María Pérez, 22 February 1788, NA/CO123/6, pp. 130–32; Deposition of María Pérez [signed with her mark], submitted to Col. Despard, Bay of Honduras, 29 October 1787, f. 151, NA/CO/123/5, p. 117.

29. Regarding the slave uprising, see *Newport Mercury,* 9 September 1765.

30. For voyages of the *Rising Sun* and *Swordfish,* see, for example, 26 November 1764, 6 May 1765, and 9 November 1767, *Newport Mercury; Boston Gazette and Country Journal,* 8 December 1760; Aaron Lopez Papers, Ledger 554 (O), 1767–1770, NHS. Regarding the Cards' purchases, see account entries for 1766–1767, 136, 143, 162, 176, 188, 193 and Ledger 555, 1766–1775, 158. Regarding purchase of tables, see 8 September to 25 October 1768, Folder 2, MSS 1140, RIHS.

31. James Card to Oliver Ring Warner, Deposition regarding the loss of the sloop *Swordfish,* 4 September 1769 and 29 July 1770, Folders 4 and 5, MSS 1140, RIHS; *Pennsylvania Gazette,* 21 September 1769.

32. Warner's Instructions and Power of Attorney for James Card; Estate of William Cahoone Esq. deceased in Acct. with Oliver Ring Warner, 26 February 1770, notarized by Warner in Newport; 1 May 1770, 29 July 1770, and 15 August 1770, James Card to Oliver Ring Warner.

33. Receipt for 3,384 feet mahogany on the *Betsy* on Warner's account, 29 July 1770 and Receipts for slaves, 10 April 1771, 2 April 1771, and 14 August 1771, Folder 5; 22 July 1772, Jonathan Card to Sarah Card, Folder 8, MSS 1140, RIHS.

34. Anthony Van Dam, Memorial "on behalf of his Correspondents Major Richard Hoare and Mssrs. Thomas Potts & Jonathan Card, his majesty's Natural-born Subjects of Great Britain & Ireland," 25 March 1786, NA/CO123/4, ff. 31–34.

35. While the exact date of Jonathan Card's death is uncertain, Van Dam's 1786 petition suggests it occurred during the 1779 attack. Likely because of disruptions in the Bay settlement, Card's will was not officially entered into probate until 1788 along with that of his wife. See also 18 August 1783 petition signed by "Francis Hickey, Administrator of the estate of Jonathan Card and Dorothy Taylor deceased," NA/CO123/6, pp. 261–62; Van Dam, "Third Memorial . . . 25th March, 1786;" Van Dam, Memorial "on behalf of his Correspondents Major Richard Hoare and Mssrs. Thomas Potts & Jonathan Card," 25 March 1786, NA/CO123/4, pp. 31–34, 53; *Rivington's New-York Gazetteer,* 10 October 1774; *Providence Gazette,* 31 December 1808.

36. *The New-Hampshire Gazette, and Historical Chronicle,* 28 September 1776.

37. "Speeches . . . in favour of the Rights of America. Viz. Gov. Johnstone, Mr. Cruger," (New York: James Rivington, 1775); Julie M. Flavell, "Cruger, Henry (1739–1827)," *ODNB* (Oxford University Press, 2004; Morgan, "Bristol and the Atlantic Trade," 632, 636.

38. Will of Thomas Potts, 12 June 1807, NA/Prob11/1463; Will of Richard Hoare, 18 July 1796, NA/Prob11/1277; Despard to Lord Sydney, Secretary of State, 2, 17 November 1789, NA/CO123/7.

39. Agreement between Jonathan Card and Francis Hickey, 27 March, 1788, Private Papers, 1: 84, BNA. On Sarah Card's marriage, see "New York City Marriages, 1600s–1800s," http://www.ancestry.com.

40. María Pérez to Despard, [signed with her mark], 29 October 1787, NA/CO123/5, pp. 117; Col. Lawrie's report about María Pérez, 22 February

1788, NA/CO123/6, pp. 130–32; Edward Marcus Despard, "A Narrative of the Public Transactions in the Bay of Honduras from 1784 to 1790," 8 March 1791, NA/CO123/10, p. 163.

41. Baymen's protest of Despard, signed by Jonathan Card, 30 May 1789, NA/CO123/8, p. 94.

42. "List of Inhabitants . . . permitting them to cultivate Gardens," 1790, NA/CO123/11, f. 261.

43. William S. Coker, "The Moreno Family of the Gulf Coast," in Ann L. Henderson and Gary Ross Mormino, eds., *Spanish Pathways in Florida* (Sarasota, FL: Pineapple Press, 1991), 224; NA/CO123/6, f. 249, List of Small Craft in the Bay of Honduras, 1 June 1788 lists Card and Hickey as co-owners of a vessel. Will of Francis Hickey, 3 October 1792, NA/Prob11/1224; NA/CO123/17, f. 40, 1806, Census of the Honduras Inhabitants; NA/CO123/14, f. 168, 1790, "Inventory of Honduras population," lists men available for the settlement's defense; Charter Party to Michael Henley and Son from Robert Hunter, Jr., 1802, HNL/94/6:4, Henley Papers, NMM; Daniel P. Finamore, "'Pirate Water': Sailing to Belize in the Mahogany Trade," in *Maritime Empires: British Imperial Maritime Trade in the Nineteenth Century,* ed. David Killingray, Margarette Lincoln, and Nigel Rigby (Rochester, NY: Boydell Press, 2004), 43; George Hyde to Bathurst, 3 February 1827, NA/CO123/38.

44. James Card's executor was his wife, Sarah Card, 3 December 1774, Folder 8, MSS 1140, RIHS.

5. Slavery in the Rain Forest

1. Cahoone's lease agreement with Warner, 21 April 1764, Oliver Ring Warner to James Card, 23 February 1770, James Card to Oliver Ring Warner, 4 April 1770, 23 February 1770, 1 May 1770, Folders 4 and 5, MSS 1140, RIHS.

2. Ira Berlin, *Many Thousands Gone: The First Two Centuries of Slavery in North America* (Cambridge, MA: Belknap Press of Harvard University, 1998), 1–14. On slavery in rain forest settings, see also Warren Dean, *With Broadax and Firebrand: The Destruction of the Brazilian Atlantic Forest* (Berkeley: University of California Press, 1995).

3. Given the dearth of sources, evidence of enslaved people in the Bay must be gleaned, often indirectly, from potentially biased reports.

Primary sources include Baymen's correspondence, travelers' accounts, trade and court records, Board of Magistrates and Public Meeting minutes, and governmental records at the Belize National Archives (BNA) and the National Archives (NA) in England; some records are also published in *Archives of British Honduras* (*ABH*), ed. John Alder Burdon (London: Sifton, Praed, 1931).

4.   O. Nigel Bolland, *The Formation of a Colonial Society: Belize, From Conquest to Crown Colony* (Baltimore: Johns Hopkins University Press, 1977), 52–53.

5.   Bolland, *The Formation of a Colonial Society*, 52; Narda Dobson, *A History of Belize* (Port of Spain, Trinidad, and Tobago: Longman Caribbean, 1973); George Henderson, *Account of the British Settlement of Honduras* (London: R. Baldwin, 1811), 85; Herbert S. Klein, *African Slavery in Latin America and the Caribbean* (New York: Oxford University Press, 1986), 54–55.

6.   Olaudah Equiano, *The Interesting Narrative* (London: n.p., [1789], repr., New York: Penguin Books, 1995), 214–215; Jeffrey Bolster, *Black Jacks: African American Seamen in the Age of Sail* (Cambridge: Harvard University Press, 1997), 8–9; Marcus Rediker, *Between the Devil and the Deep Blue Sea: Merchant Seamen, Pirates, and the Anglo-American Maritime World, 1700–1750* (Cambridge: Cambridge University Press, 1987); Emma Christopher, *Slave Ship Sailors and their Captive Cargoes, 1730–1807* (Cambridge: Cambridge University Press, 2006); Henderson, *Account*, 99.

7.   Bolland, *Formation of a Colonial Society*, 56; Thomas Graham, "Journal of my Visitation," 1790, NA/CO123/9; *Honduras Almanack* (Belize: Magistrates, 1827), 8–9, both quoted in Daniel Finamore, "Furnishing the Craftsman: Slaves and Sailors in the Mahogany Trade," *AF* (2008) 79–80.

8.   Henderson, *Account*, 56–59.

9.   Jacob Nagle, *The Nagle Journal: A Diary of the Life of Jacob Nagle, Sailor, from the Year 1775 to 1841*, ed. John C. Dann (New York: Weidenfeld & Nicolson, 1988), 282–284; Daniel Finamore, "'Pirate Water': Sailing to Belize in the Mahogany Trade," in *Maritime Empires: British Imperial Maritime Trade in the Nineteenth Century*, eds. David Killingray, Margarette Lincoln, and Nigel Rigby (Rochester, NY: Boydell Press, 2004), chap. 3; Henderson, *Account*, 70.

10. Richard Sheridan, *Sugar and Slavery: An Economic History of the British West Indies, 1623–1775* (Baltimore: Johns Hopkins University Press, 1974); Philip D. Curtin, *The Rise and Fall of the Plantation Complex: Essays in Atlantic History* (New York: Cambridge University Press, 1990); Robin Blackburn, *The Making of New World Slavery, From the Baroque to the Modern* (New York: Verso, 1997); Eric Williams, *Capitalism and Slavery* (Chapel Hill: University of North Carolina Press, 1944, repr., 1994); David Watts, *The West Indies: Patterns of Development, Culture, and Environmental Change since 1492* (London: Cambridge University Press, 1987).

11. Regarding woodcutters' contact with indigenous peoples, for example, see Frank Griffith Dawson, "William Pitt's Settlement at Black River on the Mosquito Shore: A Challenge to Spain in Central America, 1732–87," *HAHR* 63, no. 4 (1983): 677–706; regarding foraging and occupational hazards, see Henderson, *Account,* 61, 86, 131.

12. Henderson, *Account,* 56–59.

13. Henderson, *Account,* 61; *ABH,* 2:89.

14. On cosmological significance of trees in African and Afro-Caribbean traditions, see Nicholas J. Saunders, *The Peoples of the Caribbean: An Encyclopedia of Archaeology and Traditional Culture* (Santa Barbara, CA: ABC-CLIO, Inc., 2005), 289–290.

15. Bolland, *Formation of a Colonial Society,* 50, 95–96; Henderson, *Account,* 61.

16. Extract from 1765 Annual Register, *ABH,* 109–110; Jane Landers, "Cimarrón Ethnicity and Cultural Adaptation in the Spanish Domains of the Circum-Caribbean, 1503–1763," in *Identity in the Shadow of Slavery,* ed. Paul E. Lovejoy (London: Continuum, 2000), 42. On patterns of marronage in the Americas, see Jane Landers, "Acquisition and Loss on a Spanish Frontier: The Free Black Homesteaders of Florida, 1784–1821," in *Against the Odds: Free Blacks in the Slave Societies of the Americas,* ed. Jane Landers (London: Frank Cass, 1996), 88–93; John Thornton, *Africa and Africans in the Making of the Atlantic World, 1400–1800,* 2nd ed. (Cambridge: Cambridge University Press, 1998), chap. 10 and Bolland, *Formation of a Colonial Society,* chap. 4–6.

17. Governor Knowles to Lord Holderness, 6 and 18 November 1752, NA/CO137/59, *ABH,* 79; Letter from Lord Shelburne to James Gray, Ambassador to Spain, 22 July 1768, State Papers Foreign, Spain, 180, *ABH,*

1: 115; "Abstract of a letter from Mr. Thomas Potts," 28 May 1792, f. 126, NA/CO123/13; Magistrates Meeting, 11 December 1795; W. White of *Shelburne Packet* to Lord Sydney, 17 April 1785 and Robert White to the Secretary of State, 26 November 1785, NA/CO123/3, f. 149, 332–334; John Christopher's Report from meeting with Francisco Aybar, 11 September 1765 to 9 January 1766, NA/CO123/1, 97; Joseph Otway, Black River to Don Francisco Aybar, Commandant of St. Fernando de Omoa, 2 September 1765, NA/CO123/1, 105.

18. 26 April 1792, *ABH,* 1: 199.

19. "Appendix 103: Copy of letter from Bartlett to Despard, [December 1786]" in Edward Despard, "Narrative of the Public Transactions in the Bay of Honduras from 1784 to 1790 . . . ," 8 March 1791, NA/CO123/11; "Letter from the Inhabitants of the Bay of Honduras to Major Caulfield," 8 June 1745, NA/CO137/48, *ABH,* 1: 72; "Account of the Spaniards' Landing at and Taking of St. George's Key . . . ," Edward Felix Hill, 1 October 1779, NA/CO137/75, *ABH,* 1:129.

20. "The Inhabitants to the Earl of Balcarres," 12 October 1797, *ABH,* 239.

21. Dobson, *History of Belize;* Bolland, *Formation of a Colonial Society,* 77, 83; *The Defence* [sic] *of the Settlers of Honduras . . . Relative to the Condition and Treatment of Slaves at Honduras* (Jamaica: Alexander Aikman, 1824, repr., London: Baldwin, Craddock, and Joy, 1824).

22. While the case was not brought until 1822, the allegations dated back to the transition of ownership following Cahoone's death, circa 1768. Superintendent Arthur to Magistrates, 24 October 1821, NA/CO123/32, and Superintendent Arthur to Magistrates, f. 44, 1822.

23. Testimony of King's Advocate, John Cratqueline, 1822, f. 46, NA/CO123/32.

24. Excerpt from trial of Dr. Bowen, 22 October 1806, and Superintendent Arthur to Magistrates, 24 October 1821, NA/CO123/32; Superintendent Arthur to Brathurst, 10 January 1823, and Superintendent Arthur to William Bullock, Jamaica, 26 November 1821, "Bond of Commissioner's Report . . . to Investigate Indian Slaves," 8 January 1822, Superintendent Arthur to Brathurst [copy], 22 February 1822, ff. 7, 14, 48, 97, NA/CO123/31.

25. Order of the Commandant of Bacalar, Almanac 1828, 22 February 1764, State Papers Foreign, Spain, 167, *ABH* 1: 90; "Translation of Spanish Commissioner's certificate of seizure of above property found beyond the limit," Juan B. Gaul to Despard, 16 June 1789, f. 65, NA/

CO123/8; O'Brien and Bartlett to Despard, f. 237, NA/CO123/7; Despard to Juan B. Gaul, 19 June 1789, NA/CO123/8, 76.

26. "Minutes of . . . Board Council held at Black River . . . ;" Colonel Lawrie, Black River to Gabriel de Hervias, Commandant of Truxillo, 22 January 1787, and Col. Lawrie to Gabriel de Hervias, 31 July 1787, NA/CO123/6, ff. 43–47, 74, 82–84, 149–150.

27. Report of Superintendent Arthur to Earl Brathurst, 2 December 1814, NA/CO123/23.

28. Captain Davey to Admiral Rodney, 21 June 1773, and Committee of the Baymen to Admiral Rodney, 11 October 1773, NA/Adm1/239, *ABH,* 1: 121–124.

29. Deposition of Cudjoe, 30 November 1790, and Deposition of Mattias Gale, 16 December 1790, ff. 175, 180, NA/CO123/3.

30. "Memorial of his Majesty's Subjects Settled on the Mosquito Shore," submitted by Robert White, 28 October 1784, NA/CO123/3, 41–43; Despard, "Narrative," NA/CO123/10, ff. 182–188, 190–192; Emma Christopher, *A Merciless Place: The Lost Story of Britain's Convict Disaster in Africa and How it Led to the Settlement of Australia* (New York: Oxford University Press, 2011), 265–274.

31. "Appendix 82: David Hill's Affidavit," of Despard, "Narrative," f. 161; Inhabitants to Lord Barthurst, 26 February 1817, NA/CO123/26.

32. "Deposition by Thomas Potts," 31 March 1794, *ABH,* 1: 209, Public Meeting Minutes, 29, 30 June, and 5 July 1802, *ABH,* 2: 55.

33. Bolland, *Formation of a Colonial Society,* 79; Superintendent Arthur to Brathurst, 19 November 1816, NA/CO123/27; 3 May 1806, ff. 72–77, NA/CO123/17.

34. A. M. H. Hamilton to the Magistrates, 23 September 1807, f. 76, NA/CO123/17.

35. "Abstract of a letter from Mr. Thomas Potts," Author's emphasis added, 28 May 1792, f. 126, NA/CO123/13; Despard, "Narrative," f. 163, NA/CO123/10.

6. Redefining Mahogany in the Early Republic

1. Quote from Franklin's letter (13 November 1780) to Edward Nairne, a London instrument maker, in Benjamin Franklin, "On Hygrometers," *Transactions of the American Philosophical Society* (Philadelphia: Robert Aiken, [1786]), 2: 56.

2. *Pennsylvania Evening Post,* 5 July 1777.

3. Gillow to John Burrow, Kingston, 3 May 1784 and Gillow to Christopher Parkinson, 15 February 1760, cited in Adam Bowett, "The English Mahogany Trade, 1700–1793: A Commercial History," (PhD diss., Brunel University, 1996), 106; Susan E. Stuart, *Gillows of Lancaster and London, 1730–1840* (Woodbridge, Suffolk: Antique Collectors Club, 2008), 1: 234.

4. Robert Mussey and Anne Haley, "John Cogswell and Boston Bombé Furniture: Thirty-Five Years of Revolution in Politics and Design," *AF* (1994): 73–105.

5. Bowett, "English Mahogany Trade," 99, 101–103.

6. Maxine Berg, "From Imitation to Invention: Creating Commodities in Eighteenth-Century Britain," EcHR 55, no. 1 (2002): 13–14.

7. Franklin, "On Hygrometers," 53–55; Joyce Chaplin, *The First Scientific American: Benjamin Franklin and the Pursuit of Genius,* (New York: Basic Books, 2006), 303, 317.

8. Page Talbott, "The House that Franklin Built," *Antiques and Fine Art* (2006): 233; John Thomas Scharf and Thompson Westcott, *History of Philadelphia, 1609–1884,* (Philadelphia: L. H. Everts, 1884), 2: 911; John M. Huffman, "'I, as a Republican Printer,' Benjamin Franklin, Printing, and the Mission to France, 1776–1785," Florida State University D-Scholarship Repository, no. 25 (2004): 1–123; Page Talbott, "Franklin's Legacy: Documented Furnishings," *The Magazine Antiques* (December 2005): 64–73.

9. William B. Wilcox, ed., *The Papers of Benjamin Franklin* (New Haven, CT: Yale University Press, 1972–87), 19: 336–37; Morrison H. Heckscher and Leslie Greene Bowman, *American Rococo, 1750–1775: Elegance in Ornament* (New York: Metropolitan Museum of Art and Harry N. Abrams, 1992), 5.

10. Sheila L. Skemp, *William Franklin: Son of a Patriot, Servant of a King* (Oxford: Oxford University Press, 1990), 139, 272.

11. Jonathan Green to Leammi Baldwin, Woburn, MA, 1 September 1773, MHS, 1771–1777.

12. Quoted in Eleanore P. Gadsen, "When Good Cabinetmakers Made Bad Furniture: The Career and Work of David Evans," *AF* (2001): 80.

13. Eleanore P. Gadsen, "From Traditional Cabinetmaking to Entrepreneurial Production: David Evans, 1748–1819," (master's thesis, Winter-

thur Museum and the University of Delaware, 2000), 1, 6, 82–83; Coxe Papers, 18 June 1782, HSP; "Excerpts from the Day-Books of David Evans, Cabinet-Maker, 1774–1811," *Pennsylvania Magazine of History and Biography* 27, no. 1 (1903): 49–55.

14. Daniel Preston, ed., *The Papers of James Monroe: Selected Correspondence and Papers, 1776–1794* (Westport, CT: Greenwood Press, 2006), 2: 5, 276, 328.

15. Harlow Giles Unger, *The Last Founding Father: James Monroe and a Nation's Call to Greatness,* (Cambridge, MA: Da Capo Press, 2009), 61, 64–65, 278–280; Preston, ed., *Papers of James Monroe,* 2: 328, 373, 375.

16. Preston, ed., *Papers of James Monroe,* 2: 380, 382.

17. Chaela Pastore, "Mahogany as Status Symbol: Race and Luxury in Saint Domingue at the End of the Eighteenth Century," in *Furnishing the Eighteenth Century: What Furniture Can Tell Us about the European and American Past,* eds. Dena Goodman and Kathryn Norberg (New York: Routledge, 2007), 37–48; Madeleine Dobie, *Trading Places: Colonization and Slavery in Eighteenth-Century French Culture* (New York: Cornell University Press, 2010), 68–78; Cathy Matson, "Accounting for War and Revolution: Philadelphia Merchants and Commercial Risk, 1774–1811," in *The Self-Perception of Early Modern Capitalists,* eds. Margaret C. Jacob and Catherine Secretan (New York: Palgrave Macmillan, 2008), 190.

18. Laurent Dubois, *Haiti: The Aftershocks of History* (New York: Henry Holt and Company, 2012), 49; Steeve Coupeau, *The History of Haiti* (Westport, CT: Greenwood Press, 2008), 39; Frank Moya Pons, *History of the Caribbean: Plantations, Trade, and War in the Atlantic World* (Princeton, NJ: Markus Wiener Publishers, 2007), 173.

19. Eugenio Matibag, *Haitian-Dominican Counterpoint: Nation, Race, and State on Hispaniola* (New York: Palgrave Macmillan, 2003), 92–96; Frank Moya Pons, *The Dominican Republic: A National History* (Princeton, NJ: Markus Wiener Publishers, 1998), 113–117; Samuel Hazard, *Santo Domingo, Past and Present, with a Glance at Hayti* (New York: Harper and Brothers, 1873), 357.

20. Matson, "Accounting for War," 190; Thomas M. Doerflinger, *A Vigorous Spirit of Enterprise: Merchants and Economic Development in Revolutionary Philadelphia* (Chapel Hill: University of North Carolina, 1986).

21. Reinaldo Funes Monzote, *From Rainforest to Cane Field in Cuba: An Environmental History since 1492,* trans. Alex Martin (Chapel Hill: University of North Carolina Press, 2008), chap. 2, 144–146, 160, 270.

22. Peter M. Kenny, "Opulence Abroad: Charles-Honoré Lannuier's Gilded Furniture in Trinidad de Cuba," *AF* (2004); Monzote, *From Rainforest to Cane Field,* 170, 124, 301, 303, 327.

23. Adam Bowett, "Myths of English Furniture: Cuban Mahogany," *Antique Collecting* 32, no. 8 (1998): 10–13.

24. Michael Camille, "The Effects of Timber Haulage Improvements on Mahogany Extraction in Belize: An Historical Geography," *Journal of Latin American Geography* (2000): 103–116; John Lyon Gardiner Journal and Farm Book, 1798, EHFL; Dean F. Failey, *Long Island Is My Nation: The Decorative Arts and Craftsmen, 1640–1830* (Cold Spring Harbor, NY: Society for the Preservation of Long Island Antiquities, 1998), 197.

25. John J. McCusker and Kenneth Morgan, eds., *The Early Modern Atlantic Economy* (New York: Cambridge University Press, 2000), 132–134; David Hancock, *Oceans of Wine: Madeira and the Emergence of American Trade and Taste* (New Haven, CT: Yale University Press, 2009, chap. 8; Anne C. Golovin, "Daniel Trotter: Eighteenth-Century Philadelphia Cabinetmaker," *WP* 6 (1970): 151–184, 166–167; Henry Drinker Journal, 1791–1798, XV: 58, 59, and 63, HSP; Dean Thomas Lahikainen, "A Salem Cabinet-maker's Price Book," *AF* (2001): 155, 194.

26. *Pennsylvania Chronicle,* 9 September 1767, 12 June 1769, and 2 June 1773 in Alfred C. Prime, compiler, *The Arts and Crafts in Philadelphia, Maryland and South Carolina, 1721–1785* (Topsfield, MA: The Walpole Society, 1929); *Rivington's New-York Gazetteer,* 2 September 1774 in *The Arts and Crafts in New York, 1726–1776: Advertisements and News Items from New York City Newspapers* (New York: NYHS, 1938), 111; Rita Susswein Gottesman, compiler, *The Arts and Crafts in New York, 1800–1804* (New York: New-York Historical Society, 1965), 137; Barnard cited in David Jaffee, "Sideboards, Side Chairs, and Globes: Changing Modes of Furnishing Provincial Culture in the Early Republic, 1790–1820," in Goodman and Norberg, *Furnishing the Eighteenth Century,* 84.

27. Gottesman, *Arts and Crafts in New York,* 143; Mary Ann Hollihan Apicella, *Scottish Cabinetmakers in Federal New York* (Lebanon, NH: University Press of New England, 2007), 44.

28. *Dunlap's American Daily Advertiser,* 14 March 1793, cited in Golovin, "Daniel Trotter,"166; *Philadelphia Monthly Magazine,* June 1798, lists prices current for both Boston and New York; *New York City Directory,* 1829–30, accessed on http://www.ancestry.com.

29. *The Daily Advertiser,* 31 March 1801 and 9 November 1803, in *Arts and Crafts in New York, 1726–1776,* 151–152; *New York Evening Post,* 6 April 1802 in *The Arts and Crafts in New York, 1800–1804,* 138.

30. Cited in Peter M. Kenny, Frances F. Bretter and Ulrich Leben, *Honoré Lannuier, Cabinetmaker from Paris: The Life and Work of a French Ébéniste in Federal New York* (New York: Metropolitan Museum of Art, 1998), 156; *New York Gazette,* 12 April 1805 and 14 March 1809, and *The Evening Post,* New York, 13 June 1809.

31. Regarding labeling practices, see Margaretta M. Lovell, *Art in a Season of Revolution: Painters, Artisans, and Patrons in Early America* (Philadelphia: University of Pennsylvania Press, 2005), 248.

7. Mastering Nature and the Challenge of Mahogany

1. John Oldmixon, *The British Empire in America* . . . (London: John Nicholson, Benjamin Tooke, Richard Parker, and Ralph Smith, 1708), 330; Pat Rogers, "An Early Colonial Historian: John Oldmixon and *The British Empire in America,"* *Journal of American Studies* 7, no. 2 (1973): 113.

2. Patrick Browne, *The Civil and Natural History of Jamaica* (London: printed for the author, 1756), 18, 158–159; Edward Long, *The History of Jamaica. Or, General Survey of the Ancient and Modern State of that Island* (London: T. Lowndes, 1774), 3: 354–355.

3. *Oxford English Dictionary Online,* accessed 9/7/2011; Raymond Williams, "Ideas of Nature," in *Nature: Thinking the Natural,* eds. David Inglis, John Bone, and Rhoda Wilkie (New York: Routledge, 2005), 49; William Cronon, ed., *Uncommon Ground: Rethinking the Human Place in Nature* (New York: Norton, 1995), introduction; Charles Leslie, *A New History of Jamaica from the Earliest Accounts to the Taking of Porto Bello,* 2nd ed. (London: J. Hodges, 1740), 327.

4. On the importance of natural history during the Enlightenment and its connections to imperial strategies, see Richard Grove, *Green Imperialism: Colonial Expansion, Tropical Island Edens and the Origins of Environmentalism, 1600–1860* (New York: Cambridge University Press, 1995); Londa Schiebinger, *Plants and Empire: Colonial Bioprospecting in the Atlantic World* (Cambridge, MA: Harvard University Press, 2004); Londa Schiebinger and Claudia Swan, eds., *Colonial Botany: Science, Commerce, and Politics in the Early Modern World* (Philadelphia: University of Pennsylvania, 2005); Richard Drayton, *Nature's Government: Science, Imperial Britain, and the 'Improvement of the World'* (New Haven, CT: Yale University Press, 2000; Raymond F. Stearns, *Science in the British Colonies of America* (Champaign, IL: University of Illinois Press, 1970); James Delbourgo and Nicholas Dew, eds., *Science and Empire in the Atlantic World* (New York: Routledge, 2008); Susan Scott Parrish, *American Curiosity: Cultures of Natural History in the Colonial British Atlantic World* (Chapel Hill: University of North Carolina, 2006); Lucile H. Brockway, *Science and Colonial Expansion: The Role of the British Royal Botanic Gardens* (New York: Academic Press, 1979); Neil Safier, *Measuring the New World: Enlightenment Science and South America* (Chicago: University of Chicago Press, 2008); Daniela Bleichmar, et al. *Science in the Spanish and Portuguese Empires, 1500–1800* (Stanford: Stanford University Press, 2009); Antonio Barrera-Osorio, *Experiencing Nature: The Spanish American Empire and the Early Scientific Revolution* (Austin, TX: University of Texas Press, 2009); Pamela H. Smith and Paula Findlen, *Merchants and Marvels: Commerce, Science, and Art in Early Modern Europe* (New York: Routledge, 2002); Pamela H. Smith and Benjamin Schmidt, eds., *Making Knowledge in Early Modern Europe* (Chicago: University of Chicago Press, 2007); Paul L. Farber, *Finding Order in Nature: The Naturalist Tradition from Linnaeus to E. O. Wilson* (Baltimore: Johns Hopkins University Press, 2000), chaps. 1–2; Carol Kaesuk Yoon, *Naming Nature: The Clash between Instinct and Science* (New York: W.W. Norton, 2009), chap. 2; Kay Dian Kriz, "Curiosities, Commodities, and Transplanted Bodies in Hans Sloane's 'Natural History of Jamaica,'" *WMQ* 57, no. 1 (January 2000): 37.

5. Chandra Mukerji, *Territorial Ambitions and the Gardens of Versailles* (Cambridge: Cambridge University Press, 1997), 73–82; Philip P.

Boucher, *France and the American Tropics to 1700: Tropics of Discontent?* (Baltimore: Johns Hopkins University Press, 2008), 124; Harold J. Cook, *Matters of Exchange: Commerce, Medicine, and Science in the Dutch Golden Age* (New Haven, CT: Yale University Press, 2007); Drayton, *Nature's Government,* 135–137; Bleichmar, et al., eds., *Science in the Spanish and Portuguese Empires, 1500–1800* (Stanford: Stanford University Press, 2009); Barrera-Osorio, *Experiencing Nature;* Michael Hunter, *Establishing the New Science: The Experience of the Early Royal Society* (Woodbridge, UK: Boydell, 1989); Stearns, *Science in the British Colonies,* chap. 4.

6. Anthony Pagden, *Lords of All the Worlds: Ideologies of Empire in Spain, Britain, and France, c. 1500–c. 1800* (New Haven, CT: Yale University Press, 1995); Robert P. Marzec, "Enclosures, Colonization, and the Robinson Crusoe Syndrome: A Genealogy of Land in a Global Context," *Boundary* 29, no. 2 (2002): 129–156; Joan Thirsk, *Economic Policy and Projects: The Development of a Consumer Society in Early Modern England* (Oxford: Clarendon Press, 1978); Keith Thomas, *Man and the Natural World: A History of the Modern Sensibility* (New York: Pantheon Books, 1983), chap. 6.

7. Alix Cooper, *Inventing the Indigenous: Local Knowledge and Natural History in Early Modern Europe* (New York: Cambridge University Press, 2007); William Hanbury, *An Essay on Planting . . .* (Oxford: S. Parker, 1758), 35; on English tree planting traditions, see Thomas, *Man and the Natural World,* chap. 5.

8. Leslie, *New History of Jamaica,* 23, 287.

9. Michael Craton and James Walvin, *A Jamaican Plantation: The History of Worthy Park, 1670–1970* (Toronto: University of Toronto Press, 1970), 5; Alfred W. Crosby, *Ecological Imperialism: The Biological Expansion of Europe* (New York: Cambridge University Press, 1986); Sheridan, *Sugar and Slavery,* 378–379; David Watts, *The West Indies: Patterns of Development, Culture, and Environmental Change since 1492* (Cambridge: Cambridge University Press, 1987); Higman, "The Sugar Revolution," 213–236; Hans Sloane, *A Voyage to the Islands Madera, Barbados, Nieves, S. Christophers and Jamaica, . . .* (London: Printed for the author, 1725), 3; Richard Ligon, *A True and Exact History of the Island of Barbadoes* (London: Humphrey Moseley, 1657), 66.

10. Richard Blome, *A Description of the Island of Jamaica...* (London: Dorman Newman, 1678), 6; Oldmixon, *British Empire,* 330; John Lunan, *Hortus Jamaicensis* (Jamaica: St. Jago de la Vega Gazette, 1814), 2: 67; Browne, *History of Jamaica,* 248; Long, *History of Jamaica,* 1: 600; Higman, *Jamaica Surveyed,* 192.

11. Henry Barham, *Hortus Americanus: Containing an Account of the Trees, Shrubs, and Other Vegetable Productions... of the Island of Jamaica* (Kingston, Jamaica: Alexander Aikman, 1794), 86, 90–91.

12. Schiebinger, *Plants,* chap. 7; Schiebinger and Swan, eds., *Colonial Botany;* Judith A. Carney and Richard Nicholas Rosomoff, *In the Shadow of Slavery: Africa's Botanical Legacy in the Atlantic World* (Berkeley, CA: University of California Press, 2010); Sloane, *Voyage,* vii; Barham, *Hortus Americanus,* 86, 90–91.

13. Mark Catesby, *The Natural History of Carolina, Florida, and the Bahama Islands,* (London: n.p., 1731–1743 and Appendix, 1747), 2: 66

14. Joshua Lerner, "Science and Agricultural Progress: Quantitative Evidence from England, 1660–1780," *Agricultural History* 66, no. 4 (Autumn 1992): 11–27; Albert Edward Musson and Eric Robinson, *Science and Technology in the Industrial Revolution* (London: Gordon and Breach Science Publishers, 1969, repr. 1994), 58; Craton and Walvin, *Jamaican Plantation,* 80, 92; *London Magazine,* April 1758, reprinted in *The Pennsylvania Gazette,* 10 August 1758; *Premiums by the Society...* (London: Society for the Encouragement of Arts, Manufactures, and Commerce, 1760); Grove, *Green Imperialism,* 268; *Maryland Gazette,* 7 February 1765, 1; *Newport Mercury,* 8 April 1765, microfilm, 344; Joyce Chaplin, *An Anxious Pursuit: Agricultural Innovation and Modernity in the Lower South, 1730–1815* (Chapel Hill: University of North Carolina Press, 1993), 138; Walter Edgar, *South Carolina: A History* (Columbia, SC: University of South Carolina Press, 1998), 150.

15. Long, *History of Jamaica,* 2: 136, 75.

16. Catesby, *Natural History,* 2: 81; Amy R. W. Meyers and Margaret Beck Pritchard, eds., *Empire's Nature: Mark Catesby's New World Vision* (Chapel Hill: University of North Carolina Press, 1999), 228–261; Michael Craton and Gail Saunders, *Islanders in the Stream: A History of the Bahamian People* (Athens, GA: University of Georgia Press, 1992), 88, 135.

17. Catesby, *Natural History,* 2: 42, plate 81.

18. Meyer and Pritchard, eds., *Empire's Nature*, 10, 34–90; Alan Feduccia, ed., *Catesby's Birds of Colonial America* (Chapel Hill: University of North Carolina Press, 1985), 166; R. W. J. Keay, "Introduction: The Future for the genus Swietenia in its Native Forests," *BJLS* 122 no. 1 (1996): 3.

19. Browne, *History of Jamaica,* 158–159; Keay, "Introduction: The Future for the genus Swietenia," 4.

20. Nicolai J. Jacquin, *Enumeratio systematica plantarum quas in insulis Caribaeis vicinaque Americes continente . . .* (Leiden: Theodore Haak, 1760), 20; Linnaeus quoted in Frans A. Stafleu, *Linnaeus and the Linnaeans: The Spreading of their Ideas in Systematic Botany, 1735–1789* (Utrecht: A. Oosthoek, 1971), 185.

21. Jacquin, *Selectarum Stirpium Americanarum Historia* (Vienna: Joseph Kurtzbock, 1763), 1: 127 and 2: frontispiece.

22. See, for example, William Woodville's *Supplement to Medical Botany* (London: James Phillips, 1794), 4: 63–65; Schiebinger, *Plants,* 3, 36, 37–39, 105, 253; Schiebinger and Swan, eds., *Colonial Botany,* 2; Pratik Chakrabarti, "Empire and Alternatives: *Swietenia Febrifuga* and the Cinchona Substitutes," *Medical History* 54 (2010): 75–94; Saul Jarcho, *Quinine's Predecessor: Francesco Torti and the Early History of Cinchona* (Baltimore: Johns Hopkins University Press, 1993); Fiammetta Rocco, *The Miraculous Fever-tree: Malaria, Medicine and the Cure that Changed the World* (London: Harper Collins, 2003); Mark Honigsbaum, *The Fever Trail: In Search of the Cure for Malaria* (New York: Farrar, Straus and Giroux, 2002).

23. Philip Miller, *The Gardener's Dictionary,* 9th ed. (London: G. Henderson, 1835).

24. Drayton, *Nature's Government,* chaps. 3–4; Lucile H. Brockway, *Science and Colonial Expansion: The Role of the British Royal Botanic Gardens* (New York: Academic Press, 1979); Robert Olwell, "Seeds of Empire: Florida, Kew, and the British Imperial Meridian in the 1760s," in *The Creation of the British Atlantic World,* eds., Elizabeth Mancke and Carole Shammas (Baltimore: Johns Hopkins University Press, 2005); Society for the Diffusion of Useful Knowledge, *A Description and History of Vegetable Substances used in the Arts and in Domestic Economy,* 2nd edition (London: Charles Knight, 1830; Boston: Wells and Lilly, 1830), 25: 163.

25. Richard A. Howard, "The St. Vincent Botanic Garden—The Early Years," *Arnoldia* (Winter 1997–1998): 17; Joseph Dennie and John Elihu Hall, *The Portfolio*, (1809), 2: 507.

26. John Dovaston, "Agricultura Americana, or Improvements in West-India Husbandry Considered . . . ," 1774, unpublished manuscript, JCB; Jan Golinski, "American Climate and the Civilization of Nature," in Delbourgo and Dew, *Science and Empire*, 169.

27. Joseph Priestley, "Observations on Different Kinds of Air," *Philosophical Transactions* 62 (1772): 195–200, includes Franklin quote.

28. Long, *History of Jamaica*, 3: ii–iii; Dovaston, "Agricultura Americana," 85–89.

29. Dovaston, "Agricultura Americana," 85–89.

30. Long, *History of Jamaica*, 1: 355–356, 3: 725.

31. Long, *History of Jamaica*, 1: 354–355

32. Laura K. Snook, "Sustaining Harvests of Mahogany *(Swietenia Macrophylla King)* from Mexico's Yucatán Forests: Past, Present, and Future," in *Timber, Tourists, and Temples: Conservation and Development in the Maya Forest of Belize, Guatemala, and Mexico*, ed. Richard B. Primack (Covelo, CA: Island Press, 1997), 61, 75–76; Terrence D. Pennington, "Mahogany Carving a Future," *Biologist* 49, no. 5 (2002): 204–208; T. Helgason et al., "What is Mahogany? The Importance of a Taxonomic Framework for Conservation," *BJLS* 122 (1996): 47–59; Joel Hagen, *An Entangled Bank: The Origins of Ecosystem Ecology* (Rutgers, NJ: Rutgers University Press, 1992), chaps. 1 and 9.

33. K. S. S. Nair, *Pest Outbreaks in Tropical Forest Plantations* (Jakarta, Indonesia: S. M. T. Grafika and Center for International Forestry, 2001), 36–37.

34. Jamaican Agricultural Society, "Medical and Philosophical News . . . ," (August–October 1806), 4.

35. John K. Francis, "Mahogany Planting and Research in Puerto Rico and the U.S. Virgin Islands," in *Big-Leaf Mahogany: Genetics, Ecology, and Management*, eds., Ariel E. Lugo, Mildred Alayón, et al. (New York: Springer Verlag, 2002), 330; Kathryn Robinson, *Where Dwarfs Reign: A Tropical Rain Forest in Puerto Rico* (San Juan: University of Puerto Rico Press, 1997), chap. 8; Griffith Hughes, *The Natural History of Barbados* (London: printed for the author, 1750), 1; William Bishop to Nathaniel Elliott, Josiah Whalley, and John Adam (London merchants), 11 June 1798, West Riding Archives, Sheepscar Branch, Leeds,

Harewood Manuscripts, Letters & Papers on West India Affairs, 1795–1873; John Wood Nelson to Edward, 2nd Earl Harewood, Harewood House, Yorkshire, West India Papers, Correspondence. David Watts, "Biogeographical Variation in the Mahogany (Swietenia Mahogani (L.) Jacq.) Woodlots of Barbados, West Indies," *Journal of Biogeography* 5 (1978): 347, 351, 360.

36. Edgar, *South Carolina,* 150; Chaplin, *An Anxious Pursuit,* 138.

37. Paul Leland Haworth, *George Washington: Farmer* (Indianapolis: Bobbs-Merrill, 1915), 74, 157; William Rasmussen, *George Washington* (Charlottesville: University of Virginia Press, 1999), 86–87; Don Higginbotham, ed., *George Washington, Reconsidered* (Charlottesville: University of Virginia, 2001), 71.

38. François Crouzet, "America and the Crisis of the British Imperial Economy, 1803–1807," in *The Early Modern Atlantic Economy,* eds. John J. McCusker and Kenneth Morgan (Cambridge: Cambridge University Press, 2000), 289–291; "Agricola," *The Gentlemen and Ladies' Town and Country Magazine . . . ,* May 1789: 193.

39. Monsieur de Casux, Bordeaux to Marshall, 12 September 1789, Dreer Collection, Marshall Corres., II, 1, HSP. Cited in Louise Conway Belden, "Humphry Marshall's Trade in Plants of the New World for Gardens and Forests of the Old World," *WP* 2 (1965): 113, 123; Humphry Marshall, *Arbustrum Americanum: The American Grove* (Philadelphia: Joseph Crukshank, 1785), ix.

40. Gilbert Chinard, "Recently Acquired Botanical Documents," *American Philosophical Society Bulletin* 101, no. 6 (1957): 508–522; William Kingsley Taylor and Eliane M. Norman, *André Michaux in Florida: An Eighteenth Century Botanical Journey* (Gainesville: University of Florida Press, 2002); Gilbert Chinard, "André and François-André Michaux and their Predecessors: An Essay on Early Botanical Exchanges between America and France," *Proceedings of the American Philosophical Society* 101, no. 4 (August 1957): 344–361; H. Savage, Jr. and E. J. Savage, *André and François-André Michaux* (Charlottesville: University of Virginia Press, 1986).

41. Ray Desmond, "Roxburgh, William (1751–1815)," *ODNB* (Oxford: Oxford University Press, 2004); Grove, *Green Imperialism,* 309–407; Pratik Chakrabarti, "Empire and Alternatives," 78–86; Mark Harrison, *Medicine in an Age of Commerce and Empire: Britain and Its Tropical Colonies* (Oxford: Oxford University Press, 2010), 136–137; Society of

Physicians in Edinburgh, *Medical and Philosophical Commentaries* 17 (1792), 546–547.

42.   P. L. Simmonds, "The Teak Forests of India and the East, and Our British Imports of Teak," *Journal of the Society of Arts* 33 (February 1885): 345; James Fergusson, et al. to the Revenue Department, Secretary of State for India, 30 June 1880, f. 32, "India, Economic Products, Mahogany," RBG.

43.   William Beinart and Lotte Hughes, *Environment and Empire* (New York: Oxford University Press, 2007), chap. 7; Michael Williams, *Deforesting the Earth: From Prehistory to Global Crisis* (Chicago: University of Chicago Press, 2003), chap. 11; *Journal of the Society of Arts* 29 (1881): 91; Ramachandra Guha and Madhav Gadgil, "State Forestry and Social Conflict in British India," *Past and Present* 123 (May 1989): 141–177; K. Sivaramakrishnan, "Colonialism and Forestry in India: Imagining the Past in Present Politics," *Comparative Studies in Society and History* 37, no. 1 (January 1995): 3–40.

44.   "Proceedings of the Board of Revenue, 27 January 1885 . . . on the Subject of Mahogany," f. 80, James Cleghorn, "Report on the Cultivation and growth of the Mahogany Tree . . . in Bengal," 5 February 1885, ff. 86–88 , "India, Economic Products, Mahogany," RBG; *Nature* 11 (1874–1875): 18.

45.   George King, *A Guide to the Royal Botanical Garden, Calcutta* (Calcutta: Thacker, Spink, 1895), 9.

46.   Philip Zea and Donald Dunlap, *The Dunlap Cabinetmakers: A Tradition in Craftsmanship* (Mechanicsburg, PA: Stackpole Books, 1994), 29–32.

47.   *The London Magazine, or Gentleman's Monthly Intelligencer* 32 (December 1763): 640–641.

48.   *Lancaster Gazette*, 5 January 1805; *Literary and Philosophical Intelligence . . .* (February 1805), 113; Susan E. Stuart, *Gillows of Lancaster and London, 1730–1840* (Woodbridge, Suffolk: Antique Collectors Club, 2008), 135; George Birkbeck, *A Lecture on the Preservation of Timber by Kyan's Patent for Preventing Dry Rot* (London: John Weale, 1834) cited in Charles M. Haines, "The Industrialization of Wood: The Transformation of a Material," (PhD diss., University of Delaware, 1990), 95.

49.   Alexander Garden, "The Effects of the Opuntia, or Prickly Pear, and of the Indigo Plant, in Colouring the Juices of Living Animals, Communicated by H. Baker, F.R.S.," *Philosophical Transactions* 50 (1757): 296–297.

50. "Method of Staining Wood in Imitation of Mahogany," *The American Museum; or Repository of Ancient and Modern . . .* 4, no. 6 (December 1788): 506; "Mahogany," *The New England Farmer, and Horticultural Register,* 30 August 1823.

51. J. H. Plumb, "The Acceptance of Modernity," in *The Birth of a Consumer Society: The Commercialization of Eighteenth-Century England,* eds., Neil McKendrick, John Brewer, and J. H. Plumb (Bloomington, IN: Indiana University Press, 1982), 326.

52. C. D. Adams, *Flowering Plants of Jamaica* (Mona, Jamaica: University of the West Indies, 1972), 162; William Jackson Hooker, *Botanical Miscellany* (London: John Murray, 1830), 1: 32; Society for the Diffusion of Useful Knowledge, *Description and History of Vegetable Substances,* 25: 147; on hybridization see, Ariel E. Lugo, Mildred Alayón, et al, *Big-Leaf Mahogany,* chaps. 6 and 7.

8. Democratizing Mahogany and the Advent of Steam

1. Daniel R. Headrick, *The Tentacles of Progress: Technology Transfer in the Age of Imperialism,* 1850–1940 (New York: Oxford University Press, 1988); Daniel R. Headrick, *The Tools of Empire: Technology and European Imperialism in the Nineteenth Century* (New York: Oxford University Press, 1981).

2. Maria M. Portuondo, "Plantation Factories: Science and Technology in Late Eighteenth-Century Cuba," *Technology and Culture* 44, no. 2 (April 2003): 243.

3. Thomas N. DeWolf, *Inheriting the Trade* (Boston: Beacon Press, 2008), 63.

4. Entry dated 16 May 1832, George Howe's Diary and Letterbook, 1832–1834, BHPS.

5. Undated speech, circa May 1832, George Howe's Diary and Letterbook, 1832–1834, BHPS.

6. December 1832, George Howe's Diary and Letterbook, 1832–1834, BHPS.

7. Reinaldo Funes Monzote, *From Rainforest to Cane Field in Cuba: An Environmental History since 1492,* trans. Alex Martin (Chapel Hill: University of North Carolina Press, 2008), 3, 156, 270, 327; Clifford L. Staten, *The History of Cuba* (New York: Palgrave Macmillan, 2005), 20; Dale Tomich, "World Slavery and Caribbean Capitalism: The Cuban Sugar Industry, 1760–1868," *Theory and Society* 20, no. 3 (June 1991):

297–319; D. C. & W. Pell Co. Advertisement, 28 Aug, 1840, *New-York American* (New York); D. C. & W. Pell Co. Auction Broadside, 12 October, 1847, Joseph Downs Collection of Manuscripts and Printed Ephemera, Winterthur Museum Library.

8. Julius S. Scott, "The Common Wind: Currents of Afro-American Communication in the Age of the Haitian Revolution" (Ph.D. Dissertation, Duke University, 1986); Laurent DuBois, *A Colony of Citizens: Revolution and Slave Emancipation in the French Caribbean, 1787–1804* (Chapel Hill: University of North Carolina Press, 2004).

9. Léon Dénius Pamphile, *Haitians and African Americans: A Heritage of Tragedy and Hope* (Gainesville: University Press of Florida, 2001), 40.

10. [Zephaniah Kingsley] *The Rural Code of Haiti . . . with Letters from that Country . . . by a Southern Planter* (Granville, Middletown, NJ: George H. Evans, 1837). The second edition (New York: G. Vale, 1838) includes a map of Cabaret; Frank Moya Pons, *The Dominican Republic: A National History* (Princeton, NJ: Markus Wiener Publishers, 1998), 133; Loring Dewey and Jean Pierre Boyer, *Correspondence Relative to the Immigration to Hayti of the Free People of Colour in the United States together with Instructions to the Agent sent out by President Boyer* (New York: Mahlon Day, 1824) 12, 16, 19, 25, 35; James O. Horton and Lois E. Horton, *In Hope of Liberty: Culture, Community, and Protest Among Northern Free Blacks* (New York: Oxford University Press, 1997), 194–196; Gary B. Nash, "Reverberations of Haiti in the American North: Black Saint Dominguans in Philadelphia," *Pennsylvania History* 65 (supplement 1998): 44–73; Eric Foner, *Nothing but Freedom: Emancipation and Its Legacy* (Baton Rouge: Louisiana State University Press, 1983), 40–41; James Sidbury, "Saint Domingue in Virginia: Ideology, Local Meaning, and Resistance to Slavery, 1790–1800," *The Journal of Southern History* 63, no. 3 (August 1997): 531–551; Alfred N. Hunt, *Haiti's Influence on Antebellum America: Slumbering Volcano in the Caribbean* (Baton Rouge: Louisiana State University Press, 1988), 157–163; Lester Langley, *The Americas in the Age of Revolution* (New Haven: Yale University Press, 1996), 142–144.

11. Pons, *Dominican Republic,* 134; Samuel Hazard, *Santo Domingo, Past and Present, with a Glance at Hayti* (New York: Harper and Brothers, 1873), 307–308.

12. Quoted from an account in the *New York Tribune,* reprinted 28 September 1855, in *Frederick Douglass's Paper,* Rochester, New York; J. Theodore Holly, "A Vindication of the Capacity of the Negro Race for Self-Government and Civilized Progress," (1857), reprinted in *Pamphlets of Protest: An Anthology of Early African American Protest Literature,* eds. Richard Newman, Patrick Rael, Phillip Lapsansky (London: Routledge, 2001), 276.

13. Hazard, *Santo Domingo,* 234, 275.

14. Cited from letter published in the *Working Man's Advocate,* 13 September 1835; repr., *The Colored Freeman* (New York), 15 March 1838; Benjamin Hunt, *Remarks on Hayti as a Place of Settlement for Afric-Americans; and on the Mulatto as a Race for the Tropics* (Philadelphia: T. B. Pugh, 1860), 7; Hazard, *Santo Domingo,* 357, 378.

15. Daniel L. Schafer, *Anna Madgigine Jai Kingsley: African Princess, Florida Slave, Plantation Slaveowner* (Gainesville, FL: University Press of Florida, 2003); Lydia Maria Francis Child, *Letters from New-York* (London: Richard Bentley, 1843), 162.

16. [Kingsley], *The Rural Code of Haiti,* 45–48. Zephaniah Kingsley, "Hayti," *African Repository* (July 1838): 215.

17. Silvio Torres-Saillant and Ramona Hernández, *The Dominican Americans* (Westport, CT: Greenwood), 21–22; Hazard, *Santo Domingo,* 307, 357.

18. Craig S. Revels, "Timber, Trade, and Transformation: A Historical Geography of Mahogany in Honduras," (PhD diss., Louisiana State University, 2002), 195; O. Nigel Bolland, *Colonialism and Resistance in Belize* (Belize: University of the West Indies, 2003), 160.

19. Revels, "Timber," 189; Craig S. Revels, "Concessions, Conflict, and the Rebirth of the Honduran Mahogany Trade," *Journal of Latin American Geography* 2, no. 1 (2003): 4–13.

20. *ABH,* 2: 374–375, 379, 398.

21. Revels, "Timber," 13, 195; Bolland, *Colonialism and Resistance in Belize,* 162; Anne Sutherland, *The Making of Belize: Globalization in the Margins* (Westport, CT: Bergin and Garvey, 1998), 19–20.

22. Edward H. Knight, *Knight's American Mechanical Dictionary* (New York: Hurd & Houghton, 1876; repr., [Missouri]: Early American Industry Association, 1979), 2702.

23. *Poulson's Daily Advertiser,* August 1825; cited in Charles F. Montgomery, *American Furniture: The Federal Period* (NY: Viking Press, 1966),

32; Society for the Diffusion of Useful Knowledge, *A Description and History of Vegetable Substances used in the Arts and in Domestic Economy,* 2nd ed. (London: Charles Knight, 1830; Boston: Wells and Lilly, 1830), 1: 171; Jonathan Coad, *The Portsmouth Block Mills: Bentham, Brunel, and the Start of the Royal Navy's Industrial Revolution* (Swindon: English Heritage, 2005); Clive Edwards, "A History of Veneer Cutting," *Antique Furniture and Conservation Guide* (Dorchester: BAFRA, 2008), 45–50; Carolyn C. Cooper, "A Patent Transformation: Woodworking Mechanization in Philadelphia, 1830–1856," in *Early American Technology,* Judith A. McGaw, ed. (Chapel Hill: University of North Carolina Press, 1994), 285.

24. Society for the Diffusion of Useful Knowledge, *Description and History of Vegetable Substances,* 1: 171; "Progress of Practical and Theoretical Mechanics and Chemistry: Cutting Veneers," *Journal of the Franklin Institute* 18, no. 4 (October 1836): 261; "Machine for Cutting Wood into Thin Leaves," *Journal of the Franklin Institute* 20, no. 6 (December 1837): 418–419.

25. Gray Williams, *Picturing Our Past: National Register Sites in Westchester County* (Elmsford, NY: Westchester County Historical Society, 2003).

26. John C. Callahan, "The Mahogany Empire of Ichabod T. Williams & Sons, 1838–1973," *Journal of Forest History* 29, no. 3 (July 1985): 120–130.

27. Journal of Edward Jenner Carpenter (1844–1845), Manuscript Collection, AAS; Christopher Clark, ed., "The Diary of an Apprentice Cabinetmaker: Edward Jenner Carpenter's 'Journal' 1844–45," *Proceedings of the AAS* 98, part 2 (Worcester, MA: 1988), 303–394.

28. Letter from Joseph Willoughby (New York) to John Milton Cargill (Providence), 20 February 1837, Folder 1, Cargill Family Papers, 1725–1923, AAS; Richard D. Brown, *Knowledge is Power: The Diffusion of Information in Early America, 1700–1865* (New York: Oxford University Press, 1989).

29. Michael Ettema, "History, Nostalgia, and American Furniture," *WP,* 17, nos. 2/3 (Autumn 1982): 143.

30. Society for the Diffusion of Useful Knowledge, *Description and History of Vegetable Substances,* 1: 172–173; William Cobbett, *Cottage Economy* (New York: Stephen Gould and Son, 1824), 8–9; William Cobbett, *Advice to Young Men and (Incidentally) Young Women* (New

York: John Doyle), 97; William Cobbett, *Rural Rides* (London: William Cobbett, 1830), 241; Neil McKendrick, John Brewer, and J. H. Plumb, eds., *The Birth of a Consumer Society: The Commercialization of Eighteenth Century England* (Bloomington, IN: Indiana University Press, 1982), 28.

31. Emma Jones Lapsansky, "'Since They Got Those Separate Churches': Afro-Americans and Racism in Jacksonian Philadelphia," *American Quarterly* 32, no. 1 (Spring 1980): 54–78; Patrick Rael, *Black Identity and Black Protest in the Antebellum North* (Chapel Hill: University of North Carolina Press, 2002), 148.

32. *The Colored American* (New York), 9 September 1837; Ralph Waldo Emerson, "Manners" (1844), in *Essays by Ralph Waldo Emerson,* ed. Irwin Edman (New York: Harper & Row, 1981), 352.

33. *The Colored American* (New York), 27 May 1837 and 21 July 1841.

34. *U.S. Gazette* (Philadelphia), August 1834, cited in John Runcie "'Hunting the Nigs' In Philadelphia: The Race Riot of August 1834," *Pennsylvania History,* 39, no. 2 (April 1972): 187–218; *Commercial Herald* (Philadelphia), 15 August 1834; Sean Wilentz, *Chants Democratic: New York City and the Rise of the American Working Class, 1788–1850* (New York: Oxford University Press, 1984); David Roediger, *The Wages of Whiteness: Race and the Making of the American Working Class* (New York: Verso, 1999); Leonard L. Richards, *"Gentlemen of Property and Standing": Anti-Abolition Mobs in Jacksonian America* (New York: Oxford University Press, 1970).

35. Lapsansky, "Separate Churches," 54–78; Runcie "Hunting," 187–218; David Grimsted, "Rioting in its Jacksonian Setting," *AHR* 77 (April 1972): 361–397.

36. G. R. Burnell, "Of Building Woods: The Causes of their Decay and the Means of Preventing It," *Journal of the Society of Arts* 8 (1 June 1860): 56.

37. George J. Henkels, *Household Economy* (Philadelphia: King and Baird, 1867), 21.

38. P. Thomson, *The Cabinet-maker's Assistant: A Series of Original Designs for Modern Furniture* (Glasgow and New York: Blackie and Son, 1853), 31–32.

39. Catherine Lanford Joy, "Reflecting Refinement: The Making and Meaning of Silver Metal in Antebellum Boston, 1800–1875," (PhD diss. in progress, Yale University).

40. Anon., "Miscellaneous Domestic Matters. Veneered Tables," *The Magazine of Domestic Economy* 3 (1838): 345–348.

41. Robert E. Park, in Park, Ernest W. Burgess, and Roderick D. McKenzie, *The City* (Chicago: University of Chicago, 1925), 40–41; Karen Halttunen, *Confidence Men and Painted Women: A Study of Middle-Class Culture in America, 1830–1870* (New Haven, CT: Yale University Press, 1982), 33–34, 39; William Wordsworth, letter to John Stuart, 1817, cited in Alistair M. Duckworth, *The Improvement of the Estate: A Study of Jane Austen's Novels* (Baltimore: Johns Hopkins University Press, 1971), 81; *The Colored American* (New York), 9 September 1837.

42. William Bayle Bernard, *The Evil Genius: An Original Comedy in Three Acts* (London: T. H. Lacy, [1856]), 39; William Bayle Bernard, *The Passing Cloud: A Romantic Drama in Two Acts* (London: T. H. Lacy, [1850]); Anon., Letter to the Editor, *Frederick Douglass Paper* (Rochester, New York) 1 July 1852.

43. Charles Dickens, *The Uncommercial Traveller and Other Papers, 1859–1870,* eds. Michael Slater and John Drew (Columbus: Ohio State University Press, 2000), 352; Charles Dickens, *The Mystery of Edwin Drood: Master Humphrey's Clock, and Sketches by "Boz"* (Philadelphia: Porter and Coates, 1871), 361; Charles Dickens, *Our Mutual Friend* (Philadelphia: T. B. Peterson and Brothers, 1865), 30; T. S. Arthur, *Trials and Confessions of a Housekeeper* (Philadelphia: Lippincott, Grambo, 1854), 37–42, 49–50; Society for the Diffusion of Useful Knowledge, *Description and History of Vegetables Substances*, 1: 174.

9. An Old Species of Elegance

1. Irving Jenkins, *Hawaiian Furniture and Hawaii's Cabinetmakers* (New York: Routledge, 1985), 3–6; Leopold G. Blackman, ed., "Report of the Committee on Forests,"*The Hawaiian Forester and Agriculturalist,* 5 (1908): 340.

2. Roxann Wheeler, *Complexions of Race: Categories of Difference in Eighteenth Century British Culture* (Philadelphia: University of Pennsylvania Press, 2000), 1–49; Deirdre Coleman, "Janet Schaw and the Complexions of Empire," *Eighteenth-Century Studies* 36, no. 2 (2003): 169–193; William Makepeace Thackeray, *Vanity Fair: A Novel Without a Hero,* ed. John Carey (London: Penguin Classics, 2003), 61, 233, 227–228, 234.

3. Gayatri Chakravorty Spivak, "Three Women's Texts and a Critique of Imperialism," *Critical Inquiry* 12 (1985): 243–261; Henry Louis Gates, Jr., *"Race," Writing, and Difference* (Chicago: Chicago University Press, 1985), 262–280; Erin O'Connor, "Preface for a Post-Colonial Criticism," *Victorian Studies* 45, no. 2 (2003): 226; Edward W. Said, *Culture and Imperialism* (New York: Knopf, 1993), 93, 95; Jon Mee, "Austen's Treacherous Ivory: Female Patriotism, Domestic Ideology, and Empire," in You-me Park and Rajeswari Sunder Rajan, eds., *The Postcolonial Jane Austen,* (London: Routledge, 2000), 75; Elaine Freedgood, *The Ideas in Things: Fugitive Meaning in the Victorian Novel* (Chicago: University of Chicago Press, 2006), 50; Harvey M. Feinberg and Marion Johnson, "The West African Ivory Trade during the Eighteenth Century," *The International Journal of African Historical Studies* 15, no. 3 (1982): 435–453; Ruth Perry, "Jane Austen, Slavery, and British Imperialism," in *Approaches to Teaching Austen's Emma,* ed. Marcia McClintock Folsom (New York: Modern Language Association, 2004), 27, 29–31; Mary Poovey, "Ideological Contradictions and the Consolations of Form: The Case of Jane Austen," in *Critical Essays on Jane Austen,* ed. Laura Mooneyham White (New York: G. K. Hall, 1997), 75–76. On themes of empire in Jane Austen's work, see also Maaja A. Stewart, *Domestic Realities and Imperial Fictions: Jane Austen's Novels in Eighteenth-Century Contexts* (Athens, GA: University of Georgia Press, 1993); Felicity A. Nussbaum, *Torrid Zones: Maternity, Sexuality, and Empire in Eighteenth-Century English Narratives* (Baltimore: Johns Hopkins University Press, 1995); and Moira Ferguson, *Subject to Others: British Women Writers and Colonial Slavery 1670–1834* (London: Routledge, 1992).

4. Charles Dickens, *American Notes for General Circulation* (London: Penguin Books, 2001), 127; Charles Dickens, "The Lazy Tour of Two Idle Apprentices," in *Oliver Twist; The Lazy Tour of Two Idle Apprentices* (New York: University Society, 1908), chap. 3. On Dickens's attitudes towards slavery, see Wendy S. Jacobson, ed., *Dickens and the Children of Empire* (London: Palgrave, 2000).

5. "Mrs. America Answers Mrs. Britain," *Provincial Freeman* (Windsor, Canada), 24 March 1854; reprinted from *Lloyd's Magazine,* 16 January 1853.

6. "Foreign News, India. How Ruffianism was Punished at Allahbad," *Harper's Weekly,* 26 December 1857: 822.

7.   Harriet Guest, "Curiously Marked: Tattooing and Gender Difference in Eighteenth-Century British Perceptions of the South Pacific," in *Written on the Body: The Tattoo in European and American History*, ed. Jane Caplan (Princeton: Princeton University Press, 2000), 87; Matthew Consent's "Remarks on a Tour through Lapland [in 1786]," *The New York Magazine or Literary Repository*, April 1793, reprinted from *The Times* (London), 8 July 1790; Henry J. Finn, *Montgomery; Or, the Falls of Montmorency* (Boston: Wills and Lilly, 1825), Act I, 18; James Kirk Paulding, *John Bull in America* (New York: Charles Wiley and Sons, 1825), iii; James Hall, *Legends of the West*, (Philadelphia: H. Hall, 1832), 116–118; Edna L. Steeves, "Négritude and the Noble Savage," *The Journal of Modern African Studies* 11, no. 1 (March 1973): 91–104; Sharon Harrow, *Adventures in Domesticity: Gender and Colonial Adulteration in Eighteenth-Century British Literature* (New York: AMS Press, 2004), 84; Park and Rajan, eds., *Postcolonial Jane Austen*, 45–48.

8.   Joyce E. Chaplin, "Natural Philosophy and an Early Racial Idiom in North America: Comparing English and Indian Bodies," *WMQ* 54, no. 1 (January 1997): 229–252; Karen Ordahl Kupperman, "Fear of Hot Climates in the Anglo-American Colonial Experience," *WMQ* 41, no. 2 (April 1984): 213–240; Karen Ordahl Kupperman, "The Puzzle of the American Climate in the Early Colonial Period," *AHR* 87 (1982): 1262–1289; D. S. Neff, "Bitches, Mollies, and Tommies: Byron, Masculinity, and the History of Sexualities," *Journal of the History of Sexuality* 11, no. 3 (2002): 395–438; Tobias George Smollett, *The Adventures of Peregrine Pickle* (Oxford: Oxford University Press, 1983), 369; Jane Austen, *Persuasion* (Mineola, NY: Dover Publications, 1997), 14; Charles Frederick Briggs, *The Adventures of Harry Franco, A Tale of the Great Panic* (New York: F. Saunders, 1839), 158; Charles Dickens, *The Uncommercial Traveller and Other Papers, 1859–1870*, ed. Michael Slater and John Drew (Columbus: Ohio State University Press, 2000), chap. 21; Mark Twain, *Roughing It* (New York: Signet Classic, 1962), 334; Simon P. Newman, "Reading the Bodies of Early American Seafarers," *WMQ* 55, no. 1 (January 1998): 59–82; William Cummings, "Orientalism's Corporeal Dimension: Tattooed Bodies and Eighteenth-Century Oceans," *Journal of Colonialism and Colonial History* 4, no. 2 (2003): 19–20; Kathleen Wilson, *The Island Race: Englishness, Empire, and Gender in the Eighteenth Century* (New York: Routledge, 2003); John

Stedman, *Narrative of a Five Years Expedition against the Revolted Negroes of Suriname* (London: Johnson, 1806), 57.

9. Barbara Novak, "The Double-Edged Axe," *Art in America* LXIV (January–February 1976): 44–50; Nicolai Cikovsky, Jr. " 'The Ravages of the Axe': The Meaning of the Tree Stump in Nineteenth-Century American Art," *AB* 61, no. 4 (December 1979): 611–626; Leo Marx, *The Machine in the Garden: Technology and the Pastoral Ideal in America* (New York: Oxford University Press, 1964); Frances Trollope, *Domestic Manners of the Americans* (1832), ed. Donald Smalley (New York: Alfred A. Knopf, 1960), 378; Phil Patton, *Made in USA: The Secret Histories of the Things That Made America* (New York: Penguin Books, 1993), 166.

10. Edward Johnson, *Life, Health, and Disease* (London: Sanders & Otley, 1837); repr., New York: John Wiley & Sons, 1850), 102.

11. Alexander Von Humboldt, *Personal Narrative of Travels to the Equinoctial Regions of America, During the Years 1799–1804* (London: H. G. Bohn, 1851–1853), 1: 215–216 and 2: 154; Katherine Manthorne, "The Quest for a Tropical Paradise: Palm Trees as Fact and Symbol in Latin American Landscape Imagery, 1850–1875," *Art Journal* 44, no. 4 (Winter 1984): 374, 377; "Three Weeks in Cuba," *Harper's Monthly* (July 1857): 150.

12. Cikovsky, "Ravages," 611–626; Novak, "Double-Edged Axe," 44–50; Charles Dickens, *A Tale of Two Cities* (London: Penguin Books, 2003), 22–23; Charles Dickens, "The Lazy Tour of Two Idle Apprentices," in *Oliver Twist. The Lazy Tour of Two Idle Apprentices*, chap. 4; Louise Chandler Moulton, *This, That, and the Other* (Boston: Philips, Sampson, 1854), 226; Edward Bulwer Lytton, "What Will He Do with It?" *Harper's Weekly* (8 August 1857); Archibald Robertson Gibbs, *British Honduras: An Historical and Descriptive Account of the Colony from its Settlement, 1670* (London: S. Low, Marston, Searle, & Rivington, 1883), 122–123.

13. M. M. Bakhtin and Michael Holquist, eds., *The Dialogic Imagination: Four Essays* (Austin: University of Texas, 1981), 84–258; John Francis McDermott, "The Spirit of the Times Reviews Moby Dick," *NEQ* 30, no. 3 (September 1957): 392–295, 394; Herman Melville, *Moby-Dick,* eds. Harrison Hayford and Hershel Parker (New York: W.W. Norton, 1967), 169–170.

14. "Trees," *Southern Literary Messenger* 14, no. 1 (January 1848): 13. Author's emphasis; Von Humboldt, *Personal Narrative of Travels,* 1: 215–216

and 2: 154; Manthorne, "The Quest for a Tropical Paradise," 376, 381. Author's emphasis added; Felix Driver and Luciana Martins, *Tropical Visions in an Age of Empire* (Chicago: University of Chicago Press, 2005).

15. James Macfadyen, *The Flora of Jamaica* (London: Longman, Orme, Brown, Green, & Longman, 1837), 176.

16. Nathaniel Hawthorne, *Passages from the American Notebooks* (London: Smith, Elder, and Co., 1868), 92.

17. Grant McCracken, *Culture and Consumption: New Approaches to the Symbolic Character of Consumer Goods and Activities* (Bloomington, IN: Indiana University Press, 1990), 31–44.

18. Jane Austen, *Mansfield Park* (London: Penguin Books, 2003), 79–80; Charlotte Brontë, *Jane Eyre* (New York: Signet Classic, 1997), 398; John Neal, *The Down-Easters* (New York: Harper & Brothers, 1833), 2: 125; "Regardless of Expense," *Harper's Weekly*, 18 April 1857, 241.

19. John F. Watson, *Annals of Philadelphia and Pennsylvania . . .* (Philadelphia: J. P. Lippincott, 1870), 607.

20. Kathleen L. Catalano, "The Longfellows and their 'Trumpery Antiquities,'" *American Art Journal* 15, no. 2 (Spring 1983): 21–31; Henry Wadsworth Longfellow, "The Old Clock on the Stairs" (1845) in *Henry Wadsworth Longfellow: Poems and Other Writings* (New York: Library of America, 2000), 51; *Longfellow Remembrance Book: A Memorial for the Poet's Reader-Friends* (Boston: D. Lothrop, 1888), cited in Matthew Gartner, "Longfellow's Place: The Poet and Poetry of Craigie House," *NEQ* 73, no. 1 (March 2000): 46. Author's emphasis added; Walt Whitman, "Old Poets" in *The Collected Works of Walt Whitman*, ed. Floyd Stovall (New York: New York University Press, 1964), 2: 659.

21. Herman Melville, "The Paradise of Bachelors and the Tartarus of Maids" in Herman Melville, *Pierre, Israel Potter, The Piazza Tales, The Confidence-Man, Billy Budd, Uncollected Prose* (New York: Library of America, 1984), 1261.

22. Hershel Parker, *Herman Melville: A Biography* (Baltimore: Johns Hopkins University Press, 1996), 1: 31; Thomas Norman DeWolf, *Inheriting the Trade* (Boston: Beacon Press, 2008), 64; Barbara M. Tucker and Kenneth H. Tucker, *Industrializing Antebellum America: The Rise of Manufacturing Entrepreneurs* (New York: Palgrave Macmillan, 2008), 32–34.

23. Anon., "Uncle Ben," *Harpers Weekly*, 25 July 1857; Jennie A. Kassanoff, *Edith Wharton and the Politics of Race* (New York: Cambridge University Press, 2004); Edith Wharton, *Crucial Instances* (London: J. Murray, 1901), 53–54.

24. "Snoqualmi Realty Co., Appellant, v. Moynihan, et al," (October 1904), *Report of Cases Determined by the Supreme Court in Missouri, 1903–1904*, 179: 629, 633–644, as cited in *The Southwestern Reporter* 78 (Feb. 10–March 23, 1904) (St. Paul: West Publishing Co., 1904).

25. Ibid.

26. "Homes and Haunts of Edward Fitzgerald, by his Grand-Niece," *Blackwood's Edinburgh Magazine* 174 (October 1903): 439–452.

27. "Hurricane Rips Through Florida and Heads Into Gulf," *New York Times,* 25 August 1992; "Storm Offers Chance to Rethink Everglades," *New York Times,* 29 September 1992.

28. Juan Forero, "A Swirl of Foreboding in Mahogany's Grain," *New York Times,* 28 September 2003, 8; Samuel Bridgewater, *A Natural History of Belize: Inside the Maya Forest* (Austin, TX: University of Texas Press, 2012), 171–175; Michael Williams, *Deforesting the Earth: From Prehistory to Global Crisis* (Chicago: University of Chicago Press, 2003); Sandra Brown and Ariel E. Lugo, "Tropical Secondary Forests," *Journal of Tropical Ecology* 6: 1 (Feb. 1990): 1–32; "Can Sustainable Mahogany Stem from CITES Science?, *BioScience* 53, no. 7 (July 2003), 619; A.G. Blundell and B.D. Rodan, "Mahogany and CITES: Moving beyond the Veneer of Legality," *Oryx* 37 (2003), 85–90.

29. For a comprehensive bibliography of the twentieth-century scientific literature on the ecology and cultivation of *Swietenia* species, see J. E. Mayhew and A. C. Newton, *The Silviculture of Mahogany* (Wallingford, Oxon: CABI and the Institute for Ecology and Resource Management, University of Edinburgh, 1998) which represented the state of knowledge at the time of its publication. See also Sheila E. Ward, David Boshier, and James Grogan, eds., special issue on Meliaceae in *Forest Ecology and Management* 255 (2008); Ariel E. Lugo, Mildred Alayón, et al., *Big-Leaf Mahogany* (New York: Springer, 2003); F. Bruce Lamb, *Mahogany of Tropical America: Its Ecology and Management* (Ann Arbor: University of Michigan Press, 1966), chaps. 7 and 8; J. P. Cornelius, et. al., "Swietenia (American Mahogany)," in *Encyclopedia of*

Forest Sciences (2004), 1720–1726; Terrence D. Pennington, "Mahogany Carving a Future," *Biologist* 49, no. 5 (2002): 207; Nick Brown, Steve Jennings, and Tom Clements, "The Ecology, Silviculture and Biogeography of Mahogany (*Swietenia macrophylla*): a critical review of the evidence," *Perspectives in Plant Ecology, Evolution and Systematics* 6, no. 12 (2003): 37–49.

30. The scientific literature on the DNA and medical research on *Swietenia* is vast and rapidly expanding. See for example, Ariel E. Lugo, Mildred Alayón, et al, *Big-Leaf Mahogany*, A. C. Gillies, et, al. "Genetic Diversity in Mesoamerican Populations of Mahogany (Swietenia macrophylla), assessed using RAPDs," *Heredity* 83 (1999): 722–732; R. Maristerra Lemes, et al., "Chloroplast DNA Microsatellites Reveal Contrasting Phylogeographic Structure in Mahogany (Swietenia macrophylla King, Meliaceae) from Amazonia and Central America," *Tropical Plant Biology* 3, no. 1 (2010): 40–49; B. H. Goh and H. A. Kadir, "In vitro cytotoxic potential of Swietenia macrophylla King seeds against human carcinoma cell lines," *Journal of Medical Plants Research* 5, no. 8 (2011): 1395–1404; Subhadip Hajra, et al. "Antioxidant and Antidiabetic Potential of Ethanolic Extract of Swietenia Mahagoni (Linn.) Seeds," *International Journal of Pharmaceutical Research and Development* 3, no. 3 (May 2011), 180–186.

31. S. D. Sprenkle, "Community-Based Forestry in Haiti: Overcoming Extreme Erosion and Poverty," Hôpital Albert Schweitzer Haiti Timber Re-Introduction Project Report (2006); Forero, "A Swirl of Foreboding," 8.

32. Lamb, *Mahogany*, chaps. 7–8; Mayhew and Newton, *The Silviculture of Mahogany;* Francis, "Mahogany Planting," 330; Kathryn Robinson, *Where Dwarfs Reign: A Tropical Rain Forest in Puerto Rico* (San Juan: University of Puerto Rico, 1997), chap. 8; Bridgewater, *A Natural History of Belize* 171–176.

33. Melissa H. Morris, et al., "Sowing date, shade, and irrigation affect big-leaf mahogany (*Swietenia macrophylla* King)," *Forest Ecology and Management* 132 (July 2000): 2–3, 173–181; M. Mahroof, et al., "Effects of Artificial Shade on Attack by the Mahogany Shoot Borer, Hypsipyla robusta (Moore)," *Agricultural and Forest Entomology* 4, no. 4 (November 2002): 283–292; K. S. S. Nair, *Pest Outbreaks*, in *Tropical Forest Plantations* (Jakarta: Center for International Forestry Research, 2001), 36–37.

34. Edward F. Gilman and Dennis G. Watson, "Swietenia mahagoni Mahogany," Forest Service, Department of Agriculture, Fact Sheet ST-608
(October 1994); on the decline of the mahogany industry and current
conservation and reforestation efforts in Belize, see Bridgewater, *A
Natural History of Belize: Inside the Maya Forest,* 171–176.

Acknowledgments

One of the more thrilling moments of my research for this book was flying in over Belize and seeing the same landscape that I had studied on maps in the British archives suddenly come into sharp focus and living color. The lagoons and streams plied by the mahogany woodcutters that I had been studying were all still there. As I explored the environs of Spanish Creek where they were once active with their axes, however, it was immediately apparent that the area, although still ecologically diverse, was not quite the same. Within a few hours one can see an amazing variety of plants and birds—including every member of the heron family—but the huge mahogany trees that once punctuated the surrounding forest are largely absent. What mahogany trees remain in Belize are mostly farther from the coast, where some controlled logging is still done, mostly on lands owned privately, in many cases by large lumber companies. Many of the woodcutters' descendants still live in the region, however, and it is their history written on the landscape. I extend special thanks to the people of Crooked Tree who graciously welcomed my family to join them at a very enjoyable weekend cricket match, and especially our hosts at the Bird's Eye View Lodge, Verna Gillett Samuels, proprietor, and Leonard Gillett. Thanks as well to the staff of the Belize Archives and Records Service, especially assistant archivist Mary Alpuche.

My first glimpse of Jamaica was from the deck of the *Corwith Cramer* as the Blue Mountains rose up out of the sea. After spending Christmas in the lively town of Port Antonio, where Santa Claus arrived on a motorcycle with bunches of balloons for the children, I spent a productive time at the

Jamaica Archives and Records Department. Special thanks to Linda Sturtz and James Robertson for their wonderful hospitality and a most memorable tour of Spanish Town. My thanks as well to the Sea Education Association for allowing me to teach aboard ship during their Caribbean voyage in 2004.

Many thanks as well to the staffs at the British Library; the Royal Society; the Natural History Museum in London; the British National Archives; the Royal Botanic Gardens at Kew; the National Maritime Museum in Greenwich; Harvard University's Houghton Library; Winterthur Museum and Library, especially Wendy Cooper, Greg Landrey, Susan Newton, and Neville Thompson, librarian emeritus; Bristol Historical and Preservation Society; Newport Historical Society; the Metropolitan Museum of Art; the Museum of Fine Arts, Boston; the New York Public Library; New-York Historical Society; and Historic Deerfield, especially Amanda Lange, David Bosse, Philip Zea, Josh Lane, and Penny Leveritt. In addition, I am grateful to the following institutions for fellowship support for my research: The Library Company of Philadelphia; the Historical Society of Pennsylvania; the New England Regional Fellowship Consortium; the Massachusetts Historical Society; the Rhode Island Historical Society; the New Hampshire Historical Society; the John Nicholas Brown Center; the John Carter Brown Library; and New York University. Special thanks as well to the American Antiquarian Society where I spent a rewarding post-doctoral year and to the New York Botanical Garden, where I studied botany and occasionally visited the skinny *Swietenia mahagoni* that resides in their glass house.

I am eternally grateful to my advisor and friend Karen O. Kupperman, whose wise counsel, unflagging curiosity, and generous spirit have been an inspiration. Also at New York University, I thank my doctoral committee who offered invaluable feedback: Walter Johnson, Thomas Bender, Lauren Benton, and Nicole Eustace. Thanks as well for the camaraderie of my fellow Atlantic Seminar participants: Christian Crouch, Noah Gelfand, Michael LaCombe, Jenny Shaw, Kristen Block, and Heather Kopelson. Thanks to the Society of American Historians for their recognition of my dissertation and to my undergraduate mentors: Eric Foner at Columbia University and Herb Sloan at Barnard College. I am especially indebted to the faculty, past and present, of the Historic Deerfield Summer Fellowship Program and the Winterthur Program in Early American Culture where I began my studies of material culture.

Among the joys and the hazards of interdisciplinary research is that one must venture into areas beyond one's own primary areas of expertise. In the course of my research, I have sought out a wide range of specialists—cabinetmakers, furniture conservators, curators, antiques dealers, auctioneers, botanists, wood identification specialists, forestry managers, geographers, historians, and archivists—who were generous in sharing their knowledge and passion for their subject areas. I conceived this work very much as a gathering of diverse perspectives and methodologies, which I hope may illuminate each other in some intriguing and thought-provoking ways. In some cases, I benefited from personal conversations. In cases where I was not able to meet someone personally, I was nonetheless grateful to draw on their publications, which are cited throughout my text and without which my own work would be much diminished. I gratefully acknowledge their scholarly contributions, although any errors are my own. Among those whose work has been especially helpful, I thank Adam Bowett, John Cross, O. Nigel Bolland, David Hancock, Trevor Burnard, Richard Bushman, Cathy Matson, Philip Morgan, Kathleen Murphy, Daniel Finamore, S. D. Smith, Michael Jarvis, and Emma Christopher. Thanks as well to Robert Mussey, Robert Trent, and Allan Breed. During my fellowship at the American Antiquarian Society, I was grateful to the following persons who recommended useful revisions to my dissertation: Caroline Sloat, Nancy Shoemaker, Seth Rockman, Jeffrey Sklansky, Kevin Sweeney, David Hall, Margaretta Lovell, Philip Gura and John Bezís-Selfa.

Thank you as well to my friends and colleagues at Stony Brook University, especially Alix Cooper, Jared Farmer, and Ayesha Ramachandran who read chapter drafts and to Susan Grumet who taught me the ropes. I was fortunate to land in such a supportive, intellectually stimulating History Department; since I cannot list everyone, I hope you well know how much I value you all as friends and mentors.

For helping to reshape my unwieldy manuscript into a book, I am most grateful to Joyce Seltzer, my editor; Brian Distelberg at Harvard University Press; Michael Haggett, production editor, Westchester Publishing Services; and Lisa Roberts who designed the beautiful book jacket. Thanks as well for the welcome assistance of David Luljak, indexer, and Philip Schwartzberg, map-maker. Special thanks as well to Jane Rubin and the Reed Foundation for providing a generous subvention for the book's images.

Portions of Chapter 4 are reprinted by permission from "The Card Family and the Mahogany Trade: From New England to the Bay of Honduras," in *New England and the Caribbean*, Peter Benes, ed., Dublin Seminar for New England Folk Life (Summer 2012).

A preliminary version of parts of this work entitled, "Nature's Currency: The Atlantic Mahogany Trade and the Commodification of Nature in the Eighteenth Century," appeared in *Early American Studies* (Spring 2004) and I am grateful to Daniel Richter, George Boudreau, and the Editorial Board for their early encouragement.

On a personal note, this book would not have been possible without the faith and encouragement of my friends and family. Special thanks to Marla Miller, Felice Batlan, Tristan Kirvin, Marie Duryea, Steve Reiter, Fiona and Gary Eden, and Mac Griswold. My family—the Andersons, Ahlbäcks, Pearces, Eakles, and Stattlers—extends its embrace across the oceans. Much love to Rachel, Ben, and Max—in hopes we will share many happy adventures still to come. My greatest thanks go to my parents, Raymond and Gunlög Anderson, who have been my constant sounding boards. And, last but not least, words cannot express the depth of my love and gratitude to Rick Stattler who after years of research is still my best discovery! Along with our son William, he has joined me on this life's journey as a true partner.

Index

Note: Page numbers in italic type indicate illustrations.

29; trade in, 37; care of, 51, 54; informed
consumption of, 59–60, 188–195;
women as buyers of, 59–60; historical
periods of English, 321n16. *See also*
cabinetmaking
fustic, 216

Gambia, 287
Gansevoort, Peter, 307
Garden, Alexander, 246
Gardiner, Sylvester, 55
genetics of mahogany, 312
George III, King of England, 115
Gibbons (doctor), 28
Gifford, Andrew, 205–206
Gillow, Richard, 186
Gillow, Robert, 103
Gillows Company, 78, 186
Girard, Stephen, 196, 198, 203
Goddard family (Newport). *See*
Townsend-Goddard family of
cabinetmakers
Godolphin, William, 106
Goldthwait, Elizabeth, 55
Goldthwait, Samuel, 44
González, Peter, 179
Gordon, James, 72
Gosse, Philip Henry, 87–88
grain patterns, 11–12
Grant, Samuel, 41–42
Grant, Ulysses S., 268
Gray, William, 132
Grayson, William, 194
Greater Antilles, 5, 33, 235
Green, Jonathan, 191–192
Grenada, 97, 102
Grove, Richard, 99
growth patterns, 5–6, 11, 157
growth rings, 9
Guadeloupe, 97
Guatemala, 269
Guy (slave), 174

Haiti: post-revolution situation in,
196–198, 201, 260; France and, 197–198,

262, 264, 268; mahogany trade in, 197,
260, 262–268; United States and, 197,
260, 264–268; cultivation of trees in,
312–313. *See also* Hispaniola; St.
Domingue
Haitian mahogany, 14
Haitian Revolution, 181, 196, 260
Hallowell, Benjamin, 62
Hamilton, William, 229–230
Hanbury, William, 215, 239
Hancock, David, 203
hardwoods. *See* tropical hardwoods
Harper's Weekly (magazine), 297, 301,
305, 307
harvesting: growth patterns' impact on,
5–6, 157; growth methods of, 6–7; labor
involved in, 12–13, 64; restrictions on,
16; early, 20; difficulties of, 158; process
of, 160–164, *161*, *163*; timing in, 162–163;
in Cuba, 199–200; steam power's effect
on, 251–252
Havana, Cuba, 22, 199, 258
Hawaii, 293
Hawthorne, Nathaniel, 303–304
Hazard, Samuel, 268
Hazen, Edward, *The Panorama of
Professions and Trades, or Every Man's
Book, 278*
Head, John, 41, 45
health, tropical trees' effect on, 24, 102,
231–232. *See also* medicinal uses
Henderson, George, 162, 166
Henkels, George J., 286; trade card of, *284*
Henley Company, 153
Henry, Edward Lamson, 306
Herculaneum, 187
Hercules (ship), 180
Hickey, Francis, 143, 144, 150–151
Hispaniola, 5, 20, 98, 185, 195–198. *See also*
Haiti; St. Domingue history, mahogany
and, 303–308
Hoare, Richard, 114, 147–148, 150
Honduran big-leaf mahogany. See
Swietenia macrophylla King
Honduras. *See* Mosquito Shore

West Indian mahogany. See *Swietenia*
    mahagoni Jacquin
W. F. Pell and Co., 207. *See also* D. C. &
    W. Pell Company
whales, 301–302
Wharton, Edith, 308
Wharton, Thomas, xi
Whitaker, John, 85
White, Robert, 112, 114, 180
whiteness, 298
Whitman, Walt, 306
wholesalers, 204
Williams, Jesse, 193
Williams, Samuel, 205, 206
Williams, Thomas, 276–277
Willoughby, Joseph, 277–278
Windsor chairs, 60–61
wine, 203
Winslow, Isaac and Jemima, 55, 63
Winterthur Museum, 49
Winthrop, Hannah Fayerweather, 55
Wolfe (ship), 129
women: furniture buying by, 59–60; as
    runaway slaves, 166

woodcutters: itinerant, 71–73, 84; on
    Jamaica, 71–73, 79, 83–84; compensa-
    tion of, 72; costs for, 83; attitudes of,
    104; in Bay of Honduras, 104–124,
    144–145, 268–269; enslaved, 136, 141,
    158, 269; problems caused by, 136; trade
    dealings with, 139; daily life of, 159–168;
    housing of, 161–162; advantages of,
    164–165; risks for, 165; as runaways,
    169; technology's effect on, 252; in
    Haiti, 262–265. *See also* Baymen;
    sawyers and sawmills
Woodlands estate, Pennsylvania,
    229–230
wood surveyors, 35–36, 186, 208
Wordsworth, William, 288–289
Wright, John, *West-India Merchant,
    Factor, and Supercargoes Daily
    Assistant*, 125
writing desks, 188

Young, Aaron, 122
Young, William, 102
Yucatán, 103, 112, *121*